THE CHANGING MUNDA

By the same Author

- **City of Patna** (Census of India, Monograph No. 2, Series-I, Part VI-B)
- **Culture Change in Tribal Bihar:** Munda and Oraon
- **Profiles of Tribal Culture in Bihar**
- **Sarat Chandra Roy** (Builders of Indian Anthropology Series)
- **Sarvodaya and Development:** Multi-Disciplinary Perspectives from Musahari (along with Pradhan H. Prasad, Jai B.P. Sinha and S. Akinchan)
- **Social Dimensions of Agricultural Development**
- **The Harijan Elite**
- **The Tribal Voter in Bihar**
- **Tribal Village in Bihar**

About the Author

SACHCHIDANANDA D. Litt. is Professor of Sociology and Director of the A.N. Sinha Institute of Social Studies, Patna. Born in 1926 and educated at Patna and London, he has taught Anthropology and Sociology at the University of Patna, Ranchi and also at the City University of New York. He started the University Department of Anthropology at Ranchi in 1953 and was the Director of the Bihar Tribal Research Institute from 1962-65. He has contributed a large number of papers and book reviews to research journals in India and abroad and published nine books important among which are *Culture Change in Tribal Bihar* (1964), *The Tribal Village in Bihar* (1968), *Social Dimensions of Agricultural Development* (1972), *Tribal Voter in Bihar* (1976), and *Harijan Elite* (1977). Professor Sachchidananda is President, Bihar Sociological Society, Vice-President Council of Social Research and is the past president of the Anthropology and Archaeology Section of the Indian Science Congress. He is associated with a number of Social Science research Institutions in the country in an advisory capacity.

The Changing Munda

SACHCHIDANANDA

CONCEPT PUBLISHING COMPANY PVT. LTD.
NEW DELHI-110059

ISBN: 978-93-5594-817-5

Edition 2024

Published and Printed by

Since 1974

Concept Publishing Company Pvt. Ltd.
A/15-16, Commercial Block, Mohan Garden,
New Delhi-110059 (India)
T: 91-11-41101460
E: publishing@conceptpub.com, *W*: www.conceptpub.com

PREFACE

IN MAY 1972 a conference was held at New Delhi to discuss research priorities which had a bearing on social policy in the study of scheduled tribes. The conference was jointly sponsored by the Indian Council of Social Science Research and the Indian Institute of Advanced Study at Simla. One of the recommendations of the conference was to take up restudies of some important tribes in India. Enormous changes have taken place in the country and the tribal regions since the first monographs on these communities were published. One of the tribes selected for the restudy was the Munda. Since I had worked among the community for more than two decades, I decided to take up this assignment.

The concept of "restudy" is indeed a difficult one. There are certain limitations inherent in a restudy. Since the two studies, the original and the restudy, are made at different points of time, they are different not only in scope but also in their approach and methodology. In fact, the restudy is not diachronic and it is difficult to say how a truly diachronic study can be made if constrained to rely upon the normative framework used by the original author. The use of Roy's framework and categories, even when supplemented by more ethnography leads to difficulties. The study could not be conceived as a double synchronic study. Doing so would have meant closing one's eyes to fresh light that had been thrown on different aspects of Munda culture by different authors between the time when Roy wrote and the present study. The scope of the present work has been enlarged to accommodate the concerns of more recent social anthropology. However, it has not been possible to discuss Munda ethnographic data with reference to different concepts in social anthropology. As a matter of fact, it is not possible to attempt this in the present work. Care has been taken, however, to see that different aspects of Munda life and culture receive balanced attention so that a rounded picture of Munda life emerges.

The research personnel consisted of a Research Associate and a Research Assistant besides myself. Manoharlal Sharma joined as Research Associate in January, 1975, while the Research Assistant, Rajendra Kumar Besra joined in April that year. The two formed a very amiable team and remained constantly together in the three villages where field work was conducted from April, 1975 to March, 1976. Besra had the advantage of being a tribal himself. Thus, there was no communication gap between the team and the informants. This factor also helped in impression management. While the team was in the field, I visited them twice at each location. Since I am known in the Munda areas on account of my earlier work and continued interest, these visits did not only help clarify factual or methodological issues but also boosted the team's rapport with the people at large.

Besra left at the conclusion of the field work to teach anthropology in one of the colleges at Ranchi, while Sharma continued to be with me and helped in the preparation of the first draft. On account of my other preoccupations the finalization of the report took an unexpectedly long time. The effort was all the more painstaking because of my desire to prepare it eventually for publication in the form of a book.

I am grateful to Sharma and Besra for doing the arduous field work and suffering all kinds of deprivation in the Munda villages for about a year. Sharma has ungrudgingly borne with me in the even more painstaking task of producing the first draft. Both these scholars can have the satisfaction that the rigorous training that they received while working on this research project would stand them in good stead in any future research that they might undertake on their own.

I am grateful to the ICSSR for having funded the project, releasing the grants in time as well as extending the life of the project by three months.

A.N. Sinha Institute of Social Studies, PATNA

SACHCHIDANANDA
Director

CONTENTS

LIST OF PLATES

1

INTRODUCTION

ANTHROPOLOGY for Sarat Chandra Roy was a labour of love. He was moved by the oppressions and hardships of the Munda and other tribes at the hands of aliens. The tribals could not get justice even in courts of law as the people dealing with their cases had no knowledge of their language, culture and customary laws. He, therefore, made it a point to study tribal culture in depth. Roy did not have any formal training in anthropology as, when he began his work, it was not taught anywhere in India as a distinct discipline. However, Roy kept himself abreast with the latest developments in anthropology throughout his life.

When Roy was working among the Munda to collect material for his book, all anthropological learning was basically historical. It is not surprising, since most other disciplines were also inspired by the evolutionist approach. There was an effort to look for the origin of everything—origin of species, origin of religion, origin of law, origin of particular tribe, etc. Franz Boas wrote that the science of anthropology deals with the history of human society. He spelt out the problems of anthropology as the reconstruction of human society, the determination of types of historical phenomenon and their sequences and the dynamics of change.

Roy believed that a knowledge of history and of the tribe should help us appreciate better the culture of the people. It is thus not surprising that Roy's monograph contains only one chapter on ethnography and five chapters on history. In the earlier chapters he makes an effort to trace the origin of the tribe from cues drawn from folklore, linguistic and pre-historic evidences. He then proceeds to reconstruct the history of the tribe from the time of the Vedas to the beginning of the Christian era. It is only in the early mediaeval and modern periods that some historical evidences are available. In the modern period he brings the narrative down to the Birsa movement. In this chapter on the modern history of the Munda he stresses in detail various social movements that raged in the Munda country in the nineteenth century.

The section on ethnography deals with physical appearance, dress, ornaments, weapons, material culture, the description of the Munda village, details of tribal agricultural operations, social and political organizations of the Munda, religion, festivals, superstition, etc. He also gives some details about the Mundari language, folk-tales and proverbs, folk-songs, etc. The book starts with a short and generalised account of Munda life and culture and does not take into consideration the regional differences of customs and practices in the tribe.

Sixty-five years have elapsed since Sarat Chandra Roy first wrote on the Munda. The orientation and the concerns of anthropology in his days and those at the present day are vastly different. After the decline of the evolutionist and diffusionist approaches, the structural-functional school held sway for a number of decades. Malinowski proposed the abandonment of historical conjecture and its replacement by functional sociology. Radcliffe-Brown followed up by rectifying the functional theory to include social structure and substituted what might be called the needs of the structure of its essential interdependencies for Malinowski's biological needs. The structural functional approach affected not only the methodology of social anthropology but significantly altered its aims and objectives. It was soon discovered that the science of man in its structural-functional perspective could not explain the problems of man's unity nor his practical problems. The concept of relativism undermines the problems of man's unity. The practical problems are disposed of, as relativism is conservative and omnitolerant, since the assumption is that the societies which have survived are harmonious and do not need reform. The past was rejected as being irrelevant. This anti-historicism was considered an error by Evans-Pritchard and Worsley. Evans-Pritchard charged that the functionalists had thrown out the baby of valid history along with the bath water of conjectural history. The expanding horizons of social anthropology began to include complex societies which had built up great civilizations and which could be studied in time depth. It was, therefore, necessary to look at the history of the civilizations so as to comprehend more easily the problems of social and cultural change.

For a long time anthropologists studied areas and peoples. The methods that they used were eminently suited to such studies. The functionalist approach further strengthened the interest of anthropologists in the integrated and rounded study of peoples This was supposed to bring up the functional interdependence between various parts of a culture. The anthropologists turned out, every year, a good number of ethnographic monographs on different tribal societies. These provided in turn, a large amount of information which was of great use to administrators. The essential orientation in these monographs was, however, descriptive. Each study consisted of a series of chapters which treated in detail different aspects of social life, environment, racial characteristics, demography, technology, economy, social organization, law, religion, magic, etc. Evans-Pritchard insisted that field work monographs should aim at giving more than a description of the life of the people. They should involve an interpretation of culture. The analysis would then bring out those features of social life which were significant for an understanding of its structure and for general theory. Like Acton and Collingwood, he advised his students to study problems and not peoples. Thus, the anthropologist was expected not only to describe but also to explain the social phenomenon he came across.

However, ethnography is still important in some parts of the world because of the fact that there are many populations about whose culture very little is known. It is, therefore, necessary to have a detailed account of their culture so that they can be recorded before they vanish under the impact of the strong forces of modernization. Even now there are some communities in India which need a detailed ethnographic account. It is only after the ethnographies have been produced that the problems in these cultures can be picked up for detailed analysis or even for a comparison with similar problems in other cultures.

In recent years, works in social anthropology have been characterised by intense specialization. Social anthropology itself has become a distinct discipline. Even in social anthropology scholars are specialising in economic anthropology or anthropology of religion or social structure, etc. The second trend is that social anthropologists are discovering links with theories in sociology, psychology, economics, political science, etc. There are very few standard social anthropological works which do not take into account ideas and concepts familiarized by Durkheim, Weber, Parsons and Merton. In the field of methodology there is a feeling that certain concepts that were acceptable in preceding decades are now too gross to be useful and have to be refined, otherwise they may even block further analysis. There is also the feeling that more work should be done to pull together in a comparative framework, observations that are discrete in terms of subject-matter or of ethnographic milieu. The need has been felt for the refinement of standard concepts in the hope of penetrating more deeply into the structure of social life. All this is being done to discover better tools for analysing the various dimensions of social reality with which anthropologists are confronted. While British anthropologists on the whole, confine themselves to a narrow range of social science disciplines, their American colleagues are readier to move outside the restricted range of the social sciences to draw on disciplines which employ quite different techniques and concepts.

In some of the modern works there is an increasing concern with the communication patterns in society with particular reference to the study of social structure. There is also a growing concern with the ecosystem and how it influences the life of the people. In the various facets of life, although the topics covered are the same, there is some change in the content and emphasis. In the study of social structure there is greater stress on inter-personal relations rather than on determinants of kinship terminology. On the subject of marriage, the details of ritual are comparatively less important than the interaction between the two kin groups connected by marriage. In the field of tribal economy, the description of material culture, types of boats and canoes, different kinds of implements receive less attention than the production processes, the production relationship involved and the problems of exchange. In most cases details about poverty and underdevelopment receive a greater amount of attention. In the field of religion. details of worship, tribal pantheons, totems and taboos, descriptions of festivals are, of course, mentioned but greater stress is laid on the social functions of religion and on nativistic movements, if any, in the community concerned. In political organization a description of the traditional system is there no doubt; but there is greater concern for socio-political movements in the community and the motivations thereof. The impact of modern institutions on the traditional set-up is also considered in detail. In addition to this, questions of ethnic identity are coming to the fore. Industrialization, urbanization and general development have only served to accentuate the problem. The overall orientation in modern studies is not to treat aspects of life as self-contained entities; it is more important to deal with their interdependence.

In India, the social anthropology of tribes has witnessed a radical change in perspective. For a long time anthropologists studying tribes were interested in bringing out points of difference between regional cultures and the tribal cultures in those regions. While some differences between them cannot be ruled out, it may be pointed out that there are significant differences between cultures of non-tribal communities as well as between cultures of different tribes themselves. In mixed areas like those of middle India the tribals have long been living side by side with non-tribal populations. The constant and close interaction between them has led to the convergence of many aspects of their cultures. There has been an acculturation of the tribals to non-tribal norms and customs. There has also been tribalization of the non-tribal castes and communities. There is a constant transition from the tribal ranks to caste Hindu society. Some common Hindu values and customs have been so thoroughly internalized by the tribals that they are scarcely distinguishable from purely tribal traits. Similarly many Hindu traits have tribal origins. Thus instead of treating the tribal cultures of India as quaint, bizarre freaks on the cultural canvas of India, it would be more fitting to treat them as dimensions of Indian civilization which itself is a mosaic of various strains.

FACTORS OF CHANGE

In all living cultures, change is inevitable. The difference between one culture and another under the aspect of change is that some may change faster than others. In some cultures there may be more resistance while others may be more receptive to innovation. Some innovations and their consequent effects may change the face of the receiving culture beyond recognition. Some cultures may be selective in their response to factors of change. In them, changes may occur in certain aspects of culture only while the fundamentals remain intact. All these phenomena of cultural dynamics give important leads to investigation and study both from the theoretical point of view and from the angle of applied anthropology.

Munda culture is fast changing because of contact with an alien people and alien ways of life. The process has been continuing for a very long time and as facilities for communication have increased, the isolation of the tribal villages has been broken. Constant living with non-tribal castes in the village, growth of education, the growth of townships in the interior of the tribal regions, the increasing industrialization of the area due to its wealth of mineral resources and the growth of new industries, the work of various missionaries as well as the growth of political consciousness have brought about a great deal of change in the life of the tribes in this area. Administrative agencies, forest officials, businessmen, contractors, and money-lenders have given further stimulus to culture change. The Munda had been studied earlier by S.C. Roy and a monograph on them was published sixty-five years ago; but since he first described them, enormous changes have occurred among the Munda. A study of culture change among the Munda and Oraon was published in 1964 (Sachchidananda : 1964). The object of the study was to trace the factors and forces which led to culture change and the extent to which the lives of the tribes were affected. An attempt was made to investigate whether the changes were wholesome or whether there was some maladjustment consequent upon culture contact. The impact of urbanism, Community Development Projects, Christianity, Hinduism and education on tribal villages was also studied.

Efforts to isolate the effects or changes brought out by different agencies did not always prove successful. It is rather hazardous to analyse the cause and effect relationship in a dynamic process. In places where the existence of urbanism was sought to be assessed, the influence of the Church and the school could not be left out. Where the influence of the Church was sought to be studied, the impact of the tribal markets and that of non-Christian schools could not be neglected. Similarly, where the influence of a big educational centre was sought to be studied the impact made on the life of the people by the military camps in that area could not be ignored. Above all, in all cases, the influence of non-tribal Hindu castes living side by side with the tribals for centuries in their own village could not be minimised. These people have a slightly different source of inspiration. They take pride in following the popular form of Hinduism and maintain a lively contact not only with their own kin in other villages but also in distant towns. It is likely that before the coming of the Community Development Projects, these non-tribals provided a most effective means of culture contact.

The Munda response to the cumulative effect of these forces of change is felt through their changing life style, material culture, social and economic relations, political organisation, beliefs and rituals etc. Such changes have been dealt with in the present work at appropriate places. In the following pages, we have attempted to delineate the different factors of change such as education, urbanization, industrialization and community development programme which have affected the Munda way of life.

Education has made rapid strides since independence. During the days of Sarat Chandra Roy education was confined to very few Mundas. Except for some missionary schools which were also few and far between there were no other agencies. Now not only have the missionaries enlarged their educational effort, but government schools and schools run by voluntary agencies have reached the remote corners of Munda country. The spread of education has not only been lateral but horizontal and there is now a university and large number of colleges and schools catering to the needs of the Munda. The light of learning has not left the Munda women untouched.

They are also taking to education in a big way. The process has been accelerated by the opening of separate schools for girls and by the provision of post-matric scholarships for all tribals at the university stage.

Education enables people to be geographically mobile, and once they move out of their rural habitat and get an urban foothold, they try to stick to the urban way of life. This generally leads to their occupational mobility. Urban residence not only provides them with opportunities for occupational mobility but also those of social mobility. Even those people who do not go out of the village to make a living show a definite change in behaviour, outlook and orientation on account of education. Education is one of the most important factors in forming the personality structure of an individual. Educated persons become more empathic *i.e.*, they are able to see themselves in other people's situations. Education also tends to make a person more rational than otherwise. An educated man makes a rational choice whether it is of individuals, roles or situations. An educated individual has a high level of participation. He takes part in all the social, economic and political affairs of the society. Educated people show higher achievement motivation than the uneducated and aspire for better social and economic positions.

The educated and the uneducated are exposed to different types of media of mass communication. The former are exposed to the mediated and the latter to oral types. The educated go in for newspapers, radio and films which do not create much interest among the uneducated. Thus in all spheres of life the educated are at a premium and the uneducated at a discount.

Community development was conceived as a co-operative partnership between the people and the government for an all-round development of the community. In the Munda area, community development has done a lot to expand the people's horizon. It was started in selected areas from 2 October, 1952, by taking up a programme affecting all areas of activity, such as agriculture, animal husbandry, social education. Co-operatives, rural industries, health and sanitation as well as work among women and children. Community development affected people's life style and ways of thinking in a substantial measure. This affected the social solidarity of the Munda village as people had to make a choice between tradition and progress. If they chose the latter, their enthusiasm for traditional customs, dances, worship at the Sarna etc. wanes. One precludes the other. Everything that is old is sought to be discarded for the new. The respect shown to the traditional leaders and the regard for the village Panchayat have greatly diminished.

In the field of agriculture, due to the impact of community development, some Munda started using a few modern implements such as the paddy thresher and straw-cutter. Villagers now mostly do not like to make their own modern implements as they did in the past. They now prefer to buy them at the markets. Evidently modern youth has not learnt the art of making agricultural tools. The use of chemical fertilizers has resulted in people's increasing dependence on outside supply. If the supply is not available in time, the yield suffers. The same is the case with improved seeds. Formerly people depended upon their own resources in agricultural operations. This increasing dependence on supplies makes people feel that their world has expanded and that they are part of the larger socio-economic system of the region.

Formerly, when the Munda were short of credit they got it from moneylenders. If they were short of grain they borrowed from the old grain *gola* maintained in the village. Now for loans some of them approach the Block authorities or the co-operative society also and for paddy loans they have to go to the government grain *gola*. But the bulk of their credit still comes from the moneylenders, friends and their kin.

Community development in some villages has led to the growth of factions and bad blood between the tribals and non-tribals and in general resulted in a decline of the community spirit. This has been brought about by a number of factors. In most of the Blocks the extension workers were non-tribals. They were new to the tribal way of life. They did not understand the tribal language. They were avoided by the tribals who suspected them of some evil designs. These workers had to fulfil a number of targets in the different programmes within a limited time. Hence the influential non-tribals living in a tribal village took advantage of the different schemes.

They ingratiated themselves into the favour of officers with the result that the erstwhile exploiters of the tribals became the greatest beneficiaries of these programmes. They used their prosperity and increased opportunities to tighten their hold on the ignorant Munda people who began to look upon Block authorities as friends and patrons of the exploiters. The extension personnel became suspects in their eyes. In some areas, the Munda village leaders have been found trying to make personal gains by securing contracts for minor construction works being done on behalf of the Community Development Block. These self-seeking leaders have become unpopular among their own people.

An important factor which held the benefits of community development from reaching the poor tribals is the conspiracy and corruption of the vested interests and higher-ups in the villages and the implementation authorities of the Government. For instance in Amlesa, the Panchayat Mukhia, a Munda, was given a loan for an irrigation pump by the Block authorities. The loan has not been redeemed even after the expiry of the date of recovery. In this case Block authorities have done a favour to the Mukhia by not realising the loan. The Mukhia is a representative of the people but he has no guts to criticise the Block administration on account of the favour shown to him and does not point out irregularities in the functioning of the Block since his own economic interest is served. He and the Block administration thus become indifferent to the general good of the people.

In recent times, industrialization and urbanisation have come to Chotanagpur in a big way. The tribals have suddenly come into contact with people from all parts of the country. They have been thrown into the vortex of industrialism and have been exposed to new influences, values, attitudes and beliefs. Rapid industrialization has resulted in the employment of a great many tribals, including Mundas, in the industrial centres, as some of the unskilled labour for the new industries is drawn from the local tribal population.

With the world's largest deposit of mica and India's largest deposit of coal, iron, copper and other important minerals, Chotanagpur has attracted thousands of local tribals as well as outsiders to work in the various types of mining and mineral-based industries.

The Hatia industrial complex near Ranchi in the Munda area is one of the largest industrial zones of Chotanagpur. The Heavy Engineering Corporation Ltd. (HEC) was established in 1958 at Hatia for developing the manufacture of heavy capital equipment in India. Although the considerations of locating the industrial complex at Hatia were not social but wholly economic, it was bound to have a tremendous impact on the local tribal population.

The initial problems in the way of industrialization were those of acquiring the land from the villagers and settling the compensation rate with them. The other problem lay in the rehabilitation of the uprooted families. Thus, the first wave of industrialization in Hatia caused great misery to the local villagers. Twenty five villages, inhabited largely by the Munda were adversely affected. They had to face numerous odds and obstacles, cultural crises, economic and social disorganisation. Although compensation was paid to displaced tribals, in the absence of any training in wise investment, the amount was lost to swindlers and cheats. Happy families who earlier had lived by agriculture in the evacuated villages were reduced to destitution. The poor tribals did not have any technological skills and so could not get ready employment in the plant. With the passage of time, however, and the opening of technical training institutes, large numbers of tribals of nearby areas have found employment at various levels in the main plant of the HEC or in the several ancillary industries that have sprung up in the area during the past two decades. Within a radius of ten miles around the industrial complex the industrial ethic holds its sway, although the bulk of the Mundas in the villages still depend on agriculture as their mainstay.

CONTRIBUTIONS TO THE ANTHROPOLOGY OF THE MUNDA

It is evident that a number of significant changes have taken place in the Munda country since Sarat Chandra Roy wrote his book. Some of the prime movers of change have already been discussed above. These have made a deep impact on the life and culture of the Munda. Some of these changes have been recorded by scholars who have written on the Munda.

The first comprehensive work on Munda life, language and culture after Sarat Chandra Roy's book was the Encyclopaedia Mundarica. The work runs into thirteen volumes and took a long time to compile. The editors are Hoffman and Emelin. The book is in the nature of an Encyclopaedia dealing with words in the Mundari language. Some of the words and concepts dealing with institutions and philosophical ideas have been given at some length. Turning over the pages of the Encyclopaedia one cannot but be impressed by the wealth of detail provided by the authors. It is not possible to delineate here all such references but a few illustrations can be given. Writing about the Munda *Kili* or the clan system, Hoffman names 106 clans. He does not regard the clans as being totemistic since members of the same clan do not have a sense of brotherhood with the totem nor do they observe any religious ceremony connected with it. He gives examples to show how some Munda clans even consume the objects signified by the clan name. But these, to my mind, are exceptions and do not disprove the fact that the bulk of the Munda show a deep respect for the clan object. Hoffman gives details about the *Khunt* but does not realise its implications as a lineage. He thinks that it has nothing to do with the clan system. He has classified the Mundari kinship terminology into eight meaningful categories. At another place, he gives details about the changing fortunes of the Munda and Pahan in the affairs of the village. Among the philosophical ideas, Hoffman deals at length with certain terms and rituals connected with mortuary rites and Munda eschatology.

In the early sixties, Koichi Sugiyama made a detailed study of village life among the Munda. The work was published in 1969. It was part of a cross-cultural research on the relationship between agriculture and culture. A number of communities practising wet-rice cultivation in several parts of the world was taken up. Emphasis was laid on the study of the economic base, social organization and religious life with particular reference to the role of rice-cultivation in each aspect. The village studied was in the Erki Block of the Ranchi district. This is in the heart of the Hasada area. One of the main reasons for the choice of the village in this region is the fact that the *Khutkatti* or the communal tenure is still extant in that area.

Sugiyama gives full details of the agricultural activities round the year. He also details other means of cash income such as the sale of lac, timber and daily wages. He also writes about the disparity in the income of households and has noted the existence of certain affluent families.

Dealing with the social organization of the village he gives details about the Sole clan, the privileges of the Khutkattidars, the details of the two lineages and the social status of other Mundas living in the village as *parja* or tenants of the original settlers. The functional role of people belonging to other castes is also depicted. He mentions the existence of separate sleeping house or *gitiora* but notes that it is not an independent and fixed house and does not have an institutional role comparable to that of the *dhumkuria* in Oraon villages.

In connection with the village organization, Sugiyama describes the role and functions of the Munda, the *hatu panchayat*, factions in the village, friction between two hamlets and also the influence of the Block Development Office over the political affairs of the village.

The religious beliefs and practices of the Munda concerning agriculture, such as rituals of sowing, transplanting, prayers for rain, offering and eating of new corn, cattle festival, festivals at the start of threshing and the *Buru Bonga* festival are given in extenso. A number of characteristics of the agricultural rights of the Munda have been noted. These are complexity, the Corn-spirit, the role of deities, the performers of rites, the symbols of the deity, thanksgiving rites, and divination, dances and songs as part of the ritual and avoidance of the evil eye on crops.

Since the book deals with only one village the descriptions are graphic and intimate. The book contains a large number of tables, maps, figures and photographs.

N.C. Choudhary's book on the Munda social structure appeared in 1977. It embodies results of fieldwork done between November, 1965 and April, 1966 in the village of Sode, forty miles from Torpa. Sode is a multi-ethnic village in which the Kompat Munda predominate. The bulk of the Munda belong to the Surin clan, whose ancestors founded the village. Mundas of ten other clans also live in the village but do not have a voice in village affairs. As Choudhary is dealing only with social structure, he gives a detailed description of unilineal descent groups such as clan, sub-clan and lineage. He also gives an analysis of Munda kinship terminology, the role of kin, the cycle of life and the distance of marriage alliances. He gives details about the working of the village and the *Parha Panchayats*. The two *Parhas* he has chosen to deal with, are the Kandulna and Surin. At the end of the book, he attempts to give an idea of the social stratification obtaining among the various tribal and non-tribal groups inhabiting the village.

Another work, which is largely historical but throws a flood of light and gives a new perspective on the movement of Birsa Munda is the doctoral thesis of Kumar Suresh Singh. Parts of this dissertation were published under the title *Dust storm and Hanging Mist*. Besides laying his hands on hitherto unused material, *e.g.*, mission records and archives in India and Europe, records of the trials of Birsa and his followers and notices of the Birsa movement in Indian newspapers of the day, he established rapport with living Birsaite Bhagats and recorded whatever oral history was available. He also used many indigenous accounts such as that of Bharmi Munda, the Rogoto manuscript and the account of Julius Tigga. Suresh Singh· brought out the socio-economic background provided by the disintegration of the agrarian order. He has brought out the interaction between the tribals and the non-tribals during the various phases of the conflict. He has collected a large number of folk songs on Birsa and his movement and analyses them in a way that reflects the movement in retrospect.

One of the main contributions of Suresh Singh is the detailed description and phase-wise analysis of the long drawn Sardari movement, which served as the back-drop of the Birsa movement. He holds that the attempt to represent the movement as primarily agrarian or politico-religious, the first directed against the *dikus* and the second against the authorities. European officials and missionaries were both partial and apologetic (1 966 : 204). Although the Birsa and Sardari movements had the same agrarian roots, the former aimed at a total reconstruction of Munda life. "Birsa's religion and raj, the politico-religious ends and means were inseparable" (1966 : 205). In its anti-British sweep Birsa included in his movement both non-Christians and Christians. Birsa's emergence as a leader represented a phase in the evolution of tribal leadership of such large scale movements. Birsa was not a hypocrite or a trickster as depicted by Sarat Chandra Roy but a determined rebel. Singh makes a plea to judge the movement in the background of contemporary ideas and events rather than in the context of nationalism and non-violence. Although the Birsa movement was anti-British, it was at the same time against local exploiters and the missionaries. It was by no means non-violent.

Besides these major works, a number of Master's dissertations have been written in the Ranchi University Department of Anthropology. In 1955 Kala Rani wrote a dissertation on 'Munda Women'. Similarly, B.D. Gupta wrote on 'Munda Labourers', S.S. Jerai on 'Community Development Among Munda of Two Villages', Ashok Kumar Jain on 'Munda Adolescence', Arif Kalim on 'Munda Economy in the Two Villages', P. Kiro on 'Political Organization Among the Munda of Two Villages' and B.B. Nag on 'Magic, Religion and Festival Among the Munda'. In 1957-58, the author made a study of "Culture Change among the Munda and the Oraon" and the book based on this work was published in 1964. In 1963 a socio-economic survey of the Karra Block, which is a predominantly Munda area, was completed under the author's direction in the Bihar Tribal Research Institute. In addition to these, several scholars have published papers on the Munda in learned journals on one theme or the other.

However, there is no comprehensive work dealing with all aspects of Munda life and culture. It is for this reason that this restudy was commissioned. Another reason for the restudy is the change in the concerns of social anthropology today. Aspects of life that attracted the attention of anthropologists in the days when Roy worked do not appear as significant to anthropologists today. This restudy does not confine itself to changes taking place in such aspects of life and culture that Roy dealt with, but also attempts to cover those that deserve description and analysis at the present day. The bulk of the restudy is based on the field work done in three Munda villages during the years 1975-76. Thus the work is a synchronic as well as diachronic study of the Munda. Care has been taken to show horizontal variation in culture evident in the three distinct sub-culture areas. In Roy's work this has been overlooked and a generalised picture of Munda culture has been presented.

At certain places in the present study there is a reappraisal of Roy's views on events and processes witnessed by him. Roy saw to it that his views fell in line with those of the government of the day. He was all praise for the efforts of the British administrators to raise the living of the Munda. Anything that smacked of criticism of the British point of view was abhorrent to him. Since then historians have laid their hands on non-government sources of data, a perusal of which leads to a different version of the events and their motivating factors.

SCOPE OF THE STUDY

The study aims at providing a rounded picture of Munda life and culture. Three chapters deal with the background for such a study. The first relates to the Munda ecosystem and details the adaptation of the Munda to the total environment as well as a description of the geographical area, flora and fauna, minerals, climate as well as such non-Munda communities among whom the Munda live in villages. The second deals with the demographic perspective and includes such items as age and sex distribution, marital status, literacy, religion, distribution by economic activity, rural and urban population break up, fertility, mortality and migration. The third is a very brief account of the Munda in history. This is an outline of the four periods through which the Munda passed from the earliest times to the present day. Details have been avoided as they can be looked up elsewhere.

The web of kinship and marriage is delineated in the next two chapters. The first, opens with a description of the two branches of the Munda community, deals with the formation of the clan organization, kinship terminology, rules of descent and inheritance as well as size and composition of the domestic group. It also includes the status of women and fertility and family planning in Munda areas. The next chapter opens with a discussion of pre-marital sex and leads on to rules of marriage, kinds of marriage, distance of marital alliances and then proceeds to describe marriage rituals among the traditional as well as the converted Munda. Towards the end of the chapter widow re-marriage and divorce have been considered.

The Munda economy is analysed in the next two chapters. The first deals with different kinds of economic activities in which the Munda are engaged. Since the most important economic activity is agriculture, the land system is sought to be analysed in detail so as to get a correct picture of the complicated nature of land tenure prevalent in the Munda country. This is followed by a description of the land, soil, main crops and the agricultural operations. The discussion is rounded off with a mention of functional interdependence between tribal and non-tribal communities in Munda villages which is analogous to the *jajmani* system in the non-tribal areas. The last section of the chapter deals with agro-industries and the growth of entrepreneurship among the tribals. The second chapter on the Munda economy deals with markets, exchange and credit. The weekly markets have been described in detail and their functions have been analysed. A section of the chapter is devoted to the problem of indebtedness and the role of credit agencies including co-operatives.

The next three chapters are devoted to the traditional political organization, socio-political movements, the development of modern political consciousness and the growth of the Jharkhand movement. The traditional political system has been analysed in terms of the village panchayat, the Parha Panchayat and the newly evolved Parha Mahasabha with Parha Hadri as its executive organ. It bears testimony to the genius of the Munda to remould their traditional polity to meet the challenges of modern times. The next chapter deals with socio-political movements in the Munda country in the nineteenth century beginning with two Kol insurrections and the Sardari agitation which finally culminated in the form of the Birsa movement. The last chapter in the series deals with the rise of modern political consciousness, the genesis and growth of the Jharkhand party, its transition from an ethnic party into a regional one and the emergence of sub-nationalism in the form of the demand for a separate state.

The world of the supernatural follows next. The first chapter in this section deals with Munda cosmology and cosmogony, the Munda pantheon, their hierarchy of gods and goddesses, their ritual functionaries, the seasonal cycle of rituals and festivals and a brief description of Munda eschatology and the social functions of religion. The second chapter deals with the impact of Hinduism and Christianity on tribal life and thought.

The final chapter details the trends of change in Munda life and culture and ends with some reflections on the future of the community.

METHODOLOGY

The Study Area

The Munda country mainly comprises the Khunti sub-division in Ranchi district of Bihar State. Culturally, it is divided into three distinct regions, Hasda, Naguri and Panch Parganas. The heart of Munda culture is found in the Hasda area, corresponding to the Maranghada region of the Khunti sub-division. The bulk of the Munda in this area are non-Christians and are deeply attached to their mother tongue, Mundari. The Munda in the Naguri area, which lies to the west of the Ranchi Chaibasa Road, are mainly Christian converts and speak Naguri, Mundari and Sadani. The Munda in the Tamar area are known as Panchpargania as they speak the Panchpargania dialect and most of them are profoundly influenced by Hinduism. There are regional variations in usage and custom in different areas. As mentioned earlier, S.C. Roy's book, *The Munda and Their Country* (1912), does not mention the areas from where data was collected for the book. It proceeds as though what is said about the Munda holds true for all sections of the tribe living in different areas.

Three different centres have been selected for intensive study, here, one each from the above three cultural sub-regions so as to reflect the regional variations in usage and custom. These were Salehatu near Maranghada in Hasda area, Gutuhatu near Tapkara in Naguri area, and Amlesa near Tamar in the Panchpargania. All the three villages were approachable by road. Their social and ecological setting have been described in the next chapter.

Research Methods

Before being sent to the field the two research workers went through all the available published material on the Munda and took copious notes. They also studied recent field-work monographs, both Indian and foreign to get an idea of the concerns of modern social anthropology. The Research Associate and the Research Assistant, both trained in social anthropology, lived in each of the three villages roughly for three to four months during 1975-76. The methods employed for study were : (i) observation, both participant and non-participant, as conditions permitted ; (ii) interviews, both individual and group, (iii) filling in household census schedules for each family ; and (iv) case studies were also made in certain cases to provide depth wherever needed. The researchers were supplied with a schedule for observation and interview on the basis of which they collected material. They kept daily field-work diaries for the entire period of field-work. Besides concentrating on the villages chosen they often used to move about in the neighbouring areas to make an intensive study of some aspects of culture in which one village did not suffice for a rounded picture. The study of clan, *Parha* organization and the political organization could not be complete except through the regional approach. In the processing of the quantitative data simple statistical tools were used. An effort was made to see that in the course of field-work the regional variation was taken into account.

Regular visits were made to each centre to provide on-the-spot guidance. The research staff were periodically called to Patna for discussion. This helped in clarifying their ideas.

After the field-work was over, it was processed and the quantitative data were coded and tabulated. Percentages and averages were calculated wherever required to make the data meaningful for interpretation.

Field-Work

As mentioned earlier, field-work for the restudy was conducted in the Munda area in Ranchi district during 1975-76. The Research Associate and the Research Assistant lived at three different places, *viz*. Salehatu, Gutuhatu and Amlesa altogether for almost one year. A brief account of field experiences at these three places will help understand the nature of field work and the problem related with accessibility to the area, acceptability of the researchers to the study population, establishment of rapport, working with the people and finally data collection.

Salehatu is situated about 14 miles east of the sub-divisional town of Khunti. It is connected with Khunti by an all-weather road which has been metalled recently. A bazar bus, taxis and trucks ply between Khunti and Maranghada (an important market place near Salehatu) on market day. The villagers usually come to Khunti town either on foot or on bicyele. Gutuhatu is about 20 miles north of Khunti and about 2 miles north of Tapkara, an important market place and bus terminus. A regular daily bus service runs between Tapkara and Ranchi. Amlesa is about 37 miles east of Ranchi on the N.H. No. 33—Ranchi-Tata Road. It is about one mile south-east of the nearest bus stop near Tamar. The village is accessible by bus all the year round.

A number of factors helped the entry of our team in the Munda area. The Munda country has already been opened up by the social scientists, especially from the Department of Anthropology, Ranchi University, Ranchi and the Tribal Research Institute, Ranchi. The tribals are aware of the type of work done and information collected by the researchers. The present author has been working in the Hasda and Naguri areas off and on since 1956 and has not only been known to important Munda leaders but also to local leaders, school teachers etc. Some of these leaders were already aware of his writings. The research team, therefore, had no problems of entry. The key leaders introduced the research-workers to other people in the villages concerned. One of the members of the team was a tribal himself, belonging to the Gond tribe. Many of his educated college friends were from the areas of field-work and these provided convenient contact points.

At the outset the villagers were told clearly about the objectives and were requested to co-operate in the task. On all occasions an attitude of respect and understanding towards their norms and values was displayed. It was essential to neutralise their contempt for outsiders, if any, and gain acceptability. While one member of the team knew Mundari, the other picked it up with some effort. This helped in making friends and establishing cordial relations with villagers. Appropriate kinship terms suited to their age, sex and level of intimacy were used to address them or refer to them. This friendliness helped in participant observation. The research team went with the informants to their homes, weekly markets and to their relatives on friendly visits, and were invited to Church meetings, and other social events.

Friendly relations were promoted by sharing meals, tea, cigarette, *biri*, chewing tobacco and even rice beer with some of the informants at their homes and markets. Just keeping the eyes and ears open, made it possible to get plenty of information unsolicited.

Finally, living among them for months together established our bonafides. It helped in other ways also. A complete picture of the community in which one lives and works does not emerge in a day or a week. One arrives at a preliminary understanding, then makes fresh observation which corrects one's first impressions, and this makes the picture a little more complete. The team's stay among them helped check and recheck data and reduced ambiguity in the information so collected. Moreover, the people among whom one works always try to fit one into their community. It is not as if only the anthropologist has views about the people he or she is investigating. They also have their views about the anthropologist and sometimes they reveal a great deal about themselves by the manner in which they seek to accommodate the outsider within their own social and cultural world. The team's long stay among the Munda made for a good deal of sympathy and understanding to outsiders which was a great advantage.

The experience at the three centres strengthened the conviction that working with the functional leadership in the Munda area was the most effective method for conducting research among the tribals. Informal contact was developed with these influential people during the field-work. They acted as bridges between the team and the common man during the initial stages of field-work and aided in creating direct rapport with the latter in course of time.

Household survey was conducted in all the three villages for intensive study. It was carried out by filling household schedules by interviewing either head of the household or any other adult member of the family through house to house visits. In most of the cases tribal friends invariably acted as catalysts in gaining informants' confidence during interview. A list of Munda households was prepared before conducting the household survey in the three villages. Four situations proved useful in contacting the householders for the survey. These were (1) visiting people at home along with a common friend, (2) village Panchayat meetings on a particular week day, (3) Sunday service at the village Church, and (4) social events like feasts after paddy sowing etc. Some informants were contacted while working in the paddy fields.

The social events taking place in the village during the field-work were observed and recorded along with gathering relevant information for filling in gaps in our knowledge. Case histories were recorded to get a deep understanding of the phenomena. Notes were taken down from records of Panchayat registers, literature, Karamchari's register, and unpublished historic accounts of the Munda written by a knowledgeable old Munda. The study team used to visit the village fields, farms, weekly markets, fairs and festivals, and participated in situations and events like village meetings, Church meetings, ritual ceremonies such as mortuary feasts, *chhati*, baptism and sacrament, marriage in the church, *lota-pani* ceremony, *Devi bonga* worship, festivals like *Phagu*, *Sarhul*, *Dasai*, *Pus-Mela*, *Chho-Nach* etc. These situations provided an opportunity to get first hand knowledge of the events and insight into the life ways of Munda people. The field centres were revisited to collect more information for plugging the gaps in our knowledge and to take account of the new developments and events which would have occurred after we left that area. The bond that grew in the field has outlived the period of the research. All the informants have turned into long standing friends.

No field-worker may claim to have foreseen all the problems he faced or to have solved all of them to his complete satisfaction. The research experiences are not success stories as such. Like other researchers, in this instance field-work was also made up of successes as well as failures, of trials as well as joys. There were times, when the surest procedures failed to produce results, and times when the most obscure facts revealed their true significance.

The account of the field-work among the Munda of Chotanagpur certainly gives some idea of the variety of experiences through which anthropologists work towards understanding human society and culture. Field-work by itself does not provide, or even aim at, a final or complete understanding of the principles by which society and culture are governed. But it provides one of the bases of this understanding. The larger task of synthesis requires that there should be some common elements in the work being conducted by different investigators at different times and places.

2

THE LAND OF THE MUNDA : THE MUNDA ECOSYSTEM

WHETHER we study man or any other living creature, the dimension of space is as important as that of time. Recognition of this has created the discipline of ecology, which studies the relationship between animals and their habitat. In the case of man, where culture, as Forde puts it, intervenes as "a middle term between the physical environment and human activity" (1950 : 643), the problem becomes essentially one of assessing the interaction between the natural environment in which a people live and their culture. Human ecology has thus come to signify the study of this relationship rather than the investigation of how man, the biological organism, has adapted himself to his geographical setting.

THE ECOSYSTEM

The Munda ecosystem may be described in terms of population, topography and communication, natural resources, climate and seasonal variation and the interacting non-Munda cultures.

The density and distribution of population over a given territory necessarily affects its culture. Whereas a sparse population of a desert dwelling community of hunters and food gatherers may limit social organisation, an environment which will support a large and dense population makes possible the development of a stratified society, economic specialisation and hence a well-developed external trade. The Munda are spread over Bihar, Orissa, West Bengal, Madhya Pradesh and Tripura. The major concentration is however in the

Ranchi district in Bihar (Table 2.1), especially the southern, south-western and eastern parts of the district.

TABLE 2.1

Distribution of Munda Population and General Population - 1971 & 1901

	1971		1901	
	Munda	General Population	Munda	General Population
All India	1,181,151	547,950,000	466,668	238,337,313
	(0.21)	(100.00)	(0.19)	(100.00)
Bihar, W.Bengal, Orissa	1,161,797	122,609,995	438,143	54,554,870
	(0.9)	(100.00)	(0.8)	(100.00)
Bihar	723,166	56,353,369	—	27,311,865
	(1.3)	(100.00)	—	
Chotanagpur	714,927	11,040,225	344,373	4,263,707
	(6.5)	(100.00)	(8.1)	(100.00)
Ranchi district	521,095	2,611,445	287,105	1,177,611
	(20.0)	(100,00)	(24.4)	(100.00)

Sources : (1) Census of India 1971, Series I, Paper I of 1975 SC&ST, pp. 140-162.
(2) Roy, S.C., 1970 *Munda and Their Country*, pp. 205-6.

The Munda population in the country has more than doubled during the 70 years between 1901-1971. The share of the Munda in the population of India and States has increased while in Chotanagpur and Ranchi district it has declined during 1901-1971. A large number of non-tribals have entered Chotanagpur during the 1950s and 1960s to work in newly established industries in this area, thus, reducing the Munda to a minority in their own land. The Munda are settled agriculturists and live in villages. Their subsistence on agriculture in the absence of any other alternative source still holds 95 per cent of the population. Only 5% of them live in towns and pursue non-agricultural occupations.

The influence of topography on culture is fairly obvious. The character of the country inhabited by a given people determines the natural resources available to them, and thus influences their culture by limiting the range of its alternatives. The human need most directly affected by topography is that for defence. Topography likewise affects political organisation and the expansion of tribes under primitive conditions. The picturesque Chotanagpur plateau continues to be the natural abode of the Munda as well as that of numerous other tribal communities. It is characterised by undulating uplands, with an average elevation of 2000 feet above sea level, broken by hill ranges and river valleys. The plateau was formerly covered by dense forests which have gradually disappeared as a result of unmindful cutting of trees by the inhabitants, reclamation of forest land for cultivation, exploitation of the forests for commercial purposes and damage caused by fire and grazing. The net result has been extensive soil erosion and gully formation by which land adjoining the streams has been cut into typical bad land topography, locally known as *Tanr*. In the south-eastern portion, however, there is still a large stretch of forest. The plateaus are interconnected by rugged and steep hill passes, locally known as *Ghats*.

The main rivers of the Munda country are Subarnarekha, South Koel, Sankh and North Koel fed by numerous tributaries. These effectively drain the whole area and are sufficient to carry off even the heaviest rainfall. No part of the Munda country is prone to floods. The waterfalls or *ghaghs* formed by the rivers are magnificent, the most famous of these are Jonha on the Subarnarekha, Dasom on Kanchi river and Perua and Sadani on Sankh. These rivers and streams are well stocked with fish during the monsoon and remain so till January when smaller ones get dry and the larger ones have but little water. These rivers do not offer much scope for irrigation, however, during the last two decades some medium irrigation schemes were executed benefiting the Panchpargana area of Munda country.

Minerals and other natural resources in a given region enhance the industrial potential. The important minerals of economic value which occur in the district are coal, limestone, laterite, barytes, fireclay, china-clay, bauxite etc. About fifteen coal seams making a total of about 250 feet of coal and carbonaceous matter are associated in the Barakar strata in the Ray and Liapara area of north Karanpura coalfield in Ranchi district and contains approximately a reserve of about 275 million tons of coal down to the depth of 500 feet. Eight collieries are working at Khelari and Ray in Ranchi district.

Industries based on minerals are, *e.g.*, Khelari Limestone quarries, Silwai Barytes Mines, Tatisilwai, Ray Bishejhapa Fireclay Mines, etc.

The discovery of this rich mineral wealth in this area and the subsequent development of large scale industries in the post-independence period brought with it an influx of people from all parts of India. Industrial towns have grown up in areas that were not so long ago covered with forest and the hum of machines is now heard in the very heart of what was once tribal country. Industries like the Heavy Engineering Corporation of Hatia near Ranchi have changed the face of the areas around them. Rapid industrialization has resulted in the employment of a great many tribals in the industrial centres and most of the unskilled labour for the new industries is drawn from the local tribal population. This had far-reaching effects on the life-ways and thought-ways of the tribals.

The climate and seasonal variation affect adjustments particularly in clothing and habitation. The community must plan its activities in relation to anticipated seasonal changes, which often entails a considerable amount of organised co-operation. This is not only important for an understanding of the economic adjustment of a given community, it usually has also a profound effect on other institutional activities, particularly in the fields of ceremonial, religious rituals and recreation.

The climatic conditions in Ranchi have changed a lot during the last sixty years. Earlier there used to be rains every month, but now there are well defined seasons such as summer, rainy and winter seasons. The climate has become relatively dry and warm due to deforestation and the coming up of industrial complexes in the area. Earlier the climate of the Ranchi plateau used to be cool and pleasant. The rains break usually before the end of the second week of June. Due to perfect natural drainage rain water flows away very quickly. The rainy season usually ends in the last week of September, though there may be a heavy rainfall during the first fortnight of October. The winter sets in by the first week of November. January is colder with strong cold winds blowing throughout the month but the climate remains dry during this period. The day temperature starts rising by the end of February through March and April and reaches its maximum in May. The temperature, in the lower plateau, is considerably higher than in the rest of the district and the climate is moist and enervating. The peak period of precipitation is in the monsoon months of June to September with 82 per cent of the annual rainfall. The annual rainfall is nearly 60". The region around Tamar-Sonahatu-Silli near the eastern border of the district receives the least amount of rain as compared to other parts.

The most significant of the natural resources of a given environment are the flora and fauna which provide the food supply. These place limits upon the type of ecology adopted, by the human population, and, therefore, partially determine their culture. At one time, the major portion of Ranchi district was covered with dense forests. Today the central and eastern plateaus are almost denuded of forests, and only small scrub jungles, with a few big trees, are found on the hills. In the eastern plateau, large blocks of forests now are found only in south-eastern corner in Tamar area bordering Singhbhum.

Forests in the district cover an area of 1,679 sq. miles or 23.83 per cent of the total area. As reported by S.C. Roy (1912) about one-third (32.10) of the area of the district was under forests during the first decade of this century. Thus, one-fourth of the forests which existed then had been destroyed during the last fifty years.

The forests of the area come under "Dry Tropical type" and sub-classified under "Dry Sal type" in which Sal (Shorea robusta) is gregarious. In the valleys the species other than Sal are Kend, Asan and Simal (Bombax malabaricum). Karam, Paisal and Tun are the important timber trees, Kusum, Palas, Bair, Karanj are also abundant. Tetar (Tamarindus indica) and the mango groves (confined to hills) are found around the village sites. Mahua, Pipal, Jack fruit and Bamboo are of great economic importance to the inhabitants.

Timber and firewood are the major forest produce. Timber is hard and durable and is used for railway sleepers, beams, rafters etc. Due to destruction of local forests, the inhabitants in certain areas burn cow-dung cakes to supplement the fuel need. These areas are mainly in Sonahatu Block, central and eastern regions of Tamar Block, the region around Khunti, Karra, Torpa and certain areas between Ranchi and Lohardaga by the main road.

Kendu leaf (*Diospyros melanoxylon*) is available in large quantities for making *biris*. Lac is also an important forest produce and occupies a significant position in the export trade. The Indian Lac Research Institute at Namkum near Ranchi has been working for the improvement and working of the lac industry. Tamar, Bundu and Silli areas produce a large quantity of lac. Palas, Kusum, Bair, Ficus and Croton are its principal hosts. Mahua flowers are eaten and also used for the preparation of country liquor. Jack fruit is also one of the major food items and after boiling, is consumed as food by poorer families.

The forests have diminished under the axe of the inhabitants. The indiscriminate commercial exploitation of forests, particularly during and after the Second World War is also one of the major factors of deforestation. Reclamation of suitable land for food crops has further reduced the area under forests. Fire and grazing have also contributed towards it. Since the last century, various Acts have come up to regulate the cutting of forests. Most of the area under forests in the district is under the Bihar government control, but villagers in certain areas are given special rights over the forests.

Chotanagpur was known, in earlier times, to be a happy hunting ground for the sportsman, but on account of progressive reduction of the forest area due to the reasons mentioned earlier, the fauna has greatly diminished. Moreover, the large scale killing of smaller game has driven away the larger carnivorous animals to remoter parts of the jungles. Therefore, big game like bison, tiger or wild elephants may wander across the borders of this district only rarely. One often comes across bears. Wild cat, hyenas, jackals, fox, wild boars, porcupines, scaly anteater, mongoose, sambar, Chital (spotted deer), Kotra (Antelope), Nilgai and hare are other wild animals found in the forests. Some of the animals are a menace to the crops. Peafowl, some patridge and quail are the most common among the game birds. Among reptiles, snakes of both poisonous and non-poisonous varieties are found. The rivers, streams, and tanks are well stocked with fish during monsoon and afterwards. Fishing is a favourite pastime and also an economic activity among the people.

Till about the turn of the present century, communications

between Chotanagpur and other parts of Bihar were so difficult that common travellers might have had no clear indication of the route to Ranchi. Previously there was a well established trade route between Lohardaga and Gaya, passing *via* Balumath and Chatra, for the transportation of local goods as also from Jashpur and Sarguja to Calcutta. This remained in use till the advent of railways in the present century. The traditional route for pilgrims from Bengal to Puri passed through Ranchi. The bulk of the trade of the district except on roads, was carried on pack-bullocks. Bullock-carts were numerous on the metalled roads radiating from Ranchi and much of the trade with the Gaya district and South Bihar was carried in carts along the road to Hazaribagh, instead of the circuitous railway route *via* Purulia and Asansol. The tribals usually carried their goods by means of *bhar* or *bahangi.* Well-to-do people travelled in a *Sagar* (a low cart with two solid wheels) or on country ponies.

By 1910 the chief roads emanating from Ranchi were. Ranchi-Purulia-Jamshedpur (133 miles); Ranchi-Ramgarh-Hazaribagh (57 miles); Ranchi-Chaibasa-Jamshedpur (126 miles); Ranchi Netarhat (96 miles); Ranchi-Daltonganj (102 miles) and Ranchi-Gumla-Simdega-Rourkela (199 miles). During 1960s Ranchi-Tata (N.H.-33) has been constructed extending over 75 miles. The roads managed by the Public Works Department measure 1,991 miles of which 525 miles are metalled. Municipal roads are maintained by the municipalities at Ranchi and Lohardaga and Notified Area Committee of which only 60 miles are *Pucca* and the rest are *Katcha* roads. About 470 miles of new village roads have been constructed and 782 miles of old roads have been repaired by Gram Panchayats. The Forest Department has constructed about 434 miles of fair-weather forest roads. Although Ranchi district has a good number of metalled roads, many Anchal headquarters are still unconnected by such roads.

The common conveyance on roads at present are bullock carts, ponies, cycles, cycle-rikshaws, hand carts, motor-cycles, scooters, motor-cars, taxis, buses and trucks. Bullock-carts still remain as the main conveyance for transport of grains and goods in the remote interior of the district.

The opening of the Purulia-Ranchi Branch of the then Bengal-Nagpur (now South-Eastern) Railway in 1907 brought the railways to Ranchi. Earlier, Ranchi was about 70 miles away from a railway station. This railway runs for forty miles in the district. The Gomoh-Barkakana-Daltonganj section of the Eastern Railway (opened in 1927) runs for 16 miles through Ranchi district. With the opening of the Chandrapura Main section in the South-Eastern Railway in 1960, Ranchi is directly connected by train with the State capital at Patna. Besides above-mentioned broad gauge lines, there is a metre gauge line running from Ranchi to Lohardaga over a distance of 42 miles. A new line from Ranchi to Rourkela has been opened a few years ago. The total running kilometres of railways in this district is about 296 of which 227 are broad gauge and 69 are narrow gauge. The bulk of the area in Khunti, Gumla and Simdega sub-divisions have no railway system.

There are no navigable rivers or canals in the district. The larger rivers are crossed during the rains by boats. Indian Airlines operates scheduled services connecting Ranchi with Patna and Calcutta.

The origin and subsequent development of the road, railway and air communication in the district were the results of various factors such as military necessity and administrative convenience in the British period, the production of goods of economic importance such as tea, coffee, lac and jungle fruits, the advantageous physiography of Chotanagpur plateau and, last but not the least, the exploitation of rich mineral resources in the district and industrialization since the 1960's.

The postal communication in the district has increased over time. In 1977-78 there were 446 post-offices against 35 post-offices in 1914-15, including one head post-office, sub-post offices and branch post-offices. In the tribal area, the post is usually distributed in the weekly *hats* on market days when the tribesmen attend the markets for shopping. There are telegraph offices in the district. Besides, there are post offices which send and receive telegrams through phones.

All India Radio established a broadcasting station at Ranchi town in 1957. In 1978 there were 82,300 licensed radio sets in the district. The Public Relations Department of government had distributed community listening sets in rural areas, specially to Panchayats, libraries and schools. The number of receiving sets must have increased in the wake of industrialization and urbanization during the last decade. The army and the police have wireless stations for their own use.

For administrative purposes, Ranchi was divided into four sub-divisions, however, a fifth sub-division of Lohardaga was carved recently from Gumla sub-division. Other sub-divisions are Sadar, Khunti and Simdėga. The district had 43 Community Development Blocks in 1968, 16 being tribal Blocks of which Karra, Khunti, Murhu, Tamar, Sonahatu and Erki are in the Munda area of Khunti sub-division. Each Block is headed by a gazetted officer either from State Civil or Agricultural Service. There were 39 Anchals in 1968 each in the charge of an Anchaladhikari for the collection of government revenue in the district.

The present scheme of development administration is a three tier system, comprising the Gram Panchayat at the grass-roots level, the Panchayat Samiti at the block level and the Zila Parishad at the apex. Most of the development works have to be performed through the agency of Panchayats subject to the supervision and control of the Panchayat Samiti and Zila Parishad. The Zila Parishad allots funds received from government and directs as to how a particular scheme should be implemented. The Panchayat is headed by a Mukhia and the Panchayat Samiti has a Pramukh at the apex. Each Panchayat has a Gram Sewak, who along with the Mukhia takes care of development and welfare programmes in the area.

NEIGHBOURING TRIBES

The Munda do not live in isolation. There are other Mundari tribes like Kharia, Ho, Santal, Birhor and Bhumij and non-Mundari tribes such as Oraon who share the Munda ecology. The Munda village is generally inhabited by Hindu service castes with whom the Munda have functional interdependence, a sort of *jajmani* system.

The tribes of Chotanagpur differ not only from the non-tribal populations, but also from one another. These differences relate to means of subsistence, social organisation and language, but no consistent correlation can be established between any of, these features. Two tribes speaking languages which belong to the same linguistic group may differ in their means of subsistence, while there may be two tribes on the more or less same economic level which have no linguistic affinities.

The share of tribals in the population of Ranchi district declined from 70% in 1941 to 58% in 1971; it was mainly due to a comparatively higher rate of change in the district population during that period. While the district population increased by 59% in 1941-71, the tribal population registered only a 31% increase during the same period. The higher rate of change in the district population may be attributed to large scale immigration of non-tribals in the wake of rapid industrialization in Ranchi district during the last decade.

Among the tribes sharing the Munda ecology in Chotanagpur the Santals are the most numerous of all and mainly inhabit in Santal Parganas district. The Ho and the Bhumij are mostly found in Singhbhum, while the Birhors are generally dispersed in the forests of Hazaribagh district. The respective population of these tribes in 1971 in Bihar State was such as Santal (1,801,304), Oraon (876,218), Ho (505,172), Kharia (127,002), Bhumij (124,918), and Birhor (3,464).

All the tribes belong to the Proto-australoid racial stock and linguistically, except the Oraon, come under the Mundari group of Austro-asiatic family of languages. The Oraon, on the other hand, belong to the Dravidian language family.

Except for the Birhor all other tribes live in permanent mixed villages. The Birhors are largely a nomadic tribe with no fixed habitation. Of the Uthlu and Jaghi Birhors the latter are of a more settled type and live in a settlement, called *Tanda*, comprising a few families. However, most of the Uthlu Birhors are now settled in government colonies.

All other tribes except Birhor are settled agriculturists practising both dry and wet cultivation. They look towards forests during times of scarcity. They also supplement their deficit economy by working in mines and industrial centres during agricultural off season. The Birhors are food gatherers, hunters and rope makers and live close to nature because of their simple technological and economic pursuits. Among the Kharia, the Hill Kharias live on the inhospitable hills and practise shifting cultivation.

A comparative analysis of the kinship systems of all these tribes reveals a certain uniformity transcending linguistic differences. Though the terms designating kin in the different tribes vary with their language, the general method of reckoning is classificatory. Joking and avoidance relationships between kin follow the same pattern among the Munda, Oraon, Ho, Santal Kharia, Bhumij and Birhor. So also do the specific duties assigned to certain kin on the occasion of birth, marriage or death. All these tribes share the system of ritual friendship. The practice of sororate and levirate is also common to all tribes and so is the practice of bridewealth payment.

All the tribes are divided into exogamous totemic clans. All the members of a clan are supposed to be descended from a common ancestor, a mythical figure. Stratification of clans is found only among the Dhelki Kharia, who are divided into eight clans, two of which are believed to be lower in status than the rest and one of them is by common consent considered the highest. All the tribes are endogamous and clan exogamy is practised. In villages which are composed of a single clan, village exogamy automatically results from clan exogamy. But even in villages inhabited by more than one clan, there is among most of the tribes, a latent prejudice against marriage within the same village. Instances of inter-tribal marriage among Munda and Kharia and Munda and Oraon as well as among tribals and non-tribals are found these days. Instances of love marriages within the same village and clan are also found. Such couples are allowed to live together after paying a fine and giving a feast to the Panchayat.

All the tribes are patrilineal and patrilocal. The tribal family is generally nuclear, though in some cases parents and married children continue to live together till the death of the parents. All the tribes are generally monogamous, though instances of polygyny are also found. Most common form of marriage is through negotiation. Examples of other matrimonial forms, such as marriage by exchange, marriage by intrusion, love marriage, by capture and by service are also found in some of these tribes.

Tribal religion is a potent force in strengthening the social solidarity of the people. All the tribes believe in supernatural powers. Relationship with them is established through the village priest. These tribes have evolved a system of beliefs and practices to cope with the supernatural world, the intimate relationship between the tribals and their deities is concretely manifested in their various rites and ceremonies. Their pantheon includes various classes of deities with a Supreme God at the apex. These constitute nature gods, village gods, clan gods, lineage gods and family gods. There are a number of Hindu deities such as Mahadev, Devi Mai etc., which have become the part of tribal pantheon. Hinduism and Christianity have greatly influenced their religious beliefs and rituals. Christian converts are found among the Munda, Santal, Oraon, and Kharia. The Bhumij have got Hinduised on a large scale. Among the Oraon reformist sects such as Tana Bhagats and various other Bhagats are found. The Hinduised and Christian tribals have transformed their life-ways and thought-ways and respectively look towards Hindu castes and Christian missionaries for inspiration.

In the social life of some of these tribes, specially the Oraon, the youth dormitory is an important institution and an integral part of the village organisation. Among the Munda, the Kharia and the Birhor it has been known as Gitiora, and among the Oraon as Dhumkuria. The Dhumkuria is a school of social training from which the tribal youth learns not only the tribal lore but imbibes all the qualities which will make him a useful member of the tribal community. Today the youth dormitory has lost its significance in most of the tribal villages and it has ceased to exist in many others.

All the tribes have an elaborate system of social control. They have a village Panchayat which deals with disputes, breaches of peace and social offences at the village level. In some of these tribes there are inter-village organisations based either on kinship or territorial unity. In some the villages are grouped in loose unions such as Birhors, while among others such groupings relate only to the administration of tribal justice, several villages being represented on one Panchayat. The bonds that unite such a group of villages vary in strength, but in all cases, the legal authority of the group is vested in a Panchayat known as Parha among the Munda, Oraon and Kharia, Pir among Ho, and Pargana among Santals. This institution forms a court of appeal from decisions of the village Panchayat. Moreover, it is the only authority competent to try certain types of offences. Serious action is taken on those guilty of clan incest and witchcraft and the offender may be excommunicated. The punishment for an offence may vary from public disapproval, imposition of a fine to excommunication, depending upon the nature of the offence. Re-admission to the tribe is also effected through this regional organisation after undertaking a purificatory ceremony and giving a feast to the community.

Among the Santals an extreme form of punishment, *Bitlaha*, is prevalent. It follows the sentence of formal excommunication and is a social expression of the extreme disapproval of the community as a whole. In case of clan or kin incest and of sexual intercourse with non-Santal, eating with forbidden kinsmen or touching tabooed relatives, *Bitlaha* may be taken recourse to when no other measure could impress upon the offender the seriousness of the offence.

In the Munda area non-tribal Hindu and Muslim communities have been living among the tribals for several hundred years. There is no tribal village where a few Hindu caste families do not exist. They speak the tribal language and are in many cases indistinguishable from the tribals. Beside these, in many areas of Tamar in Panch Parganas there are high caste Hindus residing in the tribal villages. It is through these channels that Hindu culture permeates into the tribal areas.

In a Munda village there is a close economic relationship between the Mundas and the other tribal (Lohra) and non-tribal communities. The Mundas work as agricultural labourers, borrow money from and mortgage land to the non-tribal landlords and money-lenders. There is a kind of *jajmani* system or functional inter-dependence among the Mundas and the lower Hindu castes in addition to sharing of common habitat. The presence of government offices (like Block Development Office, Health Centre, Anchal Office etc.), largely manned by non-tribal personnel, offer another opportunity for the Munda and other tribals in the area to interact with the outsiders. The spread of roads and railways in the tribal area has exposed them quite a lot to outside influence.

The following table gives an idea of the social anatomy of

the three Munda villages where field-work was concentrated :

TABLE 2.2

Caste' Tribewise Distribution of Households

Tribe/Caste	Number of Households		
	Salehatu	Gutuhatu	Amlesa
Munda	99	101	61
Brahmin	—	—	8
Kumhar	—	2	12
Hazam	—	—	10
Puran	—	—	50
Sau	—	—	4
Rautia	—	7	—
Chik	—	2	—
Swansi	2	—	30
Ghasi	4	—	40
Lohra	1	1	3
Total	106	113	218

In Salehatu about 13 miles east of Khunti, there are about a hundred (99) households belonging to the Munda dispersed in three different hamlets. In addition to these four households belong to Nayak or Ghasi, two to Swansi (both Scheduled Castes) and one household to the Lohra tribe. The Ghasi are musicians of the Mundas. The Swansi are weavers. The Lohra are traditional blacksmiths who sharpen and repair the agricultural implements of the Munda. The Ghasi, the Swansi and the Lohra have a type of *jajmani* relationship with the Munda,but occupy a lower social and ritual status than the latter. The Munda do not accept water or cooked meals and rice beer from these people, while the latter can accept these from the Munda. There are three Munda households belonging to the Christian fold. The non-converted Munda do not share food and water with the converts.

In Gutuhatu village of Torpa Block there are 113 households of which 101 belong to the Munda. A majority of the Munda are converts to Christianity and the rest are *Sansar* (unconverted). There are 7 households of Rautias, two each of Kumhar and Chick Braik and a single household of Lohra. Rautias are agriculturists and the Munda and other caste people borrow money from them on interest or by mortgaging their lands. The Kumhar are potters and supply the villagers with earthernware on festive occasions. Chick Braiks are the village weavers ; however, in Gutuhatu in one of the households all the adult members are in service, while the other household is engaged in weaving and agriculture labour. The Lohra household serves the village by making and repairing agricultural implements. The Lohra is paid annually by each household at the harvest on the basis of the number of ploughs in a household. The non-convert Munda can accept water at the hands of Rautia and Kumhar but do not accept it from the converted Munda, Chiks and Lohra.

Amlesa in Panch Parganas has as many as 8 communities sharing the habitat with the Munda. The different communities are: Munda Brahmin, Kumhar, Hajam, Puran, Sau, Swansi, Machchua (Ghasi) and Lohra households. The Hajam (barber), Lohra, Kumhar, Swansi and Ghasi have functional interdependence with the Munda, Brahmin, Puran and Sau in terms of socio-religious and economic functions. The Mundas in this area are Hinduised and worship Hindu deities along with some tribal gods and goddesses. They do not accept water and cooked food from the Ghasi, Swansi, Lohra and converted Mundas.

The three villages exhibit the distinctive composition of Munda villages in each area. Social anatomy influences the culture and level of development in each area.

3

A DEMOGRAPHIC PERSPECTIVE

THE POPULATION of the Munda in Bihar stood at 723,166 in 1971. This accounts for nearly 15% of the State's tribal population. The Munda are largely confined to the South Chotanagpur Division. Their main areas of concentration are the districts of Ranchi and Singhbhum. These two districts account for 91% of the Munda and the rest of them are found in Hazaribagh, Palamau and Dhanbad. The south and the south-eastern part of Ranchi district is considered the chief abode of the Munda. A sprinkling of the Munda population, a little more than 1%, is also found outside the Chotanagpur region. The number of such Mundas has risen considerably during the decade 1961—71. Some of them work as wage labourers, while others are engaged in government services outside their homeland.

Ninety-five per cent of the Munda population lives in rural areas. In the decade 1961-71 the percentage of people living in the urban areas rose by nearly 2%. The figures thus reveal that the extent of urbanization among the Munda is half that of the general population in Bihar. The rise in the urban population among the Munda is generally the consequence of growing industrial complexes in and around Ranchi during the sixties.

Decennial Variation in Population (1941-71)

During the first two decades from 1941 the Munda population rose by 19.13%. In the last decade the rise was 15%. Compared to the population trends in Bihar during the same period, the rise in the Munda population lags behind that of the general population. This may be due to the fact that the death rate in tribal areas has not been brought down as in the non-tribal areas, since the number of children born to tribal couples is nearly the same as to non-tribal couples. In many such areas it has not been possible to provide medical services. The variation in the population of the Munda in this period as well as that of the general population is given in Table 3.1 below :

TABLE 3.1

Variation in Population (1941—1971)

Category of Population		1941	1951	1961	1971
Munda	(a) Population	527,116	—	628,931	723,166
	(b) Variation	—	—	+101,815	+94,235
	(c) Percentage Variation	—	—	+19.31 (1941-61)	+14.98
General Population of Bihar	(a) Population	35,174,146	+38,786,184	46,455,610	56,353,369
	(b) Variation	—	+3,612,038	+7,669,426	+9,897,759
	(c) Per cent Variation	—	+10.27	+19.77 +32.07 (1941-61)	+21.33

Source : Census of India 1961, Bihar, Part V-A. Census of India, 1971, Bihar.

Age and Sex Composition

The age and sex composition of the population at a given point has considerable effect on the potential for population growth. A population that has an extraordinarily high proportion of persons in the age bracket 45 and above reflects a low birth rate and high death rate. The net increase will be slow in such a case. According to Sundburg, the proportion of persons in the age-group of 0—14 gives an indication of the trend of population growth. If in any population 40% are in the age-group below 15, it is regarded as progressive ; if it is 30%, it represents a stationary trend, and if it is only 20%, the population trend is regressive.

Among the Munda the percentage of people in the age-group 14 and below is 42% and as such the Munda population

TABLE 3.2

Percent, age and sex composition of Population

Category of Population	Age group	1961			1971		
		P	M	F	P	M	F
Munda	0-14	41.49	41.99	41.01	42.05	42.31	41.66
	15-44	42.61	42.31	42.59	41.49	41.01	42.08
	45+	15.90	15.70	16.40	16.46	16.68	16.26
	All ages	100.00	100.00	100.00	100.00	100.00	100.00
General Population	0-14	42.30	—	—	42.60	—	—
	15-49	46.00	—	—	45.60	—	—
	50+	11.70	—	—	11.80	—	—
	All ages	100.00	—	—	100.00	—	—

Source : 1. Selected Plan Satistics Bihar, Govt. of Bihar, 1976.
2. Census of India, 1961, Bihar, Part V-A.
3. Unpublished S.T. Tables, C of I Bihar, 1971, Table ST-II.

may be placed in the progressive category. In the general population of the State the same trend is noticeable. There has been a slight fall in the proportion of the population among the Munda in the reproductive age-group (15—44) from 42.61% in 1961 to 41.5% in 1971. The general population in Bihar also shares this trend. The young and the old age-groups (below 15 years and above 45 years) gained at the cost of the age-group 15—44. This signifies some decrease in the working population and an increase in the proportion of children and of old men. The increase in the number of people in the age-group 45 and above shows a trend towards better longevity.

Sex Ratio

The sex ratio in the Munda population in 1961-71 is given in the table below :

TABLE 3.3

Sex Ratio (Females per 1000 Males)

Category of population	Age-group	0—14	15—44	45+	All ages
Munda	1961	989	1,029	1,068	1,018
	1971	995	1,037	985	1,010
Age groups		0—14	15—49	50+	All ages
General Population of Bihar	1961	945	1,027	1,053	994
	1971	919	989	942	954

Source : Computed from Age and Sex Data given in Table 3.2.

The table shows a decline in the over all sex ratio among the Munda from 1,018 females per thousand males in 1961 to 1,010 in 1971. The same trend is to be seen in the general population of Bihar during this period. However, it is important to note that the sex ratio is much more adverse in the general population than among the Munda. Among the Munda the females outnumber the males in the 15—44 years age-group in 1961 as well as in 1971.

Age, Sex and Marital Status

The precentage distribution of the Munda and the general population by marital status for both sexes is given in Table 3.4.

Marital status is influenced by age and socio-economic characteristics of the population. Distribution by age and marital status for males and females among the Munda is given in Table 3.5.

Never Married

In the 1971 Census 55% males and 48% females were returned in this category. These percentages are higher than the corresponding figures in 1961. In the age-group 0—14, 99% of the males were not married. In the age group 15—44, 32% were in this category and in the age-group 45 and above only 1.38% were not married. Among women, nearly 98% were unmarried in the age-group 0—14; 18% in the age-group 15—44 and 1.46% in the age-group 45 and above. During the last two decades there has been a rising trend in the age at marriage and also a slight increase in the percentage of persons who are not married.

Married

The percentage of married among males and females in 1971 was slightly more than 40% and less than 44% respectively. The change for males was negligible, while the females registered a slight increase in the married category. Among the males less than 1% in the 0—14 age-group were married, more than 64% in the next group were married and among those in the 45 and above age-group 83% were married. Among women in the three successive age-groups, 2%, 76% and 57% were married.

TABLE 3.4
Per cent distribution of population by sex and marital status

Category of Population		Never Married		Married		Widowed		Divorced/ Separated		Unspecified		Total Population	
		M	F	M	F	M	F	M	F	M	F	M	F
Munda	1961	53.96	45.71	40.84	42.27	4.55	11.36	0.58	0.56	0.07	0.10	100.00	100.00
	1971	55.36	48.39	40.55	43.85	3.73	8.76	0.27	0.31	0.09	0.05	100.00	100.00
General	1961	49.78	39.57	45.93	49.22	3.94	10.91	0.29	0.24	0.06	0.06	100.00	100.00
Population	1971	NA	NA	NA	NA	NA	NA	NA	NA	NA	NA	NA	NA

Source : 1. Census of India, 1961, Bihar, Part V-A.
2. Census of India, 1971, Bihar, (Table S T. II-unpublished).

TABLE 3.5

Distribution of population by age and marital status

Age groups	Year	Never Married		Married		Widowed		Divorced/ Separated		Unspecified		Total	
		M	F	M	F	M	F	M	F	M	F	M	F
0—14	1961	97.07	96.42	2.70	3.40	0.10	0.09	0.05	0.07	0.06	0.02	100.00	100.00
	1971	99.18	97.70	0.71	2.19	0.01	0.02	0.01	0.01	0.09	0.06	100.00	100.00
15—44	1961	29.95	14.40	65.06	76.35	3.90	8.32	1.04	1.02	0.05	0.17	100.00	100.00
	1971	32.20	17.71	64.41	76.50	2.84	5.13	0.52	0.59	0.12	0.06	100.00	100.00
45+	1961	2.83	1.65	77.99	50.19	18.40	47.49	0.74	0.55	0.04	0.12	100.00	100.00
	1971	1.38	1.46	82.96	57.63	15.28	40.55	0.32	0.35	0.05	0.01	100.00	100.00

Source : Same as in Table 3.4.

Widowed

The population of widowed among the Munda were 3.7% and 8.8% for males and females respectively in 1971. These were less than the corresponding figures for 1961. The proportion of widowed (for both sexes in all the three age-groups) declined during the sixties. The proportion of widows was almost three times higher than the corresponding figure for widowers. The population of widowed person is highest in the age bracket 45 and above. The sex differential in widowhood could be traced to differential mortality which is comparatively higher for males at higher ages.

Divorces and Separated

The proportion of divorced and separated in a population largely depends upon its socio-economic and cultural characteristics. Among the Munda cases of divorce are settled at the level of the traditional Panchayat. Either spouse may remarry soon after a divorce. Thus the, actual number of divorces tends to be underrated.

Economic Activities

The proportion of workers among the Munda was higher than in the general population, both in 1961 and in 1971. This was true for both the sexes. The table below gives a

TABLE 3.6

Percentage of economically active people

Category of Population		1961			1971		
		P	M	F	P	M	F
Munda	T	60.57	62.18	58.98	34.26	55.89	12.86
	R	61.26	62.64	59.92	34.22	56.33	12.52
	U	40.01	49.38	29.89	35.04	48.04	19.97
General Population							
	T	41.40	55.60	27.10	31.00	52.40	10.58
	R	42.20	56.00	28.50	32.25	52.26	11.00
	U	33.20	51.70	10.40	29.33	47.80	6.42

Source : Census of India, 1961, Bihar, 1971 Census Bihar ; Table ST-I-Bihar, 1971 (unpublished).

comparative picture of the tribal and the general population, both in rural and urban areas in 1961 and 1971.

Age-sex differential was found in the participation rates. It is always higher for the males than the females, both in rural and urban population. The overall participation rate declined considerably over the decade in both populations. The change was more pronounced among the rural rather than urban workers and among the female rather than male workers. Some 90% of the workers among the Munda, as compared to 82% of the general population, were depending on agriculture, either as cultivators or as labourers. Among the Munda there was a decline in the proportion of cultivators by 17%. This was accompanied by a rise in the percentage of agricultural labourers, but the participation in the agricultural sector remained almost the same over the decade. Only a little over 2% of the Munda were engaged in livestock, mining and quarrying. The table 3.7 gives classification of workers by occupations in 1961 and 1971.

Primary Sector

An overwhelming majority of workers (92.61%) among the Munda are engaged in the primary sector.

Secondary Sector

Less than 3% of the workers among the Munda belong to the secondary sector. Of these, half are engaged in the manufacturing in other than household industry. During the sixties there was an overall increase in the proportion of workers in these sectors. There has been a shift from household industry to non-household industry and construction work.

Tertiary Sector

4.42% of Munda workers were engaged in the tertiary sector. Among these, the bulk belonged to other services. The proportion of workers in the tertiary sector increased by more than 20% during the sixties. The increase was most marked in the categories of trade, commerce and transport. During the past years there has been a rise in landlessness among the Munda. This accounts for a decrease in the percentage of cultivators and an increment in the proportion of

TABLE 3.7

Industrial classification of workers—1961 & 1971

Category of Population/ Category of workers		Cultivators	Agricultural labourers	Livestock	M & Q	Primary	Secondary	Tertiary	Total workers
		I	II	III	IV	I—IV	V—VI	VII—IX	
Munda	1961	84.75	6.05	—	3.61*	94.41	1.94	3.65	100.00
	1971	70.46	19.81	0.63	1.72	92.61	2.97	4.42	100.00
General Population :									
	1961	53.90	23.00	—	3.40*	80.30	8.20	11.50	100.00
	1971	43.30	38.90	0.90	1.50*	84.60	5.70	9.60	100.00

*Joint figure for categories III and IV.

Source : Same as in Table 3.6.

agricultural labourers. More and more people are shifting from livestock, fishing, mining and quarrying. They are moving towards trade, commerce, transport and industrial labour.

Literacy and Levels of Education

The literacy rate for the Munda is lower (16.31) than for the general population (19.97). The rate of literacy increased during the sixties. Among the Munda the literacy rate during this period increased by more than double and at this rate the Munda literacy figures may surpass the general population during the next ten years.

Urban literacy rates were more than double than those for rural areas, but these high urban literacy rates did not contribute significantly towards the total literacy rate, because only 5% of the Munda live in urban areas. Both rural and urban areas experienced an increase in the literacy rate during the sixties. The female literacy rate is almost the same among the Munda and the general population. The male literacy rate is three times that for the female although the gap is narrower in the urban area. The urban female literacy increase among the Munda was higher as compared to the increase in the same category in the general population. The figures reveal that literacy rates for both the sexes, both in rural and urban areas, increased during the sixties. The literacy rate showed faster progress in urban rather than rural areas and for females as compared to males. In both these aspects the Munda fared better than the general population.

In 1971 of the 16.31% of literates and those with other educational levels among the Munda, 7.23% were literates without any educational level, 8.13% had read up to the pirmary and less than 1% were matriculates and above. If we analyse the increase at various levels from 1961, we find that in 1971 the total literacy rate increased by more than 18%. In the level of literates without any educational level, the increase was 13.4%. At the primary level the increase was 108% and in the matriculation and above level the increase was 160%. Although the total increase was not very significant, the trend shows an inclination towards educational levels higher than literacy. This is on account of the provision of better educational facilities, opening of new schools and the popularity of post-matric

TABLE 3.8

Per cent distribution of illiterates, literates and those with education levels among the Munda and general population of Bihar for the years 1961 and 1971.

Levels of Education		Munda				General Population			
		1961		1971		1961		1971	
		%	No.	%	No	%	No	%	No.
Illiterates	P	86.20	(542,083)	83.69	(605,249)	81.60	(3790,7765)	80.06	(45,115,756)
	M	78.62	(244,990)	76.12	(273,814)	70.17	(1635,0482)	69.36	(20,007,549)
	F	93.62	(297,093)	91.18	(331,435)	93.10	(2155,7283)	91.28	(25,108,207)
Literates without educational level	P	9.51	(59,837)	7.23	(52,277)	13.60	(6,321,489)	7.60	(4,281,267)
	M	14.75	(45,976)	10.23	(36,789)	21.40	(4,978,257)	10.90	(3,145,570)
	F	4.37	(13.861)	4.26	(15,488)	5.80	(1,343,232)	4.13	(1,135,697)
Primary	P	3.92	(24,674)	8.13	(58,787)	3.50	(1,647,245)	9.57	(5,393,790)
	M	6.02	(18,723)	12.16	(43,745)	6.10	(1,430,421)	14.84	(4,280,430)
	F	1.88	(5,951)	4.14	(15,042)	0.90	(216,824)	4.05	(1,113,360)

Matric and above	P	0.37	(2,337)	0.95	(68,53)	1.30	(579,111)	2.77	(1,562,556)
	M	0.61	(1.911)	1.49	(5,350)	2.30	(542,289)	4.90	(1,413,395)
	F	0.13	(426)	0.42	(1,503)	0.20	(36,822)	0.54	(149,161)
Total	P	13.80	(86,848)	16.31	(117,919)	18.40	(8,547,845)	19.94	(11,237,613)
	M	21.38	(66,610)	23.88	(85,884)	29.83	(6,950,967)	30.64	(8,839,395)
	F	0.38	(20,238)	8.82	(32,033)	6.90	(1,546,878)	8.72	(2,398,218)
Total Population	P	100.00	(628,931)	100.00	(723,166)	100.00	(4645,5610)	100.00	(56,353,369)
	M	100.00	(311,600)	100.00	(359,698)	100.00	(2330,1449)	100.00	(28,846,944)
	F	100.00	(317,331)	100.00	(363,468)	100.00	(2315,4111)	100.00	(27,506,425)

Source :
1. Census of Bihar, 1961,
2. Special Tables for S.C. & S.T. Census of Bihar—1961.
3. Unpublished Tables for Scheduled Tribes, Census of Bihar—1971 (Table S.T.—III, Part, A & B)
4. Unpublished Tables C-III, Part A, Census of Bihar, 1971.

education.

Among the Munda, for males in the sixties there was some decrease in the rate in the first category, *viz.*, literate without educational level, but in the second there was almost 100% increase and in the third the increase was 144%. As regards females, the corresponding rates of change in the three categories there was a slight decrease in the first category, 136% increase in the second and 223% increase in the third category. The decline in the proportion of literates without education along with considerable increase in the proportion at the primary level and at the matriculation and above levels among males and females during the period 1961-71 shows the growing popularity for school education. However, from the decline in the increase at the level of literacy without any educational level, it seems that larger numbers of Mundas are not coming into the educational net. For this special efforts have to be made.

Higher Education

Among the Munda in 1961 in urban areas there were only 66 who had received education higher than the matriculation level. 58 of them had obtained a university degree. In 1971 the total number of persons with higher education went up to 525, *i.e.*, an almost eight-fold rise over the 1961 figures. The number of those with university degrees increased from 58 in 1961 to 460 in 1971. In categories such as technical diplomas not equivalent to degrees and in technical degrees there was also an increase. This tremendous increase during the 1960's and the number of those competing for higher education is evidence of the high aspirations of the Munda. During this period the number of colleges in the Munda areas went up and since post-matric education is not only free but gets everyone a scholarship, the boost for higher education is significant.

Religion

Table 3.9 shows the changes in the percentages of the Munda belonging to Hinduism, Christianity and tribal religions during the last sixty years, *viz.*, 1911-1970. The table shows a steady increase in the proportions of those professing Hinduism and Christianity. There was a steady decline in the percentage of those subscribing to tribal religions from 1911 to 1961, but in 1971 this percentage went up. This is on account of the fact of resurgence of ethnicity among the Munda. They are now showing an increasing awareness of affinity with their tribal beliefs and customs. The increase in the number of those professing tribal religion has been at the expense of those professing Hinduism. In 1911 there were almost equal proportions of Christian and Hindu among the Munda, but after sixty years they were almost twice as many Hindu as Christian. Almost half the Munda population has been returned as Hindu and the rest were almost equally divided among the Christian and those professing tribal religions. This decline in the category of Hindu and an increase in the category of tribal religion is not only peculiar to the Munda, but the trend is shared by all the Scheduled tribes in Bihar taken together.

TABLE 3.9

Religious affiliations of the Mundas (1911-71) and All S.T. in Bihar (1961-71)

Year	Population	Number per 100 returned as		
		Christians	Hindu	Tribal religion (Sarnaism)
1911	Munda	16.4	18.1	65.5
1921		20.4	27.4	52.2
1931		24.3	29.8	45.9
1961		26.3	53.7	20.0
1971		26.0	49.0	25.0
1961	All S.T.	10.6	72.1	17.4
1971		11.1	69.4	19.6

Source : Census of India, 1961, Vol. IV, Bihar, Part V-A, Special tables for S.C. & S.T.

2. Unpublished tables (S.T.V.) Census of India, 1971, Bihar.

It is seen that between those who professed Hinduism and those reported to be belonging to the tribal religion or Sarnaism there is a very thin line of demarcation. A shift from Hinduism to tribal religion and vice versa is easy for them. Even those who professed Sarnaism take part in the worship of Hindu deities and join Hindu festivals.

4

THE MUNDA IN HISTORY

THE ORIGINAL habitat and migrations of the Mundari speaking peoples of middle India is shrouded in a thick veil of mystery. We do not have a well substantiated account of their migration and arrival in Chotanagpur. Their myths and legends, rites and customs provide us with some clues, but these are not very clear and such a reconstruction would be no more than conjecture. Sarat Chandra Roy has produced a plausible account of their migrations through time. Originally he held that the Munda and other Mundari speaking communities lived around the Aravalli hills in Rajasthan and from there they dispersed in two streams towards the Vindhya mountains and the Kaimur hills. From there they spread to the district of Sarguja in Madhya Pradesh and further on to the southern and eastern parts of the Chotanagpur plateau. In 1931, however, Sarat Chandra Roy changed his position and held that like other tribal people the Munda also arrived in Bihar through the north-western mountain passes. On the basis of his studies in the *Rig Veda*, the *Ramayana* and the *Mahabharata*, he traced the history of these communities till they were driven east wards by the advancing Aryan hordes and came to settle in the Azamgarh district of U.P.

According to Munda tradition they migrated from the southern part of north India to modern Bundelkhand and middle India, spread over Rajasthan and north-western India and finally, entered Chotanagpur through modern Rohilkhand and Oudh. Their last place of dispersal was Rohtas in the Kaimur hills. The Munda and the Santal crossed the river Sone and advanced towards the south-east and reached that place which now separates the district of Hazaribagh from Ranchi and

Palamau. It is at this stage that the Santal parted company with the Munda. They crossed the river Damodar and settled in Sikharbhum (modern Hazaribagh) and passed into Santal Parganás through Manbhum. On their arrival in Ranchi district the Munda had to wage sanguinary struggle against the Asur, another Mundari speaking tribe which had settled there earlier. The struggle continued for a long time till the Munda drove them into the north-western corner of the Ranchi district. Echoes of this conflict are found in the folklore of the Munda. Relics of Asur settlements have been found in the south-eastern parts of Ranchi district. Later the Oraon pushed the Munda from the north and north-western part of the Ranchi district. This is evident from the existence of Munda Pahan (religious headman) in a large number of villages in this area which at present do not have any Munda population.

Another clue to the origin of the Mundari speaking peoples may be an investigation of their linguistic affinity. The Mundari speaking peoples do not form a composite racial stock. They are a large language family and differ in physical characteristics from each other. In the first half of the nineteenth century the Mundari group was regarded as a branch of the Dravidian group of languages. However, in 1854 Max Muller expressed grave doubts about this classification and gave the Mundari language family a separate and distinct identity. Early in the present century Wilhelm Schmidt established the relationship of the Mundari languages with the Mon-Khmer languages of Thailand. The language of the Khasis of Assam also belongs to the Mon-Khmer group. Schmidt regarded it as part of the Austro-Asiatic languages, a stream of the Austric language family which extends from Madagascar, India, Malaysia, Indonesia, Polynesia and touches the shores of South America. Efforts were made in subsequent years to examine the relationship between Austric and other language families in the world. Trombty tried to explore the relationship between the Austric and some of the African continental languages. The close affinity between Mon-Khmer languages and Mundari languages is, according to Schmidt and Hevesy based on four reasons : (1) closeness between pronunciation and spelling, (2) symmetry in word formation, (3) grammar, and (4) vocabulary. They found that 200 word roots were the same in these languages. Hevesy did not agree with the views of Schmidt and tried to explore the affinities between the Mundari languages and Finno-ugric language family. Gordon Bowles, who made a deep study of the Mundari language and the anthropometry of the Munda, rejected the contentions of Schmidt and Hevesy. Schmidt's contention, however, has sometime back received the support of F.B. Kuiper, the famous Dutch linguistic expert and, as such, is the only accepted theory on this subject. Thus, looking for the linguistic affinities of Mundari speaking people is not very helpful in tracing their origin in migrations, especially when we know that a close correspondence between language and ethnic characteristics may not always exist.

The long history of the Munda in their present habitat can be divided into four periods : (a) primordial age in which the Munda were more or less isolated from outside influences and were characterized by non-monetised circulation of goods and services, (b) State formation and the onset of feudalism, (c) colonial rule, and (d) the post-independence period.

The Primordial Age

In this period the Munda lived for many centuries unmolested in their isolated mountain fastnesses. They were able to lead a peaceful and undisturbed life. They built up a polity suited to their environment. Land acquired from the forests was owned generally by a group of agnatic families living in distinct villages called Hatu. The boundaries of the villages were well recognized and sacrosanct. They were guarded by boundary deities. Each village had its *Sarna* (sacred grove) where the Hatu Bangako (village gods) were lodged. Authority in the village remained with the Khutkatidars from whom the village headmen, secular and sacerdotal, were chosen. With the passage of time, some affinal relations of the Khutkatidars came to settle in these villages but they did not enjoy equal rights with the descendants of the original settlers. In course of time, some service castes, such as blacksmith, weavers etc. came to settle in the village. All the non-Khutkatidars were known as the *Praja Horoko*. During this time agriculture came to be the main occupation of the Munda. Part of their subsistence, however, continued to be drawn from hunting and foodgathering. During this period outsiders could only be found along the well established trade and pilgrim routes. In the district of Manbhum, Beglar, who passed through various parts of the province in 1872-73, discovered the remains of many settlements along the various routes. Since, however, the tribals were in the interior neither the pilgrims nor the traders seem to have had any contact with them.

State Formation and Adoption of Feudalism

The tribals were living in village communities under patriarchs. The patriarchs were frequently involved in conflicts with the invading forces. Some of these patriarchs decided to elect a king. Most scholars think that this must have been soon after the fall of the imperial Guptas in the fifth century A.D. (Roy Choudhary, 1957, : 66). The first king, as mentioned in the chronicles of the Chotanagpur Raj, was Phani Mukut Rai. He is reputed to be the foster son of Madra Munda, the patriarch of Sutiambe. Phani Mukut Rai was said to be the son of a serpent father and a Brahmin mother and was fostered in a tribal home. It was said that on the birth of the child his father the great serpent Pundarik Nag was guarding the deserted baby with its expanded hood. Thus started the Nagbansi dynasty after whom the region came to be known.

It is, however, not clear whether the Mundas were able to immediately set up a full-fledged state administration with the king as its head. For a long time the king only received *chanda* or contribution from the different village communities and he was regarded as the leader of the people and not the master of the land. The Khutkatidars regarded him more or less as an honorific head. The chief function of the Raja may have been to coordinate the relations between the different patriarchs as also their relations with the aliens passing through Chotanagpur. It is, however, clear that the advent of the king must have set in motion the process of state formation, the principal conditions for which were the extension of cultivation through reclamation of land and introduction of better agricultural skills by contact with advanced agricultural communities from the plains. The Nagbansi Rajas, like the Gonds and Chero chiefs, invited non-tribal peasant communities like Kurmis and Koeris to settle in the villages. These communities introduced superior agricultural technology and raised the level of the economy from one of subsistence to that of surplus which the creation of a new state urgently required. Such state formation was accompanied by a new mode of production. This resulted in the imposition of the feudal superstructure on the tribal society and was the beginning of the break-down of the tribal polity characterized by joint ownership of land. Social stratification based on command over economic resources and defined in terms of ritual status began to emerge. State formation promoted trade and commerce, developed trade routes and facilitated the growth of small urban centres. A variety of castes ranging from Brahmins, Routias and many artisan communities flocked to these new centres. Thus, in this period a complex socio-economic system had developed in all the Munda country.

During the reign of Emperor Akbar in 1585, the Raja of Chotanagpur was forced to become a tribute paying vassal. During the time of Jahangir, Durjan Sal, the Nagbansi chief who was 46th in descent from the founder of the dynasty was defeated by Mughal forces, captured and taken to Delhi. He was released only when he showed his skill in recognizing real diamonds from fake ones. During his sojourn outside Chotanagpur the simple Nagbansi chief was dazzled by the pomp and grandeur of the Mughal court and on his return to Chotanagpur he began to copy the Mughal court style. He gathered a large number of courtiers and retinue and built a large palace at Doisa. He also began a system of granting villages as Jagirs to his loyal supporters. Service or maintenance grants of villages were made in case of members of the royal family. Some of these Jagirs were also given to alien elements in return for loans which the chief needed for the heavy expenditure in the courts and for other services rendered. The earliest of these grants is dated A.D. 1676. Some of the later chiefs built a number of Hindu temples. Within a short time a new class of people consisting of up-country businessmen, money-lenders, Brahmin priests and others came to be settled in various parts of Munda country. Jagirdars or tenure holders brought in rent contractors and exacted all kinds of dues and forced labour from tribal tenants. In many areas, therefore, the original settlers lost their proprietorship over their villages and were reduced to the status of Bhuinhars or ordinary tenants.

The process of state formation in the Munda country

promoted sanskritization in a big way and stimulated commercial activities, developed trade and the growth of small urban centres. These developments led to the creation of a stratified structural base for the integration of the tribes with the higher order of Indian civilization. Roy-Burman, however, doubts whether a causal relationship can be established between state formation and the integration of the tribes with Indian civilization. It can, however, be stated that the adoption of Hindu customs and the feudal model helped in mobilizing external support for effectively building the coercive apparatus of the state. The political authority of Parha head, the Manki, evaporated in the entire area west to the Ranchi-Chaibasa road. The more conservative and uncompromising Munda migrated to the south and south-east of the Bihar and clung to their original institutions. The entire process led to the break-up of the traditional Khutkati system. The right of the village community over a large part of the village lands was appropriated by the Jagirdar as the Raja's share or *Rajhas*. Out of Rajhas land some plots were cultivated by the farm servants of the Jagirdars and such lands were known as the *Manjihas*. Some of the waste jungles were left as vestiges of the common property of the village community. Thus, the Bhuinhari tenure came into being in the broken Khutkati villages. Kumar Suresh Singh gives another reason for the break-up of the Khutkati tenure. According to him the Oraon, who displaced the Munda from many areas in Ranchi district, showed an inclination towards development of kingship and had no interest in the communal agrarian system of the Munda. Since the break-up of the Khutkati system was spread over a long period of time, a unidimensional explanation of the phenomenon does not seem to be plausible. The reason adduced by Singh may have been a contributory factor in the entire process.

Colonial Period

The third period is covered by the colonial rule. After the grant of the Diwani in 1765, the British laid their claim to the entire state of Bihar including Chotanagpur. In 1771 the Maharaja of Chotanagpur became a vassal of the East India Company. The then Maharaja, Durpnath Sahi obtained his recognition on condition that he paid Rs. 6,000 a year as tribute and another Rs. 6,000 as rent. The internal administration of his dominion was left entirely in his hand. The recognition by the East India Company buttressed the position of the Nagbansi chief. The government recognized him as the owner of the entire land and not just as the leader of the people. The influx of up country merchants, money-lenders and petty officials unacquainted with the customs, land tenure and language of the people, multiplied the sufferings of the Munda. The unrest came to ahead in Tamar itself where disturbances continued from 1789 to 1795. In 1809 the Raja was ordered by the Company to maintain police stations in his dominions and appoint Thanadars and Chaukidars. This further aggravated discontent among the Munda. Around the year 1817 the Munda country was brought under the direct administration of the East India Company as part of the Ramgarh district and the Raja was deprived of his position as a tributary chief. After the Kol insurrection in 1832-33, the new district of Lohardaga came into being and the system of Zamindari police was introduced.

Police stations began to be maintained at headquarters at government expense and at Palkot, Govindpur, Tamar, Silli etc. at the expense of the landlords of the area. A number of other developments took place during this period, which broke up the communal character of the village. In the olden days, the Pahan was the village headman. He was assisted in his secular duties by the Munda When the new government structure came into being with the police, civil, revenue and criminal courts, the Munda came in closer contact with these officials. In the eyes of these officials the Munda came to be recognised as the legitimate representative of the village. He did take advantage of this impression and came to be regarded as the owner of the whole village. In some villages there was conflict between the Munda and the Pahan symbolised by having different *sasans* (bone burial grounds) for the descendants of the two officials, even though they belonged to the same clan.

The deterioration in the condition of the tribals may be attributed to the establishment of a new system of law and order which facilitated the entry of aliens in tribal areas and stopped up the exploitation of the tribals. These newcomers enjoyed the patronage of the administrative machinery. Thus, the newly established administration only gave legitimacy to the exploiters in the form of money-lenders and land grabbers. An important development of the period was the extinction of the tribal tenure of the land and the mode of assessment of rent. Tribal custom recognised the right of a *Khutkatidar* to reclaim and cultivate as much upland as he could, but the landlords usurped this right in their interest to enhance the rent.

Forced labour and exactions of various kinds were the order of the day. The first Settlement Officer of Ranchi district, Reid detailed twenty-one kinds of duties which were exacted by the landlords. Attempts were made to mitigate the sufferings of the tribals but these only touched the surface. However, it took a violent and armed uprising to convince the authorities that the discontent could not be contained (K.S. Singh, 1969 : 554). The dues and exactions were abolished and commuted in the first decade of the present century.

One response to the continued pressure of population and diminishing resources in the Munda country was that the upcountry people introduced new crops, implements and practices relating to both wet and dry land. The tribes had adopted terrace and wet cultivation and had developed an excellent technology suited to both communal and private family land. It was possible with the help of the new technology introduced by the outsiders to extend cultivation. Multicaste and ethnic village settlements came into being in which tribal peasants and artisans and functional castes joined in the process of production. Thus, the isolation of the tribals had more or less gone. Even though they continued to derive a part of their sustenance from the forest, by and large, in the Munda country the tribes were emerging as a community of peasants. The process of peasantisation was further promoted by the tribal markets. The colonial system created a demand for cash to pay the land revenue and other dues and to meet the expenditure of various kinds to buy some necessities which could only be acquired by ready cash. Simple barter or even money barter gave place to monetary transactions. The Munda country was rich in the production of lac and this was a cash crop. The rise and fall in the international price of lac affected the fortunes of the Munda. Thus, even the most primitive communities came to vibrate with the operation of the world market.

The market in turn brought the middlemen, merchants and intermediaries of various kinds. In the Munda area this was a period marked by the emergence of the Diku, a term of reference for the alien exploiter. The Diku was a product of the colonial system. On account of his role as middleman in administrative matters, as a moneylender, petty official or as a trader, he was in a position to control the disposal of foodgrains and ultimately came to be dubbed as a land grabber. The term Diku, however, was not confined to the non-tribals alone. A new class of insider Diku and professional money-lender emerged as an unintended consequence of such legislation against land alienation which restricted the transfer of lands from tribal to non-tribals. Singh has shown how a rich stratum of tribal moneylenders emerged as land grabbers.

The period also witnessed the process of depeasantisation. As years rolled on, more and more tribals were alienated from land. The tribal handicrafts declined. Although the figures from the Munda are not available, the outmigration from Chotanagpur which stood at 33,000 in 1891 jumped up to 707,000 in 1911 and reached 947,000 in 1921. This only refers to more or less permanent migrations. But in addition to this, every year a large number of tribals left their villages for four months to work in road construction, brick kilns, jute mills or as agricultural labour in areas close to their homeland. Singh holds that had this vast number remained at home the process of depeasantisation would have been much faster in Chotanagpur. The homogeneity and the egalitarian character of Munda society weakened. Some distinctions between high and low in terms of prestige and status which were inherent in the Munda social system were strengthened by the developments in the colonial period. These distinctions led to the creation of a three-class society. At the head of a society were the chiefs and landlords; in the middle ranks came the well-to-do headmen or the tribal bourgeoisie and at the bottom were the general mass.

The colonial period was also marked by stepping up of the process of sanskritization. Even before this period Vaisnava saints and preachers had begun visiting the eastern part of the Ranchi district. It was said that Chaitanya Mahaprabhu had passed through this area on his way from Bengal to Orissa. The impact of Vaisnavism can be traced to the Lahsua songs sung at the time of the Karma festival. The Karma puja is not conducted by the religious headman, there is no animal sacrifice involved, and ghee and incense, reminiscent of Hindu festivals are used on this occasion. Zide and Munda (1970) have found the structural influence of the Bengali Vaisnava songs on the traditional Mundari folk songs. Many of the farming and artisan castes, which had penetrated even the interior areas of the Munda country slowly influenced the tribal way of life.

There were, however, two factors which impeded the tribals from being completely assimilated in the Hindu ethos, one was the stigma of lowliness associated with the Hindu caste system, which might have attached to them if they were absorbed in Hindu society. This was, however, as experience showed, an unwarranted fear. Besides this, the economic exploitation systematically carried out by the Hindu immigrants increased the social distance between them and the tribals. However, as time passed, most of the Munda realised that in order to get entry into larger society, they had to imbibe some of the values of Hinduism as also to give up some of the customs and practices which were obnoxious to Hindus at large. Thus some of them under the influences of indigenous nativistic cults adopted vegetarianism and gave up beef eating. The bulk of the Munda in the various censuses reported their religion as Hindu. The entire process of Hinduisation was slow and not very deliberate, though in small pockets, at different points of time, some Hindu divines and preachers did exist and exert their influence on the area around.

Equally important during the period is the role of Christianity as an ideology in the colonial context. There was always a close relationship between Christianity and colonialism. As the imperial powers acquired or conquered territory across the seas, Christianity moved in to "civilise" the primitives. Besides the task of evangelisation, they engaged in activities of economic nature as well as of social welfare, such as running of schools and hospitals, even in the deep interior of tribal areas. Their efforts were buttressed by their missionary zeal as also by the supply of funds raised abroad for their work. It has been observed that the funds available to the missionaries were in size next only to the direct investment of foreign capital in India. The missionaries worked in close association with the colonial administrators. They believed that the converts, because of their religious affinity with the colonial power, were their loyal subjects and as such they were entitled to certain protection and privileges from the masters. Although after the Mutiny the Government adopted the policy of religious neutrality and non-interference, many of the local officers felt that it did not apply to the tribal population and actively supported the missionaries in all their activities. A distinguished administrator, Sir Richard Temple, observed in 1881:

> I may remind you of the fortunate fact that in India out of 200 million British subjects (exclusive of native stock), 18 million are of aboriginal races and 9 million are no caste at all. Thus, 27 million are beyond the pale of the principal oriental religions and their minds present a tabula rasa on which Christianity may work.

There were many other administrators who thought likewise and helped the missionaries to the best of their ability.

In the first phase of contact, missionary activities had an adverse affect on the tribal social system. The missionaries believed that the tribals must adopt all their norms, values as also their way of life. They tried to impose a puritanical ethic on the permissive tribal society. The approach of various churches to social questions varied between themselves from time to time. It was only later that educated tribals began to rediscover some of the values and social practices in their own culture. The missionaries promoted the growth of the notion of private property in land and espoused their cause against the oppressions of the landlords. In certain cases converted tribals under the leadership of missionaries, made violent protest against the landlords, and it was only when these protests assumed proportions in which a confrontation with the administration became imminent that the missionaries desisted. The Christian tribals underplayed their identity as tribals and forged a wider identification as members of a universal fraternity symbolised by their denomination. For the first time they felt that they could expect support from a community outside their own tribal fold. Thus, the Munda came to gain a new sense of self-esteem as also legitimate pride in their own society. Sahay (1973) has identified five cultural processes associated with the spread of Christianity in Chotanagpur. These have been termed as oscillation, scrutinization, combination, indigenisation and retroversion. The last three phases can still be seen in many places.

While the missions rendered great service to the tribals, they could not hold the tribe together or bring various tribes under one organization. As they belonged to various denominations, each village was divided firstly between Christians and non-Christians and secondly between non-Christians and various denominational factions. Thus, Christianity did not bring peace to the Munda village but it created a house divided against itself. The traditional Munda village organization gave way to the onslaughts of the more educated and economically better off converted tribals acting on the advice of the local missionaries.

The colonial period also witnessed a number of socio-economic movements in the Munda country. Some of them were purely economic in nature, while the others had important social, political and religious content. These movements were attributed not only to the economic exploitation of the Munda, but also to the operation of the process of sanskritization and conversion to Christianity. These represented the violent reactions of the Munda to fact that changes were taking place in their area during this period. A detailed account of these movements and their nature and their long-term impact on the region has been given in a later chapter.

The Post-Independence Period

The post-independence period saw the unfolding of some of the trends already in evidence during the closing years of the colonial period. It witnessed the emergence of infra-nationalism, protonationalism and sub-nationalism. It also saw the penetration of industrial capital and the wide ramifications of industrialisation in certain pockets of the Munda country. Most important of all, however, was the large scale social welfare schemes undertaken under the aegis of both governmental and voluntary agencies in the area. This was made possible by injection of large amounts of money for the welfare of the tribal people as well as of the tribal region. In the period after independence the tribals became a concern of the nation and large scale socio-economic programmes were undertaken by the new Welfare State.

Infra-nationalism is in evidence among tribal people living in comparative isolation. At this stage they are generally ignorant about the broad national goals and symbols enshrined in the Constitution. They are, however, eager to modernise with the help of new technology and bring themselves up to the level of the non-tribal population with whom they are in close interaction. This process enables them to expand their own identity and see it in relationship with the larger national community.

Proto-nationalism is the fruition of this process. The community is aware of the national goals and symbols. A new elite has, by this time, grown and developed vested interest in consolidating the expanded identity of the tribal community. The operation of this process depends to a large extent on inspiration drawn from the traditions, myths and legends of the primitive past. It is the stage in which the tribals seek to rediscover certain norms, values and practices which they like to cherish. The next stage in the process is sub-nationalism in which the national symbols are accepted in principle. But parochial loyalties continue to be the prime mover for political action. In the case of the Munda, the sub-nationalism took the shape of demand for the creation of a separate state of Jharkhand.

It is only after independence that industrialisation came to the Munda country. In the fifties the Heavy Engineering Corporation was established in the neighbourhood of Ranchi. In course of time a large number of ancillary industries came to be established in that area. This large industrial complex not only affected the life of the people who were displaced from their villages but also those who got some work either in the industrial complex itself or in the constructional activities being carried out by the contractors. A large number of people were uprooted from their hearth and home. In the absence of requisite training, they could not be absorbed in the industry. Thus, industrialisation did not bring prosperity for the tribals living in the area and national interest had precedence over tribal interest. In some areas, however, tracts could be found of the development of entrepreneurship among the Munda. Formerly, the Munda were only an agricultural community but the ramifications of industrialisation led to a welcome diversification of occupation. It is obvious that in these developments the educated section of the community derived more advantage than the others.

The Constitution of India provided a number of provisions for protective discrimination whose objective was to raise the level of living of the Scheduled Tribes (of which the Munda are one), so as to bring them on par with the non-tribal population of the country. This made for reservations not only in the legislatures but also in services both at the State and Central levels. Steps were also taken for the preservation and promotion of the culture of the tribal people. The Constitution also required special efforts to be made for promoting the economic and educational interests of Scheduled Tribes. During the successive Plans, a special outlay was made for the benefit of the tribal people in addition to the benefits accruing to them from the general sector schemes. In order to look after the special interests of Chotanagpur and Santal Parganas an Autonomous Development Authority was set up with a tribal leader as its Deputy Chairman. Great strides were taken to raise the educational level of the tribals. A large number of schools were opened in the tribal areas with the efforts of both the Government and the Adimjati Seva Mandal, a voluntary agency working in this area. The missionaries also stepped up their educational effort. The result was a spurt in the rate of literacy in the Munda country. The provision of post-matric scholarships for any tribal going in for university education helped the growth of higher education. The result is that in the course of twenty-five years a new strata of educated Munda emerged. Since the jobs have not multiplied in the same proportion as higher education, unemployment has raised its head in the tribal area producing frustration and unrest. The impact of education is specially to be seen among tribal women.

The schemes undertaken for socio-economic development in the Munda country have not benefited them to the extent it was expected. The bulk of the schemes were cornered by the small percentage of non-tribals living in the area. Among the tribals, it was the converts who gained from the schemes. The unconverted, uneducated and relatively backward Munda, remained more or less unaffected by these welfare schemes. Thus a new elite emerged. They got education, entered government service or took employment in industries and claimed leadership roles in moments of crisis. By and large, this elite is alienated from the bulk of their own brethren and are keen to preserve their privileges and position. It is these members of the elite who are active in the movement inspired by sub-nationalism in the area.

The problem of land continued to plague the consciousness of the tribals. All through the nineteenth century land alienation occurred at a fast pace. Recurrent tribal movements forced the authorities to check the process. In 1908 the Chotanagpur Tenancy Act was passed to restrict this process as far as possible. The Act, however, did not succeed in stemming this process and the Dhebar Commission in 1960 discovered many loopholes which facilitated land transfer from the tribals to the non-tribals. The poverty of the Munda, their indigence and the rapacity of the money-lenders hastened the land transfers. An effort was made to plug the loopholes in the Act by an Ordinance in 1969 but by that time the mischief had been done. Amendments were made in the Law of Limitation so as to enable scrutiny of alienation up to 30 years backwards, but not much results have flowed from such action.

Munda politics was for a long time dominated by Christian leaders who, on account of their education and enlightenment, were more vocal than others. The bulk of the legislators were drawn from their ranks. It is only lately that non-Christian leadership has begun to show results. In some areas this had led to creation of some amount of tension between the Christians and the non-Christian tribals. Along with this, tensions have developed between different strata of tribals on account of industrial disputes and trade-union activities. A new development is the forging of new links between Munda leadership and the leadership of other tribal communities. Strangely enough, this leadership is also teaming up with non-tribal leadership in this area. The motivation for this is the spirit of sub-nationalism inspired by the cry for the new state of Jharkhand. Some of these non-tribal leaders belonged to such social categories from which the erstwhile exploiters were drawn. Thus, the varied and complex forces obtaining in the Munda country have paved the way for a transition from ethnicity to regionalism. From a politics of compliance, the Munda have turned to a politics of protest and defiance.

5

KINSHIP, FAMILY AND DESCENT

THE NAME 'Munda' seems to have been given to these people by their ancient Hindu neighbours. The Munda call themselves Horoko (men) and their tribe Horo (mankind). The appellation 'kol' generally used for the Munda and other Kolarian tribes is now strongly resented by them simply because it is regarded as derogatory. The term 'Munda' is liked by them as in their own language it signified the well-to-do secular village head man (Hatu Munda).

THE BRANCHES OF THE TRIBE

The Munda tribe consists of an elder and younger branch, the Mahali Mundako and the Kompat Mundako. The former are found mainly in the Tamar area of Ranchi district and are known as Patar. They are also known as Khangars in the Bhuinhari area, Mahali in parts of Khunti, Tamarias in Singhbhum and Marang Mundas in some other parts. The Kompat Mundako or the ordinary Munda form the bulk of the Munda population. The Munda of Bhuinhari Patti are considered to be an off-shoot of the Kompat Munda. The villages in which the present study was conducted were mainly inhabited by the Kompat Munda.

Both branches are endogamous and the former is regarded as socially inferior to the latter. The reason for this lower status of the former is attributed to the eating of a piece of umbilical cord by the progenitor of this group. But the real reason is to be found in the fact that this has come less under the influence of Hinduism. Thus the distinction between

Kompat Munda and Mahali Munda, which was observed by S.C. Roy more than sixty years ago, is still found among them.

KILI ORGANISATION

The tribe is divided into a number of clans known as Kili which are exogamous. All the members of a clan are considered to be descendants of a common ancestor. The Kompat and the Mahali Mundas have similar clans among themselves.

Origin and Identification of Clans

Clans are known after some animal, plant (or a part thereof), soil and certain event etc. In course of time, the number of Mundas swelled resulting in the expansion of clan membership. Each clan was further sub-divided into separate clans. S.C. Roy thought that the sub-division of the clans was perhaps necessitated to check the need of members of a clan having to travel long distances to find marriage mates for their children. There are a number of popular stories or legends about the origin and name of particular clans. S.C. Roy has related the stories of the origin of various clans such as Tuti, Mundu, Soe, Clan and its sub-divisions, Horo and Nag.

S.C. Roy (1970 : 71) referring to a Munda tradition said that a Munda Sardar, Risa Munda, along with 2,100 Mundas reached and first settled at Muruma village near Ranchi. These 2,100 Mundas, it is said, belonged to 21 clans. The names of the 21 original clans were, Kachua, Topno, Bhengra, Sandigura, Dungdung, Lipi, Honre, Hau, Kandir, Kerketa, Barla, Tuti, Hemrom, Kongari, Sanga, Kujur or Kujri, Soi, Tiru, Tuyu, Orea and Purthi. Subsequently, the number of clans seems to have multiplied by segmentation or otherwise. According to another legend, Sutia Pahan (who established Sutiambe village) divided the Mundas into 21 clans such as Hemrom, Suren etc. The two legends, contradict themselves for the original clans like Hemrom, Soren etc. are also found among the Santals and Bhumij which once formed one tribe with the Munda before the latter entered Chotanagpur. (Hoffmann, 1950 : 2415).

In the Bhuinhari Patti, the appellation, Bais Parha is in vogue which assumes that initially there were 22 clans and 22 uniclan Parhas. The Parha Raja of Barla clan used to be the

Parha-Maharaj of the Bais Parha. Sutiambe and Korambe villages are still named by the Mundas of this area to have been earlier settlements of the Kompat Munda. Sutiambe is still referred to as the place where they were formed into 22 distinct clans and Parha.

Whatever may be the origin and the number of original clans of the Munda, S.C. Roy (1912) mentioned almost 50 clans then present in the Munda country. Hoffmann (1950 : 2411) mentioned the names of 106. The names of sixty have a known meaning, those of thirteen have a doubtful meaning and those of thirty-three do not have even a fancied meaning. Among the names, the meaning of which is known there are 11 names of animals, 11 names of birds, 3 of fishes, 2 of reptiles, 2 insects, 3 names (Guria, Sandiguri, Hemrom and Taraeba) of trees and a shrub nothing of which is eaten, 4 trees (Baru, Jojo, Kunda and Sirka) the fruits of which are eaten, 3 food grains and a pulse, 2 pot herbs, 2 edible tubers, 1 plant with edible oil, 1 condiment (Bulung), 4 inanimate objects, and 2 adjectives (See, Bodra).

Now the number of clans among the Munda has reached almost one hundred and fifty and new clans come up as a result of division and sub-division of original clans. A detailed list of various clans among the Mundas is given in the appendix.

Some clan names have been transformed beyond recognition under the Hindu influence. For instance, in Panch-Parganas, Sandi clan has been changed into Sandil *gotra,* a clan name common to many Hindu families which is said to have sprung from saint Sandilya. This clan name seems to be very popular with the semi-Hinduised Mundas of Panch Parganas. Examples are known in which a Munda of the Sandil *gotra* has married in the same *gotra*. This probably shows that this new clan name was adopted by several originally distinct clans (Roy, 1970 : 234). This was corroborated by our findings among the Mundas of village Amlesa in Tamar. Binod Singh Munda of Sandil *gotra* in village Amlesa married a girl of the same *gotra* from a village in W. Bengal. Similarly, his two widowed sisters were also married in the Sandil *gotra.* It was learnt that Munda of Sandil *gotra* marrying in the same clan abstain from choosing a marriage mate from a family originally having a common burial ground with them. The descendants of a common ancestor belong to a single clan and they bury their dead in the same *sasan*. Thus the rule of clan exogamy is maintained. It is quite probable that Sandil *gotra* might have been adopted by several originally distinct clans. Bhojroj clan in Tamar Thana, was also mentioned to be a metamorphosis of Jom-Tuti clan.

Roy's observation that in rare cases members of one clan were known to have been incorporated into another clan is corroborated by us. Roy mentioned how some members of Bando clan were incorporated into the Hereng clan. Similarly the ancestors of the Munda of Tola Baruhatu (village Salehatu), who belonged to Barai-ood clan in the beginning, changed to Hassa—the dominant clan of the Khutkatidars of Salehatu. Irrespective of the fact that the Munda of Salehatu and Baruhatu belong to Hassa clan, instances of intermarriage between them against the general rule of clan exogamy, helped in revealing the distinct original clans of the two groups. The villages of Chandor and Maranghada near Salehatu were originally established by two Munda brothers of the Hansda clan. It is said that the descendants of the elder brother who lived at Maranghada, changed their clan name to Nag under the influence of Christian missionaries. In another instance, the ancestors of Mansukh Guria of Gutuhatu in Torpa Block originally came from Serdikel village of Tiru clan. During their long stay at the present village, they adopted the Guria clan, the dominant clan of the Bhuinhars of the village. However, they do not have any Bhuinhari rights over the village land.

Original Homeland and Regional Distribution of the Clans

Each clan is supposed to have an original homeland in a village established by their ancestors. When they multiplied they dispersed in different directions and settled in new villages. In this original village of the clan their ancestors established all the political, socio-economic and religious institutions. All of them had equal right to the village land and were known as Khutkatidars. They had equal access to the village burial ground or *sasan* and the Mundas, even to the present day, erect *sasan diris* or burial stones in the memory of their dead. The members of a clan long after their dispersion from the original village, used to bury the bones of their deceased members in the *sasan* of the old village. With the passage of time, they established *sasans* in their new villages, though they erected *sasanadiris* in their former *sasan*. As a result of formation of new villages, the knowledge about the original homeland of many of the clan has become obscure and no connection can be established between their present village and the cradle of their clan. In some circumstances the original home of a clan could be traced, e.g., ancestors of Tuti clan and Mundu clan lived in the beginning at Chutia near Ranchi ; those of Soy clan lived at village Balgi. In the Bhuinhari area there are uniclan *Parha* headed by the respective Parha Rajas. The seat of Parha Raja is generally in the village first established by their ancestors and this Raja village is considered the original home of the clan members from where they migrated to other places. The original home of Guria clan is at Kalet, Kandulna at Khatanga, Kongari at Garai Digri, Topno at Kotbo, Bhengra at Angrabari, Bodra at Latauli, Aind at Echa, Barla at Gopalpur, Horo at Chalngi (near Govindpur), Surin at Pushatoli and Kerketta at Bangroo near Govindpur and so on.

The regional distribution of different clans is as follows. In the study village of Salehatu all but three families of Mahali Munda belong to the Hassa clan. Jojohatu, Ganamana, Hende-ba, Gutuhatu and Janum Pirhi also belong to Munda of the Hassa clan. Other clans found in this area are Hans, Hansda, Nag, *Purti*, Bhalu, Soy, *Purti*, Horo and Runda etc.

The Munda of village Gutuhatu in Torpa Block mainly belong to the Guria clan. The other clans in the village are Kandulra, Hemrom, Horo and Topno. There are 16 contiguous villages including Gutuhatu, which belong to the Guria clan. Similarly other such groups of villages are inhabited by the members of Topno, Lang, Barla, Kandulna, Kongari, Hemrom, Horo, Bhengra, Bodra, Dahanga, Aind, Surin, Kerketta, Baba Dhan clans respectively.

In Tamar village Amlesa is a multiclan Munda village. Kamal is the dominant clan. Other clans in the village are Sandil, Nag, and Kachchap. The mission tola of Amlesa village is mainly inhabited by migrants, most of them being converts to Christianity. They come from distinct clans such as Purti, Bhengra, Guria, Soy, Hans, Hasso, Horo, Bodra, Sirka, Mundu and Somla respectively. Other clans found in Panch Parganas are Sal, Bhojroj, Tau and Sanga etc.

There is hardly any social stratification among the various clans of the Mundas. Like Santals and Oraons and unlike Dudh and Dhelki Kharias and Hos, all clans are reported to have equal social status.

Functions of the Clan

The clan is significant as a reference group for all those who claim to be descendants of one common ancestor. The primary function of the clan is to regulate marriage relationships, for all marriages must be contracted outside the clan. In most cases the clan also bestows the surname on a person. For instance, among the converted Mundas, especially in Bhuinhari Patti, the clan name (such as Guria, Topno, Kandulna etc.) is suffixed, after the personal name. Members of a clan look back to a common past, claim descent from a common ancestor, claim a particular area as their place of origin, revere the same totemic object, plant or animal, observe the same food taboos and in some areas (as 22 Parhas of Bhuinhari area) form uniclan organisations like the Parha such as the Topno Parha, Guria Parha, Bhengra Parha, Sanga Parha etc. Social offences may be taken to this clan organisation for disposal. It may also discuss matters of common concern, for instance, the attitude to be adopted towards the forest policy of the government, consolidation of holdings or voting in elections and so on.

The Munda belonging to distinct clans have separate burial grounds (*sasan*) where they bury the bones of their dead. The *sasan* is situated in one corner of the village and the descendants of the original settlers of the village only can make use of it. In the villages which are settled by members of more than one clan, each clan has its separate *sasan*. Similarly, Munda of different villages, but of the same clan, possess a common *sasan* with distinct corners reserved for each village, *e.g.*, Buruhatu *sasan* is used by three villages, *viz.*, Buruhatu, Bichagutu, and Dandeya, all belonging to Nag clan. The bones of a Khutkatidar or Bhuinhar dying away from his village, will be taken to the *sasan* of his original village by his relatives. The Munda of a clan other than that of Khutkatidars or Bhuinhar but of long standing is allowed to bury their dead in the village *sasan*, but will not be permitted to put up a *sasandiri* which is a memorial stone erected for the Khutkatidar or Bhuinhar of the village. S.C. Roy has observed that the Munda regard these *sasandiris* as the title-deeds of the Khutkatidars and Bhuinhars of each village (1970 : 222).

LINEAGE (KHUT)

In a Munda village the clan of the original settlers is the dominant clan which is further divided into two lineages, the Munda Khut and Pahan Khut and the village officers are usually drawn from them. These two lineages are more or less equally important and enjoy greater prestige than the rest of the village community. In the Bhuinhari area in addition to these lineages, there is a third lineage known as Mahto Khut.

S.C. Roy (1970 : 92) observed that during the eighteenth century when the alien landlords were introduced into the land tenure system of the Munda, they preferred to select a member of the original village family to manage the affairs of the village in its relation to the new landlord. Thus, the Mahto was introduced as a new functionary and gradually a Mahto Khut was evolved in many villages probably out of the Munda Khut. Similarly, Hoffmann (1930 : 2381) observed that in Naguri area a third Khut, Mahto Khut, came into being from the third or fourth son of the original settler. Mahto helps Pahan and especially the Munda.

These lineages may not take part in each other's sacrifices to the ancestors; when such a sacrifice is offered by a member of one *khut* no member of the other *khut* is allowed to partake of the sacrificial rice, meat or rice-beer. Both *khuts* in any village, belong to the same clan, have the same totem and may not intermarry. It has, however, a repercussion on the marriages with other clans. Suppose that a marriage has taken place between the Munda Khut of one village and the Munda Khut of another (belonging to a different clan). In the same generation further unions may be arranged between them, but the next generations are debarred from inter-marriage as long as members of the set of people who contracted relationship through these marriages are alive, and even after the extinction of that first generation, as long as the two *khuts* remain on visiting terms. However, the Pahan Khut of one of these villages may freely intermarry with either *khut* in other villages. However, it should be noted that avoidance relationship between a man and his wife's elder sisters and cousins and a woman and her husband's elder brothers and cousins respectively does not make a distinction between the *khuts* and covers the village as a whole.

In the Khutkatti area especially in the intact Khutkatti villages in Khunti and Tamar area Mahto and his *khut* are unknown. In village Salehatu three lineages *viz.*, Munda, Pahan and Kuar Khuts were found to exist. The Kuar Khut is the lineage of younger branch of the Munda Khut and the Kuar assists the Munda in the performance of his duties.

The Munda and Pahan lineages of the Purti clan in Anigara village live in separate blocks in the village and there is a long history of struggle for supremacy between these two groups in the village. Generally, the members of all the lineages bury their dead in the corner earmarked for each *khut* in the village *sasan.* However, sometimes a quarrel between two lineages of one clan may lead to the setting up of two *sasans.* An example of this was seen in village Anigara which has two *sasans*, one for the Munda Khut and the other for the Pahan Khut lying on two sides of the road passing through the village.

In the village Salehatu proper, the Chetan Tola (upper Tola) is inhabited by the Mundas of the Hassa clan. They claim to be the descendants of a common ancestor who came from Kadaldih long ago. There are three lineages or *khuts* among them, *viz.*, Munda Khut, Pahan Khut and Kuar Khut. Similarly there are three lineages in Lattar (Lower) Tola, Baruhatu and Maddih Tola. It was reported that religious and social rituals at the village level are celebrated by members of Munda and Pahan Khuts (excluding Kuar Khut) together. Similarly the Kuar Khut is excluded from the Karma festival celebrations in which the first two *khuts* join. As regards the interrelationship between these three *khuts*, it was revealed that during negotiations for marriage, in addition to name of the tribe and clan, the *khut* affiliation is also enquired about.

However, *khut* affiliation is not very significant in this regard and the member of a Munda Khut of a clan may marry a girl of either of the three Khuts belonging to another clan and *vice versa*. As regards status, Munda and Pahan Khuts are considered of equal status but higher than that of Kuar Khut.

Formerly, when a family died out, its land reverted to the members of its own lineage, and could only be appropriated by the members of the other lineage when no member of that lineage survived. But this custom has been overruled by the settlement and record of rights at the beginning of this century.

There are cases of inter-lineage conflict. A case in point was found in Serengdih. There was a conflict between the Munda lineage and the Pahan lineage as each of these considered itself superior to the other. When the authority of the Munda was challenged by the Pahan, the Munda lineage united with the Munda. Dondo Munda, who made much money in Assam and who was influential in the village affairs, accepted Birsa religion along with all other members of his lineage. This was to show to the Pahan that they were no less religious than the latter. However, the people of the Pahan lineage are in a better economic position than those of Munda lineage. The Birsites have lost their land and have, therefore, to get assistance from the members of the Pahan lineage. In the Panchayat also the members of the Pahan lineage play a dominant role. The Birsites felt so isolated that seven families from the village have since given up the Birsa religion. It appeared that they were disillusioned as their original claim of being at par with the Pahan lineage was never recognised by the villagers.

SOCIAL STRATIFICATION

In Tamar although the Munda belong to a single tribe, deep seated social stratification has come to be formed. Such special distinction may be the result of their long contact with the semi-feudal Hindu castes living among them. Six distinct classes may be distinguished. These may be grouped into two *e.g.* (a) the zamindars or landlords, and (b) the tenants. In group (a) there are at the apex, landlords called Thakur who hold above fifteen villages each. Next come Manki who are lesser landlords holding up to ten or eleven villages each. Some of these then got themselves enumerated as Kshatriyas in the 1961 Census with a view to raise themselves in the eyes of their Hindu neighbours. But for all practical purposes they are Munda. Both these classes are endogamous and only in rare cases does an intermarriage take place between the two. In the third class may be placed Munda or the village headman who owns only one village either in Khutkatti right or as a lessee of the landlords. He settles land with some members of his family and these landholders known as Babu form the fourth class of the social hierarchy. Similarly, the respective agnates of Thakur and Manki are also known as Babu. In group (b) are Munda tenants. Intermarriage between Munda tenants and the above-mentioned four classes is unusual due to great disparity in economic and social status. At the bottom of the Munda society in Tamar are the Patar, who belong to the Mahali-Mundakȯ branch of the tribe. Though they hold small bits of land, there is no social intercommunication between them and the upper five groups. Not only is intermarriage unthinkable, but even water cannot be taken from the hands of a Patar.

KINSHIP TERMINOLOGY

Munda kinship terminology is to some extent classificatory and the relatives are ordered in a wide-ranging system of kinship. In a nuclear family with parents and their unmarried children (sons and daughters), the father is termed as Apu, the vocative term is Aba. The term for mother is Eanga, and Kora and Kuri are used for son and the daughter respectively. Among the siblings, use of kinship terms is affected by its own internal structure such as the social distinction between sexes and the order of birth thus distinguishing senior from junior. There are different terms for elder and younger brothers and sisters. The elder brother is known as Marang Haga or Dada and the younger is known as Huding Haga, Bhai, or Unding. The elder sister is known as Didi, Dai, Aji, or Nana and the younger sister is spoken of as Eahin, Misi or Unding. As is true of classificatory system, the terms which apply to lineal relatives are also applied to certain collateral relatives, *e.g.*, father's brother is known as father (Marang Apu and Huding Apu respectively for elder and younger brothers of the father) and mother's elder sister is Marang Eang and younger is Huding Eang. However, there are different terms for mother's brother (Mamu, Kuma) and Father's sister (Hatum, fufu, gungu) respectively. The Munda do not distinguish between parallel and cross-cousins and use the same terms of kinship and keep them in a single category of brothers (Dada, Bhai), and sister (Didi, Bahin etc.). Therefore, the principle of classification has been applied over a wide range of relationship in which nearer and more distant collateral relatives are arranged into a few categories and a person has many relatives to whom he applies the terms father, mother, brother or sister.

This system of dividing relatives into categories, determines or influences social relations expressed in behaviour. For example, putting two relatives in one and the same category (mother and mother's sister, father and father's brother, father's father and mother's father, father's mother and mother's mother) shows that there is some significant similarity in the customary behaviour in social relation between them; while inversely the placing of two relatives in different categories implies some significant difference in customary behaviour or social relations.

It is interesting to note that the Munda kinship terminology distinguishes between immediate family circle and classificatory relatives (such as father, mother, brother or sister) by the use of word *anjh* (own) (before or after the kinship term) for one's own parents and siblings.

The Munda like many other societies, show a relation of social inequality between proximate generations and this is commonly generalised so that a person is expected to show respect to his relatives of the first ascending generation – that of his parents. This relation between the two generations is usually generalised to extend beyond the range of kinship. Some measure of respect for persons of the generations or age of one's parents is required from them.

The relationship between parents and children is asymmetrical. Symmetrical relationship is one in which two persons observe the same pattern of behaviour towards each other, e.g., between grandparents and grandchildren. Similarly, terminology can also be symmetrical or asymmetrical. In the former case each applies the same term of relationship to other and in the latter there are two different reciprocal terms. Both types of terminology are found among the Munda, e.g. *nana* and *nani* are the common terms for male and female grandparents and grandchildren respectively. Similarly *bada* and *badi* are the symmetrical reciprocal terms for father's elder brother and his spouse and younger brother's children respectively. The grandparents are also known as *aja* (for grandfather) and *aji* (for grandmother). Where terminology in a relationship is symmetrical it is frequently an indication that the relationship is thought of as being approximately symmetrical in respect of behaviour.

The wife's parents and the husband's parents are treated on an equal footing. The father-in-law is *apu hunjar* and the mother-in-law is known as *hanar eang*. The terms for the son-in-law and the daughter-in-law are *aratani* and *kimin* respectively. The siblings of the husband and of the wife are also designated by one term such as *bau hunjar* and *eril kura* for elder and younger brothers respectively, *aji hanar* and *eril kuri* for elder and younger sisters respectively. Brother's wife is known as *haga kimin* by his elder and *hiling bu* by his younger siblings. Similarly sister's husband is *aratani* to her elder siblings and *bonoi* (*bahnoi* Hindi) or *bhatu* to her younger siblings.

Certain relations are obliged to perform specific duties at the time of name giving, marriage or death of some of their kinsmen. For instance father, brother, or father's brother of the expectant mother is supposed to perform *garasi-bonga* ritual for the well-being of the expectant mother. *Sakhi* or *mita* of a child takes leading part in his *lutur-tuku* (ear-boring ceremony). A son (or a nephew or brother in the absence of a son) of the the deceased performs the ritual of putting burning charcoal in the mouth of the dead, where the practice of cremation is prevalent among the Munda.

Regional variations are found in the kinship terminology in the three villages of Salehatu, Gutuhatu and Amlesa respectively. The influence of Hinduism is observed in the use of various kinship terms for different relatives such as *beta, beti, bhai, bahin, dada, didi, ma, bap, mamu, fufu, bhagina, bhagini, mausa, mausi, nana, nani, nati, natin, damad, bahu,* etc. The Hinduised Munda of Amlesa use terms which resemble Hindu kinship terms.

Artificial kinship terms are used to address the unrelated persons on the pattern similar to that for the kindred and they are held in the same esteem as the latter.

KINSHIP USAGES

As in all other societies, the Munda exhibit certain types of co-active behaviour patterns with regularity and more or less permanent and definite structure. These kinship usages are expressed both at verbal and non-verbal levels. While two proximate generations observe some distance in interaction, there are certain types of kin between whom avoidance relationship exists. Such a pattern of relationship exists between a woman and her father-in-law as well as husband's elder brother. Similarly, there is avoidance between a man and his mother-in-law as well as his wife's elder sister. The intensity of avoidance is most between a person and his younger brother's wife. He cannot sit on the same mat by the side of his younger brother's wife or take bath in the same tank where she is bathing. The woman is even expected to avoid the shadow and the clothes of the husband's elder brother. The elder brother in turn has to observe these restrictions. This is a taboo whose infringement is beset with dangerous consequences. It makes no difference whether the infringement is intentional or unintentional. The avoidance relationship between a woman and her father-in-law is not so strict obviously because the brother poses a more serious threat than the father-in-law. The frequency of interaction between a person and his mother-in-law, and his wife's elder sister, is poor. Thus, we experience avoidance relationship at different levels between specific groups of kin among the Munda.

The reverse of avoidance relationship is an extreme degree of familiarity expressed through a joking relationship. Such joking may extend to abuse and banter as well as obscene and vulgar references to sex in each other's presence. Joking relationship is indicative of equality and mutual reciprocity. It is also indicative of potential sexual relationship. In Munda society there is joking relationship between a man and his wife's younger siblings and also between a woman and her husband's younger siblings. The pattern of joking also extends between grandparents and grandchildren. The joking relationship between a person and his wife's younger sister or between a woman and her husband's younger brother can easily be explained as they are looked upon as each other's potential mates on account of the prevalence of junior levirate and junior sororate. The joking by no means goes to the extent of sexual access. The existence of such a practice among the Santal led to a surmise about the existence of polyandry in that tribe by a foreign missionary. This was obviously wrong in view of the all India pattern of joking relationship between a person and his elder brother's wife. The joking relations between the members of alternate generations may signify a sense of equality and solidarity between the two against the intervening generation. At the name-giving, a child usually receives the name of one of his grand-parents. There is also a belief that grand-parents are reborn as grand-children and thus the family line is maintained. Two persons bearing the same name are known as *mita* or friend. Sometimes grand-parents and grand-children address each other as *mita* or as *nana* or *nani* as the case may be. There is no joking relationship between cross-cousins as marriage between them is not the preferred marriage among the Munda.

As all over rural India and among some tribal groups, teknonymy is prevalent among the Munda. A person is referred to as the father, mother, brother or sister of some one else. This is on account of the fact that it is taboo for a woman to utter the name of her husband, her husband's elder brother and her husband's father. Among the Munda, a daughter-in-law is generally addressed by the name of her natal village. Although there is no avunculate among the Munda, the mother's brother does play an important role on various occasions in the life-cycle of the individual. He has some special obligations towards his nephew and his presence is a must in his nephew's marriage. The father's sister does not have any role whatever as far as pattern behaviour is concerned among the Munda. The practice of *couvade* is unknown.

FAMILY

S.C. Roy held the viewpoint that the dominant pattern of family among the Munda was the nuclear family. I have shown elsewhere (1964 : 37) that there were large numbers of patrilineal extended families, though the majority of the families were nuclear in character.

TABLE 5.1
Types of family

Village	Nuclear		Polygy-nous	Extended	Joint	Others	Total
	Simple	With depen-dent					
Salehatu	56	9	2	9	14	9	99
	(56.6)	(9.1)	(2.0)	(9.1)	(14.1)	(9.1)	(100.0)
Gutuhatu	33	27	—	11	28	2	101
	(32.7)	(26.7)	—	(10.9)	(27.7)	(2.0)	(100.0)
Amlesa	41	3	2	—	9	6	61
	(67.2)	(4.9)	(3.3)	—	(14.8)	(9.8)	(100.0)
All	130	39	4	20	51	17	261
	(50.0)	(15.0)	(1.5)	(7.6)	(19.5)	(6.4)	(100.0)

The present study shows that the dominant form of family among the Munda is still nuclear with almost two-thirds of the total families falling in this category. Among the three villages of Salehatu, Gutuhatu and Amlesa, the last has the largest number of nuclear families. In Gutuhatu more than one-fourth of the families are those where either of the parents (widowed) lives with the nuclear family of their son. Almost one-fifth of the families are patrilineal extended or joint in nature where members belonging to three generations with at least two lineally united couples with their children live together. The largest number of such families are in Gutuhatu.

The collateral extended families or those where two married brothers live together with their spouses and unmarried children were 7.6% of the total families in all the villages. In Amlesa such families were conspicuous by their absence.

Two examples of the polygynous family, with one husband and two wives and their children were found in Amlesa and Salehatu. No such families were reported from Gutuhatu. In an earlier study four polygynous families were reported from Jojohatu and one from Serengdih.

SIZE AND COMPOSITION OF THE FAMILY

In almost all villages more than half of the families comprise 1-5 members. Three-fourths of the families fall in this category, while in Gutuhatu only one-fourth of the families are such. On an average, four out of every ten families comprise 6-10 members; Gutuhatu and Koenara have each more than half of such families and less than 30% of the families in this category. The families with 11-15 members are more than 6% in all the villages ; Gutuhatu has about 14%, while Koenara does not have families of this size. There are two families from Gutuhatu and one family each from Amlesa and Selda which consist of more than 16 members respectively. The average size of the family is highest, *i.e.*, 7.3 persons in Gutuhatu and lowest, *i.e.*, 4.2 persons in Jojohatu. In other villages the average size of the family is between 5.2 to 6.4 persons. A common average for all the villages is 5.8 persons per family (Table 5.2).

TABLE 5.2
Size and Composition of the Family*

Size of	Per cent distribution of families							
family	Salehatu	Gutuhatu	Amlesa	Birhu	Jojohatu	Koenara	Serengdih	Selda
1—5	56.6	25.7	57.4	50.0	71.4	46.2	55.7	52.5
6—10	41.4	58.4	37.7	39.3	28.6	52.4	40.0	35.7
11—15	2.0	13.9	3.3	10.7	—	1.4	4.3	9.5
16 +	—	2.0	1.6	—	—	—	—	2.3
Total No. of families	100.0 (99)	100.0 (101)	100.0 (61)	100.0 (28)	100.0 (62)	100.0 (71)	100.0 (47)	100.0 (42)
Total Population	521	740	332	165	263	409	257	270
Average size of the family	5.2	7.3	5.4	5.9	4.2	5.7.	5.4	6.4

* Data for villages of Birhu, Jojohatu, Koenara, Serengdih and Selda were from Sachchidanan da, 1964, *Culture Change in Tribal Bihar*, p. 39, Tables 2 & 4.

THE ROUND OF LIFE

Institutions of marriage and family play a primary role in the life of an individual from birth to death. These events are marked by distinct religious ceremonies and rituals. Among the Munda these ceremonies and rituals are largely influenced by Hinduism. Such rituals begin with pregnancy where the expectant mother's father offers a red or grey fowl to the Garasi Bonga for her well-being and that of the child in the womb. The birth of a child brings joy to the parents and close relatives, but it puts the entire family in a state of ritual pollution. Usually it ends on the eighth day but in special cases the period may be reduced to five days. The purification ceremony called *chhati* is marked by feasting of near relatives. The *sakhi* or the name giving ceremony is performed on the following day and the baby is usually named after some older relative or after the day of the week on which it is born. The *lutur-tukui* or ear-boring ceremony of the baby is celebrated either in the first, second or third year of its life. The *sakhi* or *mita,* after whom the baby has been named, plays the leading role. In the end the guests are entertained with food and drink. There is little formal instruction in traditional Munda society. All that the children learn is through informal socialisation, tradition, myth, riddles, dance and music. They are mostly learnt at the *Akhra.* Now opening of schools, even in remote tribal villages, have provided them an opportunity for better learning.

Among the converted Mundas similar religious ceremonials are associated with childbirth. A prayer is held along with the pregnant woman's father when first signs of pregnancy appear. The *chhati* ceremony and name giving are conducted on the eighth day of birth. During this period the child and the mother remain under ritual pollution. The child is baptised after the *chhati* ceremony is held. Among Munda belonging to the Lutheran mission, the priest baptises the newly born either in the church or in the house on a written request from the child's father. A godfather and a godmother are chosen for the child from the same Christian denomination. Similarly, among the Roman Catholic and Society for the Propagation of Gospel missions the father or the parish priest baptises the child. The boys and the girls are confirmed usually after 12 years of age and before marriage by the Bishop among the Mundas of R.C. and S.P.G. missions. Among G.E.L. Christian Munda the girls are given confirmation at 15-16 years of age and boys at 17-18 years of age. In this case, for the first one and a half months, the boys and the girls are given religious instruction from the Pracharak and then for next 15 days by the Priest. All the boys and the girls among the converted Mundas are supposed to be baptised and confirmed before marriage.

The Munda believe in life after death. They burn or bury their dead according to the season of the year and socio-economic status of deceased. Only in summer and winter can the body be cremated if money can be spared, in other cases it is buried. Death also places the family in a state of ritual pollution. On the third, fifth, seventh or ninth day depending on the area in which death takes place the blood relatives of the deceased gather for the *umbu-lader* ceremony. This is the purificatory rite after which the spirit of the dead is housed in the *ading* and is worshipped in the form of Ora-bonga or house god. Once a year the *Jangtopa* ceremony is held in which the bones or relics of the dead are deposited in the clan *sasan* of his Bhuinhari village and *sasandiri* is erected for the dead in the *sasan*. Among the converts the dead are buried in the ground specially meant for them and *sasandiri* may be erected in the clan *sasan*. Those who die unnatural deaths are buried away from the *sasan* and *sasandiris* for each of them are erected somewhere in the village outside the *sasan*. Due to large expenditure involved in putting up a *sasan-diri* this practice has declined considerably in the Munda area.

DESCENT AND INHERITANCE

S.C. Roy has described in detail the process of partition and inheritance and the customary rules governing these events among the Munda. No major changes have taken place in these rules since his time. The joint family system of the Munda resembles the Hindu system. In the lifetime of the father, the sons do not generally separate from the common kitchen or property and the members share all they have, in common, till the death of the father. The father is regarded as having almost absolute control over the family property, and handles income and expenditure. Women have exclusive right over their ornaments. The splitting of the domestic group is generally accompanied by partition of the family property. In case the partition takes place during the father's lifetime, the property is divided equally among the sons and the father, while the eldest son gets slightly more than the equal share. On the death of the father, his share is equally divided among his sons. An unmarried son, however, will get, in addition to his proper share of both real and personal property, some cash or cattle or both by way of provision for his marriage. Women amongst the Munda are not entitled to inherit, but the father may in his lifetime make presents of cash or otherwise to a daughter, but not land. When, however, the father effects a partition during his lifetime, the unmarried daughter usually gets some land to be held by way of maintenance till her marriage. Almost invariably, an unmarried daughter, after such partition lives either under the protection of her father or one of her brothers, and the land allotted to her by way of maintenance till her marriage remains till then in the possession of her chosen guardian who supports her. The bride-price received at her marriage too will go to that guardian if he bears the expenses of her marriage. This maintenance land of the sister, however, will be repartitioned amongst the brothers, after her marriage.

After the death of the father, if the sons do not agree to live together, a Panchayat is convened and the property is divided according to Munda rules of inheritance. When the deceased has left behind him a widow and grown-up sons and daughters, the Panch will first set apart some land, generally equal to a younger son's share, for the maintenance of the widow in which she can only have a life interest. If she lives independently and not with any of her sons, the land allotted to her will be equally distributed among the sons after her death. In most cases the widow prefers to live with one of her sons who cultivates and enjoys the land of her share and if he meets all her funeral expenses, he becomes entitled to that land.

The real and personal property left by the deceased father is divided by the Panchayat in equal shares among the sons of the deceased except that the eldest son will, in most cases, get a little land in excess along with more paddy and other articles. When the deceased leaves no son but only a childless widow or a widow with daughters only, she is allowed a life interest in the property left by the husband. She may dispose of movable articles in case of necessity and give temporary leases such as usufructuary mortgage etc. of the real property left by her husband, but she has no authority to sell any such real property without the consent of the agnates of her dead husband. In case the widow goes to live with her parents permanently she is deprived of her right on her deceased husband's land which then goes to his nearest agnates. If the widow remarries, she loses all rights to all movable and immovable property left by her dead husband. She is just allowed to take away with her ornaments and clothes.

Daughters among the Mundas do not inherit. The sons are, however, bound to support unmarried sisters till their marriage. She may decide to live with one of her brothers who is allowed some additional land which is repartitioned equally among brothers after her marriage. The bride-price, however, goes to the brother or brothers who have borne the expenses of her marriage. If a Munda leaves an unmarried daughter or daughters and no widow or son, the unmarried daughter is entitled to the personal property, left by the father, and remains in possession of the land left by the deceased till her marriage. Neither a daughter's husband nor a daughter's sons are entitled to inherit.

In the absence of sons, or widow or unmarried daughter of a deceased Munda, his property goes to the nearest male agnate or agnates. The son-in-law (ghar-dijoa or ghar-damad), who lives with his son less father-in-law till the latter's death, gets all the movable property left by the deceased and such share of the land, if any, as, according to the circumstances, the Panch may think proper to give him, the rest going to the nearest male agnates. He can enjoy the share of the land so long as his wife is alive after which the inheritance passes to the nearest agnate. In the absence of such agnates of the dead, the Panch may give the inheritance to the *ghar-damad.*

Illegitimate sons of the deceased owner or sons of the deceased wife by a former husband, do not have a legal right in the property left by the deceased. They may be given small plots

1. Munda farmer going to the field

2. Ploughing and sowing

3. Women selecting ornaments in a market

of land to cultivate, for maintenance, although they cannot claim this as a matter of right. The adopted son (from among the agnates) of a sonless Munda will inherit all his property after the latter's death to the exclusion of all other agnates, he may be allowed only his marriage expenses and the inheritance will pass on to the nearest agnates of the deceased, and he may be allowed to inherit only in case there are no agnates of the deceased.

THE STATUS OF WOMEN

The status of women among the Munda is equal to that of men in almost all the spheres of life. Munda women take their full share in the economic activities of the family. They are given light work in comparison to men. They work both in the field and at home—cleaning, washing, bringing drinking-water from the village spring, tending cattle, cooking, spinning and looking after children. They help the menfolk in agricultural operations such as preparing the soil, sowing, transplanting, harvesting, threshing and husking of paddy etc.

They grow vegetables in the kitchen-garden or *bari* and sell these in the market. During sowing and harvesting seasons they work on other's fields also, for wages. The wages for women are less than those for men. Young Munda women also work as construction labourers in the industrial cities like Ranchi, Bokaro etc. where they fall a prey to unscrupulous outsiders who deceive these simple tribal womenfolk with false promises of marriage.

Some women, especially young married girls and widows, work as maidservants or *dai* (*dhangrin*) in rich Munda families, where they are treated like family members. There, they perform household work as well as work in the fields. They work up to the harvesting time when they are given new clothes and some cash as remuneration for their work. They take vegetables, paddy, rice, *hanria* (rice-beer) and *daru*, firewood, cut grass etc. for sale in the nearby markets.

There is no segregation of the sexes among the Munda. There is free mixing between the sexes. Young women participate in the dances and songs in the village *akhra* along with men on the occasion of festivals and *jatras*. The dress of women, like the dress of men, varies with their means, age and education. Old women cling to the traditional costumes. Some of the middle-aged women whose husbands earn money outside, put on mill-made saries. By and large, within the house middle-aged and old women rarely wear anything above their waist, outside the house those who can afford it, wear blouses. Christians of all ages, however, wear a blouse at all times. Young women wear a sari and blouse when they go to weekly markets or to dance-meets like *jatra*.

In villages, in the interior, both men and women take keen interest in personal decoration. The girls deck their hair with flowers at the time of dances. Their hair-do is also distinctive. Among unconverted Munda both men and women put on ornaments. Most women wear ear ornaments called *taro*. This is made of rolled palm leaves sometimes fitted with little mirrors. Necklaces of different varieties are also worn by women. In bazars, which they often visit, they go in for cheap trinkets and other silver or brass ornaments they can afford. Christian women are more particular about their dress than about their ornaments. Education has made them look upon heavy ornaments as waste. They are keen about wearing good saries and blouses, and in keeping themselves tidy and smart.

The practice of putting vermilion in the parting of their forehead has been adopted by such tribal married women as have been deeply influenced by urban contacts, specially with Hindu women. Other married women may be seen putting vermilion only when they go out. Among women tatooing is common on the face and other parts of the body, but the practice is dying out and is not popular in highly acculturated areas. Colour consciousness is developing among the tribals and the girls with light skin are preferred to the dark-skinned as wives by the young men. The women, like men, relish rice-beer and Mahua liquor.

Women do not participate in the worship of the deities, like Kali and Saraswati along with their husbands. They are not allowed to go to the *sarna* where worship of the deities is strictly confined to men-folk only. Women cannot even worship household gods in the *ading*. However, they may do so in the absence of men and may offer vermilion to the deity. They cannot offer sacrifice.

The Munda are a patrilineal society. The rights of women

in certain fields are fewer than that of men. She can own only her clothes, ornaments and certain materials of daily use. She is also allowed to keep the income from the sale of paddy, rice and other things in the nearby market. While reaping, some stalks of paddy are left untouched in the field to be gathered by the unmarried daughters of the family for their personal use. Women do not hold or inherit real property though a daughter is entitled to maintenance and her marriage expenses from the heirs of her father. But in certain cases the daughter of a sonless Munda was found to inherit the real property of her deceased father amidst constant threats of litigation by her deceased father's agnates who claimed to be the real successors. Similarly, a widow is allowed to have life interest in the lands of her deceased husband only if she does not go to live permanently with her parents or does not remarry. In Tamar area instances were met where the childless widow of the deceased Munda (head-man) succeeded to the office of her husband and became *mundain* and inherited his real property.

Women are considered polluted during menstruation ; they are not allowed to enter the kitchen and cook meals. They do not take bath or wash their clothes. They do not sleep with their husbands and do not work in the fields during this period.

Among the Munda, the daughters are valued as much as sons. Sons are important as they support the parents in old age and worship them, even after death, in the form of ancestor worship. Daughters also play a significant role in household work and in the fields. Parents receive bride-price on their daughter's marriage which they can use for getting a bride for the unmarried son. The women have an important role in household activities and in the bringing up of children.

Christianity has played an important role in the spread of education among the tribals. The general literacy and female literacy among the Mundahave gone up. A large number of boys and girls in the school age-group attend school. Educated girls mostly opt for the teaching professions. Education has brought general awareness among the women. Though she has no political rights in the traditional village Panchayat, she may express her opinions if the need arises. The coming up of statutory Panchayats has given the women right to be elected as a Panch. In Tamar area the widow of a village Munda succeeded to her deceased husband's office. In the 1972 elections one Mrs. Barla who was a graduate and was married to a Hindu stood as a Congress candidate for the legislative assembly from Torpa constituency. Men and women participate equally in casting their votes during elections. The women cast their votes as directed by their men-folk.

Munda women are respected in the family as wife, mother and daughter. They play important roles in social, cultural and economic and ritual fields. Their position is better than that of women in the neighbouring communities. They lead a comparatively free and uninhibited life.

FERTILITY AND FAMILY PLANNING

The average number of children ever born to married Munda women in Gutuhatu, Amlesa and Salehatu villages were 3.6, 2.9 and 2.8 respectively. The average for all the villages was 3.2. children. Similarly the average number of living children per married woman in the three villages were 2.8 in Gutuhatu, 2.4 in Amlesa and 2.3 in Salehatu respectively. The common average for all the villages was 2.5 living children. About 12% of the couples never had a child and 15% had no living child at the time of survey. Only 8% of the married women gave birth to seven and more children.

The Munda have traditional methods of birth control. Many old women know of effective abortificients which they use in case of necessity. These are, however, used to prevent illegitimate births only. A *dai* (mid-wife) of Bhandartoli, Tapkara possesses knowledge of wild herbs for conducting abortion and for inducing temporary sterility. She also knows about displacing the uterus in case a woman wished not to conceive for a desired period. Some indigenous medicines from wild herbs which either induce or check fertility are also known among the Munda.

In all the villages we studied, people know about modern family planning. Kalyan Guria, an educated Munda of Gutuhatu knew about sterilization, loop and Nirodh. Sterilization is known in all the villages as a second name for family planning. Since a man in a neighbouring village died in 1974 after undergoing vasectomy operation, the attitude of the people in that area is not favourable to modern methods of family planning. In Gutuhatu, which is a Christian Munda village where the tribals belong to the R.C. Mission, the attitude about family planning is unfavourable and no one has accepted any method of family planning.

In all the three areas family planning sub-centres are functioning with one auxiliary nurse and midwife deployed specially for this purpose. None of the villages under study was ever visited by the family planning workers.

Vasectomy camps were held at Torpa, Khunti, Bundu, Karra, Rania and Tamar from time to time where the poor tribals and non-tribals were attracted by monetary incentives. The average number of living children in an average Munda family was less than three showing an orientation towards a small family norm. Thus, the problem is one of raising their standard of living rather than limiting their number.

6

SEX AND MARRIAGE

LIKE OTHER communities the Munda realise that sex is not the sole or the most important foundation upon which the edifice of marriage and family stands. Sex is not taboo and they have very few inhibitions in talking about it. Even before the onset of puberty children get some idea about sex. The physical differentiation between male and female is more than obvious to them since the bulk of the Munda children remain naked till the age of five or six. At a somewhat later stage, since they sleep in the same room with their parents they have an idea even of the sex act. Earlier there was the institution of youth dormitory known among the Munda as *gitiora*. There were very few *gitiora* even in the days of Sarat Chandra Roy. One does not know whether even at that time it served only as a sleeping house for youth or it had certain socio-economic functions like the *dhumkuria* in the Oraon areas. Either it was an incipient form of the *dhumkuria* or it was in a state of disuse. At the present time there is no *gitiora* worth the name in any village. In most villages, however, there are certain empty houses where a number of youths sleep. In Jojohatu, for example, a number of youth sleep on the verandah of the school hostel. Similarly, girls sleep in the house of some widow. Thus, by and large, most of the children at the age of adolescence and above sleep outside the home.

In Munda society, there is no segregation between the sexes. There is no bar on mixing between the boys and the girls. They run into each other in the agricultural field, forests, in the weekly markets, at the *akhra* dances and at the *jatras* and festivals. Boys and girls do different kinds of work in the agricultural operations. The girls go to collect firewood, while the boys are given the task of grazing the cattle in the forests. In the weekly markets boys and girls go in their best dresses. A visit to these markets would reveal the presence of many dandies who have made appointments with their girl friends to meet them in the market. The market thus is a meeting place for boys and girls. They make a few purchases and at dusk return to their village in small groups. No one questions the boys and girls regarding visits to the market. Thus, the market functions also as a love mart. In the dances at the *akhra* the boys and girls dance together. In some dances boys and girls dance separately, while in some others they dance together.

The Munda do not have an attitude of prudery in their attitude to sex. Parents talk about the sexual affairs of their children as a matter of course. In fact, it is a permissive society where pre-marital relations are tolerated. The Hindu notion of pre-marital chastity is not at a premium in Munda society. Young boys and girls are expected to have their sweethearts. They must take care that as far as possible they avoid members of their own clan, village and people of another tribe. However, cases of pre-marital relations with members of the prohibited groups mentioned above are not unknown. Sometimes boys and girls lose sight of the reserve and restraint prescribed for them in this regard. Earlier they feared the authority of their parents and the Panchayat which used to punish offenders by expelling them from the village. Now this strictness is not always observed.

Though pre-marital chastity is not considered important, conception of an illegitimate child is condemned socially. In such cases either the offending couple or the girl's parents try to induce abortion. In every village there are knowledgeable old women who can do this. Sometimes, however, many girls lose their lives in this process.

Educated youths and girls were found passing notes in the market. Girls visited young men sleeping in the Jojohatu school hostel premises late at night and boys and girls disappeared in the school building. Many Munda youths (single or married) with whom a friendly relationship was established during field work narrated the story of their sex-relations with young and unmarried girls during their youth. They also narrated stories of young girls of the villages around this area having love affairs with the young men of their own or different clan or village.

Such sexual contacts may be within the village itself, among people belonging to different villages within or outside the clan or with persons outside the tribe. In the village Salehatu sometime back an unmarried young girl became pregnant through the boy of an adjoining village. The matter was kept secret and the young man gave the girl a drink mixed with some poisonous element for aborting the child. The girl died in the process of abortion. The brother of the girl declared her death to be due to dysentery. He wanted to bury the dead in the *sasan.* The villagers especially the Munda of the village suspected it to be a case of death due to abortion and forced him to bury the dead body away from the *sasan.* He was fined Rs. 150 for giving incorrect information to villagers.

A girl of Jojohatu developed sex-relations with a Munda school boy of Maranghada High school staying in the Adivasi hostel, Jojohatu. Their relationship was steady for a long time and some months later the girl conceived. The girl's parents knew of this relationship, but they did not press him to marry her. An abortion was secretly arranged at home by using indigenous medicine. This leaked out. The girl was emaciated and died later.

An unmarried girl of village Salehatu Tola Maddih had relations with the young men of Pirihatu, Ganamana and Jojohatu. Subsequently she conceived through one of them and a male child was born to her illegitimately. She claims to have this child from a youth of Jojohatu an army man who developed relations with her and who used to meet her during his two-month annual leave. These three young men have got married in the course of time leaving this unmarried mother and her child to face the scorn of the society.

A young married Munda of village Jojohatu admitted liaison with many young girls prior to his marriage. He had affairs with many of them without any intention of marrying them. He recalled his relations with one of the girls belonging to his own clan and his own village. When she conceived her parents kept it secret for the fear of bad name. The loving pair aborted the child using some local medicine and continued their relations even after that. The girl's parents arranged for her marriage but on the day of marriage she ran away with her lover towards Tamar.

Similarly, in the Tapkara area, cases of pre-marital sexual contacts, between persons belonging to the same or different clans, same village or among the Munda and non-Munda, were found. In certain cases the Parha Panchayats punish the culprits with heavy fines. In a multi-caste village of Bhengra Parha an affair developed between a Munda girl and a Hindu boy. In another village under Guria Parha, the pre-marital sex relations between a boy and a girl though of different clans, but of the same village resulted in conception. The couple tried and failed to abort the child and the boy left the girl. She delivered a male child. She approached the Guria Parha and a joint meeting of Guria and Kandulna Parhas directed the boy to give the produce of a specific portion of land for the maintenance of the mother and the child for three years. In the village Amlesa, many a Munda youth admitted having pre-marital sex relations.

MARITAL STATUS

Marriage is considered obligatory for the Munda. Even spirits and deities are supposed to have consorts. Even though pre-marital sex is permitted the Munda accept the restrictions of the married state readily as it gives both men and women a higher status than otherwise. Marriage is not regarded as an affair between two persons but between two groups of kin. This relationship is emphasized at different rituals and life crises occasions by the exchange of gifts of food and clothes.

In the three villages of Salehatu, Gutuhatu and Amlesa about 60% of the males were unmarried and 70 to 80% of them belonged to ages below 15 years. Similarly, 50% of females were unmarried of which 60 to 70% were below 15 years of age.

Among persons of both the sexes below 15 years all except two females were unmarried. Percentage of married among males was higher than that for females. The respective figures were 60% and 50% for males and females. The percentage of

TABLE 6.1
Distribution of Population by sex and marital status in three villages

Village / Marital status	Salehatu	Gutuhatu	Amlesa	All villages
		MALES		
Never Married	163 (59.3)	212 (57.6)	108 (63.5)	483 (59.4)
Married	99 (36.0)	139 (37.8)	59 (34.7)	297 (36.5)
Widowed	10 (3.6)	14 (3.8)	2 (1.2)	26 (3.2)
Divorced/ Separated	3 (1.1)	3 (0.8)	1 (0.6)	7 (0.9)
Total	275 (100.0)	368 (100.0)	170 (100.0)	813 (100.0)
		FEMALES		
Never Married	111 (45.1)	192 (51.6)	84 (51.9)	387 (49.6)
Married	99 (40.2)	135 (36.3)	60 (37.0)	294 (37.7)
Widowed	36 (14.7)	43 (11.6)	17 (10.5)	96 (12.3)
Divorced/ Separated	— —	2 (0.5)	1 (0.6)	3 (0.4)
Total	246 (100.0)	272 (100.0)	162 (100.0)	780 (100.0)

widowed males was less than 4% in all villages and it was highest for Amlesa. The percentage of widowed females was almost four times that of males and it was highest (14.7%) in Salehatu.

The divorced and separated among males were around 1% with 3 cases each in Salehatu and Gutuhatu and one case in Amlesa. Similarly, among females the corresponding figure was around 0.5% with two such persons in Gutuhatu and one person in Amlesa respectively.

RULES OF MARRIAGE

The Munda do not have any system of preferred marriages. A person can marry into any clan other than his own. All clans are considered equal in status. There is no fancy for contracting marriage alliances between particular clans.

The Munda generally practise clan exogamy and tribal endogamy. Instances contrary to this general rule were found in all the three settings of the study. The wife of the Pahan of village Jojohatu belonged to the Sawansi caste. He was excommunicated by the Munda villagers because he did not agree to pay the fine and give the feast imposed by the Panchayat which had allowed him to keep the Sawansi woman provided he paid the fine and made separate cooking arrangements for her. Cases of valid marriages of Munda with Oraon and Kharia were also reported. In Amlesa two Munda school teachers have Oraon wives. In Tapkara, a multicaste village, some Hindus were married to Munda girls and begot children from them. Within the tribe the unconverted Munda do not like to marry the Christian Munda as well as Mahli Munda. In the case of a Christian girl marrying a non-Christian boy, the girl is incorporated into the tribal religion through ritual purification. Last year a Munda girl of village Salehatu (Tola Maddih) went to live with a Lohra boy of another village. A group of elders led by the Munda went to the Lohra boy's house and held a Panchayat. They realised Rs. 600 as fine and allowed the girl to live with him. Half of this money was spent on feasting the members of the Panchayat, while rest of the money was spent on feasting the Munda of all the three tolas of Salehatu by the excommunicated father of the said girl. The father was readmitted to the Munda fold as he had given a feast to all his collaterals.

Cases of breach of clan and village exogamy were met in all the three settings, especially in Salehatu area. Such couples were allowed to live together and the village Panchayat realised a nominal fine from them. Obviously, these inter-clan marriages resulted from pre-marital love affairs. It was reported from Salehatu that the Mundas of the lower tola, Baruhatu and Maddih tolas were originally from Baray-ud clan who changed to Hassa, the dominant clan of Salehatu, for acquiring *khutkatti* rights. Therefore, marriage alliances are tolerated between these two groups, however, the village Panchayat imposes a fine for breach of village exogamy which is considered desirable for the social solidarity of the village.

Similarly, the Munda in Salehatu area said that marriage within the Hassa clan was allowed among certain villages of Hassa and clan exogamy was observed in some villages thought to be *bhayads* or agnates. Perhaps the reason for such unions may be that either the two groups within the clan belonged to two or more distinct stocks and any possible agnatic relationship could not be traced or some of them must have belonged to a different clan earlier and changed to the present clan for one reason or another. Similarly, in Tamar area marriages between persons belonging to Kamal *gotra* but of different villages were found to exist. The reason given was that marriages within Kamal *gotra* were valid if the negotiating parties never had a common *harsari* or *sasan* (burial ground), *i.e.* the concerned parties should not be the descendants of a common ancestor. For example, Binod Singh Munda of Kamal *gotra* was married in the same clan. Similarly his mother was Kamal and his elder sister was also married in Kamal *gotra*. All the three females above belonged to three different villages which never had a common *sasan*.

As regards preference for marital alliances a lineage similar to one's own (of a different clan) is preferred. Similarly the Munda and the Pahan would like to marry in families of the same social status. In Bhuinhari Patti, the uniclan Parha system is in vogue. It has a standing body with hereditary officials like Parha Raja, Lal, Dewan Pande etc. The different villages are known after these officials as these are inhabited by the descendants of a particular ancestor holding the official status. They prefer to marry in a family of similar social status from other clans.

In Tamar area social stratification is found among the Mundas such as the landlords (Thakur, Manki, Munda, Babu), the tenants or Raiyat (Mundari) and Patar (who belong to Mahali Mundako branch). All these four classes among the landlords are endogamous and only in rare cases does an intermarriage take place between them. Intermarriage between the landlord class and the ordinary Munda is impossible due to great disparity in their social and economic status. Marriage with the Patars is considered unusual. If somebody from one of the higher classes takes a fancy for a girl of the lower class he may keep her as a mistress without marrying her. A separate apartment in the house may be given to her and the man would not accept cooked food from her hands.

These days, emphasis is placed on the social and economic status of the family and the person's education while selecting a marriage partner. Relationship of some sort, direct or indirect, must be traced before starting the negotiations. The parents generally take the final decision and the boy's consent is frequently asked and generally obtained. Certain factors are taken into consideration in the selection of marital partner for a boy among the Mundas. In those marriages where the boy's parents try to find girls as suitable mates for their sons the nature, disposition and ability of the girl to do household work are taken into consideration. She must also be healthy. Now-a-days beauty and education are also considered important, specially if the groom is educated.

POLYGYNY

Monogamy is the usual practice among the Mundas. Instances of polygynous marriages were also found with two cases in Salehatu and Amlesa and in the traditional villages of Jojohatu and Serengdih. Infertility of the first wife generally leads to the second marriage. But in exceptional cases a man can take another wife for reasons other than this. Rattan Munda of Salehatu has two wives and begot children from both of them.

KINDS OF MARRIAGE

Most of the marriages in all the villages under study were arranged with bride-price, where parents took the initiative and the formal consent of boys and girls was taken at a later stage. In Birhu, Selda and Koenara which are Christian villages almost all the marriages were arranged by parents. In Jojohatu and Salehatu, both the traditional villages, more than half of the marriages were of the arranged type.

Raji khusi marriage (love marriage) is the marriage, settled by the boys and girls themselves. Later on the stamp of recognition is accorded by the parents. 15% of total marital unions in all the study villages were of this type. Salehatu and Jojohatu had the highest percentages of such marriages. Amlesa and Gutuhatu each have 7% of such marriages, while Selda and Koenara have each 3% of such marriages. A solitary case of intrusion marriage came to our notice in 1958 in Jojohatu. Not a single marriage by intrusion was reported from the villages covered in this study.

TABLE 6.2
Different Types of Marriages Among the Munda

Name of village	Types of Marriage						
	Arranged with bride price	Love Marriage (*Raji khushi*)	Intrusion	By Capture	By Service	Not Specified	Total
Salehatu	86 (55.1)	60 (38.5)	— —	1 (0.6)	— —	9 (5.8)	156 (100.0)
Gutuhatu	179 (87.3)	14 (7.0)	— —	— —	— —	12 (5.7)	205 (100.0)
Amlesa	74 (86.0)	6 (7.0)	— —	1 (0.2)	— —	5 (5.8)	86 (100.0)
Birhu*	85 (100.0)	— —	— —	— —	— —	— —	85 (100.0)
Selda*	30 (97.0)	1 (3.0)	— —	— —	— —	— —	31 (100.0)
Koenara*	94 (97.0)	3 (3.0)	— —	— —	— —	— —	97 (100.0)
Jojohatu*	66 (68.0)	30 (31.0)	1 (1.0)	— —	— —	— —	97 (100.0)
Total	614 (81.1)	114 (15.0)	1 (0.1)	2 (0.3)	— (0.0)	26 (3.5)	757 (100.0)

**Source* : Sachchidananda, 1964, *Culture Change Among the Munda and Oraon*, p. 45.

Two instances of marriage by capture in the market place or *Jatra*, were reported from Salehatu and Amlesa respectively. In such cases the girl's consent is always implied. As such it is a case of simulated capture.

Marriage by service is unknown in all the villages.

AGE AT FIRST MARRIAGE

It was observed that the mean age of marriage was higher for males than females in Salehatu, Gutuhatu and Amlesa. The corresponding ages were above 20 years for males and below 20 years for females. Both the males and the females marry at a later age in Amlesa than in Gutuhatu. In Salehatu the age of marriage is lower than at Gutuhatu. In an earlier study it was found that among the Munda, the largest number of boys married after 21 years of age in Serengdih and Selda while in Birhu and Koenara 40% and 30.4% respectively, married after 21 years of age. In Selda, Birhu and Koenara most of the girls married between 16-20 years of age.

TABLE 6.3

Distribution of Population by Sex and Age at first marriage

Age at first marriage	VILLAGES					
	Salehatu		Gutuhatu		Amlesa	
	Male	Female	Male	Female	Male	Female
10-14 years	3(2.6)	11(8.2)	1(0.6)	4(2.3)		3(3.9)
15-19 ,,	46(41.0)	82(61.2)	37(23.5)	82(46.3)	6(9.8)	36(46.7)
20-24 ,,	49(43.2)	22(16.4)	70(44.5)	52(29.5)	30(49.2)	22(28.6)
25-29 ,,	9(8.0)	1(0.8)	28(18.0)	5(2.8)	16(26.2)	5(6.5)
30 and above	1(0.9)	1(0.8)	7(4.4)	2(1.1)	7(11.5)	1(1.3)
Age not stated	5(4.3)	17(12.6)	14(9.0)	32(18.0)	2(3.3)	10(13.0)
All ages	113(100.0)	134(100.0)	157(100.0)	177(100.0)	61(100.0)	77(100.0)
Mean age at first marriage (in years)	20.6	18.0	22.7	19.7	24.5	19.8

In Amlesa none of the boys married below 15 years. A small proportion of boys and girls married below 15 years in Gutuhatu and Salehatu. Child marriages or marriage below 10 years of age were not found in any of the three villages. Some cases of child marriages in case of girls were reported from Jojohatu.

DISTANCE OF MARITAL ALLIANCES

Marriages within the same village were found in all the villages, *viz.*, Salehatu, Gutuhatu, Amlesa, Serengdih, Selda and Jojohatu though very few in number. In Salehatu, the marriages were largely contracted within the same Block. Marriages beyond Ranchi district were not found in Salehatu. Gutuhatu, which is a Christian Munda village of Torpa Block was different from Salehatu as 45% of marriages took place in other adjoining blocks of Ranchi district. Marriages beyond Ranchi district as well as outside Bihar were also reported. In village Amlesa of Tamar Block marriages within Tamar area were only 30%. Other Blocks of Ranchi accounted for about 42% of the marriages.

TABLE 6.4

Percentage Distribution of Marriages by village of Marital Alliances

Village of Marital aliance	Salehatu	Gutuhatu	Amlesa	All villages
Same village	3.8	4.4	2.3	3.8
Within the block	68.6	39.0	30.2	47.7
Within the district	16.0	44.9	41.9	34.2
Within the State but outside the district	—	1.0	8.1	2.0
Outside the State	—	1.5	8.1	2.3
Village not specified	11.6	9.2	9.3	10.0
Total	100.0	100.0	100.0	100.0

TABLE 6.5

Percentage Distribution of Marriages by Distance of Marital Alliances

Distance of Marital Alliance (in miles)	Salehatu	Gutuhatu	Amlesa	All villages
Same village	3.8	4.4	2.3	3.8
Up to 5 miles	43.6	24.4	15.1	29.3
6 — 10 ,,	24.5	34.5	26.7	29.5
11 — 19 ,,	11.5	19.0	15.1	15.7
20 and above	5.1	6.3	31.5	10.7
Distance not specified	11.5	11.3	9.3	11.0
Total	100.0	100.0	100.0	100.0

As regards proximity of marital alliance, 44% of marriages in Salehatu took place within its five miles radius. In Gutuhatu 35% marriages were arranged within 6—10 miles distance. 32% of marriages were contracted beyond 20 miles in case of Amlesa.

An analysis of marital alliances among the Mundas of Serengdih, Selda, Jojohatu, Birhu and Koenara revealed that there were very few marriages in which both the partners belonged

4. Munda farmers preparing a storage bin for paddy

5. Reaping the harvest

6. A village sasan

7. Guests at a marriage party

to the same village. From village Serengdih cases of marriage within the same tola were discovered as also those of marriages in the same village. The reason is that most of the marriages reported are from Birsite families. Birsites are not found in the neighbouring areas. So most of the marriages took place among them in the same village. No case of intra-village marriage was reported from the Christian Mundas of Birhu and Koenara. Half of the marriages in Selda and Serengdih took place within 6 miles of the respective villages. In Jojohatu and Koenara about two-third of the marriages were contracted up to a distance of 9 miles. In Birhu about three-fifths of marriages took place in villages at a distance of 10 miles and above.

The analysis of marriages by place and distance of marital alliances among the Munda of different villages may be explained as : The tradition of village exogamy is not very strictly followed, thus resulting in inter-clan marriages within the same village. These marriages are mostly love marriages. However, among Birsites of Serengdih, these might be directly settled by the respective parents.

The Munda in the three areas, *viz.*, Khutkatti, Bhuinhari and Panch Parganas usually have marital alliances in the villages within their respective areas.

In the Khutkatti area, marriages are settled at comparatively shorter distances than in Bhuinhari area. In Panch Parganas marriages take place in which the partners are separated by long distances. The Khutkatti area have different clans living in neighbouring villages which facilitates inter-clan affinal ties at shorter distances. The Munda of the Bhuinhari area live in groups of uniclan villages with single clan dominant in a number of adjoining villages. Munda of the Panch Parganas also have marital relations with those of West Bengal. In Amlesa one-third of the Munda families are migrants from Bhuinhari and Khutkatti areas, and prefer to marry in their own respective areas. These two factors certainly contribute towards marital relations at comparatively longer distances than in the first two areas.

MARRIAGE RITUALS

The marriage rituals among the Munda have been greatly affected under the impact of Hinduism and Christianity. Certain changes have taken place in these rituals since S. C. Roy's time. His description of marriage gives a generalised account without considering the regional variations. Also, he did not write about the marriage rituals among the Christian Mundas.

Since S.C. Roy's work, the marriage ceremonials among the traditional Mundas have become less elaborate by cutting short and eliminating many rituals to suit changing times. Earlier the Pahan used to be the main functionary at marriage, while now Brahmin, barber, *Gosain* etc. have been introduced. Among the Christian Mundas, the parish priest or *padri* performs the marriage in the Church. In Panch Parganas, the Hinduised Mundas imitate their Hindu neighbours to a large extent and have adopted Hindu names for the ceremonials as well. At their marriages a Brahmin officiates.

Among the Mundas, generally, the pre-requisite for marriage is the existence of some kinship relationship (*kutumb*), direct or indirect, between the negotiating parties. An *agua* (*dutam*) or intermediary is selected by the parents of the boy to look for a girl for their son. The *agua* talks to the interested party and the *rashi mala* of the potential groom and the bride are matched by a Brahmin.

CEREMONIES PRIOR TO ACTUAL MARRIAGE

S.C. Roy has mentioned four rituals before marriage, such as the *chenre-uri* (omen reading), the *bala* (Betrothal), the *gonong taka idituka* (carrying or presentation of bride-price), and the *logon tol* (selection of a suitable date for marriage). These ceremonials required four visits for *chenre-uri*, then a visit to the groom's house by the bride's guardians for betrothal, and finally the groom's party visit the bride's house for presentation of bride-price.

Now only two alternate visits are required during negotiations for marriage. The first visit is paid by the boy's party to the girl's house to see the girl and then the girl's party reciprocates by paying a visit to the former for the *bala* or betrothal.

Kuri-hon-lel (*Kanya Dekhna*)

The boy's guardians accompanied by senior members of their village and the *agua* go to the house of the potential bride on a fixed date. The groom may or may not accompany the party. The party arrives at the bride's house at night. On their way they observe omens* (*chenre-uri*, *ere-uri* or *hora-pari*) from groom's house to his village boundary, and then from the boundary of the bride's village to her house.

If the party happens to come across a bad omen on the way, they forthwith return home and the negotiations fall through. If no bad omen is encountered, the party proceeds to the house of the intended bride. On their arrival they are made to sit on mats spread in the courtyard. The omens are discussed and if declared favourable, the umbrellas and sticks of the boy's party are tied in a bundle and the *agua* keeps the bundle inside the house for safety. The womenfolk of the girl's house now wash the feet of the guests.

If the boy has acompanied the party, the girl is brought in the courtyard to meet the boy. Both of them are asked by the elders of both the sides, whether they like each other or not. In case they accept each other, the bride presents a *lota* of water and then *kheni* (tobacco) in a Sal leaf, and some burning charcoal in a pot. The boy accepts the present in case he likes the girl. The eldest among the visitors presents clothes and ornaments brought for the girl. *Gonong* or bride-price may be fixed during this visit, otherwise it is settled when the girl's party will pay a visit to the boy's house for the betrothal. Now the visitors are feasted with *hanria* (ricebeer), country liquor and a meal. Next morning after mutual greetings or *johar*, the boy's party takes leave of the girl's guardian and relatives. Before the guests leave they invite the girl's guardian and relatives to return the visit.

An informant of Amlesa in Panch Parganas said that in his marriage during this ceremonial his party started at night so as to reach girl's house the next morning. Before starting they took mustard oil in a plate and sprinkled it thrice on the ground in the name of God and prayed for their smooth journey. Similarly, when the girl was taken out before the

*A detailed list of good and bad omens is given in Chapter XII.

guests, she was dressed nicely. She along with her girl friends (*lukundis*) anointed and washed the feet of the guests. The feet of the oldest among them are washed first. He presented the girl with clothes (sari, blouse etc.) brought from the boy's house. The girl and her friends were given some cash by each guest when they washed their feet. The guests and hosts cut jokes with each other. A goat was killed in the honour of the guests and its meat was served along with the meals.

The Bala (Betrothal)

The next preliminary ceremony in connection with a Munda marriage is the '*bala*' or betrothal. On an appointed day, the bride's guardian with a number of relatives arrives at the bridegroom's house and is accorded a hearty welcome. Before leaving the house, the girl's party asks the girl whether they should proceed for further negotiations. They set out after taking her consent. The party takes rice-beer at the girl's house before leaving. Then thrice they pray to Singbonga for getting His blessings in making the negotiations successful. They take mustard oil in a plate and observe it for a few moments. If the oil remains clear, it is a good omen. During this period they listen carefully for any bad omen such as the barking of a dog, a man sneezing or coughing, the sound of wood being cut, the sound of a flute or drum being played etc. If no such thing is heard they proceed on their journey and mark the omens on the way. Reaching the village boundary they again pray to Singbonga three times and look for omens. Similarly, they observe omens from the boundary of the boy's village to his house. The party arrives at night.

Now both the parties sit and omens are discussed, and if satisfactory, the intermediary takes charge of the sticks and umbrellas of the guests. The women of the boy's house wash their feet. All of them take rice-beer together. The relatives on the boy's side sing *bala* songs. If the *gonong* (bride-price) was not fixed during the previous ceremony, it is fixed on this occasion.

The bride-price is settled not by naming the demand, but by the bride's guardian signifying his demand by symbols, and the groom's guardian signifying his acceptance by the use of the same symbols. Now both the parties sit apart. The girl's party makes sal leaf cups. They put in some stone pebbles (or globules of goat dung) to signify the amount desired. Figures signifying bullocks demanded are made on the sal leaves. A number of sal leaves, each rolled up and tied round with a red or white thread, signifies the number of saris and other clothes wanted and so forth. In the beginning the bride's guardians demand a higher bride-price than what they expect. The groom's guardian takes a certain number out of these and returns the rest to signify that he agrees to give as many of each item as he has kept and begs to be excused from satisfying the rest of the demand. If not agreed this way, the matter is discussed directly to fix the exact amount of bride-price agreeable to both the parties. Earlier Rs. 6 in cash, two head of cattle and three pieces of cloth comprised the customary bride-price but these days it has been raised to Rs. 12 in cash, two head of cattle and five or seven pieces of cloth. In the case of a graduate informant of Amlesa no bride-price was given. Some dowry was given to him by the bride's parents.

Lota-Da Ceremony

When the bride-price is fixed and agreed upon, the *lota-da* (*lota-pani*) ceremony is performed. The *agua* stands with a *lota* of water covered on both sides with sal leaf-cups. The girl's guardians accept the *lota-da* by touching it and then saluting it. Then they greet (*johar*) all the persons present there. A goat is ceremonially handed over to the guests. Two persons from the girl's party sacrifice the goat. The boy's relatives throw turmeric water on them. The women wash their feet. The hosts boil the rice and cook the meat. All of them, then rejoice by drinking rice-beer. They sing *bala* songs all night. The guests are taken out for morning duties and bath. Then meals are ready and the guests are served the meals. Some persons from the boy's side also sit along with guests. The goat's head is cooked separately and an elder from the girl's party performs worship outside the courtyard with this meat and rice-beer.

When meals are served, someone from among the guests demands water as a ritual and he is served with cold water in a leaf cup. Then he says that he wants hot instead of cold water. The boy's father then puts Rs. 1.25 in that leaf-cup. The father of the bride and the bride-groom respectively sit face to face with each other and they are served water along with meals in the beginning. Now they exchange their meals and water and then everyone starts eating the meals. Afterwards, again ricebeer and country liquor are taken. The girl's party now intimate to the hosts their intention to leave through the intermediary.

It is customary to take home the goat's meat. Previously the head of the goat was not cooked and was given to the guests. Afterwards it was realised that it merely contained more bones than flesh, so they agreed to take the hind part as *dundi.* Those who do not like taking the raw meat with them, take cooked meat and boiled rice as *dundi.* The intermediary gives the *dundi* and their sticks to the guests. The guests are sprinkled with *haldi* (turmeric) mixed with oil and garlanded with *golainchi* flowers at the time of leaving. The bride-price or *gonong* may be presented at this time or promised to be paid afterwards. After a fresh exchange of hearty greetings and *johar*, the guests depart. On reaching home, they distribute the meat brought as *dundi* among those who accompanied the betrothal party.

In Panch Parganas, the girl's party is received at the boy's house by the boy himself and at that moment the elder among the visitors presents him with a *dhoti*, and the latter greets him. Bride-price may be settled now if not decided earlier. The girl's maternal uncle then ties a thread around the boy's wrist. The maternal uncle of the boy and the girl both hold each other's hands and declare that if either of them will break this engagement, his left hand will be cut by the Raja and the right hand by the Praja.

Logon Tol

An account of *logon* ceremonial as narrated by an informant from Amlesa is given below.

On an auspicious day the Pandey (Brahmin) looked into the almanac for fixing the *lagan* and the date of marriage. Nine days before the actual date of the informant's marriage eleven men went to the bride's village Erki to bring *lagan.*

They carried with them clothes, vermilion, *kajal*, bangles, etc. for the girl and *lagan* in the form of nine pieces of turmeric tied in a new piece of cloth and mustard oil. On arriving at the bride's place at night they were given a hearty welcome and treated with rice-beer and meals of boiled rice and meat.

Early next morning *lagan* was fixed. A rectangular *mandap* was made with rice flour by one of the three friends of the bride for which she was given Rs. 5 by the visitors. Then the bride was brought out by one of her friends in her lap holding the hand of another friend carrying a *lota* of water. They came out of the house and took three rounds of the *mandap* anti-clockwise and stood near the *mandap* facing east. The girl carrying the bride was paid 50 paise by the groom's party before the bride alighted from her lap. The bride was dressed in clothes brought by the visitors. The bride was made to sit in the *mandap* and she opened the bundle containing turmeric and the pot containing mustard oil with the help of the barber. Then the barber similarly collected *lagan* in the form of turmeric and mustard oil from the bride to be carried to the boy's house. The barber then demanded and was given Rs. 5. The women relatives of the bride sang *lagan* songs on this occasion. The songs were in Panch Pargania as well as in Bengali. The visitors had to pay Rs. 2 to the women singing *lagan* songs. These women would buy salt with this money and share it among themselves.

The male relatives of the bride anointed the visitors with turmeric oil and *kajal* and garlanded them with flowers. The bride and her famale relatives made use of the turmeric, oil and *kajal* etc. brought by the visitors. Similarly the barber collected turmeric, oil and cosmetics from the bride's household and the latter handed these over to the head of the groom's party or any other near relative. The visitors were seen off from the courtyard as they were not supposed to enter the house after taking *lagan*. Before leaving they were given betel, *biri*, cigarettes, matches etc. for the journey. As is customary, the visitors left the bride's place before sunrise.

The party returned to Amlesa led by the band played by Ghasis who met the party on the way. The party waited outside the house till sunset, if the day of arrival is either Tuesday or Saturday which is thought to be inauspicious.

Then girl friends of the groom made a similar *mandap* in the groom's courtyard. The groom was brought out by one of the girl friends in the same way as the bride. No money was demanded by the girl carrying him. The women sang *lagan* songs. The *lagan* brought by the party was given to the groom who handed it over to his mother. She received it in her *anchal* or a part of her *sari*. The *lagan* consisted of turmeric, mango leaf signifying the bride, betelnuts, white handspun thread, wrapped in a turmeric coloured piece of cloth and mustard oil. The turmeric oil from bride's house was anointed on their person by all the members present here. Now the mother took the *lagan* inside the house followed by the members of the party who brought the *lagan*. All of them were feasted with rice-beer and meals.

In Gutuhatu the ceremonials prior to the actual marriage are performed in four visits. In the first visit, a few male relatives of the boy along with the intermediary visit the girl's house. They observe omens on the way. On reaching the girl's house, their feet are washed *(katta-da)*. *Dalitaka* or bride-price is fixed on this day. The customary bride-price is four head of cattle, two *saris* and one *dhoti*. If three head of cattle are agreed upon, the boy's guardians have to give clothes for all the family members of the girl. Next, at least five male relatives of the girl visit the boy's house. They also observe omens on the way. They are treated sumptuously. This is called *ghar-dekhi* or seeing the house. Then on another appointed day about ten male relatives of the boy visit the girl's house for *lota-pani*. They take some clothes for the girl. The ceremony is similar to that in other traditional villages. The visitors are feasted with food and drink before they return home. Next, more than thirty male relatives of the girl visit the boy's house where they are given a hearty welcome. They are served rice-beer and then boiled rice with mutton or pork. While leaving they take the cattle head agreed upon for bride-price. The *barat* or wedding party along with the boy goes to the girl's house on a fixed day for the actual marriage. The *barat* party takes *chura* (parched rice), *gur* (molasses) and *hanria* (rice-beer) with them. Women also accompany the wedding party. The marriage takes place in the *mandoa*, and the Pahan officiates at the function. Other ceremonies related with anointing and bathing the couple are also performed. When the wedding party returns home with the bride, the couple is carried inside the house where they are given *jang-da* to drink. Then a red hen is sacrificed in the *mandoa.* It is followed by sumptuous meals and drink.

ARANDI (MARRIAGE CEREMONY)

The marriage rituals in Khutkatti area are narrated below :

The date of marriage is fixed according to the convenience of both the parties. Tuesday, Thursday and *amawas* (moonless night or newmoon) are avoided as being inauspicious for marriage. The wedding date is announced about two weeks prior to the actual celebration so that both the parties may send for their relatives and make necessary arrangements for the coming occasion.

Sasang-goso

On a day prior to the wedding both the bride and the groom are anointed with turmeric and mustard oil at their respective houses. Next morning the barber paints the feet of the bride, the groom and their family members with red liquid at their respective places. This is called *narta* ceremony. The *gosain* or the barber ties a mango leaf with a thread on one of the legs of the groom and his parents and the bride and her parents respectively at their places.

Barat

The bridegroom along with his men and women relatives and friends sets out in the form of a *barat* (wedding party) to the bride's house with Ghasis leading the music party. According to his socio-economic status, the groom travels either in a palanquin or is carried to the village boundary on the shoulders of relatives and friends.

The Bridegroom's *uli-sakhi*

After leaving his house, the groom is first taken to a mango tree on his way and the mango tree is made witness. He is accompanied by his relatives and the musicians. He ties a white thread around the stem, smears liquid rice flour on it and goes round the tree anti-clockwise three times, while he is being carried in the lap of a relative. From there, he joins the *barat* again and the party moves towards the bride's village.

Daparom (*Samdhi Bhet*)

On reaching the bride's village, the wedding party waits under a tree at some distance from the bride's house. Now the bride's guardians and relatives come to receive the guests accompanied by musicians and paiki dancers. The young men bring long sticks tied with straw which they light and go around the wedding party. The girls of both the sides sprinkle water on each other with a mango leaf. Then the joint procession moves ahead and the wedding party is led to the place (*jalom*) set for their stay. The guests are given meat, rice, pulses, and rice-beer. They cook for themselves and enjoy the food and drink.

Sasang-goso

The groom is then taken to the bride's house. There he is anointed with turmeric and oil by the female relatives of the bride. The groom is then brought to the *mandap* in the courtyard by the younger brother of the bride holding a *dhoti* tied around groom's neck.

Sinduri-Rakab

The actual marriage ceremony is performed in the *mandap*. The bride is carried out of the house and made to sit by the side of the groom. Some worship is performed by the Brahmin or Gosain and the couple then put three vermilion marks first on their own forehead and then on each other's forehead. The groom takes the initiative. Their garments are tied to each other. The Brahmin requests the bride's parents to display the presents and gifts to be given to the bride and these are ceremonially handed over to the groom's guardians. Those wishing to give gifts to the newly wedded couple offer these to them at this time.

Feast

By this time the meals are ready. The bride's relatives feast at the bride's house. The groom eats with them. The groom will not eat until the bride's parents accept his customary demand. This is called *hatthi karna.* Then the groom and the bride both go to the place where the groom's party is put up and dine with them. The bride is accompanied by one of her female friends and return home with her after meals.

Bidai

The bride's guardians then make over the bride to the groom's guardians in the presence of relatives and village elders. The bride's friends *(gati-kuriko)* do not relieve the bride unless the groom pays them some small cash present. After a demonstrative farewell and greetings by the couple individually to all present, the couple leave by palanquin or other conveyance along with the wedding party.

Ceremonies at the Groom's House

At the groom's house *chuman* ceremony is performed, while the newly wedded couple sits in the *mandap* along with all the relatives and friends. First, the mother of the groom, then father and other relatives come one by one, sprinkle turmeric mixed *arua* rice on the couple and kiss their forehead ritually and exchange greetings. They put the gifts in a brass plate kept there. At the end, the gifts and presents are counted and announced to the gathering. This is followed by feasting. If the wedding party returns at night the *chuman* would be performed the following day.

Otung-Nam

Next day, the father or guardian of the bride and a few relatives pay a visit to the groom's house to see the bride, and are received and entertained with great hospitality.

A week, or two or a month after wedding, the parents or brother/uncle of the bride take back the couple to the bride's house. There the groom dismantles the *mandoa* and the couple are feasted.

Marriage Ceremonials in Rajikhusi Marriage

In the case of *rajikhusi* or love marriages, among the traditional Mundas of Khutkatti area, the girl (on her way back from the market or *jatra*, fair etc.), goes along with the boy of her choice to live with him. The boy persuades his guardians to allow her to stay in the house. On learning this the girl's mother along with few women pays a visit to the boy's house to know whether the girl is willing. In case the girl says that she came to stay there by her own choice the visitors return without being entertained. If she does not, the girl may go back with them to her own house.

Then on an appointed day the girl's guardians accompanied by male relatives and villagers visit the boy's house. They reach there at night and are given a hearty welcome. The bride-price is negotiated. The visitors demand some fine for the loss of face due to the conduct of the potential couple and that of the host who allowed the girl to live with them without proper marriage and thus abetted the offence. When the bride-price is being settled, the guests are treated with rice-beer, boiled rice and goat's meat. The bride's party departs next morning with bride-price or a promise for that.

Sometimes a couple may elope and live away from their home if their parents are known to be against their union. Later on a nominal bride-price is paid to legitimise the union.

The boy and the girl start living as husband and wife and the actual marriage takes place sometime afterwards at the boy's house, generally before the birth of first child. A young Munda of Jojohatu who was living with his girl (through *rajikhusi* marriage) got married ceremonially after a year of stay with her before his first issue. The Brahmin (the Vaidya in the village dispensary), officiated at the marriage and was paid a fee of Rs. 5.

Among the unconverted Munda some changes have occurred in the marriage ceremonial. Though *mandap* is necessary for a marriage, it can be dispensed with for fear of witchcraft. The barber is invited from the town, instead of the Brahmin, to officiate at a Munda marriage, because the latter used to demand high fees for the work. The barber is paid Rs. 1.50 as his fee. About two decades ago the Pahan used to perform the marriage.

The Ceremonial among Converts in the Church and the Social Rites Performed in the Village

Similar to the details of preliminary ceremonials described

among the unconverted Mundas of Gutuhatu, the converted Mundas of all the three Christian denominations (*e.g.* G.E.L., R.C. and S.P.G. missions) have *kata-da* and *dalitakka, ghar dekhi, lota-da* and *barka-kutumb* rituals performed before actual marriage.

The boy's relatives visit the girl's house for *kata-da.* The *dali-takka* (bride-price) is settled there. Among the G.E.L. mission Mundas it is three head of cattle (or equivalent money), one *maisari* for the girl's mother, one *ledri* for the grandmother, one *sara-dhoti* for the bride's brother and 2 to 3 saris for other relatives. Among Mundas of the R.C. Church the usual bride-price is Rs. 200 or two head of cattle and one sari for the mother. Next, the girl's relatives visit the boy's house for *ghar-dekhi.* They are given hearty welcome there. The party observes omens on their way to boy's house. Then on an appointed date the boy along with his relatives and friends and the intermediary visits the girl's house for the *lota-da* ceremony. Two or three persons are deputed to look for omens on the way. At the girl's house the feet of the guests are washed, their sticks and umbrellas are collected from them, rice-beer and tea are served to them and then discussion on *hora-pari* is conducted. If found favourable, then *lota-da* ceremony is performed at night. In the *marwa* which is a rectangular shed made of sal saplings and thatched with green leaves and twigs the girl (dressed in the new sari presented by the groom) stands flanked by two female friends (*lukundis*). Each of them holds a *lota* (water pot) full of tea and covered on both sides by sal leaf-cups kept in a *thali* or brass-plate. The groom along with his two friends (*gati-kurako* or *lukundas*) stand face to face with the bride. All the relatives of both the sides stand in one corner. The *parcharak* says the prayer and then asks the groom and the bride whether the two like each other. If they reply in the affirmative, *parcharak* gives the *lotas* in the hands of the bride and her friends and then each of them exchange the *lota* three times with the respective male partner and then they keep the *lotas* on the ground. Now all of them shake hands, the girls give presents of handkerchieve to their partners who in turn give some money (upto Re. 1) to them. The tea in the pot is distributed to all the persons present there by the bride and the bridegroom together. Finally, they take tea from each other's hands. The guests are now feasted with rice and meat and sometimes pork also. For the whole night the *bala* songs or *bhajans* are sung separately by both the parties. In the morning the guests depart after having breakfast. The date for *barka-kutumb* is also fixed before departure.

In *barka-kutumb* (big feast) the girl's male and female relatives visit the boy's house on a fixed date. They also observe the omens on the way. On arrival their feet are washed. Then tea is served and omens are discussed. The meals are given. For the whole night the programme of songs and *bhajans* continues. In the morning the cattle for bride-price are selected. A man from among the guests touches the selected cattle with a pebble and exchanges *chuna* (lime) and tobacco with one of the hosts. A he-goat and a *banda* (pig) are slain in the honour of the guests. Lunch is served with rice and pulses, while dinner is served with meat. In the evening a Panchayat is held in which formal introduction is done. The groom is presented with a *dhoti*. *Samdhis* and the groom sit together. The two *samdhis* exchange their meals. They put some coins by the side of the meal before exchanging it. Afterwards guests are given a farewell and some rice, meat and *gurakhu* (tobacco mixed with molasses) are given to them for the bride's mother. This is called *dundi*. Earlier, the hind parts of the *khassi* or *banda* (still common among non-converts) was taken home as *dundi* by the bride's party. Four to five members of the bride's party take with them the cattle as bride-price. The bride's mother distributes the gift of rice, meat and *gurakhu* to all the relatives and agnates. After two or three days some persons from the bride's house go to the groom's house to return the chain for tethering the cattle.

Bachan-dat

Subsequently the date of engagement and marriage are fixed. Among the Mundas of the German Mission the date for *bachan-dat* is fixed three weeks before the marriage date. The applications for marriage are submitted separately by the groom and the bride in their respective church-Mandlis and their approval and recommendations are obtained. On the appointed day, the groom along with his friends and *panch* of his Mandli visit the girl's house. He presents her with a *sari*. Then both the parties along with the bride and the groom go to the parish Church of the bride's village and hand over the two recommendation letters to the priest who keeps these for furture reference. The priest makes sure that the boy and the girl agree to marry each other. If desired further negotiations may be broken at this stage. Then everyone enters the Church where prayer is offered by the priest. On the subsequent three Sundays, *pukar* (call) is given by the two Church Mandlis at the Sunday service whereby the proposed marriage is announced to all.

Among the Catholic Mundas after a similar engagement ceremony, the couple has to attend a school for marriage separately at their Mandlis between December 9 to December 25, where they are taught about their respective roles in married life.

Arandi (Marriage Ceremony)

The date for marriage is fixed in accordance with the convenience of the priest and the parties concerned. Tuesday and Wednesday are considered auspicious for marriage. Generally marriages are held in January, February and April when the house is full of food grain. The R. C. Mission and S. P. G. Mission consider Wednesday and Friday as inauspicious for marriage. In the Lent period, starting from March first, no marriage is performed among the Christians. Though theoretically all Christians may intermarry, tribal endogamy is the rule. The Roman Catholics usually do not permit marriage between its adherents and Christians of other denominations. However, they may allow such marriage (even with the unconverted Munda), if the prospective spouse would agree to become Roman Catholic. The priest at G.E.L. Church, Tapkara performed a marriage between a boy of the German Mission and a girl of the R. C. Mission. The girl was converted to her husband's church before marriage.

The marriage ceremonial among the converted Mundas is held at the Church. This is followed by a social ceremonial at the home of the bride and the bridegroom without which a marriage is not considered complete.

Barat

A wedding party led by the bridegroom with musicians playing ahead of them (*barat*) goes to the girl's house. Before starting, a prayer is held. At the girl's village, the *barat* is given a cordial reception. *Samdhi-bhet* is performed. The parents and female relatives of the bride and the groom sprinkle water on each other with mango twigs. They give *chura* or beaten rice (sometimes sweets) to each other and then wash each other's feet. The bridegroom is treated in the same way. The girls dance and sing. The groom and his *gati-Kurako* are carried by male relatives of the bride to her house. The *barat* party sits in the *mandoa.* Every one is given tea and other refreshments. The feet of the guests are then washed and they are served meals. All through the night *kirtan-bhajan* is performed.

In the Church

Next morning both the parties along with the bride and the bridegroom visit the Church for the marriage ceremony. The recommendation letters from the respective Mandlis of the two parties are produced before the priest. In the meantime, the women relatives of the groom dress the bride with clothes given by the groom. The girl puts a head-wear or *salu* on her head, along with flowers. The groom is anointed with turmeric and oil by the women relatives of the bride. The bride and the bridegroom exchange flowers. A short small prayer is held outside the Church and then the priest attired in gown leads them to the Church from the western door. Prayers are offered. The priest then gives a sermon to the couple and the marriage rules are recited to them. They are told how to lead a good married life, their duties and obligations towards each other are highlighted. The two silver wedding rings brought by the bridegroom are given to the priest for being presented to the couple. First the groom and then the bride put the wedding ring on each other's right hand third finger. They hold each other by their right hand and the priest gives them blessings by putting his hands over their heads and declares them as husband and wife. At this time the Mandli keeps standing. The priest tells them that those whom, God has united, no man should separate. The Mandli sits down and now the registration is done. The marriage certificate is signed first by the bridegroom and then by the bride and three witnesses (two from the groom's and one from the bride's side) and finally by the priest. The priest hands over the marriage certificate to the bride and keeps the counterfoil in the marriage register. The bride then hands over the certificate to the bridegroom. The certificate contains information like the names of the two spouses and their fathers, the clan name, ȧge, sex, the village, date of marriage, etc. In a marriage performed by the priest of G.E.L. Church Tapkara, Rs. 20 were collected as his fees for the work.

Among the Roman Catholic Munda, the marriage ceremony is performed by the priest. In addition to exchanging wedding rings, they apply vermilion on each other's forehead like the unconverted Munda. This custom of applying vermilion started in the early seventies. In S.P.G. Church also the Chotanagpur Bishop has allowed the application of vermilion at marriages (from 1973), but no such cases were found among the Mundas of this Mission. In the R.C. Mission no marriage certificate is issued to the couple, but it is kept in the marriage register of the Church.

After the marriage ceremony in the Church, a procession is taken out with music. The friends, relatives and co-villagers of the bridegroom join. They are received with dance and music by the bridal party. In some cases, the wedding party goes to the bride's house only after performance of the marriage at the Church where the bride was brought from her village with her women friends and relatives. The wedding party sits in the *Mandwa* and they are served meals. In the evening a Sabha (Panchayat) is held. This begins with a prayer. The couple is given presents and gifts and the nominal dowry. A record of gifts is made by the two secretaries, one from each side and in the end they announce the list of gifts to the Sabha. Then the elderly women of both the sides sit together. The clothes or saris (part of the bride-price) are presented to the bride's women relatives by those of the bridegroom and the former shake hands with everyone and display the gifts received. The Sabha is dissolved after prayer.

After the feast the bride is made over to the groom's guardians. The wedding party leaves with the bride after a ceremonial farewell.

At the groom's house, his mother washes the feet of the couple as they enter and throws water over the roof three times. Now a feast is given to all the relatives. Next day a Sabha is held at groom's place, where the newly wedded couple is given presents and gifts. A list of articles received is made and announced to the Sabha. In the evening a big feast of rice, roasted goat or pig is given to the relatives and villagers.

Bahurat

After a few weeks or so the newly wedded couple is sent for by the bride's parents. They visit the latter along with male and female friends and take rice-beer with them which is distributed among the co-villagers. They stay there for a week and are entertained with mutton and pork. A big feast is held on the eve of their departure. They are given rice-beer on their return journey which is distributed among the co-villagers of the bridegroom. They are also given rice and meat to be taken home. Important friends and villagers are invited for the feast where the rice and meat brought from the bride's house is served. This marks the end of rituals related with marriage.

EXTRA-MARITAL RELATIONS

Cases of marital infidelity whereby either of the spouses have extra-marital sex relations have been reported among the Munda. Cases of adultery are sometimes discovered but the culprits are punished with heavy fines and excommunication, when detected, by the village Panchayat and the Parha. Such relationship involves a married woman and another married or unmarried man. Earlier those indulging in extra-marital sex relations were driven out of the village, but now such punishment is not heard of. Some instances will illustrate the attitude of the Munda regarding such extra-marital relations. A man of Jojohatu admitted having extra-marital relations with Munda girls of his own clan. In Salehatu, the wife of a Munda developed extra-marital relations with a Munda of another village when her own husband was in jail. On his release he divorced her and both of them again married elsewhere. A widow in Salehatu had relations with more than one person and finally she went to live with one of them in an adjacent village. The extra-marital relations of a man in Jojohatu were the source of constant conflict and occasional fights between the husband and the wife.

In Tapkara, the headmaster of a middle school eloped with a girl of a different clan and absented himself from duty for three months. The joint meeting of the school committee and the guardians unanimously demanded his resignation for such an act. In the multicaste village of Tapkara, extra-marital relations between Munda girls and non-Munda men were prevalent and in many cases the matter was brought into the Parha, where the non-Munda man was forced to keep the girl. He was fined and the girl's parents were asked to undergo a purification ceremony to get readmitted to the Munda tribe. In Amlesa some of the married informants admitted having sex relations with married and unmarried girls of their own or other clans and in their own or other villages.

Elsewhere (Sachchidananda, 1966 : 128-132) many specific examples have been cited of adultery brought up before the Parha organisation at different times. In most of the cases the persons involved in such relations admitted their guilt. The cases were brought up to Parha, on many occasions when a girl became pregnant through such a union. In such cases both the parties were fined and they shared the expenditure on feasting the Parha Panchayat. Some examples are given here.

Mangal had sexual relations with his younger brother's widow Karuna. When the latter had been carrying for six months, she was given some abortificient as a result of which she died. The Parha found him doubly guilty for incest and for causing death.

In another case a shopkeeper of Tapkara enticed a Munda girl. One night she was seen coming out of his house. The matter was referred to the Parha. The girl confessed everything. The man too confessed after much argument. The girl could not be readmitted to the community and as the shopkeeper was responsible for her plight, he was to marry and maintain her. He was also fined Rs. 400 which he readily paid. He married the Munda girl.

In another case, Marium's husband went out of the village for a week. Daniel, a neighbour, had an eye on Marium. Marium fell seriously ill and in that condition, he succeeded in gratifying his lust. When Marium gained consciousness, she turned him out. She informed her husband on his return and then the matter was reported to the Parha Panchayat through the Munda of the village. At first Daniel denied the charge. But there was evidence of eye witnesses against him. He was found guilty and fined Rs. 50. He had to offer a feast for the whole community and undergo a purification ceremony. Marium was not fined but she and her husband had to purify themselves, the cost of which was met from the fine paid by Daniel.

Marital maladjustment does not, however, take a serious form in Munda society for the couple have an opportunity of satisfying sexual urges elsewhere. Examples of divorce because of sexual maladjustment are almost non-existent. Though extra-marital relations are not approved by society, serious notice is not taken of them unless they become a matter of common knowledge. Adultery, when discovered and proved, is severely punished. A wife found in adultery may even be killed by her husband.

WIDOWHOOD AND REMARRIAGE (SAGAI)

The widowers among males in the three villages of Salehatu, Gutuhatu and Amlesa were less than 4% while the corresponding figure among females was almost four times higher. In Salehatu about 15% of the women were widows. The survey figures are comparable with the Census figures of 1971 for the Mundas in Bihar. The sex differential in widowhood can be due to sex-differential mortality with higher death rates for males especially at higher ages. Widow remarriage is allowed among the Munda, and the males may be remarrying more frequently than females, thus producing large sex-differential in the rates of widowhood. A widow can remarry only in the *sagai* form in which the detailed ceremonies required for the *arandi* or marriage are not performed. The bridegroom goes with some of his relatives to the bride's house, the party is feasted, and the bride is taken home by the bridegroom. In some localities the bride and the bridegroom just put vermilion marks on each other's forehead and in other areas this ceremony too is dispensed with. In Tamar such marks are put on a Sal-leaf instead of on the forehead. But if the bride is a maiden, she will put such marks on the forehead of the widower bridegroom. In widow remarriage only half of the customary bride-price is paid.

DIVORCE

Divorce is frequent and may be granted at the desire of either partner. The percentage of divorced for both the sexes was almost negligible among the Munda in the three villages. Remarriage is as frequent as divorce.

Divorce may take place due to various reasons such as bad nature and laziness of wife, barrenness, if the wife is declared to be a witch, extra-marital relations of either of the spouses, if the wife is found to be a thief, on learning about some hereditary disease in the spouse or disease caused by a spirit, husband's cruel behaviour etc. The final decision on the divorce is taken by the Panchayat. When the rift between the couple widens and is referred to the Panchayat, members try to reconcile the differences and only when they do not succeed, a divorce is granted.

S.C. Roy (1970 : 260) has described the process of granting divorce by the Panchayat. The President or Head Panch of the Panchayat hands over a sal-leaf to the party who is unwilling to continue the marriage tie, and the latter tears the leaf in two, indicating the dissolution of the marriage. This ceremony is known as the *sakamchari*. In Tamar area, a piece of turmeric (*sasang*) is also similarly broken in two and this ceremony is known as *sasang had*.

A father whose daughter often runs away from her husband's home is fined by the Panchayat. If the husband is at fault, he loses his bride-price. If the wife is the unwilling party, the bride-price has to be returned.

7

MAKING A LIVING

OLDER ANTHROPOLOGISTS were interested in portraying the spectacular and the bizarre aspects of tribal life. They devoted the bulk of their attention to a description of the social structure and religious beliefs and practices of the tribal people. Human activities in the ordinary business of life did not catch their attention. It is natural therefore that in the earlier monographs, there is very little analysis of the tribal economy, particularly, about how people made their living. In his book, Sarat Chandra Roy has a small portion on agriculture detailing soil, crops and some agricultural operations. Mention is made of various agricultural implements, household utensils and furniture; some details of house construction and the pattern of food and drinks.

All communities are faced with the problem of allocating their resources within the limits set by their ecology as transformed by culture, technology and the state of knowledge, their social structure and values. The study of the economically active population is important, as the economic and social well-being of the community is influenced by the number of earners, their attainment and skills, the regularity of their employment and the amount they earn. The questions asked in this context are : What is produced and by whom ? How are the productive groups organised ? What conflicts arise in the process of production and how they are resolved ? What are the relationships between the different partners in the productive process? What are the strains generated by the working of the forces of modernization and how are the social structure and social values changing?

Agriculture being the main economic activity of the Munda,

it is necessary to know about the land, soil, main crops and their sowing and harvesting seasons, yield etc. The study of the land tenure system among them will throw light on the ownership of land, the Bhuinhari and Khutkatti land tenure, land alienation and the present day situation in regard to these. The agricultural operations show how, by whom, and when the various agricultural activities are carried out, and the socio-economic significance thereof. There are other service castes living in a Munda village. It is important to know the type of socio-economic relations that prevail between the Munda and these castes. Munda economy is based on economic cooperation and reciprocity. This necessitated the study of exchange of tools and services among these communities.

Agro-industries have been studied with a view to knowing about the diversification of occupation, various types of industries, production and marketing of the products. A number of large scale and ancillary industries have come up in the Munda area since the sixties. It is important to know to what extent it affected the tribal economy. Employment of Mundas in large scale industries will show how much they participate in this process.

The study of entrepreneurship is a recent development in economic anthropology. The role of enterprises in tribal economy, the ways of decision-making and the part played by the leadership in the organisation of economic activities are examined with reference to the Munda economy.

An attempt is made to study the dynamics of Munda economy so that a composite picture should emerge showing it as a constantly changing phenomenon through the impact of market forces rather than a static one.

ECONOMIC ACTIVITIES

One-third of the total population in all the villages was enumerated as workers. Participation in the work force differs according to age and sex. There is a higher participation rate (50%) for ages 15 years and above than those (6.7%) for ages below 15 years. The proportion of workers among males was higher than that for females.

Inter-village variations were observed in participation rates in the three villages. Highest participation rates for males were observed in Salehatu and for females in Gutuhatu respectively at all ages, below 15 years, and 15 years and above as well.

TABLE 7

Percent distribution of workers in the population by Age and Sex—village-wise

	0–14 years			15 years and above			All ages		
Village	Male	Female	Total	Male	Female	Total	Male	Female	Total
Salehatu	19.4	—	11.3	94.0	5.1	48.7	60.4	3.3	33.4
Gutuhatu	8.3	0.7	4.5	85.2	17.3	51.1	57.6	11.3	34.3
Amlesa	7.7	0.0	3.7	80.0	15.4	50.0	52.4	8.6	31.0
All villages	12.5	0.3	6.7	86.8	13.0	50.0	57.4	8.2	33.3

Agriculture continues to be the most important economic activity of the Munda. While it was so even during the time of S.C. Roy, it is evident that agriculture has not been able to support a large proportion of cultivators throughout the year.

TABLE 7.2

Percent distribution of workers by categories of occupation—village-wise

Village	Cultivation	Agricultural labour	Labour	Industrial labour	Service	Dhanger (Servant)	Petty Business	All workers
Salehatu	75.4	4.7	3.5	—	9.4	7.0	—	100.0
Gutuhatu	68.3	1.3	12.5	1.3	11.6	4.2	0.8	100.0
Amlesa	48.0	5.0	1.0	1.0	27.0	18.0	—	100.0
All villages	66.7	3.1	7.2	0.8	13.9	7.8	0.4	100.0

This is because most of the cultivation is at the subsistence level and the pressure on land has increased due to the growth of population. As a result, a large number of tribals from every village go out as seasonal migrants to nearby towns or to the jute mills in Bengal, the tea gardens in Assam, to work as labourers in the railway and road construction in other areas, as agricultural labourers to Punjab, to the iron or coal mines or for other casual seasonal employment. Generally, they leave by the end of December and return by the end of April to be in time for the *sarhul* festival. There are people who have migrated permanently particularly to the tea gardens in Assam and to the Andaman Islands, but their number is not very large. The savings they make from their income in this way help to pay the land revenue and meet their other requirements for cash such as purchase of clothes etc.

In the above table, the economically active population has been classified according to occupation. The analysis reveals that more than three-fourths of the workers in all the villages are engaged in agriculture, two-thirds of the workers are cultivators and more than 10% of the workers are agricultural labourers, seasonal or on a yearly basis. Agriculture is a family occupation where the women and the children of the house assist the menfolk in various agricultural operations. In Salehatu 80% of the working population were cultivators, while in Amlesa about half of the working population was engaged in cultivation.

The next important occupation among the Munda is service. A little less than 15% of workers are engaged in jobs such as police, forest department, army, government office, teaching, missionary work, and jobs in other government, semi-government or voluntary agencies. The proportion of those in service for males was eight times that for females. Lack of education and attachment to the hearth kept the village women from joining service away from home. In Amlesa more than one-fourth of the workers were engaged in service occupation of one type or the other.

About 8% of the workers, predominantly males, in all the villages, with half of them alone in Amlesa, were working as *dhangar* or fulltime agricultural labourers recruited on an annual basis. Those Munda families who have more land than they can cultivate keep *dhangars* all the year round. The *dhangar* is engaged in the month of *Magh* (January). He is paid annually at the harvest either in cash or in kind and is housed and fed by his employer. From the day he is engaged, he becomes a member of the employer's household and participates in all the activities of the family. There is no difference in status between the employer and his *dhangar* and the latter can even marry his employer's daughter or sister if their clans are different.

Since the early seventies, among the Munda of Khunti area

there has been a seasonal migration to Punjab where they work as agricultural labourers in the fields of rich farmers. They are recruited and transported by middlemen styled as *Sardars* who receive commission both from the Munda labourers and their employers. The agricultural labourer from Chotanagpur is a cheaper substitute to his counterpart in Punjab. He is paid Rs. 60 per month along with meals, clothing and accommodation. He has to serve his master for a period of six months which is the period of contract.

The percentage of workers engaged as labourers was only 7%. Most of them were from Gutuhatu. These labourers worked in building and road construction in local and other areas, at the dam site on Karo river, in the Andaman Islands, in the jute mills of Bengal and tea gardens in Assam.

Three Mundas of Gutuhatu and one from Amlesa worked as industrial labourers in coal and iron mines.

The Christian Mundas in Gutuhatu were petty cloth merchants. They sold cloth, readymade garments and clothes tailored by themselves. Tailoring was a secondary occupation with them in all the three villages. Sukhram Munda, a graduate teacher at Maranghada augmented his family income by making dresses at Maranghada. The other secondary occupations among the Mundas are basketry, carpentry, rearing and collection of lac, running a grocery or tea stall, preparation and sale of *arkhi*, the indigenous Mahua drink, selling firewood and grass at the weekly market, carrying loads from one market to another, selling vegetables grown in the kitchen garden, lac rearing, and keeping bee boxes for honey and wax.

Hunting is no more an occupation for the Munda, because there has been large scale cutting down of the forest. Hunting has been reduced to a ceremonial. It is not clear from the work of S.C. Roy as to how important hunting was in his time and what proportion of the food resources of the Munda was contributed by the game killed during hunts. From the elaborate account of hunting rituals given in Roy's book on the Munda, it may be considered that hunting, even though subsidiary to agriculture in his time, augmented the food resources to a considerable extent. There are details about the season of hunting, the worship preceding hunting, the organisation of a hunt, the election of the hunt-leader and lastly the distribution of the game killed during the hunt. These days since the importance of hunting has been reduced, most of the rites are not observed. There is only one important hunt among the Munda e.g. one which takes place in spring and is known as *Phagu Shikar*. In the Christian Munda villages of Gutuhatu and Koenara and in Hinduised Munda village of Amlesa people do not go out for a hunt or fishing even ceremonially, while in Salehatu, Jojohatu and other traditional Munda villages such ceremonial hunt is still found.

Women's hunt or *jani shikar* has been reported from Koenara and Jojohatu and Salehatu villages. In Jojohatu the women's hunt took place some years back. It is held once every twelve years. It is actually more a mode of recreation than anything else. Women dressed in masculine dress with bows and arrows and axes etc., take part in this hunt. They leave the village in a group in search of game and go to another village and take whatever they find. Fowl, goats, sheep and pigs are their favourite catch. People of other villages generally do not mind this expedition. When the party enters the village it is received by women who wash their feet. The wife of the Parha Raja functions as the leader of the hunt in that locality. The women of the second village then repeat the performance in a third village and thus the mock-hunt proceeds in relay till many villages have participated and the village from which the hunt started is reached. The gifts collected during this hunt are considered to be the property of the women. The women's hunt is a contrast to men's hunt in that the former engage in mock-hunt of domestic animals.

Fishing is also practised by the Munda especially for consumption and also for sale. Various types of fishing implements have been devised to catch fish from ponds, tanks and small streams. They sell the catch in the local markets. In villages of Jojohatu and Amlesa, Mundas have shown keen interest in fishery by rearing fish in their ponds with good variety of fish fries obtained from the Block Development Office.

The Munda country used to be covered by forests. Their forefathers made clearances in the thick forests of Chotanagpur and established villages and reclaimed lands for cultivation. Their gods reside on the hills and in the forests. They depend upon the forests for their fuel, timber for house building and for grazing ground for their cattle. They gather forest produce like *kendu* leaves for *biri* manufacture, honey, lac, Mahua flowers, *karanj* etc. and sell them in the market. They get their medicinal herbs from the forest. They hunt small game animals and go to the forest on ceremonial communal hunts. Indiscriminate destruction of forests in the absence of a firm forest policy has had an adverse effect on the Mundas and other tribals living around and in the forests.

In an earlier chapter it has been observed that there was a decline in the working population among the Munda in Bihar State during the 1960's, the rate of decline was higher for females as compared to males. Similarly, the workers in rural areas decreased more rapidly than their counterparts in urban areas. Again, on the one hand, the economy based on household farming, livestock, fisheries and forestry etc., mining and quarrying, household industry and other services shows a decline; on the other hand, the economy based on agriculture with the assistance of hired labour on a large scale, non-household industry and ancillary occupations has gained strength. The decline of workers in other services seems to indicate the decline of feudal relations, requiring the employment of a large number of menials and other village servants in rural society. This trend in the Munda economy during the last decade is similar to the general trend in the economy of Chotanagpur during the same decade.

It will be worthwhile to analyse the non-working population which is two-thirds of the Munda population. More than half of the non-workers are below 15 years of age, of which about one-fourth are students, one-third are children below 5 years of age. The rest of them are not exactly non-working but do petty jobs like grazing the cattle, the girls helping in household and the boys helping in agricultural work.

As regards the sex differentials among the non-workers, seven out of every ten were females of which 60% were above 15 years of age and were engaged in household work.

One-fifth of the total non-working population was students. Among the students 64% were below 15 years of age. Seven out of every ten students were males and three were females.

The process of transformation of the Mundari agrarian system was faster during the British period. They took the Maharaja of Chotanagpur to be the absolute owner of the land.

The external instruments for the breakdown of the agrarian system consisted of the Raja and his relatives, the jagirdars, zamindars, the British administrators and the local petty officials. The internal factors comprised the reversed roles of the Pahan and the Munda, the latter assuming a new authority, the break up of tribal organisation, and a general impairing of its racial character (Singh, K.S., 1966 : 1).

To the twin challenges of agrarian breakdown and culture change, the Munda responded through a series of uprisings from 1789 to 1831-32 and through the agrarian revivalistic movement of the Sardars during the later half of the nineteenth century.

The plains of Panchparganas, because of their geographic position and the influx of the peasant population into it from the east and the south were the first to witness the disintegration of the Mundari Khutkatti system. Today, in Panchparganas, only a few broken Khutkatti tenures exist. The Kol insurrection of 1831-32 was the result of their discontentment with the alien landlords who left no opportunity to usurp their land. This was followed by suitable measures to facilitate the administration of the territory. However, the crux of the agrarian problems, i.e., security of tenure for the Munda was not touched and the process of breakdown of the agrarian order continued apace.

The forty years of Sardar agitation or *muluki larai* from the late 1850's onwards, which constituted the background of Birsa's movement, was aimed at expelling alien Zamindars. They attacked forced labour and praedial conditions. The widespread disturbances during 1858-59 in the Bhuinhari area of Sonepur, Lodhma, Belkadi, Basia, Doisa and Khukhar forced the government to define and determine the Bhuinhari tenures: Lal Lok Nath Sah was deputed for the job and he completed his enquiries (before his death) in 429 villages during the two years from August, 1860 to August, 1862. However, this did not satisfy the Munda. During 1862-88 there were occasional clashes between Zamindars and their raiyats. With a view to an authoritative settlement of the title to Bhuinhari lands, the Chotanagpur Tenancy Act of 1869 was passed. It provided for the restoration of Bhuinhari lands to the raiyats who were dispossessed of them during twenty years preceding the Act on the strength of the evidence collected during the

Bhuinhari survey operations. The operations lasted from 1869 to 1880 and 2482 villages were registered in 35 Parganas of the Chotanagpur estate. Bhuinhari Settlement marked the end of disputes centering round Bhuinhari and *majhihas* tenures of lands, but its overall result fell short of the expectations of the Sardars, who would be satisfied with nothing short of a restoration of all the lands of which they or their ancestors had ever held possession. Moreover, the Act came too late and the operation was not extended to other tenures such as *rajhas*, *khutkatti* and *korkar*, which were the new sources of agrarian troubles between Zamindars eager to convert them into their personal cultivable possession and the resisting raiyat. This dispute between the Munda and their landlords continued and now and again, assumed a serious aspect. Although at this period, several special Acts relating to Chotanagpur were passed, none of them solved the real problem of the people. The Sardar agitation later on merged with the Birsa movement in the year 1895 and continued up to 1901. The Birsa movement was a resistance and a religious movement at the same time and it was centred around those Munda areas, such as Khunti, Tamar, Bundu and Sonahatu police stations, which were not covered during the earlier Bhuinhari settlement in 1869.

An immediate consequence of the Birsa Revolt was that the government became aware of the urgency of preparing a record of rights for the lands of the discontented Mundas and hence, survey and settlement were conducted during 1902—1910. As a result the Chotanagpur Tenancy Act of 1908 was passed which recognised the special privileges of the Mundari Khutkattidars aiming at the removal, as far as possible, of the causes fostering the agitation which had for a long time been disturbing them.

MUNDARI KHUTKATTI TENANCY

The terms Mundari Khutkattidar and Mundari Khutkattidari tenancy were defined in the C.N.T. Act of 1908 by which the claims of the Munda tribe to the real ownership of the country of Chotanagpur were for the first time legally recognised by the British Government. Mundari Khutkattidar may be defined as a "Munda who has acquired a right to hold jungle land for the purpose of bringing suitable portions thereof, under cultivations by himself or by male members of his family and includes the (i) heirs in the male line of any such Munda when they are in possession of any such land, and (ii) as regards any portions of such land which have remained continuously in the possession of any such Munda and his descendants in the male line".

Thus Mundari Khutkatti Tenancy means the interest of a Mundari Khutkattidar. Hoffmann wrote that Mundari Khutkatti tenancy is neither a tenure nor an under tenure nor is it a holding. This tenancy is not a tenure because this is perpetual. As the above two conditions are fulfilled a Munda will remain a Khutkattidar. It is also not under tenure because Khutkattidars are never under any landlord and in the sense of above definition it is also not a "holding".

It is a tenancy of whole brotherhood. Under the purview of the Chotanagpur Landlord and Tenant Procedure Act, 1913, "the Mundari Khutkattidars are not raiyats. Raiyat means primarily a person who has acquired a right to hold land for the purpose of cultivating it by himself or by members of his family, or by hired servants or with the aid of his partners and includes also the successors in interest of persons, who have acquired such a right, but does not include a Mundari Khutkattidar".

The benefits of the C.N.T. Act of 1908 were not limited to the official recognition of the ancient rights of the Munda; its scope was extended beyond this. It admits that all the land within the boundaries of the village is the common property of the village family because all the members of the village family are direct descendants of the original founder of the village. However, every single member of the village community keeps complete personal proprietary right over the land, he has inherited from his own father.

Khutkatti land is heritable and subject to the payment of a permanently fixed quit rent to the superior landlord through the Munda and the Manki. The Munda, the Pahan and the Manki do not have any superior proprietary right over land. The rent or Chanda of old Mundari Khutkatti tenancies can never be increased. From this it appears that no Registry Office has the power of registering transfer deeds of Khutkattidari lands to an alien except on explicit sanction of the Deputy

Commissioner (under section 49 of C.N.T Act) for public purposes and for reasonable and sufficient purpose. This Act also empowers the Deputy Commissioner to eject forcibly any alien who may have acquired lands in a Khutkatti village. The Act explicitly declares—"No transfer in contravention of sub-section (i) shall be registered or shall be recognised as valid by court, whether in exercise of civil, criminal or revenue jurisdiction" under Art. 46(3) of C.N.T. Act.

S.C. Roy (1946 : 156-180) in "Theory of Rent among the Mundas of Chotanagpur" has clearly shown that the rent payable by Munda tenants in Chotanagpur stands on a different footing and belongs to a different category altogether from the rent payable by a Bengal or Bihar raiyat or by Sadan raiyat in Chotanagpur. The Bengal theory of rent as a certain customary proportion of net produce of a holding cannot be applied to the case of tribal raiyats in Chotanagpur and that, what is called rent in the case of the holdings of tribal tenants, originated in a contribution in the nature of tribute or aid paid by their ancestors to the ancestors of the present Maharaja of Chotanagpur as their leader in war and peace. These rents were originally fixed without any reference to the yield of the holdings and at no time period of their history represented a certain proportion of the produce, or its money value and that consequently neither any permanent rise in the prices of staple food crops nor any other ground will be available to the landlord to enhance the rate of rent. This rent stands as a class apart from other types of rent and may be termed tribute rent. In order to determine the liability or non-liability to enhancement of existing rents, the origin and history of Munda tenancies and the agrarian history of Munda tenancies and the agrarian history of Chotanagpur have been dealt with by S.C. Roy.

The history of rent in every village is a history of struggle between landlord and the tenant. The landlords are mostly middlemen introduced between the Zamindars and the raiyats, who proceeded to exploit the villages and their tenantry. The great differences between the incidence of rent from village to village are principally due to the good or ill success of the exploitation—low rent of a village generally indicates that it is an old Bhuinhari village and that the old raiyats have maintained something of their Khutkatti rights and successfully resisted the landlord's encroachment. By passing the C.N.T. Act of 1908 a definite and reasonable usage of rent payment by the Munda tenants have been proved. The ancient custom of non-enhancibility has been established by the evidence of reliable witnesses, reliable public documents like village notes and the authoritative decision of courts. Section 76 of the C.N.T. Act will be a bar to any enhancement of the rate of rents of these defendants. This usage or custom was recorded at the Survey and Settlement of 1903 in the village notes of almost all the villages of the Pargana Sonepur. Thus the existing rates of rent are the outcome of a necessary compromise in the past, the result not of express contract but of necessary usage ripening into an inviolable custom.

Intact Mundari Khutkatti

During the first survey and settlement operations in Chotanagpur it was found that only 156 villages in the Ranchi district had successfully withstood the aggressions of Jagirdars and Thickadars and retained their Khutkatti character intact to that day. The village community was theoretically the joint owner of all the village lands and actually joint owner of all unoccupied and waste lands and of all rights to these villages. Of these intact villages, 87 were within the Khunti thana, 58 in Tamar thana, 9 in Bundu thana and one in thana Rahe. The total area of these villages was 153.7 sq. miles. The greater portion of intact Khutkatti area was held under the jagirdars or tenure-holders (S.C. Roy 1970 : 356-57). In the first settlement by Reid, 144 sq. miles area, of which 69 sq. miles were cultivated and 75 sq. miles were uncultivated, was recorded as intact Mundari Khutkatti. It was situated in the eastern part of Khunti police station.

Individual Khutkattidars held specific portions of cultivable village lands as their personal possessions and left them on their death to their own heirs. They paid small and permanently fixed quit rent to the superior landlord. This quit-rent was paid to the Munda by each Khutkattidar, . the former in turn paid in a Manki Patti to the *Manki* and outside the Manki Patti to the superior landlord himself or his agent. Neither the *Manki* nor the Munda, nor the *Pahan* had any superior right of property. The *Manki* got a small remuneration for collecting the contribution (*Chanda* or rent) from different villages of the Patti. Since 1950 with the abolition of the Zamindari system in Bihar, the State Government has started collecting the rent through the *karamchari* from the hands of Munda as in the Khutkatti area or directly from the Bhuinhars as in the Bhuinhari area. In the former case the receipt for the revenue is given in the name of the Munda, while in the latter case separate revenue receipts are given to each Bhuinhar.

Every Khutkattidar of an intact Khutkatti village has the right to reclaim any waste land within the village limits or take any jungle produce or timber he requires from the village jungles. Under-ground rights belong to the Khutkatti community as a whole. Khutkatti tenancies are inalienable except for certain purposes and under certain conditions and restrictions laid down by law. These tenancies are heritable and the rent or *chanda* of old Mundari Khutkatti tenancies can never be increased.

Broken Mundari Khutkatti Villages

According to first survey and settlement operations by Reid only 130 sq. miles of area, of which 119 sq. miles was cultivated and 11 sq. miles was uncultivated, was covered as broken Mundari Khutkatti in the Manki Patti situated in the east of Khunti Thana. As stated earlier the various factors in the break-down of the Khutkatti system were the role of Raja of Chotanagpur and his jagirdars, thickadars, the ignorance of British officials, the money-lenders and the internal weaknesses of the Munda system.

The first stage in the break-down of the intact Khutkatti system is visible in some villages of Tamar Thana, where although the Raja or superior landlord received at the hands of the village Munda the quit-rent payable by the Khutkattidars, the Raja succeeded in getting hold of a few acres of land as his own share and named such land as the Rajhas. He has since either been in cultivating possession of the land or settled his own tenants on such land who began to pay him rent direct.

The next stage in the disintegration of the Khutkatti system may be seen in those broken Khutkatti villages where either an alien landlord or the Munda himself, has gradually claimed to himself the proprietary rights in the village and thereby broken its communal nature. Either the superior landlord himself, or the Munda or a Zarpeshgidar (mortgagee) or a Nilamdar (auction purchaser) from him, began first by himself collecting the *chanda* from the Parja, proceeded next to enhance the *chanda* payable by the Khutkattidars, and lastly reduced most of them to the position of ordinary tenants. Finally, the Munda assumed the control of the village jungles and waste lands. The Khutkatti brotherhood has lost its joint ownership of the entire village area, but each Khutkattidar only retains his proprietary rights over the old lands he cultivates. These lands form his individual "Mundari Khutkatti" tenancy, for which he must pay his fixed *chanda* directly to his new landlord. In Tamar Thana there exists a third category of "broken Khutkatti villages" where the Raja or superior landlord, has introduced an intermediate landlord, probably originally called Manjhi who started collecting *chanda* directly from the khutkattidars. This intermediate landlord acquired the land originally held by the *parjas* under the khutkattidars. Such land came to be called the *Majihas* and became the privileged land of the lessee of the village.

BHUINHARI TENURES

In the villages now known as the Bhuinhari villages, the Khutkatti system or even the very name of *Khutkattidar* have been lost. Only a few portions of their ancestral lands were left in the possession of the members of the original village community as their privileged tenures and these are called their *Bhuinhari* lands. The rest of the village land have been absorbed mostly within the Rajhas and partly within the Majihas. The names Rajhas and Majihas, no longer have the same meaning as used in the "broken Khutkatti" villages in Tamar. The term Rajhas in the Bhuinhari and Zamindari villages are known as Prajali lands in Tamar. The Rajhas lands in the Bhuinhari area have no longer, as in Tamar, any concern with the Raja or superior landlord, where there is an intermediate landlord over the village. But the rents collected from Rajhas lands in these villages are supposed to make up the superior landlord's dues which, however, are generally satisfied with a fraction only of the profits derived by the intermediate landlord from these

Rajhas lands. Majihas lands, though originally created only in villages in which the superior landlord introduced a lessee under him, have since arisen even in villages in the direct possession of the superior landlord. Majihas lands in such villages have been created by the latter for his benefit partly out of the Rajhas and partly out of old Khutkatti or Bhuinhari lands of the descendants of the original settlers. Rajhas lands, in most Bhuinhari villages now cover the largest area of cultivable lands and are generally cultivated both by holders of Bhuinhari lands and by other cultivators as ordinary raiyats on cash rent or produce rent or both. The Rajhas land has been further subdivided into various categories such as Chhatisa, Korkar, Murli Chhatisa, Uttakar or Balkatand, Maswan Danr lands etc.

Originally there were two *khuts*, Pahan Khut and Munda Khut in a tribal village. An addition to the number of *khuts* in the Bhuinhari area was, in course of time, made by the landlords themselves to safeguard their interests in the villages. Thus, the Mahto Khut was created in most of the villages probably out of the Munda Khut.

In a Bhuinhari village, these village officials have each been allotted specific lands for his services. But it is the Mahtoi land alone which is, properly speaking, a service land. The Munda and Pahanai lands are generally practically hereditary. It is only in a few Munda villages near the Oraon area that the Pahan's office is not hereditary. In such villages the Pahan and his assistants are elected every three years from amongst the members of the Pahan Khut and in some villages even from amongst the Bhuinhars in general by certain well recognised supernatural processes.

LAND SYSTEM IN THREE MUNDA VILLAGES

Salehatu in Murhu Block is a Mundari Khutkatti village. The Mundas belong to the Hassa clan. The total land in the village is 616.21 acres out of which 488.44 acres are cultivable while the rest is not. There are three *khebatdars*, viz., Bara Sunder Munda, Chara Munda and Sudan Munda who collect rent from Khutkattidars and their tenants belonging to respective khebats. They pay Rs. 55 as rent and about Rs. 26 as cess to the Karamchari of Gutuhatu Panchayat. In addition to individual lands held by each Khutkattidar, they have settled tenants, Munda or non-Munda on their respective lands. The village community as a whole hold proprietary rights over common village land such as *sarna, akhra, sasan,* etc. The Munda and the Pahan have been given some land for the service they perform. This land grant is heritable because of the heritable status of the two offices. In the village there are some families of service castes like Ghasi, Swansi and Lohra who do not own land.

Gutuhatu, a Bhuinhari village in Torpa Block, is a Munda village with Rautia, Kumhar, Chick Baraik, Lohra, Hajam etc. Three categories of land, e.g., Bhuinhari, Rajhas and Korkar are found in the village. There are three khuts that is Munda Khut, Pahan Khut and Mahto Khut in the village. The Munda own individual Bhuinhari land for which they pay a fixed *chanda* or rent. Bhuinhari land is inalienable and the rent cannot be enhanced. Rajhas land held by them is liable for rent which may be enhanced. This type of land can be sold with the permission of the Deputy Commissioner. Korkar land is held on a low fixed rent which cannot be increased. Rautias hold Rajhas land. Chick Baraiks and Mundas of other than Guria kili (the dominant clan of the village) hold tenancy land under the Bhuinhars and give rent to their respective Bhuinhar who along with their own share directly give it to the Karamchari of the Tapkara Panchayat. There is common ownership of *sarna, sasan, akhra* and *path.* The Pahan, the Munda and the Mahto are given service lands. Only *chanda* is given for these lands. The Mahtoi and Mundai lands are heritable, while Pahanai lands are transferable with the change of office every three years, the new Pahan being selected from within the Pahan Khut. The potter (Kumhar) also holds service land. The right to the village burial ground is held by the Bhuinhars of the three *khuts.* The Munda tenants in Gutuhatu do not have right to the Bhuinhari land and the village *sasan.*

Before 1950, the three heads of the Munda, Pahan and Mahto Khuts used to collect the rent from all the Bhuinhars and once in a year at the Dasehra festival the rent in the form of cash and kind and a goat were given to the superior landlord, the Jaria Thakur. Gutuhatu, Kamra, Tali and Koenara of Guria Parha were considered as Pujar villages which contributed towards the Dasehra celebration. Now after the vesting of Zamindari, the rent goes directly from each Bhuinhar through Karamchari to the State Government. The government compensates the Jaria Thakur for the loss of the contribution by the Pujar villages for the celebration of Dasehra. These villages are still illuminated by the Thakur at Dasehra.

In Amlesa, Mundas belong to more than one clan, viz., Kamal, Sandil, Kachchap, Nag, etc. The dominant clan is Kamal and the Munda and Pahan belong to this clan. The other communities living in the village are Puran Manjhi, Brahmin, Barber, Swansi, Machchua etc. The types of land found in the village are Khutkatti, share cropper tenants land such as *Pahnai*, *Brahmanai*, *Hajamati* (to the barber) and *Panbharwa* lands, *Roka-Mal* as reward to the social workers like village doctor etc. The Khutkattidars collect rent from their tenants and pay the amount to the Munda, who in turn gives it to the Karamchari of Amlesa Panchayat. The total amount payable by the Munda to the Government is Rs. 280.

The *sarna*, *sasan*, Mahadev Mandir, the *path* etc. are jointly held by the village community. Earlier under the tenancy settlement the tenant was settled by giving a gift or by payment of actual land price to the landlord. The tenant pays rent to his landlord yearly. In case a tenant of a Khutkattidar wishes to return the land to his Khutkattidar he is allowed to do it privately or through court expressing his inability to keep it. In such a case he writes a document and the land is valued at the present level of land price. The Khutkattidar may again settle a new tenant or may keep it for self-cultivation. For instance, Anand Singh Munda, a tenant of Ghisu Singh Munda, gave up 0.45 acre of tenancy land in 1975 to reduce his burden of rent. The widow of Madho Singh Munda did the same in respect to 0.35 acre *bari* land for Rs. 220 in 1975. If a tenant dies without any direct heir or agnates, the land automatically reverts to the original Khutkattidar. Land was given to the ancestor of Duga Puran for his services as a doctor for animals. He was given the right of cultivation for Rs. 125 as annual *malguzari*, but no receipt was given for this. Service lands are given to the Pahan, and Brahmin (religious priest), Hajam, Ghasi, and Panbhara. No rent, except some form of cess, is given to the landlord (the Munda under Hindu influence is also referred to as such). At the time of the last survey these lands were recorded in the names of old functionaries. Now their descendants are cultivating these lands in Amlesa. The Khutkattidars have also given the land as Thicka-Sanjha through contract and the rent (generally about one-fourth of the produce) is fixed in the beginning. This is paid in kind annually to the landlord. A receipt is given for this. The rent is paid for a particular crop season only.

In Amlesa and Salehatu the Karamchari gives single receipt for rent in the name of the Munda who in turn gives receipts to different Khutkattidars. In Bhuinhari village of Gutuhatu all the Bhuinhars obtain separate receipts from the Karamchari for the rent paid by each of them individually to him and not through the Munda as in Salehatu and Amlesa. In all the three Munda villages many of them have mortgaged some portions of their lands to other Mundas, non-Munda tribals and non-tribals. Though the sale of tribal land to non-tribals has been restricted by the C.N.T. Act, many cases of the sale of tribal land were met in Tamar area. It was known that some of the Puran Manjhis of Amlesa have purchased land from various Munda families of the village.

MUNDARI KHUTKATTI TODAY

There are two views on whether Mundari Khutkatti system should be abolished. Those who are for abolition of this system envisage that there should be uniformity in land revenue administration everywhere and all the tenants should be brought at par with other parts of the State. Even the Bihar Law Commission is of the view that there should be uniform system to deal with the tenants. Some of the revenue officials posted in the Mundari area also have the feeling that if the Khutkattidars are not brought under them they will lose prestige in their area. The other view which is held by the Munda is that the system of Mundari Khutkatti which their ancestors had enjoyed and they are enjoying, is the product of historical evolution and particularly suited to their special conditions.

The first survey and settlement report by J. Reid during 1902—1920, and that of Taylor during 1927—35 for the district of Ranchi put the figures of intact and broken Mundari

Khutkatti villages as 156 and 449 respectively. As mentioned earlier, at present intact Mundari Khutkatti villages are found only in Erki Block of Ranchi. Out of 128 villages in Erki Block 100 villages are intact Mundari Khutkatti villages and rest are either mixed or fully vested in the State. According to S.P. Sinha (1965 : 44) this difference between the former and the current number of intact Mundari Khutkatti villages might have resulted from the interplay of various factors. One of the reasons may be that 'New Khata' has been opened and different *Bujharat* were carried on in the area which might have done the trick.

LAND ALIENATION

Land Alienation and other Problems of Mundari Khutkatti system

Earlier the process of land alienation and the laws enacted to check such alienation have been dealt in detail. The C.N.T. Act of 1908 was a major step to restrict the transfer of land to the non-tribals. However, this Act did not check the process of land-alienation completely. The various factors leading to alienation of land are industrialisation, urbanisation,mortgage etc.

The C.N.T. Act prohibited all alienation of land by gift or any other contract or agreement in respect of raiyat except (a) mortgage and lease for any period of less than five years; (b) *bhugut bandha* mortgage for any period of less than seven years; (c) mortgage to registered cooperative societies for 15 years; and (d) transfers permitted by rules subject to official sanction, the condition being that such transfer should not be from tribal to non-tribal. The Deputy Commissioner was authorised to restore within three years the possession of the land through summary procedure.

The C.N.T. Act was amended four times in 1938, 1947, 1955 and 1969. Despite the amendments brought to plug the loopholes, the exploiters have managed to find yet other means, legal or illegal, to deprive the tribesmen of their land. The implications of land alienation on the tribal life are indebtedness, displacement and unemployment of tribals, migration and feeling of insecurity. The measures to be taken to restrict any more alienation of tribal land are radical changes in the government's policy and administration, by general remedial measures such as an alternative source of credit, increase in production, altering man-land ratio etc.

The first and the foremost question is whether or not the Khutkatti system should be allowed to continue. The Munda are very proud of their tradition. In May, 1965, two subsequent meetings of Khutkattidars were held respectively at Ulihatu and at Birbanki in the heart of Munda country to discuss the future of the Khutkatti system in the light of the fear created by loose statements by administrators and leaders in the press, expressing doubts about the continuation of the Mundari Khutkatti system. They exhorted their brethren to prepare to defend it.

Though the small rent or the *chanda* paid by the Khutkattidar is fixed by law, the cess on education, health and roads has increased with time. During 1970 the road cess was 20% of the rent and the education and health cess were 40% of the rent payable by the Khutkattidars. This has caused great distress to the poor Mundas living at subsistence level. Any enhancement of rent will bring hardship and cause resentment.

The forest department controls forests in Khutkatti villages and the villagers are put to all sorts of harassment for cutting trees. The forest policy has made the government unpopular in Chotanagpur and more so in Khutkatti area. In the intact Khutkatti villages, the whole body of the cultivators are the proprietors of jungles included within the periphery of their villages. With the reservation of the forest by the Forest Department now a Forest Guard is posted in Khutkatti village, if it has a reserve forest and on the slightest pretext he makes the life of the tribals troublesome.

The land in the Khutkatti area is not transferable and under Art. 240 of C.N.T. Act 1908 the alienation of land is prohibited, but the Khutkattidars too have requirements and pressing needs which force them to go to the money-lenders. Once they go to him they always remain in his clutches. In one case cited by S.P. Sinha before 1950 there had been some auction purchase of Khutkatti land in Tamar by some non-tribals and they are still realising the rent from the Khutkatti village. Cases of illegal sale-deeds of tribal land to other tribals and non-tribals were reported from Erki Block. In these cases special permission of the Deputy Commissioner of Ranchi district was not taken at all.

It was observed in all the three villages, viz., Salehatu, Gutuhatu and Amlesa that most of the Munda families have given their ancestral land as usufructuary mortgage (*zarpeshgi* and *bhugut-bandha*) to their fellow tribals or non-tribals in and around their villages. Until and unless measures are taken to improve their socio-economic conditions, the mere enactment of tenancy laws without proper and efficient implementation, the problems associated with the land tenure system of the Munda are hard to solve.

To do away with money-lenders, a good system of credit has to be created among them by the State agencies. Mundari Khutkatti lands which have been purchased by the money-lenders, should be given back to the original Mundari Khutkat-tidars and the money-lenders be compensated for that, thus freeing the debtors from their bondage.

By taking proper and timely measures we shall save a good system which Hoffmann characterizes as one of the "wisest creations". This is tenancy of a whole brotherhood and it should be spared and protected.

AGRICULTURE

The classification of village land into different kinds of *don* and *tanr* still remains. Low lying areas are known as *don* and high lands are known as *tanr*. The former are suitable for wet cultivation and the latter for dry cultivation. A first class *don* which forms the bed of some stream, receives moisture throughout the year. It is on such *don*, that besides the usual winter rice-crop, a summer crop called *tewa* rice is grown. The importance of *tanr* is discounted as it grows only coarser varieties of rice as well as some pulses, millets, oilseeds and other products of minor values. It is very difficult to irrigate them. Though efforts have been made by the Government to increase irrigational facilities by building bunds, tanks and digging wells, the farmers are still dependent on rains for their crops. As compared to Hasda area, the Bhuinhari area and the Tamar area are more fertile.

The principal varieties of soil in the Munda country are:

(1) the *pankur*, found mostly in the Panch Parganas and best suited for rice, (2) the *nagra*, (3) the *khirsi*, (4) the *ruguri loyong*, (5) the *bala* and *lal matia* found only in *tanr* lands.

In Salehatu, Gutuhatu and Amlesa the technique of agriculture is almost unchanged. By and large, the same tools are being used as in days of S.C. Roy. Cultivation is done with the old plough driven by bullocks or buffaloes. Due to the impact of the Community Development Programme some tribals have started using a few modern implements such as paddy thresher and straw-cutter. Villagers now do not like to make their own wooden implements as they did in the past. They now purchase things at the weekly market.

In almost all the fields only one crop is grown and land is kept fallow for the year. Most of the people are subsistence cultivators and they grow food crops which they consume themselves. Among food crops, the staple is rice, which is grown both on *don* and *tanr* lands. The upland crops are generally sown by rotation. These include *gora* rice, *gondli*, *kurthi*. A recent addition in the crops is wheat and maize. Wheat is grown in small plots where irrigation is possible.

The main agricultural operations as regards the low-land rice crop and sowing, transplanting, weeding, watching, harvesting and threshing and storing of grains. S.C. Roy has described the various operations in detail. As agriculture is a cooperative activity, in all the operations the co-operation of family members and the kindness of the village brotherhood are essential. Hired labour is also engaged on payment in cash or kind. As in S.C. Roy's time, the Munda celebrate certain festivals associated with different agricultural operations. *Mage* festival is celebrated in January when the old Dhangars are relieved of their job and new ones are appointed or the terms and conditions for the old one are renewed. *Hon-ba* is celebrated in April-May, a day before sowing the paddy. In June, just before the transplantation, the *Batauli* or *Kedleta* festival is celebrated in each village. *Kolom Singh Bonga* or *Khalihan Puja* is observed in the month of November after the rope paddy has been harvested. No villager will thresh his paddy before this festival is celebrated at the Pahan's *khalihan* or threshing floor. *Jom-Nawa* is observed by the Munda in general before eating the new rice in the month of September or later.

Tribal agriculture is based on co-operation. This is evident at the time of transplanting paddy and on other occasions. Exchange of labour, tools and equipments are rendered on reciprocal basis and cash is not paid.

A person who does not have plough cattle of his own makes an arrangement with a neighbour by which, in return for these he works on the latter's field for half a day on all days that he takes the cattle on loan. By another arrangement, he may enter into service of a person who has plough cattle. He does not get any wages but works on his own and his master's land with the latter's equipment. Alternatively such a man enters into a partnership with another person having all equipment on crop-sharing basis. Some families get tools, equipment and other services from their relatives staying in other villages during the agricultural seasons.

Ploughing is taboo for women among the Munda, Oraon and Kharia, while watching of crops is done by men of the family among these tribes; transplantation and weeding is done by women of the entire village jointly in different fields by turn. While working they sing in a chorus which breaks the monotony and brings joy.

Those who render help during the various agricultural operations are given one meal for their work. In village Gutuhatu it was observed that during sowing of paddy the villagers provided help to each other for ploughing the paddy fields in turn. For instance, on a particular day Kalyan Guria prepared his field for transplantation of paddy seedlings with the assistance of eleven Mundas with plough and cattle of Lathura Toli. After ploughing they all gathered in Kalyan's house. They were entertained with rice-beer and fixed *gangai*. Afterwards they were given rice. Next day about 35-40 women did the transplantation in his fields. After work they were entertained with rice-beer and *gangai*. The hired women were given wages in kind such as 4 seers and one handful of paddy per woman for a day's work. Kalyan's wife was seen giving away *Gora dhan* to a woman and her young daughter for their work in transplantation.

During harvesting of paddy in the months of November and December in village Amlesa, the wage labourers were paid Rs. 2.50 for males and Rs. 2.00 for females for carrying bundles of paddy from fields to the threshing ground. In other cases some stalks of paddy were left unreaped in some of the fields to be collected by the labourer as wages for transporting the paddy of these specific fields. In this case the money value of the paddy obtained in wages was almost double the wages in cash.

At other times, individual labourers are employed in different families as *dhangar* who work all the year round. They are paid annually in cash or kind and housed and fed by their employers.

The wages for agricultural labourers as decided by the Gutuhatu village Panchayat in *Fagun* (during 1975) were as follows : For transplanting and weeding Rs. 1.50 per day or two seers and one handful paddy for a half day and three seers plus one handful paddy for a whole day's work. For any type of agricultural labour men were paid 3 seers and one handful for a half day and 3 seers and 4 handful for a whole day. For ploughing with bullocks Rs 3.00 and with buffaloes Rs. 4.00 per day. For helping in agricultural operations, one meal with *hanria* is given to all.

JAJMANI SYSTEM

In most of the Indian villages inhabited by a large number of castes, the *jajmani* system determines the functional relationship between them. Under this system each caste group within a village is expected to give certain standardized services to the families of other castes. Each man works for services to the families of other castes. A particular family or group of families served by an individual is known as his *jajman*, while the man who performs service is known as the *jaman's kamin*. The *jajman* pays his *kamin* in cash or grain on a daily, monthly or bi-yearly basis (Oscar Lewis, 1958 : 56-57).

The functional relationship between the tribes and castes in the tribal villages of Bihar is also characterised by a similar phenomenon, though it is not called *jajmani* system as such. The village Lohra sharpens the ploughshares of all the peasants for which he receives in Anigara 1 maund and 4 seers paddy in November, 3 seers Gondli in August and 3 seers Gora Paddy in October per plough. If any one wants any other iron implement made by the Lohra he has to pay him in cash or kind at that very moment. In Selda the mid-wife belonging to the Ghasi caste gets for each childbirth, half a seer of rice daily for six days from the day of birth to the day of *Chhati.* On the last day she gets four seers of rice, 50 paise in cash and her share of meat and rice-beer. Similarly, the Hajam in Anigara gets from every house about 20 seers of paddy at harvest time. In return he shaves all the adults in the family twice a week and gives them a monthly hair cut. Besides this, he and his wife have to attend in all ceremonies connected with birth, marriage and death in all households, tribal and non-tribal. For these services he gets his customary payment after the ceremonies are over.

In Salehatu, Swansi, Ghasi and Lohra are the three communities which have functional relationship with the Munda. In Gutuhatu, the communities other than the Munda are Rautia, Kumhar, Chick Baraik and Lohra; the last three provide services to the Munda and to the Rautia. In Amlesa the functional castes are Kumhar, Swansi, Machchua (Ghasi) besides the Lohra community. The other communities in this village are Puran Majhi and Sao. The Vaishnav and Dhobi (Washerman) of other villages also render service to the Munda in Amlesa. In Amlesa the services of the Brahmin and *gosain* are required at birth, marriage and death. The barber and washerman also render service at these occasions. At marriage the Brahmin is paid Rs. 10, Vaishnav Rs. 5, Hajam Rs. 2.50, and Dhobi Rs. 1.25 respectively. In addition to small gifts given to these functionaries at various occasions, they are given a fixed amount of paddy at the harvesting time. The barber, in addition to the occasional services shaves the adult members of the village once or twice every week.

In Gutuhatu, the Lohra is paid 20 seers of paddy per bullock plough, 40 seers per buffalo plough in November. During harvesting of Gora paddy some stalks of paddy are left in the field to be reaped by the Lohra which constitute about 10 seers of Gora paddy. Itowa Lohra of Gutuhatu said that he had 50 ploughs in his *jajmani* in the village and was paid 40 seers of paddy for each plough. Earlier the Kumhar and barber in Gutuhatu were also in functional relationship with the Munda, but now Tapkara market provides the former with better opportunities for his business. The Kumhar family, however, still holds the land which was given to it for its customary services in the past.

The midwife, who is generally from the Ghasi caste, is an important functionary at the time of childbirth. She helps during the delivery and then attends to the mother and the child for about a week up to the time of the *Chhati* ceremony. In Salehatu, the Ghasin midwife is usually paid 50 paise to one rupee for cutting the umbilical cord of the newly born. During all these days she is given one seer of rice and some uncooked vegetable for her daily meals. On the *Chhati* day she is paid 3.50 seers of paddy and 15 paise for her services. In Gutuhatu she is given some rice and a sari on the *Chhati* day. In Amlesa the washerman does the washing of unclean clothes of the child and the mother on that day while in the other to villages the *dai* performs all functions. During the *Chhati* ceremony of Vishwanath's daughter in Amlesa, the *dai* was given 3 seers of rice and some amount of lentil and turmeric. She was given a sari brought by the child's maternal uncle. She was promised a sari by the child's father also. The washerman was paid 2 seers of paddy and 12 paise for her service and a sari was promised. The barber in Salehatu is paid 3½ seers of rice and 30 paise for his services at the *Chhati*, the amount is double than that paid to the *dai*. The barber performs his customary duties at the *lagan* and marriage and he is paid according to the set rules. In Vishwanath's *lagan* ceremony, the barber from his village was paid Rs. 5 by the bride's guardians. The Ghasis are traditional musicians and play at the ear-boring ceremony and the marriage in Munda families. They are remunerated either in cash or kind for their services.

Among Christian Mundas the *parcharak* and the *padri* stand in a similar relationship as the Brahmin and *Gosain* among the non-convert. These functionaries officiate at baptism, marriage and death among converts and they are given a customary payment for their services on these occasions.

AGRO-INDUSTRIES

The 1971 Census showed that 669 Mundas, 535 males and

134 females were engaged in household industries. The percentage of such workers was only 0.27. The types of industries were carpentry, production of honey, oil extracting, livestock rearing etc.

Agriculture is the main occupation in the Munda country and some agro-industries like blacksmithy, weaving, pottery, basketry and carpentry are essential aspects of the village economy. These occupations are taken up by the artisan castes like Lohra, Sawansi, Kumhar etc. They belong to different castes and are engaged in some type of *jajmani* system with the Munda. In Gutuhatu and Amlesa villages there are three Munda households which are engaged in carpentry and basketry, respectively. The Munda build their own houses as well as make their own earthen tiles etc. Weaving and blacksmithy are considered low grade occupations and the Mundas do not practise these trades. Though, contact with modern industry and work in factories have brought some change in their traditional attitude in urban areas, in the village, such an attitude change has not come, thus putting a brake on the diversification of the tribal economy.

At Khunti in the first decade of this century a Roman Catholic Industrial School was opened in which training was given for weaving, carpentry and smithy. The prejudice of the Munda to weaving was overcome by using Japanese loom. For years the Munda were trained in this profession but they never shed their disdain for it. Many such weaver technicians who acquired skill through training did not practise their trade at all. No such prejudice is shown by the Munda to other village crafts. Some of them have opened grocery shops, cycle repair shops, tailoring and tea shops, *pan* and cigarette shops, etc. Rearing of bees and lac has always been a subsidiary occupation with them. The weekly market serves as the nerve centre of the village economy where the Munda and other local communities sell products. The proceeds from the sale of a surplus produce or commodity in the market are generally used for purchasing other necessary articles.

Employment in Large Scale Industries

It was observed in the 1971 Census that 1.72% of the Munda workers were engaged in the mining and quarrying

The total number of such workers were 4259 (3008 males and 1251 females). They work as industrial labourers in the coal and mica mines etc. in Chotanagpur.

Similarly 1.75% of the workers among the Munda in Bihar were engaged in manufacturing, processing and repairs in other than household industries. There were 4324 persons in these industries of which 3360 were males and 964 were females respectively. Most of them were employed as unskilled and semi-skilled workers in large scale industries in and around Ranchi. Some of these important large scale industries are the Heavy Engineering Corporation at Hatia ; Usha Martin, Ranchi ; Associated Cement Company, Khelari ; Bokaro Steel Plant, Bokaro ; Tata and Steel Company, Jamshedpur ; Ranchi Distillery, Ranchi ; the lac factory at Murhu near Khunti and so on. Industrialisation in Chotanagpur has provided the tribals an opportunity to be engaged in non-agricultural pursuits and has brought about some change in their socio-economic attitudes.

Growth of Entrepreneurship

Though agriculture still remains the primary occupation and main source of income among the Mundas, the more enterprising among them have always ventured into non-traditional ways of augmenting their income, such as business, industry, trade or related services. For instance, the Munda families grow vegetables in the kitchen-gardens and sell these in the weekly market for profit. The tribal women trade in rice. They purchase paddy from the market, husk it themselves and resell in the same or other markets for a small margin of profit. The money obtained from the sale of rice is used as a revolving fund to continue their business. In Gutuhatu and Salehatu a couple of Mundas tailor clothes and sell them in the weekly market. One well-to-do Munda in Gutuhatu deals in readymade clothes. A young graduate Munda of Gutuhatu opened a controlled rate cloth shop with funds from the State Government under the unemployed graduate scheme. Some enterprising Munda purchase cattle in a weekly market and sell in another market for a small profit. In the villages some have opened a groceries, *pan* and cigarette shop, tea shop and cycle repair shop respectively. A Munda ex-M.L.A. of

Khunti sells kerosene oil in the weekly markets. A graduate Munda of Amlesa opened a grocery store in his village with a loan of Rs. 6000 from the bank under the unemployed graduate scheme of the State Government. His business did not pick-up because he had to sell the commodities on credit which is not often honoured thus eating away the capital. A teacher of Amlesa deals in firewood. He purchases a cartful of fuel from an interior market at a cheaper rate and sells it in his village earning a cent per cent profit. Some other households prepare and sell country drink (from Mahua) and *hanria* (rice-beer) at home as well as in the weekly market. One household each was engaged in carpentry and basketry in Amlesa and Gutuhatu villages respectively. Some of the rich Munda families advance money and paddy on credit at a higher rate of interest like the professional non-tribal money-lenders. These illustrations of the tribal entrepreneurship reveal that the conditions for planned growth of entrepreneurship already exist among the Munda and what is needed is the right stimulus in the form of an integrated programme to promote entrepreneurship.

The Xavier Institute of Social Service, Ranchi recently completed a research project on tribal entrepreneurship at Ranchi and Khunti. The findings of the project will hold true for the Munda entrepreneurship as such for the two sampled areas (i.e., Ranchi and Khunti) are fairly representative of the Munda area.

In all 400 tribal entrepreneurs were identified of which 153 were selected for obtaining their background information, performance and attitudes. Of these, 38 were in the primary sector, 59 in the secondary and 86 in the tertiary sector of economic activity. The type of economic activity of different entrepreneurs included vegetable growing, making dairy products, manufacturing, repairs, household industries, contractors, food trade, non-food trade, transport and service. Similarly the sample was divided into small size (Rs. 1—500), medium size (Rs. 501—2000) and big size entrepreneurs based on the size of initial investment ; the number of entrepreneurs in these three categories were 93, 61 and 29 respectively.

The research findings show that (a) tribals do engage in business, to a greater extent than originally imagined. This belies the common opinion held amongst tribals and non-tribals alike, that tribals cannot do business. It must immediately be added, however, that the majority of tribal entrepreneurs occupy as yet a marginal position and operate on a very small scale ; (b) it is in the core area of entrepreneurship, i.e., decision-making and financial risk-taking that tribal entrepreneurs face considerable handicaps, arising both from their own culture and value system and also from external factors.

Handicaps arising from the internal factors are such as : (a) a weak financial basis, (b) low risk-taking, (c) absence of technical and business skills, (d) lack of awareness of opportunities, (e) lack of effective spokesmen for their interests, (f) low capability to effectively cooperate with one another on business terms, and (g) minimal level of participation by tribal entrepreneurs in the general business world. The external factors are : (a) marked communication and confidence gap between tribal entrepreneurs and the government, (b) the policy-makers in major industries and financial institutions lack knowledge about the specific nature of their problems, (c) the education system is not job-oriented and it does not equip the students for self-employment, (d) tribal entrepreneurs go in for service-especially government service, as the most desirable form of modern employment, simply because of the reservation policy for tribal candidates and the promise made by the government to provide them with jobs. Thus it takes tribals away from the field of self-employment.

The research findings further reveal that these obstacles and handicaps in the way of growth of tribal entrepreneurship are counter-balanced by certain positive features associated with them. For instance : (a) the entrepreneurs show signs of social mobility, (b) they are aware of their own shortcomings and show a desire to acquire better skills through training programmes, consultancy services and opportunities to travel around and establish new contacts. Moreover, there seems to be little discrimination on the part of other communities against tribal entrepreneurs. Resistance from non-tribals might arise, however, once tribals penetrate deeper into the field of business and engage in types of business till now monopolized by others.

In conclusion, a congenial atmosphere exists in Ranchi

and Khunti for launching an integrated programme to promote tribal entrepreneurship. Agencies like the State government, industry, business and professional organisations, banks, training institutes, research institutes, and voluntary organisations have a role to play in developing tribal entrepreneurship. They themselves can be assisted in forming an organisation of their own to function as the spokesmen and pressure group for their interests.

8

GIFT, MARKET AND CREDIT

As among other peasant communities, the Munda sustain with gifts, dormant social relationships, which distance in time and space threaten to sever. The giver gains a return in the continuance of an esteemed relationship to which for some time he has been unable to contribute. Those who desire to create a new relationship start it with an exchange of gifts. Gifts are also the foundation for establishing new social ties.

The exchange of gifts follows a pattern. At the birth of a child, certain specific kin are required to bring gifts, both for the child and the family. So strong are the cultural compulsives that all such relations have to meet these kinship obligations. The same is the case at the name-giving and ear-boring ceremonies. In the marriage rituals and at mortuary rites such gifts have to be brought.

The exchange of gifts, between two kin-groups going to establish marital relationship is spread over a long period of time and takes the form of 'prestations'. The gift mostly consists of food articles and clothes. The occasions on which such gifts are exchanged at the time of marriage have been detailed earlier. But the gifts do not stop when the marriage rites are over. Whenever the young bride leaves her natal home to go to her husband's place or at the time of certain festivals gifts are expected from the bride's house.

There is also the practice of unsystematic gifts. During the slack agricultural season large numbers of tribals go on visits to relatives in other villages. At this time also gifts are made. Such visits are known as *mehmani.* Although a direct return for the gift is never expected over a long period of time, the gifts given and received from both parties tend to equalise.

There are some gifts, however, which are in the nature of tribute. In the days of the landlords a large number of such gifts were extracted from the Munda peasants by the servants of the landlords These exactions were very troublesome for the tribals and were slowly abolished by law.

WEEKLY MARKETS

For a long time, the Munda like other tribals in Chotanagpur, frequented weekly markets held in neighbouring villages once or twice every week. In these markets they brought their surplus for sale and purchased such articles as salt, kerosene oil, cloth, spices etc. Since they were also visited by traders and businessmen from outside, they provided exposure to outside influences to such tribals who were never destined to go out to any town. As such markets are in operation for a long time, they may be viewed as one of the traditional factors of culture change.

S.C. Roy has not made even passing reference to the market and exchange system which is an important aspect of Munda economy. Earlier I have studied the weekly market in the tribal areas as to its role in culture change and its importance in the socio-economic sphere by linking one village with another. The important weekly markets in the Munda area are held at Maranghada and Tapkara respectively. The weekly markets in tribal areas function as channels through which urban ideas and influences penetrate into the interior. The market also acts as the nerve centre of the economy of the adjoining villages. It is a place of brisk business transaction. It also functions as an important place for publicity and advertisement. It is a meeting place for friends, relatives and lovers. It acts as an important agent of social change.

A village is served not only by one weekly market but by a number of them big and small, each being held on a different day of the week. People from Salehatu visit weekly markets at Jojohatu, Maranghada, Landup, Chondar, Saiko, Sarjomdih, Khunti and Marhu. Gutuhatu is in the hinterland of more than 15 markets up to a distance of 15 miles from the village. They include Tapkara, Torpa, Dorma, Khunti, Muhru, Manhatu, Rania, Garai, Raikera, Sode, Tamba, Patria, Tangarhela, Dumangduri,

Barkuli and Marcha. People from Amlesa visit Tamar, Diuri, Hemarom, Erki, Salgadih and Sindwari markets. The weekly markets at Maranghada, Tapkara and Tamar are comparatively bigger regional markets, while most others are small and visited by people from nearby villages, while the former are visited by urban traders as well. Most of these weekly markets are held biweekly. The markets at Jojohatu, Landup, Chondar, Diuri, etc. look alike on both market days of the week, while Maranghada, Tapkara and Tamar markets respectively appear less significant on Tuesday and are known as *sabjibazar* or vegetable market. On Saturday these take the form of a major market and urban traders bring their wares for sale from distant towns, like Khunti, Ranchi, Chaibasa etc. Like the hinterland villages, the urban traders also visit all the important markets in Munda area. A villager may frequent one market more than others depending upon its distance from his village, mode of communication, cycle and bus, taxi, etc., type of market—big or small, weather conditions and the type and urgency of the requirement.

The Maranghada weekly market can be taken as a typical example of the nature and functions of a weekly market in the Munda area. Wherever possible a comparison will be drawn with other important markets such as Tapkara and Tamar to illustrate regional variations in the dynamics of a weekly market.

Maranghada Weekly Market

Layout : Maranghada is situated about ten miles east of Khunti in the heart of traditional Munda country. The weekly market is held every Tuesday and Saturday at a permanent place in the middle of the village. It is called *bazar*, *hat*, or *peet*, and is identified with the name of the village and the day of the week. The layout of Maranghada market shows that the market place extends in a linear fashion from south to north passing through the main village lane flanked on both the sides by village houses and a few permanent shops. These shops sell tea, eatables, grocery, cigarettes, *pan* and *biri*. They are also engaged in cycle repairing. There is a health centre and a post-office at the market place. The market place bears a deserted look except on market days when the villagers and traders from far and near throng the place. At the northern end there are a few permanent sheds with raised platforms, owned by some traders. There are uncovered platforms also. On market days the commodities are displayed under these sheds, on the uncovered platforms and most of the traders spread their wares on the ground.

Management: The market was established in 1869. Since then it has been held at the same place except for a short time when it was shifted to a place beyond Maranghada. The Maranghada bazar is a Khutkatti bazar and owned by Khutkattidars of Maranghada village. It functions under the supervision and control of the Maranghada Bazar Samiti headed by a honorary Chairman. The other honorary office bearers include a treasurer, a secretary, two supervisors and ten members, all from Maranghada village. Every year new office bearers and members are selected for the Samiti. In 1975, Samu Pahan was the chairman and John Nag the secretary of the Samiti. The members collect a toll from the traders visiting the market. This market yields annually Rs. 1200. This amount is raised through tax imposed on the commodities coming for sale in the market. The income is equally distributed among the village brotherhood after paying Rs. 12 i.e., one per cent of the income as tax to the State Government. Some of the money is spent on improving the market place and other public places in the village. Different rates of toll are fixed for each commodity in the market. For cattle one per cent of the sale price of a cattle is exacted from both the parties involved in the transaction. The purchaser is given a receipt to validate his purchase. 5 paise per basket and 10 paise per quintal from the purchaser. A permanent shop is charged 10 paise on each market day. Cloth and hardware shops have to pay 30 and 20 paise respectively. The Bazar Samiti does not allow the resale of a commodity in the same market place.

Previously the bazar used to be held only on Wednesday and Saturday. The day of the Jojohatu bazar at a distance of 3 miles east of Maranghada was changed from Thursday to Wednesday. Therefore, Maranghada bazar day was changed from Wednesday to Tuesday. The Saturday bazar is held on large scale while on Wednesday only local people attend the market in small numbers.

Maranghada is linked with the town of Khunti by a *kachcha* road passing through the village and terminating in Sirum village east of Maranghada. There is a market bus service, popularly known as bazar bus, from Khunti trucks also ply between Khunti and Maranghada on market days bringing urban traders and their goods to the market. The transport between Khunti and Maranghada is disrupted during the rainy season due to water in the Tajna river. Recently with the completion of the bridge on Tajna and construction of metalled road, communication with Khunti has become possible all the year round.

A weekly market serves a number of villages in its neighbourhood. The hinterland served by Maranghada market covers a radius of ten miles around it. These villages are connected with the market place through footpaths, and *kachcha* roads. Villagers carry articles for sale to the market on their heads, on *bahangis* (a bamboo with hide baskets suspended at each end), on bicycles and in bullock carts. The urban traders from Khunti, Ranchi, Chaibasa bring their materials by bazar bus, private taxis and trucks. Several ethnic groups patronize the market including the Munda, non-Munda tribals, Hindus, Muslims, Christians and Sikhs. The market provides them with a place for interaction and exchange of goods and ideas.

Maranghada bazar is held in the afternoons. The bazar bus reaches the market place at about 11 A.M. with traders from Khunti. The traders, local and urban, start arranging their commodities at the usual places in the sheds and platforms already cleaned and swept. By noon, people start pouring in, and by three o'clock business is in full-swing and the market place is packed with people. Before sunset the traders pack up and leave by the transport available. The business in this market takes place on a larger scale between January and June than from July to December. On rainy days and during festivals fewer people visit the market.

A visit to the Maranghada weekly market, in April, 1975 is described below which gives a clear idea of its functioning.

We set out on bicycles from Jojohatu village, three miles from Maranghada with three young Munda friends who had put on their newly washed and ironed shirts, powdered their faces and combed their hair in great style and reached the market place at 3.30 P.M. As we approached the market at its south-eastern end, we observed some Munda women selling rice-beer and *mahua* liquor on the roadside. Moving further we found herds of goats, sheep, bullocks, cows and buffaloes for sale under the shady trees. Nearby was a shed where a member of the Bazar Samiti regulated the sale and purchase of cattle and charged one per cent on the sale of each head of cattle from the seller and the purchaser. Traders from Khunti and Ranchi purchase cattle from this market for profit. On the right the Sawansi displayed their hand-made cloth. While on the left two cycle repair shops and a tea shop were doing brisk business. Near one of the cycle shops about 50 cycles were kept by customers to the market. We also kept our cycles there.

Towards our left in front of the tea shop, Lohras were selling iron plough shares, iron axes, *baluas*, arrow-heads etc. Mundas were also sitting with wooden ploughs, ropes and bundles of firewood displayed in front of them. Towards the road leading to Khunti the local tribals and non-tribals were selling paddy and rice. From this point towards the north end tribal and non-tribal women were sitting in two rows in the middle of the road with paddy and rice. There were women who sold beaten and puffed rice. Some men and women were also selling vegetables and chewing tobacco and unleavened bread made of rice flour. There was a great rush in the market place and we pushed our way ahead. We took tea in a tea shop and then bought rice and pulses from a permanent shop and kept these in the tea shop.

While we were at the western end we saw people collected at a gambling shop run by non-tribals from Khunti and Gobindpur. Walking a few yards from the tea shop, we saw that the Health Centre on the left side of the bazar was packed with villagers waiting for medicine. Further north, on the right-hand side corner, an ex-MLA Munda from Khunti was selling kerosene oil at controlled rates. From this corner eastwards, there were four to five tea shops in a row where people were taking tea with snacks. These also sold cheap sweets. At this eastern point the footpath from Jojohatu entered the market. Around this place a few permanent sheds have been erected owned by different traders. They were engaged in the purchase of Mahua flowers, *karanj* oil seeds and tamarind. Lac is also purchased by these traders during the season. These traders come from Murhu and Tamar. As we moved ahead towards the north, we found two or three grocery shops and a gambling shop. At the extreme north-eastern end Munda women were selling rice-beer and *mahua* liquor. While moving westwards along the periphery, we could see potters displaying earthen ware. There were also locally made bamboo baskets, brooms and winnowing fans. There were chicken for sale. In one corner people were trying their luck at the dice under a shed. Traders from Chaibasa visit the market for purchasing fish. Located at the space on the northern end there were urban traders with their articles displayed in the sheds. There were Mohammaden traders from Khunti selling mill-made cloth and ready-made garments. Traders from Ranchi sold hardware and aluminium utensils. There were plastic goods, soaps, cosmetics, stationery, ladies articles like ribbon, hair pins, mirrors, cheap brass and silver ornaments etc. Adjoining these sheds on the right, on uncovered platforms, were local people who sold local grown vegetables like potatoes, tomatoes, onions, chillies, and gourds of all kinds.

The bazar was packed to capacity. Young tribals, both boys and girls, were dressed in their Sunday best. Some of them were very well groomed and decked with flowers in their hair. They were moving in the market brandishing their sticks, and axes. At some places in the market one could see boys and girls engaged in conversation. We saw friends and relatives exchanging greetings or *johar*. The common form of greeting for men is to bend slightly with folded hands and saying *johar*. Women kneel down with both hands touching the ground. It is customary for the young to respect to their elderly relatives.

We left the market place for Jojohatu late in the evening because Sukhdev Bardiar's cycle was being repaired during this period. It was dark by now and the market place was deserted except for a few persons sitting in the tea shops, gambling shops or drinking shops. The urban traders had already left by bazar bus, taxi or truck. The villagers from distant villages had left long back. At 7 P. M. we started our return journey. Due to the enveloping darkness we went on foot, walking our bicycles. Approaching Jojohatu village boundary at a place where the road from Maranghada makes a shape with roads from Jojohatu and

Gutuhatu, there was a small bazar popularly known as *gudri bazar*. Here we saw the tribal men and women enjoying drinks in *sal* leaf or aluminium cups. The tribals selling the drinks belonged to Jojohatu, Gutuhatu and other nearby villages. They had displayed their articles on the ground in the light of petromax lanterns. Some persons were also engaged in gambling there. Except in Tamar, gambling and liquor shops are integral parts of every weekly market in the Munda area.

EXCHANGE SYSTEM

Until recently the transactions in the weekly markets were in a large measure in the nature of money barter. But now most of the commodities, in the market, local as well as from urban areas, are sold and purchased for cash. The proceeds from the sale of a surplus produce in the market are generally used for purchasing other necessary articles. Though the volume of trade in the weekly market is considerable, the circulation of cash is small. The system of money barter was found in Tamar weekly market in case of parched rice and *murhi* (puffed rice). One seer of beaten rice was exchanged for one seer of rice or two seers of paddy. One seer of puffed rice was exchanged for half a seer of rice or one seer of paddy.

Standard weights and balances are used for weighing vegetables, *karanj* oil seeds, lac and other groceries. Apart from kilograms, seers, equivalent stone weights are also used. The standard iron balance as well as the wooden balance are used for weighing the commodities. Paddy and rice, *mahua* etc. are measured with a *paila* which is a local measure of volume equivalent to one seer. Most of the Munda women and local Hindu low caste women trade in paddy. They purchase paddy from the mark et with an initial capital of about Rs. 20-25. They take it home and dehusk it and then sell it as rice in the next market and make some profit. This type of business was observed in all the markets.

Non-tribal traders from Khunti, Ranchi and other places purchase large numbers of cattle from a weekly market and sell them in another market at a profit. Villagers also exchange cattle in the market. The tribals purchase goats and sheep for sacrificial purposes as well as for eating. Bullocks for ploughing and for payment of bride-price may also be purchased from the market.

Similarly, the Banias and Muslims from urban areas purchase poultry and eggs from the weekly market and sell them in the town at higher prices. The local people purchase chicken for performing sacrifices at festivals.

In Tamar area there is a good deal of business in fire wood. Some local people purchase almost all the firewood from the tribals who bring it from the forest. They transport it to different villages and thus make a profit.

Firewood from Tamar area is also transported to the adjoining districts of West Bengal. The local people have to pay a higher price for firewood for their own use. Sometimes the cost of a *bhar* (one head-load) of firewood reaches Rs. 5, while in Maranghada and Tapkara the cost of one *bhar* does not exceed Rs. 2.50. Puran Chandra Munda of Amlesa brings firewood in large quantities in a bullock cart from Hemrom market near Erki. He sells it in his own village for double the purchase price. Every Sunday he transports firewood worth Rs. 25 from Hemrom and makes a profit of Rs. 100 per month from its sale in his village.

Most of the important weekly markets in the Munda area are owned by the State government. These are given on annual contract through auction. These include the Murhu, Khunti, Tapkara and Tamar markets. The contractor collects toll from the traders attending the weekly market. The supervision and control of these markets is in the hands of contractors. The Maranghada market is a Khutkatti market and the village community owns it. The Dorma weekly market is owned by the Bhengra Parha under the sole supervision of Sukh Ram Munda. The market at Tapkara is generally taken on contract by the local Bengali landlord. In Tamar, it is the Raja of Tamar, who gets the Tamar market contract valued at Rs. 2200. The Raja uses this contract as an asset for increasing his political influence and gives employment to people loyal to him or who were in his service before the abolition of Zamindari. The Raja's interest, therefore, lies in acquiring the contract at all costs. His agents collect a fixed toll from the traders visiting the market.

All the weekly markets are linked with nearby towns like Ranchi, Khunti, Chaibasa, Jamshedpur through *kachcha* and *pucca* roads. NH 33 connects Tamar with Ranchi and Jamshedpur. Therefore, local commodities like vegetables, firewood, paddy, poultry etc. find an easy market at a higher price in these towns. This causes scarcity and price rise in the local markets.

The market place is generally situated either in the centre of the village as in Maranghada or at the outer fringe of the village as in Tamar, Tapkara and Dorma markets. It is popularly known as Bazar Tanr, especially in Tapkara and Saiko. The market place is generally provided with sheds and platforms under the shady trees. It gives a deserted look except on market days.

In small markets the trade is much less and urban traders do not visit such places. The commodities sold and purchased in these markets are locally produced paddy, rice, vegetables, *mahua*, lac, rice-beer and *mahua* liquor, pots and pans.

FUNCTIONS OF WEEKLY MARKETS

The weekly market is a multipurpose institution not restricted merely to economic functions. The post office at Maranghada, Tapkara and Tamar respectively serves the villages within a radius of 6—10 miles and the villagers collect their post on market day. The weekly market is a clearing house for all the news of the locality. Notices of meeting are distributed, the dates of *parha* meetings are notified in the market and dates for important festivals, *jatras* are announced. The contractors recruit labourers in the weekly market to be sent to different places.

The weekly market is a meeting place for relatives, friends and lovers. The young people come to the market in their best turn-out. In Maranghada and Saiko bazars most of the tribal boys and girls are seen in tribal dress ; the boys with painted faces brandishing their weapons and girls with flower bedecked hairdo and silver ornaments. Many women are draped Bengali style in a single piece sari without blouse. In Tapkara weekly market most of the men are found wearing *dhoti* and *kurta*, shirt and trousers etc. Most of the women wear a blouse and sari in the style found in rural Bihar. Due to Christianity, many women in the Tapkara area are literate. One can see educated women and school girls selling boiled gram, vegetables etc. in the market. In Tamar market it is difficult to differentiate between a tribal and a non-tribal without minute observation. In Maranghada market mostly the traditional mode of salutation, i.e., *johar* is exchanged between friends and relatives. In Tapkara area Christian Munda greet each other with handshake and say *Yishu Sahai* or Namaste. In Tamar the Hindu mode of greeting is saying *parnam* or *johar* with folded hands. In Maranghada market the language of conversation is Hasda Mundari and Hindi, in Tapkara it is Naguri Mundari and Sadani as well as Hindi, and in Tamar market mostly Hindi, Panchpargania and Bengali are used as the language for conversation.

Urban traders engage labourers for loading and unloading their commodities from the bazar bus. Labourers are also engaged to carry the belongings of a trader from one market to another, because these traders visit all the important markets of the area. Tapkara market serves the villages beyond Karo river in the south and in the rainy season the river poses a problem for these villagers to visit Tapkara market.

Villagers, on a market day, finish their agricultural work in the forenoon to be able to visit the nearby weekly market. On the market day the nearby schools, colleges and government and private concerns, change their working hours to the morning in order to free the students, staff and other employees to visit the weekly market in the afternoon.

The weekly market is an important agency of social change. Local tribals and non-tribals, urban traders, and the government officials visit the market. They belong to different religions such as the tribal religion, Christianity, Hinduism, Islam etc. They interact with each other in the local dialects like Mundari, Sadani, Panchpargania or in Hindi. Thus, a good deal of urban influence reaches rural areas through these markets. New tastes and fashions in dress, ornaments and food are diffused to the hinterland villages from the market. These influences reach the remotest corners and thereby make an impact on the tribal way of life in the Munda area.

Short-term Credit

Trade within the village is very little. Whenever a person requires something he borrows it from a neighbour or kinsmen and returns it afterwards. Such borrowing and lending is known as *paincha* a loan between friends that carries no interest. *Painchas* are asked and given for any purpose. In Gutuhatu 12 households had borrowed paddy and cash money as *paincha* from different sources such as neighbours, friends, relatives and R.C. Mission Vikas Fund of Gutuhatu. *Painchas* were taken for periods extending over some months to seven years. The reason for such borrowing is to provide food for the family, paddy seed, purchase of bullocks, purchase of land and education of children. The amount of paddy taken as *paincha* by three households in Gutuhatu was 3.50 maunds for the purpose of seed and food within the same year. Ten households were found to have borrowed Rs. 3637 as *paincha* of which Rs. 780 were taken during the previous 3 to 7 years. This shows that with the passage of time mostly after three years it becomes difficult to return the *painchas*. The reasons for the continuance of the *paincha* system may be that the lender will not claim it back unless it be urgently needed for his own consumption. The borrower would refund it, whenever it is convenient for him to do as return of *painchas* is not insisted upon. Though the borrower does not pay any interest on it, the creditor feels that the borrower is under his obligation and informal influence during that period.

Petty business

Chhota Rai Munda of Salehatu augments his income by tailoring clothes in his village. In Landup village there is a grocery store, a betel and cigarette shop and a cycle repairing shop ; the last two are owned by the Mundas. Similarly in Maranghada, where an important weekly market of the area is held every Saturday, there are a few permanent shops selling tea, groceries, betel and cigarettes. There are two cycle repair shops as well. Lucas Guria of Gutuhatu tailors clothes in his village. He also sells readymade garments in the weekly markets. In Amlesa, Vishwanath Singh Munda and Ram Singh Puran run grocery shops. In Tapkara, Torpa and Tamar there are permanent markets, where grocery, eatables, cloth and untensils etc. are sold by the non-tribal Hindus and Muslims. There are some persons in the village who work as part-time traders. They get certain goods such as cattle, paddy etc. from one market and sell it in another to make a small profit. However, most of the trading in the Munda area is done in the weekly markets.

The Mukhia of Jojohatu once borrowed Rs. 30 from a member of my team and with that money his wife bought some paddy in Maranghada market. This acted as a revolving fund for her for purchasing paddy and selling the rice made from it in the market. After four subsequent markets she made Rs. 50. Large quantities of paddy and rice are also sold in the weekly markets, especially in Tamar.

INDEBTEDNESS

Self-sufficiency, which was an important feature of tribal economy was gradually lost with the influx of outsiders who created new demands. The tribals fell into the habit of borrowing. The problem of indebtedness has assumed such large proportions that the benefits conferred by the welfare activities of the government are entirely lost. The chief factors leading to indebtedness are : (a) very small family holdings, (b) prime importance to growing of paddy, (c) failure of crops, (d) no habits of saving, (e) heavy expenses on festive and marriage occasions etc., (f) excessive drinking, and (g) effects of urbanisation.

A survey of the pattern of income and expenditure of the Munda in Karra Block sometime back reveals that their income is drawn from three sources such as : (a) food crops, (b) wages and, (c) cash crops. An average tribal household in that Block was found to produce rice, millet and pulses worth about Rs. 500 annually. An average household produce 18 maunds of rice, 10 maunds of millet, i.e., either *gondli* or *marua* and 3 maunds of *urad* pulse. Income from wage labour varied according to the availability of work. On an average it was found that a tribal household earns approximately Rs. 150 per year from this source. By selling cash crops an average tribal household was estimated to earn Rs 20.00 per year. Thus an average tribal household earned Rs. 670.00 per year from all sources.

The annual expenditure of an average tribal household was estimated between Rs. 650 and Rs. 700 per year. The main item of expenditure is rice. Besides these, there are some other occasions when a lot of expenditure is incurred. Such occasions are marriages, births and deaths in the family. Further, the payment of land revenue and other taxes also involves expenditure. Thus on the whole, a tribal household incurs more expenditure than it earns. The following table shows the expenditure pattern of a tribal family in the Karra Block :

Articles	Total expenditure (Rupees/year) (Approximate)
1. Rice and millets	400.00
2. Pulses	25.00
3. Condiments	12.00
4. Mustard oil	12.00
5. Kerosene oil	15.00
6. Tobacco	15.00
7. Clothing	50.00
8. Liquor	50.00
9. Vegetables	10.00
10. Agricultural inputs—seeds, implements etc.	10.00
11. Expenditure on Education	3.00
12. Festivals and other cermonial occasions	75.00
13. Miscellaneous	25.00
Total	702.00

If both men and women engage in wage labour for a longer period, they might remove the deficit in their current expenditure. But to meet extraordinary expenditure as on festivals and ceremonies an average tribal household has either to sell or mortgage a part of the land or take loans.

Extent of Indebtedness

Out of 261 households surveyed in three villages, 137 (i.e., 52.3%) were currently under debt. Villagewise distribution of indebted households was 70.5% in Amlesa, 67.3% in Gutuhatu and 26.3% in Salehatu respectively. In a study of 200 tribal households of Karra Block in 1965 the extent of indebtedness

TABLE 8.1

Extent of Indebtedness

Village	Total number of households	Total number of indebted households	Indebted households as proportion of total households 3/2
Salehatu	99	26	26.3
Gutuhatu	101	68	67.3
Amlesa	61	43	70.5
All villages	261	137	52.3

was found to be 52%, i.e., the same as the average for the three villages.

The total loans incurred by the 137 indebted families were 417 in number. 236 loans (56%) were in cash and 181 (44%) were in kind. While in Amlesa and Salehatu about two-third of the loans were cash loans, in Gutuhatu majority (54%) of the loans were paddy loans. The average number of loans for an indebted household in the three villages was 3.1. The average loans per household were more in Amlesa and less in Gutuhatu and Salehatu as compared to the average for all the villages. The 1965 study in Karra Block showed a comparatively lower rate of indebtedness, i.e., there was only two loans on average incurred by the tribal households.

TABLE 8.2

Extent of Indebtedness

Village	Number of indebted households	Types of loans						Average number of all loans per household
		Cash		Kind		Total		
		No.	%	No.	%	No.	%	
Salehatu	26	35	(64.8)	19	(35.2)	54	(100.0)	2.1
Gutuhatu	68	92	(46.0)	108	(54.0)	200	(100.0)	2.6
Amlesa	43	109	(66.9)	54	(33.1)	63	(100.0)	3.8
All villages	137	236	(56.6)	181	(43.4)	417	(100.0)	3.1

The aggregate amount of debt for the household surveyed in the three villages was Rs. 69,312 of which Rs. 14,490 (one-fifth) was incurred by three households in Amlesa. Two-third of the total loan was alone from Amlesa, while Gutuhatu had more than one-fourth of it and rest was from Salehatu. The average debt per household (excluding Rs. 14,490) for all villages, Amlesa, Gutuhatu and Salehatu was Rs. 406.88, Rs. 802.60, Rs. 268.20 and Rs. 161.65 respectively. In the Karra Block study (1965), the average debt per household was comparatively lower (Rs. 138.40) than that found in the present study. This can easily be explained by the higher value for money ten years back.

TABLE 8.3

Village-wise distribution of indebted households by maximum number of loans per household

	Frequency of loans per household					
Village	1	2	3	4	5	Total
Salehatu	13	8	3	1	1	26
%	50.0	30.8	11.5	0.4	0.3	100.0
Gutuhatu	14	17	19	8	10	68
%	20.6	25.0	27.9	11.8	14.7	100.0
Amlesa	6	8	10	7	12	43
%	14.0	18.6	23.3	16.3	27.9	100.0
All villages	33	33	32	16	23	137
%	24.1	24.1	23.4	11.7	16.8	100.0

Among the indebted households, more than three-fourths had taken loans more than once. In Salehatu half of the indebted households had incurred only one loan each. In Gutuhatu the maximum proportion of households (28%) had three loans, while in Amlesa the highest proportion of households (28%) had five or more loans. In all villages about one-fourth of households each had got one, two and three loans respectively. In Karra Block 37.7% households had one loan, 38.4% had two loans, 20.1% had three loans and only 3.8% had four loans respectively.

Source of Loan

There are different sources from which the Munda obtain loans at varying rates of interest. In a majority of the cases loans are taken from private sources such as money-lenders, friends or kin etc.

TABLE 8.4
Village-wise distribution of total number of loans by types of source

Village		Type of source					
		Money-lenders	Friends & Kin	Co-operative Agencies	Public sector Agencies	All sources	Amount of land mortgaged against loan
Salehatu	On Interest	—	15	1	3	19	
	On Land	—	35	--	—	35	11.23 Acres
	Total	—	50	1	3	54	
			(92.6)	(1.9)	(5.5)	(100.0)	
Gutuhatu	On Interest	—	66	42	20	128	
	On Land	—	70	2	—	72	21.53 Acres
	Total	—	136	44	20	200	
			(68.0)	(22.0)	(10.0)	(100.0)	
Amlesa	On Interest	31	7	20	42	100	
	On Land	10	53	—	—	63	54.33 Acres
	Total	41	60	20	42	163	
		(25.2)	(36.8)	(12.3)	(25.7)	(100.0)	
All villages	On Interest	31	88	63	65	247	
	On land	10	158	2	—	170	
	Total	41	245	65	65	417	
		(9.8)	(59.0)	(15.6)	(15.6)	(100.0)	

It is evident from Table 8.4 that a maximum number of loans were obtained from kin and friends. More than 15% of the loans were taken each from Co-operative Societies, village funds R.C. Church *Sirni* (contribution) and grain *golas* and the C.D. Block. Money-lenders were least important except in Amlesa where one-fourth of the loans were taken from them. In Karra Block the distribution of loans according to the agencies of loan in 1965 was 57% from money-lenders, 27.2% from block and grain *golas*, 10.7% from the Co-operative Society and R.C. Mission Co-operative Credit Society and only 4.5% from kin and friends.

60% of the loans were obtained on interest while 40% were incurred through usufructuary mortgage of their land. 93% of the loans on land were obtained from friends and kin and 6% from the money-lenders. In two cases the loans on land in Gutuhatu were taken from the R.C. Mission Vikas Fund.

A villagewise analysis reveals that in Salehatu most of the loans were taken from kin and friends and none from non-tribal money-lenders. In Gutuhatu almost two-thirds of the loans were from kin and friends, while almost one-fourth were from the village co-operative societies. Here again the professional non-tribal money-lenders did not operate among them. In Amlesa, though less than 40% of the loans were from kin and relatives, one-fourth of the loans were from professional money-lenders and government agencies respectively. Of the loans on land almost one-fifth were taken from the non-tribal money-lenders of Tamar and rest were from kin and relatives. 11.23 acres in Salehatu, 21.53 acres in Gutuhatu and 54.33 acres of lands in Salehatu were given as usufructuary mortgage or *Bhugut Bandha*—against 35, 72 and 63 loans respectively. The *Bhugut Bandha* is a kind of usufructuary mortgage in which at the end of 7 years the creditor's claim for principal and interest are supposed to be discharged and the land reverts to the original owner.

Money-lenders : As it was observed above, professional money-lenders who were generally non-tribal Hindus and Mohammedans, were found only in one of the three villages surveyed, i.e., Amlesa. In this village one-fourth of the loans were obtained from money-lenders of Tamar of which three-fourths were on interest and one-fourth on land. The money-lenders charge a high and differential rate of interest on cash and paddy loans. The rates of interest for paddy vary from 20 seers per maund of paddy per year. Similarly the rate of interest on cash loans varies from 10% to 100% per year. Some of them charge interest in kind at an annual rate of one seer paddy per rupee which is almost 100% interest. Though the money-lenders charge exorbitant rates of interest on loans, their popularity among the tribals is mainly because they are easily approachable and the whole transaction is confidential and involves a very simple procedure.

Friends and Kin : Friends and kin are the most important agencies approached for loans. Six, out of every ten loans, are obtained from friends and relatives. They include Munda (80.5%), non-Munda tribals, Lohra and Oraon (1.2%) and non-tribals (18.3%).

The rates of interest charged by them range from 20 seers to 40 seers per maund of paddy per year for the loans in kind. The cash loans from kin and friends were mainly taken as *paincha*. One such loan was taken on 6% interest, two on one seer of paddy or a rupee per year and two on 5% interest.

In each village there are certain families, Munda as well as non-Munda, who extend loan to the needy villagers. There are seven families in Salehatu, ten families in Amlesa and eleven families in Gutuhatu, who usually extend loans to neighbours.

It was observed earlier that 60% of the total loans were obtained from kin and friends. Of these, almost two-third loans were taken against usufructuary mortgage of land and these were mainly cash loans. It is obvious from the analysis that a class of money-lenders has evolved among the tribals who like the outsider non-tribal money-lenders, exploit their fellow tribals. The C.N.T. Act, 1908 has restrained the Munda from selling their ancestral land to the non-tribals. When a tribal household requires a loan, it has to give as usufructuary mortgage a plot or two of land for an amount much less than its market value. The amount once taken is hard to be returned in the stipulated period and in the mean time some more loans are taken and thus mortgaged land is seldom redeemed.

Co-operative Agencies : The Munda have village institutions like Jama Bank, Sahyog Fund etc. from where they can take loans of paddy or cash as the case may be. In Jamtoli in village Gutuhatu they collect 10 paise per household on the weekly meeting day of the village Panchayat. This amount and the amount obtained as fine for minor offences in the village have been set apart as village fund since June 1972. The amount stood at Rs. 400 by June 1975. Money can be borrowed from the village fund at 5% rate of interest. Paulus Guria maintains the records.

Jamtoli also has a paddy or *grain store* called *khajana*. It was started in the year 1973 with an initial contribution of 5 seers per household. The paddy is given on loan at a rate of interest of 20 seer per maund of paddy per year. Philip Guria keeps the accounts. Paddy is stored in bundles of 6 to 15 maunds. A bundle is opened only when there is a sufficient number of borrowers for that amount. The initial amount was only 60 seers, by 1974, it became 90 seers and by 1975 harvest this amount of paddy became 135 seers.

Village Sahyog Fund : In 1970 a Munda of the R.C. Mission bought land with a loan from the Co-operative Bank. At sowing time 21 R.C. Munda households contributed 10 seers each of paddy seed and ploughed the fields collectively. The paddy from this land was sold, and the loan was returned by the sale of the harvested paddy. The balance and the money obtained from the next harvest acted as the initial capital for the Sahyog Fund. This amount of money is lent to the Catholics of Gutuhatu at 6% rate of interest. By 1975, the amount reached Rs. 2000. The Sahyog Fund has also given loan by taking land on mortgage. The members cultivate this land collectively and the income is added to the Sahyog Fund. In Gutuhatu R.C. Mission's *Sirni* (the contribution obtained on Sunday Church service) is given on loan at a rate of interest of 25%.

Similarly in Lathura Toli, there is Village Jama Bank for paddy. There is also a girls' Jama Bank or Sanghati Bank which was started by the village girls with 5 seers of paddy each in the beginning. The rate of interest is 20 seers per maund of paddy per year. The profit is equally distributed among the member girls. This Sanghati Bank gives paddy loan mainly for seed at the sowing season.

Similar Jama Banks are present in Salehatu and Amlesa. The Co-operative Society at Amlesa charges 8% to 9.25% interest on cash loan and 10 seers per maund paddy on kind loan. People of Amlesa get loan from the R.C. Mission Tamar at 6% rate of interest. Co-operative Bank Khunti was also one of the loaning agencies operating in that area. The popularity of these co-operative societies is highest in Gutuhatu. Almost one-fourth of the total loans have been obtained from these sources. In Amlesa and Salehatu percentage of such loans are 12.3% and 2%. Among the different sources of loan, co-operative societies are only next to kin and relatives. The CCS also serves the R.C. Mission Christians in the area. The society gives productive loans such as for purchasing ploughs, cattle, seed and fertiliser etc.

Public Sector Agencies : These agencies include Grain *golas*, Block and Anchal offices. The villagers of Salehatu, Gutuhatu and Amlesa are served by grain *golas* at Maranghada, Kamra and Tamar respectively and the Block and Anchal offices at Murhu, Torpa and Tamar respectively. These agencies are as popular as the co-operative agencies with 15.6% of the total loans obtained from these. A large number of paddy loans are obtained from Grain *golas*, at a rate of 8 to 10 seers per maund paddy. 25% in Amlesa, 10% in Gutuhatu and 5.5% of such loans in Salehatu were obtained from these agencies. The Block and Anchal offices also gave cash loans for which these charged 8 to 10% interest. Mukhia of Amlesa took a pump set worth Rs. 3100 on loan from the Tamar Block office at 10% rate of interest.

Another Munda of Amlesa took Rs. 6000 at 10% interest from the Bank of India, Bundu to start a grocery store in his village.

Grain Golas : Grain *golas* are government grain depots from where villagers take grain on loan and return at the time of the next harvest. These days hundreds of grain *golas* have been opened by the Welfare Department of the State government. In Khunti Block grain *golas* are situated at Maranghada, Khunti, Fudi and Taro Silajon. The grain *gola* at Maranghada was started in 1959 and it serves 55 villages. The initial amount of paddy loaned to the tribals was 200 maunds. Various types of loans are given. Agricultural loan is given in the form of paddy for seed on a 10% rate of interest.

Paddy loan is given to the farmers at the sowing season and the collection of loan is carried out between November and March. The Welfare department in 1959, started the Maranghada grain *gola* with 200 maunds of paddy which was loaned to the tribals in that year. By 1975, the total demand was nearabout one thousand maunds. The rate of interest during 1959-61 was 25% and afterwards it was reduced to 10%. In case a person is unable to repay the paddy loan, it may be remitted by applying to the State Welfare department. The grain *gola* of Landup Panchayat which was started in 1954 was closed down in 1967 and then merged with the one at Maranghada.

The most difficult problem faced by the grain *golas* is that a major proportion of the loans remain uncovered and further expansion of this government credit agency is limited.

Duration of Loans

The loans required for a short period and paid within one

year are called short-term loans. The Munda need such loans for the purpose of cultivation or for meeting domestic expenses. Only 26% of the loans are of this type.

TABLE 8.5

Duration of loans

	Short-term Loans	Medium-term Loans						Long-term Loans			
	Less than a year	1 yr.	2 yrs.	3 yrs.	4 yrs.	5 yrs.	1 to 5 yrs.	6 yrs.	7 yrs.	6+ yrs.	Total
Salehatu	12	16	9	5	2	3	35	3	4	7	54
%	22.2	—	—	—	—	—	65.0	—	—	12.8	100.0
Gutuhatu	74	25	29	26	12	10	102	6	18	24	200
%	37.0	—	—	—	—	—	51.0	—	—	12.0	100.0
Amlesa	22	36	26	27	20	12	121	6	14	20	163
%	13.5	—	—	—	—	—	74.2	—	—	12.3	100.0
All villages	108	77	64	58	34	25	258	15	36	51	417
%	26.0	—	—	—	—	—	61.8	—	—	12.2	100.0

The maximum number of loans (61.8%) in all the villages were medium-term loans. Such loans were repaid within 5 years. These loans were generally taken for the purpose of buying cattle, agricultural implements and for improvement of land etc.

Loans for periods exceeding 5 years, i.e., the long-term loans were only 12.2% in all the villages. Such credit was required for effecting reclamation of land, fighting land disputes, liquidation of old debts etc.

Purpose of Loan

62.6% of the loans were taken for non-productive purposes, such as consumption, education of the children, festivals, land dispute, treatment of family members and repayment of an old debt. The rest were loans for productive purposes, such as purchase of land, pumping set for irrigation, plough and cattle, seed and fertilizer and for starting a grocery. In many cases productive loans were spent for non-productive purposes. The repayment of non-productive loans is mostly delayed, thus keeping the tribal families in perpetual debt.

9

THE TRADITIONAL POLITICAL ORGANISATION

THE MUNDA had evolved a polity suited to their needs from a long time. It was largely a two-tier structure headed by a traditional chief. The chief, however, did not have absolute powers but went by consensus expressed at meetings of a regularly constituted panchayat. From time to time the Munda have introduced changes in their composition and functions to meet the challenges of the situation.

Hatu panchayat and *parha* panchayat are the two important institutions of the Munda polity. The former functions at the village level, while the latter is the regional council of a group of villages. In some parts of the Munda country these institutions are in a process of decay though efforts are being made to rejuvenate them. With the introduction of statutory panchayats and courts of law in the tribal areas the significance of the traditional socio-political institutions has been undermined. A study of the composition, powers, meeting procedures and present position of these institutions will help in understanding their dynamics and their role in the political organisation of the Munda.

HATU PANCHAYAT

The Munda have a long tradition of managing their village affairs through panchayats. In olden days, before the introduction of the British courts, the panchayats were the only means through which disputes were settled and justice dispensed in the tribal areas. Though the village panchayat has remained the basic unit of Munda polity since long, S.C. Roy has not made any reference to this village organisation in his work. The dynamics of the village panchayat in the changing social and political situation in the Munda country have been studied here. Unlike the popular view in almost all the villages under study, the panchayats were found to be functioning. In some areas these were still quite powerful, while in others their activities were confined only to social matters. Since 1949, statutory *gram* panchayats have been established in tribal areas. Sometimes there is a conflict of jurisdiction between the traditional panchayats and the statutory panchayats.

The traditional panchayat suffered a lot when landlords began to control the affairs in tribal villages. By the power they wielded as landlords in the villages they ruled, only they could decide cases and for sometime traditional village officers like Munda, Mahto and Pahan were punished if they tried to hold meetings of the *Hatu* panchayat. After the first settlement, when forced labour was abolished, the tribals raised their head. The landlords lost some of their importance and the *Hatu* panchayat once again came into its own, but new organization was lightly modified in its composition. Non-tribals were also admitted to its membership. In the panchayats even the non-tribals can be elected as President.

The *Hatu* panchayat was found to be active in Salehatu and Gutuhatu, while in Amlesa it has been completely replaced by the statutory *gram* panchayat. In some villages, each *tola* or settlement has a panchayat. In Salehatu there are three separate *tola* panchayats at Maddih, Baruhatu and Salehatu respectively. Appeals from the *tola* panchayat go to the *hatu* panchayat. It is the *tola* panchayat rather than the *hatu* panchayat which is convened regularly on a particular day of the week. All the adult males of the village are its members and at least one adult male from each household is expected to attend the weekly meeting of the panchayat. The panchayat meetings are held more regularly during the agricultural season.

COMPOSITION

The *hatu* panchayat, as a judicial mechanism, deals with disputes, breaches of peace and social offences at the village level. Like Oraon and Kharia, the panchayat in a Munda village consists of the influential and elderly persons in the village. Children and women are excluded from participation in the panchayat.

In Birhu the panchayat consists of thirteen persons Munda and the Pahan select other members from among the elders of the village. As the village has a substantial non-tribal population also, these sections are represented on the panchayat. In this panchayat all kinds of disputes and offences are brought up except those dealing with social offences and clan rules which are mostly taken to the *parha* panchayat. The panchayat deals with all the cases pertaining to tribals and non-tribals in the village, but the cases which involve the Munda or the Pahan, are tried by the *parha*.

In Koenara, a Christian Munda village, people take part in panchayat meetings after attaining the age of twenty. The panchayat meeting is attended by at least one member from every house. In case of absence without showing a cause, the head of household may be fined. Besides dealing with judicial matters, the panchayat also takes up many important problems facing the village from time to time. In one meeting the panchayat expressed dissatisfaction over the management of forests by the government.

Similarly in Salehatu and Gutuhatu, the panchayat includes all adult males of the village, tribals as well as non-tribals. At least one member from each household is required to be present at its weekly meetings. Attendance is maintained by the Chairman or Secretary in a register and a fine is imposed on a person who abstains from attending it without specific reason. In Gutuhatu, the two factions in the village hold separate panchayat meetings with membership confined to the households within a faction. These panchayats are activated during cropping season to help in regulating the various activities related with agricultural operations.

Powers and Functions

Most of the cases which come under the jurisdiction of village panchayat are social and sexual offences. The most important are the offences that violate the laws of clan exogamy. Although the punishment prescribed for offenders has ceased to be deterrent, the horror of the traditional taboo has not disappeared. Such an offence is believed to bring evil in its train as well as natural calamity and is penalised with severe punishment by the village panchayat. Incest is regarded with horror and punished with excommunication. Sex relations between boys and girls of the same clan are not permissible and it is asserted that formerly such relationship when detected would be punished with the expulsion of the offending boy and girl from the village. But, these days, so long as inconvenient consequence (such as conception) do not follow, such relations appear to be often overlooked. When, however, a Munda girl is found to have conceived through a lover of her clan, the girl's family and her lover have to be excommunicated. This rule, too, no longer seems to be always strictly enforced. A fine to the panchayat and a feast to relatives often satisfies the community. In some cases the offending lovers leave the village secretly and go to the Assam tea gardens or to any urban area. In Khutkatti area, in many cases, the lovers belonging to the same clan have been allowed to live as husband and wife in the village after paying a small fine and giving a feast to the villagers. As a direct result of the rule of the tribal endogamy, sexual congress with an outsider is considered a grave offence leading to severe penalty of excommunication. Though extra-marital relations are not approved of by the society, serious notice is not taken of them unless they become a matter of common knowledge. Adultery, when discovered and proved, is severely punished. A wife found in adultery may be deserted or even killed by her husband.

The aim of social sanctions and constraints is usually not so much the enforcement of rigid rules, but the redress of injuries suffered by one member of the society at the hands of another. This may be achieved by the award of compensation, or the injured party may be satisfied with the imposition of fine on the offender and the implied condemnation of his behaviour. Penalties range from beatings to heavy fines, and unrepentant offenders unwilling to pay the prescribed fines may even be excommunicated or banished.

The cases of assault, injury and deliberate destruction of others' property are decided by the panchayat and the punishment is in the form of compensation, compromise and apology, or certain amount of fine. If the complainant is dissatisfied with the award given by the panchayat, then an appeal is made to the *parha* panchayat. Alternatively, the help of a witch is sought. Unprovoked witchcraft directed against an individual or a family is usually considered a challenge to the whole society and the victim generally counts on his fellow clansmen and co-villagers for assistance. Witches, when discovered, are severely punished and are severely beaten and driven out of the village. In Selda, a woman suspected of being a witch was secretly killed. However, such sorcerers help the villagers against the mischief of other witches by counter spells and magic and are rewarded by contributions in kind after the harvest. Witchcraft is practised in almost all houses. This is a quality acquired by propitiating spirits or Banita *bongas* (malevolent spirits). In early days a person found to be a witch was banished from the village and her lands confiscated by the village panchayat. The witch is identified with the help of a witchfinder or *sokha*.

Eating of forbidden types of food and cooked food at the hands of other tribes and castes or even at the hands of the Munda who have so eaten, or whose family have eaten such food or who are under sentence of excommunication, is regarded as an offence and the offender can be boycotted by the whole village. In Anigara there are two Munda Lohra and one Sad Lohra families. The former were Munda who ate food at the hands of a Lohra which is a defiling community as they take the meat of dead animals. From that day they formed a separate group. Now even the Munda do not take water from their hands. While there is no eating restriction between Sad Lohra and Munda Lohra groups, any marital alliances between them is unthinkable.

In another case a woman who brought false charges of a sexual offence against a person, was criticised by the panchayat and was warned of a heavy punishment for doing so. The offender had to meet the cost of the communal drink.

Stealing is considered wrong. Once the mother of Habil stole some paddy from the store of John Guria. The owner's son caught her. John reported the matter to the panchayat. The accused was found guilty and fined Rs. 15.

Niranjan Topno and Phulmani Guria fell in love and a child

was born of their union. Later on Niranjan had illicit relations with another girl, Lily Guria, with the result that the latter conceived. Niranjan told neither Phulmani nor Lily that he had had relations with both of them. But the secret leaked out and a case was instituted in the village panchayat. The panchayat decided the case as follows : (a) Niranjan had to marry one of the two girls and pay maintenance to the other ; (b) as Lily Guria had already conceived through him, she could not be married to anyone else. So Niranjan had to marry her; (c) Phulmani would have the right of full maintenance from Niranjan for herself and her son. Some land was accordingly registered in the name of her son for their maintenance ; (d) Phulmani was permitted to marry anyone she wished but would not be able to take her son along with her as he was the legitimate heir of Niranjan; (e) if Niranjan did not have any male child from Lily Guria in future, the son of Phulmani would exercise full rights of succession.

In case a person usurps someone else's land, the offender is fined by the panchayat. The fine is used for bringing rice-beer or liquor for the panchayat members. The fine does not exceed Rs. 5. The offender is asked to give up the usurped land and warned not to do so in future.

As illustrated above the judicial and social functions of the *hatu* panchayat are to settle disputes and deal with breaches of peace and social offences at the village level. The punishments which these days the panchayats usually impose are fines and excommunication. For petty theft the culprit is fined. Excommunication is usually reserved for sexual offences which violate rules of clan exogamy and tribal endogamy and also for those who offend against the rules of commensality.

All cases that come before the *tola* panchayat can be taken in appeal to the *hatu* panchayat. Further, appeals from the *hatu* panchayat and sometimes directly from the *tola* panchayat can be filed in the higher court at the *parha* level. In cases of murder, grievous hurt, theft, land dispute the statutory panchayat, police and courts enter the scene.

Meeting Procedure for Panchayats

In Salehatu and Gangudih *tola*, the panchayat meeting is held jointly under the shade of a tarmarind tree every Thursday morning and is known as *haftabar bethaki* (weekly meeting). An account of one such meeting held on 1st May, 1975 will illustrate the composition, powers and meeting procedure of the village panchayat. The meeting was held around 6 A.M. and it continued for two hours. The meeting was attended by 37 persons. Two members were absent. When everybody had gathered at the meeting place, Pandey Munda took the attendance in the attendance register. Then a general discussion began about the reasons for the recent murder of Chandra Munda of Salehatu. People put forth their own speculations about the murder mystery. Then most of them talked one by one about their programme for that day. Chota Rai and Raghunath were planning to go to attend the Khunti court with reference to a long-standing land-dispute case between Chota Rai and Achchu of Jojohatu. The village watchman Charku Nayak said that he would go to Murhu Police Station along with Madhu of Baruhata in connection with the Chandra murder case. After some time everybody dispersed discussing the murder case.

On 15 May, 1975 only two persons were absent from the village meeting. Due to a storm on the previous day a mango tree on the common village land had been uprooted and it blocked the village path. It was decided in the meeting to dispose of the fallen tree on the coming Sunday. At least one person from each household was required to participate and the firewood was to be distributed equally among the village households. At the next weekly meeting it was made known that the firewood was distributed with one full share going to those who participated in the cutting, and sawing, such households as did not have an adult male got a half share. During this weekly meeting the members dispersed without taking up any issue for discussion. They left immediately after attendance to be in time for sowing paddy and *gondli*.

The sources of income of the village panchayat are : (a) fines realised from those who commit small thefts and whose cattle graze on other peoples' crops etc., (b) fines from accused in petty quarrels; (c) interest on the paddy loans from the village grain *gola*; and (d) fine from those guilty of sexual offences.

The income of the village panchayat is spent on betterment of the village. The fine obtained by settling petty quarrels, social offences and thefts is partly spent on food and drink for the panchayat members. The panchayat also undertakes periodic cleaning of village drinking water wells. The village ponds are cleaned and deepened through the panchayat. The villagers donate their labour for such work and they are entertained with rice-beer and *mahua* purchased from the panchayat funds. During Mage (January) festival a he-goat is purchased from the panchayat funds and the mutton is equally distributed among the villagers. For widening the village paths also, the villagers offer voluntary labour and are entertained with rice-beer from Panchayat funds. Sometimes the villagers are asked to contribute some part towards the cost of entertainment incurred on the occasion of social, religious and development work in the village. In Salehatu the village panchayat has lost a part of its income from fines because the villagers refrain from stealing and grazing cattle in someone else's fields.

In Gutuhatu Khas, Lathuratoli, and Jamtoli, the village panchayat was found to be active. The composition, powers and procedures of the panchayat are similar to that described earlier about the panchayat in Salehatu. All the adult males of the village community are its members. The panchayat holds regular weekly meetings on Sunday morning in the village *akhra*. The secretary of the panchayat who is an educated young man, takes attendance before starting the discussion on the relevant issues. The specific issues discussed in the Gutuhatu panchayat during its weekly meetings in July and August 1975 were as follows : (a) Thukku Kumhar (a non-tribal) of Gutuhatu was fined because his daughter, with her grandmother's assistance, plucked fruit from the *ber* tree at the site of Manaburu (*buru-bonga*) which is a forbidden place for women and girls. To save the village from the wrath of the *bonga* it was to be propitiated by the village *Pahan*. Thukku was asked to pay a fine in the form of two chickens, one new earthen pot and some amount of rice to propitiate the *bonga*, (b) Next a decision was taken in the meeting to offer sacrifice to the Devi bonga on that day for guarding against disease and bring prosperity to the villagers, (c) Two years back Lucas Guria of Gutuhatu was excommunicated on the charge of adultery committed with a non-Christian girl of the same village. He was expelled from the panchayat. He is a rich man of the village and deals in readymade clothes. Due to his influence he, with the help of some Roman Catholic Mundas of the village, started holding a separate village panchayat and defied the decision of the general body of the village panchayat. Some more villagers also started working and eating with him. It was brought to the notice of the members in one of weekly meetings that whosoever would deal with Lucas Guria in future will be fined Rs. 20 and the informer would be paid Re. 1 as reward, (d) The existing fines for stealing or grazing others fields were also revised in the meeting, (e) In another meeting of the panchayat the main issue of discussion was the scarcity of kerosene oil in the Tapkara market which caused problems to the households and the students in Gutuhatu and other villages, (f) In one more meeting during August 1975 the panchayat was concerned about the development of agriculture in Gutuhatu. Kalyan Guria, an enlightened agriculturist in the village, suggested to the members to grow radish, cabbage, cauliflower and other seasonal vegetables to make full use of the agricultural fields soon after harvesting the *gondli* crop.

In village Amlesa, the traditional village panchayat is non-existent. The statutory village panchayat of Amlesa is concerned with cases of theft, land dispute and other social offences. However, a special meeting of the village elders is convened as and when required for planning the celebration of some religious festivals and worship of tribal and Hindu deities such as Buru Bonga, worship at the *sarna* in Sarhul festival, worship of Mahadeo and Kali or Devi etc. Similarly, the Christian Mundas in the Mission *tola* of Amlesa hold their special meetings in the Church regarding socio-religious issues involving the Christian community. In Salehatu village the secular village headman Pandey Munda is also the Sarpanch of the Gutuhatu statutory panchayat. It has given him additional political power and he holds three offices simultaneously.

S.C. Roy has described the existence of private panchayat among the Mundas which is convened by the disputants to decide the dispute. It is a mechanism for adjudication and is organised as and when required.

A look at the functioning of the *hatu* panchayat shows that it is not in a state of decay as is generally supposed, at least in some areas. These are highly effective and influential bodies and that in many villages such as Koenara, Gutuhatu, and

Salehatu, very few cases go to police stations or law courts from that area. They do nót only settle disputes, but also act as an instrument for the development and welfare of the village community. By working through traditional organisations, government could gain confidence of the tribal people and associate them in the overall development.

PARHA PANCHAYAT

Parha is an important institution in the tribal polity of Chotanagpur. It is the union of a number of villages of the same clan located around the village of origin. Among tribes like Oraon, Santal and Ho this union of villages is known as *parha*, *pargana* and *pir* respectively, though among them the villages do not be long to the same clan. The legal authority of the *parha* is vested in the *parha* panchayat. This constitutes a court of appeal from decisions of the village panchayat. Moreover, it is the only authority capable of trying certain types of offences. Though the village panchayat is in some cases empowered to pass a sentence of excommunication, readmission to the tribal fold can only be effected through the *parha* panchayat.

Composition

The basis of the formation of *parha* differs in the Bhuinhari Patti and Khutkatti Patti. This institution is not found among the Munda of Panch Pargana area.

The *parha* in the Bhuinhari area is based on kinship. It is a uniclan organisation and is named after a clan. In the Bhuinhari Patti, which at quite an early date came under the rule of the Raja of Chotanagpur, it was an increase in population which led to the formation of village groupings. When the population in a village increased and the pressure on cultivable land grew, subsidiary villages were founded in the neighbourhood. As the parent village consisted of people of one clan, the subsidiary villages also belonged to this clan. This group of villages came to be known as *parha* of the Bhuinhari area. Each *patti* or the administrative division in the realm of the Raja of Chotanagpur was co-extensive with a *parha* and comprised exclusively of one clan. In the beginning, the subsidiary villages continued to bury the bones of their dead in the clan *sasan* of the original village and joined in certain public rites in the *sarna* of the parent village, but in course of time each came to have its own *sasan* and *sarna*. However, the group continued to function as one body in social and administrative matters.

The Khutkatti Patti was colonised by those Munda who wanted to be free from the Raja's rule. They migrated with their friends and relations and founded new villages in the south and southeast of Ranchi district which were then outside the Raja's control. The population of these later colonised *pattis* comprised people belonging to different clans and in this area the *parha* unit is not co-extensive with either clan or *patti*, i.e. *parha* in this area is based on the principle of contiguity.

The unity and solidarity of the *parha* community is realised through the institution of the central panchayat known as the *parha* panchayat. This body in which both executive and judicial authority is vested, is differently constituted in the Bhuinhari and Khutkatti areas.

In the Bhuinhari area, the *parha* panchayat is a fixed body with a permanent President styled as Raja or Maharaja and a stable staff of officers. In the Khutkatti area, on the other hand, the panchayat is neither a fixed body nor has it any permanent officers. Earlier there used to be a permanent President called the Pat-Munda which has ceased to exist these days. The office-bearers of the *parha* panchayat are hereditary, the eldest son succeeding the father. Physical disability, feeble-mindedness, insanity and such other defects are considered as disqualifications for an important office. In such a case the office-bearer is replaced by one of his nearest agnates. When the eldest son of the *parha* Raja succeeds his father and takes over charge, a ceremony known as *pan-pugree* is held. To this function representatives from the adjoining *parhas* are invited. The oldest *parha* Raja among the invitees puts the *pugree* on the head of the successor and the Dewan gives him betel. The ceremony puts the seal of official recognition on the succession. In addition to the *parha* Maharaja, Raja, the other officials of the *parha* panchayat are Barlal, Majhilal, Sanjhilal, Chotlal, Kartauthani or Bamme or Purchit, Pande, Kotwar, Santari, Sipahi, Pan khwas, Ghatwar, Ghasketta and Chamar Bardaz.

They perform different duties in the *parha* panchayat. All adult members of all the villages under the *patti* are members of the *parha* by virtue of their residence. As a consequence of his birth a Munda becomes a member of the *parha* of his clan. So when a Munda settles in the jurisdiction of another *parha* he has to fulfil double obligations. The membership of a *parha* is thus not fixed but fluid. The jurisdiction of the *parha* panchayat extends over the entire area of the *parha*.

The judicial authority of the *parha* panchayat is now exercised in cases of breach of marriage laws and other social rules, disputes regarding the rights claimed by a family to bury the bones of the dead in the village *sasan*, disputes over inheritance and partition and boundary disputes between two villages. The cases referred to the *parha* are as follows :

1. Any case which the village headman does not like to try in the village panchayat.
2. Disputes between the *tola* head and the head of the village.
3. Communal disputes between two villages.
4. Disputes between parties coming from two villages.
5. Disputes concerning the rights of the Munda and the *parha*.
6. Disputes between different lineages in a village.
7. Adultery.
8. Incest.
9. Breach of other sex-taboos :
   (a) Sexual relations between members of the same lineage.
   (b) Sexual relations between members of the same clan.
   (c) Sexual relations involving Munda and non-Munda.
10. Sorcery and witchcraft.
11. Any appeal from the village panchayat.
12. Cases involving members of two different *parhas* are decided by a joint meeting of these *parhas*.

The *parha* organisation is concerned with the members of Munda tribe living in the *parha* area. Non-Munda tribals and non-tribals also come under its jurisdiction for social justice by virtue of their residence in the *parha* area. Along with the

Munda of the dominant clan, the members of other clans residing in the *parha* area come under the jurisdiction of that *parha*. The latter are also supposed to abide by the decisions of their territorial *parha*. It is not obligatory for the *parha* of the dominant clan to invite for participation or intimate their decision to the *parha* of the offending member living in its territory.

Procedure of meeting (*Parha* Panchayat)

If a case of the nature mentioned earlier occurs in any village, it is the duty of the village Munda to refer it to the *parha* Raja. The complaint may be lodged by the Munda, Mahto, Pahan or the complainant himself. The proceedings of the *parha* Panchayat are carried out in the same way as in any government court of law. The Raja orders his Dewan to make enquiries and report the findings to him. Then the *parha* Raja in consultation with the Dewan fixes the date, time and place of the panchayat meeting which is generally held in the village in which the case arises. If it is a case of dispute between the two villages, the meeting is held on their boundary. The *Pande* informs all the villagers about the date, time and place of the meeting as also about the case which is going to be taken up here. The parties to the dispute are expected to come fully prepared.

On the appointed day, representatives from all the villages under the *parha* turn up. The Munda, Pahan and Mahato of all the villages must attend. *Charpoys* are kept for them to sit on. The *parha* Raja occupies the central cot. On one side of the Raja sits the Pande and on the other, the Dewan. Other office-bearers take the seats indicated for them. Members of the village, in which the panchayat meets, sit on the ground. When the meeting is declared open by the Raja, the Dewan explains the purpose and makes the people familiar with the nature of the case and identification of the parties. If it is an appeal, the complainant is asked to state the case himself. In the case of a social offence, like breach of sexual taboo, the complaint is filed by the village headman. When the complaint has been heard the defence has its say. If the accused admits his guilt, the panchayat begins deliberations on the nature of the punishment to be awarded. But if he does not plead guilty, further examination is conducted. Witnesses may also be examined. Any office-bearer can ask questions or seek clarifications from either party. The report of enquiry by the Dewan, oral examination of the parties, and supporting evidence in the form of documentary or other materials and testimony of the witnesses, all are considered to frame the charge and the award of punishment. In case the validity of the charge is not established, a small committee called *gutu sabha* conducts further enquiry in camera. The *parha* Raja can not be a member of this Sabha. The *gutu sabha* then reports its findings to the *parha* Raja. If the committee is unanimous in its verdict and the *parha* Raja agrees with it, the question of punishment is discussed. If the committee is divided in its opinion and the *parha* Raja is of a different view, deliberations continue until unanimity is arrived at not only about the establishment of the guilt but also about the nature of punishment. The final verdict is given by the Raja who also gives reasons for the verdict. The verdict is binding on both the parties. A person who disobeys is liable to be excommunicated. The expenditure for the feast on the meeting of the *parha* Panch are incurred by both or either of the two parties as the case may be.

In case the disputing parties belong to two different *parhas* and subsequently to two different clans a joint meeting of the respective *parhas* is held to decide the case. The head of the *parha* in which the complaint has been lodged calls the meeting of his *parha*, to which representatives of the complainant's *parha* are invited to participate in the deliberations. Sometimes, if the parties are not satisfied with the decision of the *parha* panchayat an appeal is filed with the *bais parha*. In many instances, these days, the cases falling in the jurisdiction of *parha*, or the appeals from the *parha* panchayat are taken to the statutory panchayat, police station or court of law, as the case may be.

In the Khutkatti area there is no standing body of the *parha* panchayat. For deciding disputes over the burial of the dead in the *sasan*, pre-marital relations, adultery, and excommunication or readmission into the tribe, the Munda and Pahan of 10-15 adjoining villages hold a meeting of the panchayat in the complainants' village to dispense social justice and punish the wrong doer. They select a chairman and secretary to conduct the meeting. The proceedings of the panchayat are similar to that of *parha* panchayat in the Bhuinhari area. The expenditure on feasting the panchayat is borne by the complainant. After the deliberations are over, the *parha Panchayat* is dissolved. Again on another occasion a fresh panchayat is constituted to deal with a specific social offence. The number of villages taking part in the panchayat this time may differ and may not be the same as on a previous occasion.

With the coming up of the statutory panchayat, police stations and courts of law, the significance of the *parha* panchayat has been undermined. Its jurisdiction extends only over social offences connected with the breaches of tribal custom. For theft, assault, murder, disputes over property etc. people generally go to courts of law. This is because traditional socio-political institutions and leadership are gradually weakening and do not command the obedience of the emerging tribal elite. In some areas though the *parhas* are in decay, some like Guria Parha, Kandulna Parha, Topno Parha, Bhengra Parha etc. are quite active. Moreover, the educated Munda of the Bhuinhari area are making successful efforts to rejuvenate and revive the *parha* and modify it to suit the present political situation.

The *parha* panchayats in different areas still hold their occasional meetings to settle disputes related to social offences. The *parha* officials are respected in their respective areas. Among the emerging tribal leaders Sukh Ram has made constant efforts to earn a good name for the Bhengra Parha. The *parha* still acts as an indigenous political organisation of the Munda and saviour of the people against the exploitation of modern courts of law.

Guria Parha

Guria Parha comprises 16 villages of the Guria clan. Of these, Koenara is called Maharaja village, Kalet-Raja village, Kamra-Barlal, Tapkara Dewan village and so on. Guria Parha with its headquarters at Koenara was a vital force in the area due to the dynamic personality of Mangra Pahan who was the Maharaja of the *parha*. A man of strong will and domineering nature; Mangra was widely respected over the entire region. He wielded great authority and was the repository of all the ancient wisdom of the Munda. His death in 1957 left a great void.

After his death Mansidh Munda of Koenara was made the Parha Maharaja. On his death, Paulus Guria of Kalet was made the acting Parha Maharaja though he has not yet been ceremonially accorded the status of Maharaja.

Office-bearers of the *parha* are hereditary. It was found that the officials such as the Maharaja, Raja, Dewan or Pandey etc. were either the Munda, Pahan of Mahto of the Maharaja, Dewan or Pande village respectively. In case there is no direct male descendent of the office-bearer or the direct heir is incapable of holding the office, the new successor is selected from among his agnates. The new Maharaja in a *parha* is crowned by the head of the *Bais parha* and the Maharaja in turn performs the ceremonial function for the new office-bearer in his *parha*.

Along with the Guria clan, Mundas of other clans live in the villages of Guria Parha. These are Topno, Dodrai, Horo, Kandulna, Barjo, Mundu and Aind. The number of families of other clans is very small as compared to the dominant clan of the *parha*. Mundas of a clan, other than the dominant one, do not have the Bhuinhari right in the village and the clan *sasan*. But for all practical purposes they come under the jurisdiction of the Guria Parha. Similarly, the non-Munda tribals and non-tribals living in the *parha* area are tried by the Guria Parha in case of breach of tribal custom.

Guria Parha still holds some power and decides cases related to social offences. Even the government courts respect its decision. During the 1940's Lathu Sao of Tapkara took a Munda girl of the Guria clan as his wife. The *parha panch* held its meeting in which they excommunicated the girl and her parents and Lathu Sao was fined Rs. 300 for breaking the rule of tribal endogamy. Lathu Sao filed a case against Guria Parha's decision in S.D.O's court at Khunti. The then S.D.O. Khunti visited Tapkara and held talks with the Guria Parha officials. He was convinced that Lathu Sao was guilty of violating the norm of tribal endogamy. He upheld the decision of the *parha*. Lathu Sao had to give Rs. 300 as fine. The money was utilised for purification of the excommunicated family of the Munda girl. For purification an outcast is made to drink water sanctified with the blood of the sacrificed white goat or hen along with a piece of copper or a few *tulsi* leaves put into the water. This is followed by feasting and drinking. Lathu Sao was allowed to marry the Munda girl. The girl was later ex-communicated from the Munda tribe.

About a decade ago the Lohra of village Omda in Singhbhum requested Paulus Guria, the Maharaja of Guria Parha, to purify and take them back into the Munda fold. The claim was made on a popular belief that in the beginning the Lohra belonged to the Munda tribe, but as their occupation was that of blacksmith and they worked with leather bellows, they were considered of low ritual status and therefore the Munda had stopped all social intercourse with them. Paulus Guria organised a meeting of the Guria Parha in Omda. The function was attended by one thousand Mundas. About Rs. 3000 were spent on purification and feasting. The assembled Munda were divided among themselves on the question of readmission of the Lohra into the tribal fold. Half of them boycotted the meeting while the rest, led by Paulus Guria, agreed to the admission of the Lohra to the Munda tribe and enjoyed food and drink with the latter. Those who participated in this function were outcasts for all practical purposes by the rest of the Munda community. Those who boycotted the function filed a case in Chaibasa court with the help of Kalyan Guria against Paulus Guria and his followers. After a year's hearing the two groups reached a compromise. The Lohra remained Lohra due to evidence of settlement records where they were referred to as Lohra. Paulus and his followers who had eaten along with Lohras were taken back into the Munda fold and purified in a meeting of the *bais parha* held at Pakra in 1970.

Elsewhere (Sachhidananda, 1968 : 128-132) a number of cases have been cited which were brought up before the Guria Parha on different occasions. These were related to breach of incest taboo between close relatives, between members of the same clan and between a Munda and a non-Munda, extra-marital relations, stealing, and appeals from *hatu* panchayat regarding the position of property and charge of fornication. In almost all the cases the offenders obeyed the verdict of the *parha* panchayat. Punishments awarded for sexual offences were fines, excommunication, and even depriving the offender of his Bhuinhari right and right in the clan *sasan* (for clan incest) etc. For stealing, a fine was imposed on the offender. The money obtained from fines was used for the communal feast. Breach of sexual taboos invites automatic sanctions as a result of which the offender and his family are polluted. The *parha* panchayat simply puts its seal by excommunicating such persons and families so to sâve rest of the society from pollution. A part of the fine obtained from the accused is used for purification and readmission of those temporarily polluted. A Munda girl who marries a non-Munda is never taken back into the tribal fold.

Ganjhu of Dimbukel while on his way home from Tapkara Bazar took away Tiru's plough from his field. The matter was referred to the *parha.* Ganjhu denied the charge but there were people who had seen him taking away the plough and hiding it at a secret place within his village boundary. His guilt was proved beyond doubt. The panchayat sentenced him to pay a fine of Rs. 100 or to give as much paddy as would be required to hold the plough in question in an upright position with the heavy end up. The fine was heavy because the Munda consider the plough to be sacred. The theft had aroused their religious sentiment. Ganjhu began to cry. In view of Ganjhu's poverty the fine was reduced to Rs. 50 which he agreed to pay.

During the year 1974, Salomi Kandulna of Derang Churdag in Guria Parha fell in love with and conceived through Hardugan Guria of the same village. As they belonged to two different clans marriage between them was feasible. But Hardugan did not want to marry her. He tried abortion but failed. On finding that Hardugan wanted to desert her, she filed an application with the Derang *hatu* Panchayat asking for justice. The *hatu* panchayat met two days later to consider the matter. Hardugan's father did not agree with Salomi's charge against him and threatened the panchayat members with dire consequences in case they favoured Salomi's cause. The panchayat then referred the case to the Maharaja of Guria Parha requesting him to look into it. The latter directed Parha Dewan Masih Prakash, Suleman and Jakiria Guria to make enquiries in this regard and report back to him. The Dewans, after a month, reported to the Raja that the enquiry could not be completed because Hardugan Guria did not present himself before the investigating officials in spite of repeated notices. They requested the Raja to act as he wished. The Raja then ordered them to call a meeting of the *parha Panchas* and inform all concerned to attend it. He asked them to meet him for necessary discussions.

A meeting of the Guria Parha was held under the chairmanship of Parha Raja Paulus Guria at village Derang Churdag to consider Salomi Kandulna's case. The meeting was attended by 129 persons representing 14 out of 16 villages of Guria Parha. Among them were five invitees from the Kandulna Parha. Before the start of the proceedings, Dharam Prakash Guria, father of Hardugan submitted an application requesting that his son could not present himself in the meeting so the case of Salomi Kandulna should not be taken up. The application was rejected. The proceedings of the meeting started and Paulus Guria explained the nature of the case and the parties involved to the panchayat members.

First Salomi Kandulna was examined by the Barlal, John Guria and then cross-examined by Lal Kalyan Guria, and Raja Paulus Guria. Salomi Pahanain of Kalet was also examined as witness. She was approached by the parties for abortion. As Hardugan was absent his father Dharam Prakash Guria who was present in the meeting, accepted his guilt and gave a written statement to the *sabha* in this regard. The Chairman, Paulus Guria read Dharam Prakash's statement for the *parha sabha* members. A *gutu sabha* of the Munda, Pahan, Mahto, and parents of the two parties was held in camera to decide the verdict. The Chairman read the award to the members. A record of the proceedings of the meeting was prepared and signed by all the members.

It was decided to impose a fine on both the parties as detailed below :

	Hardugan Guria	Salomi Kandulna
1.	Rice—2 maunds	Rice—One maund and 20 seers
2.	Pulses—15 seers	Pulses—7½ seers
3.	One pig	One goat
4.	Rs. 30 in cash	Rs. 15 in cash

The fine was utilized for a feast to the members of the *parha* panchayat.

As Salomi had already borne a child by Hardugan she

would be given a small piece of cultivable land from Dharam Prakash's landed property, for maintenance for three years. In 1975 Salomi was living with her child in her village.

Topno Parha

Topno Parha is largest among the *Bais Parha*. There are 44 villages in its jurisdiction. It stretches from Kotbo, Kamdara to Baski. Mundas belonging to as many as 12 other clans reside in the villages under Topno Parha. Such clans are Tiru, Guria, Barla, Horo, Kandulna, Surin, Samad, Baba, Kerketta, Aind, Sanga, and Dungdung. Kotbo is the seat of Topno Parha Raja and Anand Masih Topno is the Raja. Bamni is the Dewan village and Hardugan Topno is Dewan. Urmi, Marcha and Raikera are Lal villages. Kanekera and Pokla are Chamarbardaz villages. The Kunwar is from Kamdara village. Turundu is Bhandari village. Pande belongs to Kuda and Kurmur. Sonbir is Sipahi village. Torpa and Kulda are Thakur villages. Musadi belongs to Banabira and Kartha is from Buruhatu. These villages were established by the ancestors of the respective office-bearers.

The function of these office bearers is as follows. The Raja is the permanent President of the *parha*. Lal is the younger brother of the Parha Raja. The Dewan is the public prosecutor, Kartha the official purifier, Pandey the writer, Kotwar or Daroga the police officer, Sipahi the constable, Pan khwas the officer-in-charge reception, Ghatwar the official sacrificer, Ghaskatta the man who arranges for fodder for officers' horses, and Chamarbardaz is the man who waves a fan over the head of the Maharaja.

These *parha* officials are hereditary and belong to Munda, Mahto or Pahan khut of Topno clan. Raja is supposed to belong to Munda khut, however, now a Munda of either of three khuts (but from the family of the village headman) can succeed to the coveted office of the Raja. At present there are two Rajas at Kotbo. Anand Masih belongs to Munda khut and Jura Mahto to Mahto khut of the village. The members of clans other than Topno residing in the Topno Parha villages do not have Bhuinhari right in the land in their residential village. The Bhuinhari rights of members of the Topno clan of Kotbo who had migrated to Sambalpur long back and who returned to their home village after the land settlement, were not restored. In village Ramtolya, members of Hor kili have erected *sasan diri* in the *sasan* of the Topno clan. The members of the Topno clan of that village have instituted a case against the Horo family in the Topno Parha. Samuel Topno of Marcha, who has changed his clan from Horo to Topno, does not enjoy the Bhuinhari right to land.

As the Munda of Topno clan multiplied with the passing of time, they dispersed far and wide. For the purpose of administration Topno Parha is divided into three parts : (1) Lopar Ghat —Kotbo to Baski and Raja at Kotbo, (2) Majhi Ghat—Koel to Bano, and (3) Het Ghat—Bano to Cuttack (Orissa) and Raja at Banai (Orissa). The Raja at Kotbo is also known as the Maharaja. Parha Raja Eliazer Topno of Majhi Ghat and Luthar Topno of Hat Ghat send annual reports of their activities to the Parha Maharaja at Kotbo.

Soy Parha

There are about 30 villages under the Soy Parha. These villages are Balgi, Gulu (Parha Raja and Dewan villages respectively), Rumtkel, Sankuteur, Kurki, Bande, Sokoye, Koyangsar, Basilemha, Karangka, Kumhardih, Hatu Mundi, Mamail, Konoa, Hesabera, Gompila, Unukuda, Mahraora, Dilisud, Umbua, Chatakpur, Rungduh, Habo (Pande), Lota, Uskeya (Bar Lal), Konari (Bhandari), Sunura (Thakur) etc. Mangra Soy of Balgi is the Parha Raja, Josoph Soy of Gulu is Dewan and Daud Soy of Habo is Pande. In the villages under Soy Parha some families of other clans live together with the members of the dominant Soy clan. These other clans are Bhengra, Bodra, Barjo, Hemrom, Guria, Topno, Aind, Kandulna, Dodrai, Sanga, Purti and Kongari. The Mundas belonging to these clans are tenants of the Bhuinhars of the Soy clan.

The Soy Parha does not command considerable hold over the *parha* villages these days. Earlier the *parha* officials used to hold the meeting of the Parha Sabha every month. In 1975 it was observed that the *parha* had not met for the last three years. Before that the *parha* meeting was held to decide the issues relating to social offences.

Bhengra Parha

Angarabari is the headquarters of the *parha* and Indrias Bhengra is its Raja. Though earlier the *parha* had lost its importance, but for the last few years, it has been activised under the leadership of Sukh Ram Munda. Sukh Ram Munda belongs to Dorma village in Bhengra Parha. Though he does not hold any office in the Parha Sabha, he works through the Parha Sabha. He is notorious for awarding harsh punishment to the offenders brought to the Parha Sabha meeting. Social offences against the tribal custom are dealt with severely.

Regular monthly meetings of the *parha* are held under the chairmanship of the Parha Raja. A fund has been raised in the Parha by the traditional method of collecting one *sup* (winnowing fan) of paddy from each and every household of the *parha*. Those who need are loaned paddy from this on nominal interest.

Cases relating to breach of social norms like commensality with forbidden castes and sexual offences are tried in the regular *Parha* meetings. The offenders are awarded heavy punishments such as fine, thrashing and excommunication. Sukh Ram and the Bhengra Parha are criticised by others for harsh sentences in dealing with social offences. The Bais Parha Sabha also resented Sukh Ram's severe attitude towards the offenders. Many among those who were tried by Sukh Ram through Bhengra Parha and were awarded heavy punishment, have instituted legal cases against Sukh Ram in the S.D.O's court at Khunti. Once a young boy and a girl of the Bhengra clan of a village were found to have had premarital sex relations. They were ordered to report in the Parha Sabha. There the boy was given a heavy thrashing. Both of them were asked to undress and lick each other's genitals. In another case, where a Bhengra girl was found having relationship with a Hindu boy, the latter was fined Rs. 1000. The boy's parents filed a case in Khunti court against this decision. Other tribal leaders in this area do not agree with Sukh Ram's thesis of bringing about tribal solidarity and unity among the Mundas through severe measures. His efforts at boundary maintenance have affected the relations with non-tribal communities. Yet Sukh Ram's contribution to revive the Bhengra Parha cannot be denied. He has tried his best to save the tribals of the area from exploitation especially in the weekly markets. A weekly market is held at Dorma under his control and supervision. He has opened a general store in the name of Bhengra Parha where the tribals get kerosene oil, sugar, grains, chemical fertilizer etc. at controlled rates. He organises a *jatra* every year at Dorma village under the Bhengra Parha where tribals from far and near come in colourful dress and enjoy dancing and singing. He has given a decaying institution a shot in the arm in the form of new functions and activities which are extr emely useful.

Sanga Parha

The Sanga Parha of Birhu deals with all serious cases which are not ordinarily settled by the *hatu* panchayat. All types of breaches of the rules of clan exogamy tribal endogamy are referred to the *pahra* panchayat. The panchayat selects its own Parha Raja. The Raja is the executive head of that clan in a particular area. He is the person on whose authority a *parha* meeting is called. The Parha Raja operates with the help of advice of the members of the *parha* panchayat. The *parha* organisation, however, in Birhu has grown weak. In early days the *parha* was said to be just and effective but gradually bad elements crept in and people lost interest in the affairs of the *parha*. The decisions of the *parha* no longer carry weight and its meetings are poorly attended.

FORMATION OF THE BAIS PARHA

Parha Rajas of different *parhas* and the educated Mundas in the Bhuinhari area have succeeded in bringing the various Parha Sabhas under the umbrella. The new organization differs from the traditional *parha* organisation in nature, scope and functions. It is based on the elective principle, in contrast to the old hereditary principle. The area of operation of this organisation extends beyond the old limits of Chotanagpur. An attempt has been made to build up a pan-Munda organisation thus widening the horizon of identity. It aims at working for the socio-economic development of the Munda and creating a fellow feeling with the neighbours. These new functions are political rather than judicial in nature and make the Bais Parhas distinct from the traditional *parha* organisation which till now tried only cases of social and sexual offences.

The Munda in the Bhuinhari area speak of 22 original clans of the Munda and for administrative purposes the uniclan villages were grouped into Bais Parha each *parha* named after a clan. The names of the Bais Parhas which are active at present are as follows: The name of the village to which the Parha Raja belongs is considered the original home of the clan and is given in the brackets : (1) Topno (Katbo), (2) Bhengra (Angra-bari), (3) Kongari (Garai Digri), (4) Guria (Kalet), (5) Kandulna (Khatanga), (6) Sanga (Birhu), (7) Soy (Balgi), (8) Barla (Sohgi), (9) Bage (Loykera), (10) Baba (Bala), (11) Karketta (Bangru), (12) Samad (Kanarowa), (13) Horo (Chalagi), (14) Lugun (Jarakel), (15) Dahanga (Tamba Harasuku), (16) Bodra (Latauli), (17) Aind (Echa), (18) Hemrom, (19) Surin (Pusa toli), (20) Tiru (Tirtus), (21) Herenj (Muchchia), and (22) Tani (Takutoli).

Several years ago, in a joint meeting of the different *parhas* at Pithuria, Barla Parha was chosen the chief of the *parhas*. In 1925, another meeting of the Bais Parha was held at Tapkara in which Topno Parha was chosen as its chief. Bhengra Parha was made the Secretary of the Bais Parha. In 1946, the Bais Parha met at Pithuria (Sutiambe) and elected Guria Parha as its head. Mangra Pahan (Raja of Guria Parha) was elected the Parha Maharaja of Bais Parha. In the late fifties after the death of Mangra Maharaja, at a meeting of the Bais Parha at Marcha, Paulus Guria (Kalet) was made the acting Maharaja of the Bais Parha. However, he has not yet been confirmed and given *pan-pugree*. After few years again the Bais Parha met at Marcha. The constitution of the Bais Parha was amended.

A Parha Raja Mahasabha of the Bais Parha Rajas was held in May 1970 in the village Pakra. The following Parha Rajas attended the meeting. There were more than one representative from Topno, Suren, Kandulna and Dangwar Parhas, because these parhas have further sub-divided to facilitate administration. Each new unit is headed by a Parha Raja.

Name of Parha Raja	Village	P.O.	District
1. Paulus Guria	Kalet	Barda	Ranchi
2. Imil Kongari	Digri	Marcha	,,
3. Junas Kandulna	Khatanga	Tangarkela	,,

Name of Parha Raja	Village	P.O.	District
4. Anand Masih Topno	Kotbo	Kamdara	Ranchi
5. Prabhu Dayal Suren	Kusumtoli	Kurkura	,,
6. Prabhu Dayal Bage	Loykera	Rampur	,,
7. Imil Dangwar	Harad Suku	Sodu	,,
8. Paulus Dengwar	Baki	Baki	,,
9. Esahak Dang	Kereya	Kereya	Sundergarh
10. Daniel Jojo	Orga	Orga	Ranchi
11. Silas Lugun	Jarakel	Bano	,,
12. Soma Samed	Kanarua	Bano	,,
13. Esahak Horo	Chalagi	Jariagarh	,,
14. Siril Barla	Sohagi	Mehugaon	,,
15. Gabriel Aind	Lappa	Jariagarh	,,
16. Marcos Sanga	Birhu	Khunti	,,
17. Paulus Karketta	Surhu	Kamdara	,,
18. Madho Singh Herenj	Muchchia	Karo	Sundergraph
19. Abrahm Topno	Janum Biran	Birmittar	,,
20. John Tani	Tukutoli	Rai Boga	,,
21. Sarika Suren	Kinvua	Barsaloya	Ranchi
22. Iliazer Topno	Pangloya	Lachragarh	,,
23. Indrias Bhengra	Angrabari	Bichna	,,
24. Juel Kandulna	Buru Esgi	Jitu Toli	,,
25. Turi Taromda	Marangdih	Khunti	,,
26. Silas Baba	Bala	Karra	,,
27. Bhutka Manaki	Badhia	Barsaloya	,,

The Bais Parha Mahasabha holds the meeting of its excutive on last Friday every month. The last Bais Parha Mahasabha general meeting was held at Pakra in 1974. Prabhu Dayal Bage was elected as the Chairman, Gabriel Aind of Lapra as Vice-Chairman, Masclant Topno of Kotbo as Secretary and Gunja Aind, Elisser Topno, Prabhu Dayal Kandulna, Ignis Bhengra as members. A regular fund has been started with monthly contribution of Rs. 5 from member *parhas*. A written constitution has been prepared and an effort is being made to register the Bais Parha organisation. Masclant Topno, Secretary of Bais Parha is the moving force behind the Bais Parha organisation.

The executive authority of this higher political organisation rests in the hands of Parha Mahasabha or Parha Hadri. Parha Mahasabha has an executive body constituted from among the representatives of the member *parhas*. The traditional political organisations like Hatu Sabha and Parha Sabha are being modernised to suit the social, economic and political changes taking place in the tribal area and the country. An effort has been made to incorporate modern democratic values and strengthen the existing traditional institutions so as to promote the common welfare of the tribals. A written constitution of the Bias Parha has been prepared for promoting the co-existence and interplay of the traditional and modern values and norms in the context of *parha* organisation.

Constitution

The organisation will be named as Chotanagpur, Assam, Bhutan, Andaman, Nicobar, Siam and Assam's Munda Kili Parha Sabha. The short name will be Munda Parha Sabha.

Objectives

1. To ameliorate the social conditions of the Mundas and to work for the promotion of agriculture, trade and industry in the area.
2. To work for the preservation of traditional monuments, relics, rights, language etc.
3. To work for progress in the field of education, health, living standard, character etc.
4. To create friendly relations with the neighbours and to follow the principle of peace, non-violence and patriotism towards the nation.

Rules and Regulations of Hatu Sabha Organisation

The Hatu Sabha will be formed by the Munda, Mahto and Pahan khuts of the dominant clans having at least three-fourths of the village population belonging to this clan. It will have administrative and judicial powers in the village. It will be responsible to the Parha Sabha of its clan. The Hatu Sabha will be constituted by the representatives chosen for every 50 persons or more than its half from the various khuts in the village. The representative of the Munda khut will be the Sabhapati.

Parha Sabha

Various Hatu Sabhas of the same clan will together form a Parha Sabha and elect a Parha Raja among themselves. The Parha Sabha will take care of the administration, security and progress of the *Parha* villages. It will be responsible to the Bais Parha Sabha. There may be more than one administrative area in a Kili Parha, each will have its own Parha Raja and will be responsible to the senior Parha Raja of its clan. Each Hatu Sabha will send one representative per 500 or more than half of it for the Parha Sabha. Sabhapati and Mantri will be the office-bearers of the *parha* and will be chosen from among the members. The Parha Sabha will be constituted for five years after which a new Parha Sabha will be formed. There will be at least one representative each from members of other clans residing in a *parha* area.

Parha Hadri

Constitution : The Parha Sabha, which is already functioning, will be re-named as Parha Hadri. It will look into the functioning of different Parhas and work for the progress of tribe as a whole. The Parha Hadri will be constituted with five representatives including the Parha Raja from each Parha. The office bearers of the Parha Hadri will be Sabhapati, Mantri, Khajanchi (treasurer) and two members elected for every 5000 Hatu Sabha members. The Parha Hadri will meet twice a year. It will be elected for five years.

Powers : (1) The Parha Hadri has the power to allow its members to establish or cut off relations with other friendly communities, organisations and institutions in the area for the welfare of the Munda society.

(2) The Parha Hadri can look into the internal administration of the member Parha Sabhas. If a member Parha Sabha does not conform to the rules and regulations and the orders of the Parha Hadri, the latter can punish the offending Parha Sabha by stopping monetary aid and depriving it of its powers.

(3) The Parha Hadri will hear appeals from the Parha Sabha. The appeal has to be made through the proper channel.

(4) The Parha Hadri will safeguard the social customs and norms in Munda society. It will instruct the Mundas not to

adopt customs and norms as are different from and militate against the Munda way of life.

(5) The Parha Hadri will arrange for the publication of informative books about Munda culture.

(6) It can form relevant committees for tackling various issues. It will have to make an annual budget and allocate amounts for each *parha*.

(7) It will formulate an economic policy and take up the responsibility of assisting the poor students for higher education, digging of drinking water wells, opening of dispensaries etc.

Office-bearers : (1) Office-bearers of the Parha Hadri are Parha Maharaja (Sabhapati), Pande, Secretary or Mantri and Bhandari, Treasurers or Khajanchi. They will be elected for five years through a vote in a regular meeting of the Hadri. They will be eligible for re-election for another term. They will be entitled to salaries fixed by the Parha Hadri. No other member will be paid any salary. The Parha Maharaja will always be elected from among the Parha Rajas of member *parhas*. The various officers of the Parha Hadri will be elected on the second afternoon of first Hadri Sabha in the election year. The newly elected officers will take charge of their offices immediately after the meeting.

(2) The Parha Maharaja will be the Sabhapati or Chairman in all meetings and will conduct the installation ceremony of other officials. The Parha Maharaja will see that the Parha Hadri and Parha Sabha function properly. Only after he has put his signature, a document will be valid. In case the Parha Maharaja is sick, an acting Parha Maharaja will be elected.

(3) The Mantri will keep a record of all the documents of the Hadri and Parishad. He will be responsible for notifying the members one month in advance of the place, date and time of the Hadri meeting. In special meetings he will inform the members only 15 days in advance.

(4) The Bhandari will keep accounts of the Hadri and present statements of accounts in the regular Hadri and Parishad meetings. Sanction of money for expenditure will be made with the signatures of the Parha Maharaja and Mantri. It case of the death of an office-bearer of Parha Hadri or his

resignation or suspension, the *parha* will nominate another officer till the next regular Hadri meeting when another person will be elected to the office to complete the remaining tenure of the Hadri. Any official, not abiding by the rules and regulations, can be suspended by the two-thirds majority vote of the Parha Hadri members.

Parha Parishad: (1) The Parha Maharaja, Mantri and Treasurer of the Parha Hadri will also act as the officers of the Parha Parishad. Other representatives from member *parhas* will be elected such that the *parha* having less than 5000 adult population will send one representative. Those having 10,000 or less will have two representatives and those with 15,000 three representatives. In case a *parha* sends two or more representatives, at least one of them should be the Parha Raja.

(2) The Parha Parishad cannot meet more than twice a year. It must meet at least once a year. This will be the annual meeting. In this meeting the working of different *parhas* is to be reviewed. The budget to be presented to the Parha Hadri for the coming year will also be discussed at this meeting.

(3) The executive body of Parha Parishad will have 8 elected members in addition to the Parha Maharaja, Mantri and the Treasurer. This executive body will decide issues of immediate importance in its meetings but this body cannot replace the general body of the Parha Parishad.

(4) If a member of the Parishad dies or is expelled from the Parha Sabha or is absent in two subsequent regular meetings of the Parishad, a new member will be taken from the same *parha* to replace him for the remaining period of the Parishad.

(5) The Parha Parishad will look into the administration of Parha Sabha according to following rules : (a) The Parha Parishad has the right to direct the Parha Sabhas to act according to the rules and regulations laid by the Parha Hadri and Parishad, (b) Parha Parishad can investigate into the affairs of the Parha Sabhas on a written request of the concerned *parha*, and (c) It has the right to warn the erring Parha Sabhas to mend their ways.

Representatives : (1) The Mantri of Parha Hadri is required to prepare a list of representatives to the Parha Hadri prior to every regular meeting. He will receive from each Parha Sabha the list of its members to Parha Hadri duly signed by the Parha

Raja and Mantri two weeks before the date of the meeting.

(2) A separate file for each *parha* will be maintained and no change in the list of representatives can be made without the permission of the concerned Parha Raja. The Maharaja will prepare an annual report and present it in the Parha Hadri meeting for discussion.

(3) The Maharaja can participate in a debate leaving his chair, but some other member should take the seat of Sabhapati during that period.

(4) In case there is no unanimity among the members over an issue, the Parha Maharaja will ask for their votes by raising hands or standing in favour or against it. The Chairman has the right to give a casting vote only.

Amendments : In a meeting the members and the representatives have the right to express their views only once. The Chairman's permission is required before speaking every time. Invitees can speak with permission of the Chairman. The representatives will stand while speaking.

Right to Vote : Each member and representative has the right to vote on all issues, except those relating to himself. Votes will be signified by raising hands. In cases where there are no specific rules for deciding the issue, it will be decided by a majority vote.

This brief survey of the functioning of the traditional Munda political institutions reveals their capacity to adjust to needs of new situations. From the *tola* organization limited to a small hamlet of the village, the Munda have come to set up an organization which even transcends the boundaries of Chotanagpur and brings into its ambit not only social and judicial matters as in the *parha* set-up, but also matters of education, poverty and development. Since the Parha Mahasabha and its executive organ *Parha Hadri* derive their sanction from the traditional *parha* organization, they command universal respect and legitimacy. Its objectives and functions are, however, modern. Thus, it has a better chance of success. It is an amalgam of tradition and modernity and in this the Church has played an important part. This is an evidence of the genius of the Munda to come to terms with the spirit of modernization.

10

SOCIO-POLITICAL MOVEMENTS IN THE MUNDA COUNTRY

SINCE THE END of the eighteenth century the Munda country has witnessed a number of popular socio-political movements. Before that the Munda lived in relative isolation in the hills and forests of Chotanagpur, where they had developed a polity well suited to their social and economic needs. In the nineteenth century, however, Chotanagpur witnessed two simultaneous processes, viz., the disintegration of rural communities due to the imposition of the zamindari system of land-tenure on tribal organisation and the introduction of a cash economy. These processes had far-reaching repercussions on the tribal society that surfaced in the form of a large number of uprisings and movements.

These movements in the Jharkhand region were restorative rebellions aimed at driving out the British and the Hindu zamindars installed by the British administration, and restoring earlier autonomy and social relations. Some of these tribal uprisings had a religious colour, yet they strived for the liberation of the tribals from the yoke of up-country alien landlords. A sore point of tribal grievance was provided by the forest laws and revenue levies which adversely affected the economy of the tribals.

All the revolts seem to have occurred under conditions of relative deprivation, that is, the deprivations considered outrageous in comparison to the past or to the condition of others in the present exploitative system. All of them embodied ideas of freedom from undue economic exploitation or deprivation or some form of collective independence from a domination conceived of as foreign and unjustified; and of a just social order sanctioned by some religious faith or tradition. They considered intervention by the British rulers and the Hindu landlords as an affront to the autonomy of their economy, culture and social organisation. The tribals of this area believed that they were never under any kind of dominance before the advent of the British. The very idea of being ruled by an alien people (the Britishers or the Hindu zamindars) was not acceptable to these people even if the rulers ensured better living standards and other comforts of life. Thus, these movements aimed at the re-establishment of a traditional polity with marginal changes.

With outsiders from Bengal and Bihar, ignorant of Munda customs, the language and land tenure system, in all subordinate government services, and with alien landlords ruling over the villages, the Mundas suffered a great deal. Signs of unrest among the tribal population all over Chotanagpur were evident enough. The disturbances in Tamar continued from 1789 to 1795. This first revolt against the British was that of the landed gentry, supported by the Munda, Manki and Ghatwals between 1795—1800. It was against the revenue regulations of Lord Cornwallis. The attitude of the Chotanagpur Maharaja was that of watchful silence, but the alien Thikadars did not lend any support to it (S. P. Sinha, 1964 : 17). The agrarian troubles came to ahead in the early decades of the nineteenth century and were so much further worsened by failure of crops and famine, that the Mundas in their despair resorted to violence. They had no other choice than to fight openly for their ancient rights. The Mundas rebelled against their landlords several times between 1789 to 1832, mainly in 1811, 1819-20, and again in 1832.

KOL INSURRECTION

Around the year 1817, the Munda country was brought under the direct administration of the East India Company as part of the Ramgarh district and the Maharaja of Chotanagpur was deprived of his position as a tributary chief. The number of jagirdars swelled with time and their oppression knew no limits. In 1820 the Kols revolted against this oppression. The leaders of this revolt were two Mundas, Rugdeo or

Roodan and Konta. The immediate cause of the revolt was that in the year 1819, there was a great drought in the Pargana Tamar, and the Munda with their universal belief in witchcraft assembled to locate those responsible for the calamity, and pointed out Tribhuvan Manki as the culprit. His son was killed and his house burnt. A crusade against the alien Thikadars and Jagirdars was proclaimed. The revolt was put down with the help of large scale military operations.

The second insurrection broke out in 1831-32. The immediate cause of the revolt in Sonepur was the grant made by the Maharaja's brother of a number of villages in Pargana Sonepur over the heads of the Mankis and the Mundas, to certain Muslims, Sikhs and Hindus. It was a crusade against these foreign landlords. It was crushed by the British forces by March 1832. In 1833, Chotanagpur proper and other adjoining areas were together formed into a non-regulation area known as South-West-Frontier Agency. The system of Zamindari policy was introduced. Captain Wilkinson was appointed the first Agent to the Governor-General. To pacify the Mundas and Mankis of the Panch Parganas and the Manki Pattis, he granted them confirmatory *pattas*, confirming their titles and fixing the rent for ever. Afterwards the fight between the outsiders and the tribals of Chotanagpur took another form. The non-tribals sought the aid of the police and the court of law to suppress the innocent tribals. In 1854 the South-West-Frontier Agency was wound up and Chotanagpur was made a non-regulation division of Bengal. However, these measures did not bring relief to the Munda and the pressure of the landlords under the cover and protection of the British administration became increasingly stifling.

In their sad plight, the Mundas turned in great number, especially after the mutiny of 1857, to the German Evangelical Lutheran Mission. The missionaries promised help, but they were warned by the then Government not to fight for their cause. Thus they withdrew themselves from active participation in the tribal struggle. The Mundas, on the other hand, felt themselves betrayed by the missionaries. Failing to receive adequate missionary support, they gave up Christianity in thousands and induced many others to sever all connections with them.

The better educated among these apostates, often trained by the missionaries, now formed various groups and associations looking for ways and means for achieving justice and gaining redress. They presented a dangerous potential for rebellion. They only lacked a gifted leader to unite them and lead them into concerted action (Fuchs, S., 1965 : 26).

After the Kol insurrection was crushed and the leaders surrendered in March 1832, the middlemen, who were expelled during the all out crusade against them, returned and avenged themselves on the Mundas. The greatest disturbance of peasant proprietary tenure took place and many tribals were forced to leave the country. It was this class of uprooted Mundas who constituted the core of the Sardari movement for forty years starting in the late 1850's (Ray-Burman, B.K. 1974 : 46).

SARDARI LARAI

From the middle of the nineteenth century the presence of Christian missionaries came to be felt. The spread of Christianity gave a new dimension to the agrarian question. The struggle against alien landlords escalated. Many tribals had accepted Christianity but not on account of a quest of the spirit. Their objective was merely to take the help of missionaries in their struggle against the oppression of the landlords. They expected active help from the missionaries in giving them succour from the oppressions of the landlords and the police. They believed that the day of deliverance was at hand. In 1855-57 some landlords who had been perturbed by the spread of Christianity began to give trouble to the new converts. One of the Thikadars had cruelly beaten up a missionary named Hertzog. Some of the landlords had forcibly harvested the crops of tribal cultivators. During the Mutiny, it was these landlords who led the attacks on the Christian Churches. Out of 56 villages, Christians in two villages alone were safe. The property of many of the converts was destroyed and many who had fled their villages on account of fear died of starvation in the jungles.

The Sardari agitation which began in 1859 was largely the struggle of the Christian tribals against the landlords. Sardar is not a title. It meant the leader in the agrarian struggle. Like the leaders of the Tamar and Kol insurrection the Sardar leaders also claimed to be the descendants of the original settlers. The main objectives of the agitation were to expel the Rajas, Thakurs and landlords, to end the system of forced labour and to alleviate the condition of women and hungry people. The leaders reminded people of such heroes of the Kol insurrection as Kanre and Bindrai, but they adopted legal means to improve their conditions. These included petitions, memoranda and protest. They had no faith in Dikus, non-white judges and officials since they were akin to the landlords. They did not want to pay rent to landlords. They chased away rent collectors.

Some of them went to Calcutta and consulted lawyers. On return they collected money to fight the case. They hoped that as a result of the case they would get back their rights and also their kingdom. They threatened those who did not pay contributions and said that the latter would remain slaves till the end of their lives. The Sardars wanted the intermediaries and exploiters to be removed and to be brought directly under the British administration. The Sardars were wholly loyal to the British Government and in the beginning they were not even opposed to the Raja of Chotanagpur.

Kumar Suresh Singh is of the view that the Sardar agitation later on culminated in the Birsa movement. He has identified the three phases of the movement, viz., agrarian (1859-1881), renascent (1881-1890) and political (1890-1895).

The agitation spread far and wide and engulfed both the Munda and the Oraon. Among the Munda leaders mention may be made of Nikodim of Dehkela, John of Uyur, Johan of Champadih, Tenga of Jilingkela, Eliazar of Kasmar, Martin of Nagra and Gidion of Piring. Eliazar of Kasmar and John of Chalkad exerted a great deal of influence of Birsa himself. Eliazar was so much respected that riding in a palanquin on his way to Ranchi Munda women of villages through which he passed used to wash his feet.

It is interesting to examine the ideas that inspired the Sardars. Christian education had given them an idea of a primeval golden age. They wanted that their social, economic and political conditions should correspond to the so-called picture of the golden age. The golden age was conceived as the period before the advent of non-tribal people in Chota-nagpur.

It is important that the Sardars stressed the ownership of the Bhuinhars rather than on the communal nature of the Khutkatti system. In the Bhuinhari area, the communal system was practically non-existent, Sardar leaders had imbibed many ideas from Calcutta lawyers and extracted lakhs of rupees from simple Mundas. In fact, they were responsible for changing the character of the struggle. They impressed upon the Munda that the British Government was with them, although the local officers at Ranchi were with the landlords and the money-lenders. In this way the Sardars were incited against local officers. Gradually the intentions of the Calcutta lawyers became apparent to the Munda, since the legal agitation did not produce any results.

The central area engulfed by the Sardar agitation and Birsa movement is a quadangle surrounded by hills. The people of this area had seen their lands being usurped by landlords and money-lenders. It was in this area that prominent leaders of the Tamar revolt and Kol insurrection were in hiding. The memory of those days rankled in their hearts. They also nourished intense hatred for the alien elements.

The Sardar agitation began with agrarian disturbances. The Sardars adopted an aggressive posture. They used the methods of the landlords and occupied such of their lands which the landlords had illegally usurped. The agitation slowly spread over the entire Naguri country. Sonepur, Lodma, Belkadih, Basia, Doisa and Khukhra were affected. The main targets of the Sardars were those landlords who had plundered the Christians in 1857. With the spread of Christianity the Mundas had come to understand the rights of the original settlers. They began to demand their rights with greater force. The first incident of the conflict occurred in village Jhapra. The landlord of the village, Shubh Narain Sahu captured some Christians in course of a revenue collection drive since the latter were not prepared to pay some illegal dues. Christians in the whole neighbourhood opposed this and drove away the family of the landlord. Not satisfied by this, the Christians captured the landlord and brought him to Ranchi and filed a complaint against him. But the Assistant Commissioner at Ranchi did not take any action. This encouraged the landlord and he began to wreak vengeance on the tenants. The flame of resistance spread. It gathered strength in Sonepur, Basia, Belkadih and Doisa.

There was only one incident in which blood was shed. It occurred in the area of Anand Singh the landlord of Bala. Anand Singh was harassing Christian tenants. The neighbouring tribals resisted this. In this conflict two of the landlord's men were killed. Later on cases were filed in which both parties were found guilty. Thakur Jagannath of Govindpur did not take any step to suppress the disturbance in that area. Later on, on government instructions he assembled two hundred persons to crush the mischief-makers. Thus the people of that area suffered a great deal from the depredations of the landlord and the police. During this conflict the question of forced labour also surfaced. The Christian tenants stopped offering forced labour.

To improve the state of affairs, Davis recommended that police powers should be taken away from the landlord of Govindpur and that enquiry should be made in the Bhuinhari areas by Lal Loknath Sahi, so that the conflict between the landlords and the Bhuinhars may be resolved. Government did not agree to his recommendations that the system of forced labour be abolished. Lal Loknath Sahi completed the enquiry in 427 villages within two years but the Munda were not satisfied with his work. They believed that his findings could not be correct, since he was himself a landlord and also a non-Munda. He had declared many lands as *Rajhas* which the Munda Sardars thought should be classed as *Bhuinhari*. The result of this enquiry was that peace was established in Parganas, Lodma and Sonepur and the number of agrarian disputes was substantially reduced; Loknath Sahi died in 1862 and the local government officers recommended that the work he had left unfinished should be completed. But until 1868 nothing was done. During this period sporadic disturbances took place in several villages. The conflicts between landlords and tenants and Christians and non-Christians escalated. In November, 1867 a constable named Maheshwar Das was sent to a village in Basia to prevent breach of peace. He was badly beaten up by the Christians who were engaged in harvesting the crops in a disputed field. In view of the aggressiveness of the Munda of Sonepur Pargana a small contingent of soldiers was stationed there and the culprits were given stern punishment.

In September 1867, under the leadership of Noosh Eliazar 1400 Christians submitted a memorial against Colonel Dalton and the Maharaja of Chotanagpur in which it was alleged that unjust exactions were made from them on account of their conversion and their crops were forcibly harvested. Investigations showed that only 20 Christians were connected with this petition. After some time a Munda delegation went to Calcutta to place its point of view before the British Government. The Sardars continued to file such complaints and memorials with the government. In these memorials the halcyon days of a primeval past were evoked when there was neither king nor landlord in their midst. The only result of these memorials was that in 1869 a law was passed by which the landlords were prevented from encroaching on Bhuinhari land and instructions were given to restore all the lands from which the tenants had been evicted. Arrangements were also made for the registration of their land rights. Although this law did not succeed in solving tribal problems completely, it was a significant move in that direction. Rakhal Das Halder was appointed as Special Settlement Officer. In the next eleven years the settlement work was completed in 2500 villages. All agrarian disputes were solved as far as possible.

These steps did not satisfy the Sardars. Some of them wanted a total change in agrarian relations. It is these leaders who became active in the second phase of the movement and gave it the colour of a renascent movement. In 1878, an Act was passed which raised high hopes and expectations in the tribal mind. The Sardars believed that it was the wish of the paramount power that all such land as was ever under their control or that of their forefathers should be restored to them. The Calcutta lawyers had further raised their aspirations. They wanted to re-establish the primeval system and to expel the *Dikus* from their area. Government officials however considered their demands unjustified.

Even before the settlement operations ended, the agitation

started again. In May 1876 a Christian missionary named Onash submitted a memorial to the Lt. Governor of Bengal to improve the social condition of the Munda. It was alleged that the survey work had not been done impartially. The memorial contained a threat to the government and the government took strong objection to it. The assumption in government circles was that the tribals should not get any special advantages on account of their conversion to Christianity. The missionaries were warned against inciting the tribals.

There were many shortcomings in the Bhuinhari settlement, but it revealed clearly the extent to which Mundari and Bhuinhari tenures had disintegrated. The movement to resist the settlement continued. After 1880, many of the Munda Bhuinhars made imaginary claims. The number of suits increased and the gulf between the landlords and the tenants widened. The agitationists wanted the settlement to be amended in their favour. Instances of conflicts between landlords and tenants multiplied. Violence, forcible capture, resort to illegal action, exacting forced labour etc. occurred at many places. This was the background for the second phase of the Sardari movement. Although the renascent aspect was visible even before 1880, it became clearer after that. In the petition of 1879 the following questions were raised.

"How is it that the rights of the Ilakadars were determined and not that of the Munda? If Chotanagpur does not belong to the Munda, it does not belong to anyone else; neither to the Thikadars nor to the Ilakadars or to the Nagbansis. Chotanagpur has been built up by the Munda and they are its masters. The Nagbansis who are now the rulers of Chotanagpur were servants of the Munda. In course of time, they usurped the kingdom by fraud and made a false declaration that they had received the kingdom from the Munda. What had they done for the Munda that the Munda would give them their kingdom? Do the Munda not have their own stomachs, do they not feel the pangs of hunger that they will give up their own share? Nobody gives a quarter of a seer of rice to anybody. How is it then that Munda would give such a large kingdom to the Nagbansis? If the kingdom was given to the Nagbansis, they should produce proof in support of their claim. The Nagbansis were the Bhuinhars and Tahsildars of the Munda. Such was the state of affairs in our ancient kingdom. With the passage of time such a calamity descended on us. At present whatever little Bhuinhari land we have is in danger of eviction."

In this petition it was prayed that Munda should be organized in village communities which should be directly taken over by the British Administration so that they have nothing to do with the Raja of Chotanagpur, landlords and Thikadars. For the first time in this petition, lack of confidence was shown in the Raja of Chotanagpur. The government rejected the petition and advised the missionaries to tell the Christian Munda that they should not spend their time and money in such fruitless endeavours. The missionaries acted accordingly and forfeited the confidence of the Munda Sardars.

Soon the agitation took a political and religious turn. In 1881, some Sardars organised themselves under the leadership of John the Baptist and established their "kingdom" at Doisa, the former capital of the Raja of Chotanagpur. They sent a threat to the Munsif at Lohardaga. The Deputy Commissioner of Ranchi thought that the agitation should be crushed in the beginning as it had potentialities of great disturbance. Some of the supporters of the newly established "kingdom" even confronted the Bara Lal of Palkot. In 1884 another petition containing a large number of frivolous demands was sent to the Lt. Governor. It was promptly rejected. Masihdas, Sardar of Paghi in the Oraon area, declared himself the Raja of Chotanagpur. In the Munda area Manmasih declared himself the Raja.

In 1886, another petition was sent in which the aggressive attitudes of the Sardars became more apparent. It was said in the petition that the Munda were the autochthon of the area and were not under its law. The Sardars gave this petition for transmission to the Lutheran missionaries. Like the earlier petitions, no notice was taken of this petition also. But the Sardar leaders engaged themselves in this work with great determination. In August 1887, a petition was sent to the Secretary of State for India in London in which the demand was made for the setting up of a Commission to enquire into their conditions. The Secretary of State, however, refused to consider the matter.

Though these petitions did not yield any direct dividends, the agitation was kept alive and the political objectives of the Sardars emerged clearly. The Sardari agitation had a religious dimension too. They wanted to create an independent Munda Christian Mission. The Oraon Sardars had already created a separate organisation of their own, called the Jhandia Mission. This was completely free from foreign missionaries. The anti-missionary programme of the Sardars included recalling children from mission schools. They split from the churches. Some of them even gave up Christianity, others celebrated their festivals and observed rituals outside the Church. One agitationist even solemnised a marriage according to Christian ritual outside the church. In the beginning the Sardars were opposed to the missionaries but not to Christianity. They did not give up their Christian names. Mansingh of Bagru proclaimed himself to be Christ. John of Magantoli declared that he was John the Baptist. Later on some Oraon Sardars promulgated separate rules for religious rituals which were very different from that of the missionaries.

In 1886-87 the German Lutheran Mission forced the pace of the Sardars. Its main objective was to establish direct relationship between the tribals and the government, so that they would have nothing to do with landlords. In June 1886, the Sardars submitted a petition that they should be allowed to deposit land revenue directly in the Lohardaga treasury. The petition was rejected. The missionaries of the German Mission, Notrott and Hahn, tried to convince the Sardars that their demands were not justified and dissuaded them from going to Calcutta. The Sardars wanted to know whether there was any possibility of an amendment of the settlement. They were also anxious to protect their rights in village forests, on homestead land, *Bari* land and *Korkar* and *Rajhas* lands. They asked Notrott whether he could help them get back their land. When Notrott showed his inability, they severed their relations with the mission and abused the missionaries. Some missionaries even filed a case against the Sardars for misbehaviour. This spelled the end of the Sardari movement in the Oraon area.

In 1887, the agitation spread from Tamar to Porahat. The Mundas began to recall their children from missionary schools and prevented people from attending the Church. They exacted forced contributions, defamed the local officials and incited the people in various ways. In one meeting the people came with arms. At a meeting in Tamar the Sardars declared that all Mundas would act together and not pay the rent and the rent collectors would be killed. Some Sardars forcibly grabbed the land of the landlords. Thirty-five Sardars in twelve villages of Tamar created grave disturbances. Some of them occupied the *Manjihas* land of the Rani of Tamar and divided it among themselves. The government adopted a stiff attitude and the agitation slowly petered away. The Sardars seem to have received the inspiration for the disturbances from the lawyers at Calcutta.

Catholic Sardars also took an active part in the agitation. They told the Rev. Muelender of the Sarwada Mission that if the Roman Catholic Mission helped them achieve their objectives, the entire Munda tribe would be converted to Catholicism. But he told the Sardars in very clear terms that their objectives would not be fulfilled. The Sardars did not despair however. In 1887 some Catholic missionaries began to take an interest in the land question. But the higher authorities in the Mission disallowed them. About this time Father Leivens began his work in Torpa. He had a real sympathy for the tribals. Whenever he received any news of oppression of the tribals he talked to the landlords and settled the disputes between the landlords and the tenants. In December 1889, the Catholic Munda agitation assumed large proportions. It engulfed Basia, Palkot, Sisai and Chainpur also. Some landlords filed a complaint with the government saying that Christian tribals were going about the villages cutting the hair of the non-Christians and forcibly converting them to Christianity. Four such persons were taken into police custody. A mob of 2500 Catholics armed with weapons came to free the captives. From various places news was received of illegal harvesting. The government was greatly concerned about this as until that time new disturbances were caused on account of the conflict between the landlords and the tenants; but a new dimension was emerging at that time. This new dimension comprised the Christian converts and the missionaries. For the restoration of peace a contingent of soldiers was brought in. Rainey, the Deputy Commissioner, visited the disturbed area and camped at various places. In these camps he used to hear complaints and decide the cases then and there. The Christian missionaries were severely warned not to join the fray. Many of the trouble-makers were awarded long sentences.

In 1889, 200 Catholic catechists were arrested but were later on released on appeal. In the eyes of the government the Mission had become a den of political unrest. The strong attitude of the government led the missionaries withdraw their support to the agitationists. The agitationists, therefore, turned away from the Mission. At places they even began to oppose the Mission actively. Gradually the agitation took an anti-European turn. The agitationists were inspired by political objectives. The Sardars were convinced that the Mission could not save them from the oppressions of the landlords. They alleged that the missionaries were hand in glove with local officers and that the whites had turned against the tribals. Thus they had no way left but to carry on their struggle on their own. Even when this became clear, some Sardars would not leave the apron strings of the Calcutta lawyers. In 1881, after the disturbances were quelled, many of the Sardars were given long jail sentences. Some of the Sardars went to Calcutta and arranged for a barrister named Jacob to argue their case at Ranchi. Jacob was able to get four of the accused released but the government again prosecuted them. In some cases Jacob saved many of the accused from going to prison. At this time it became known that during the past few years Calcutta lawyers and their assistants had extorted two lakhs of rupees from the Sardar leaders. When this was known to the Munda people, they gave up their Calcutta visits and declared their loyalty to their government.

The political phase of the Sardari agitation began from 1890. In this period the Munda boycotted the Mission and encroached on the lands of landlords. Gradually, the political aims and the revolutionary means of the agitation began to emerge clearly. Between 1890-95 many important meetings were held at governmental level at Ranchi in which the agrarian situation was discussed. The Lt. Governor of Bengal, the Commissioner of Ranchi, Rev. Notrott etc. met the Sardars and the tenants to know their points of view. Johan Sardar complained that the landlords and the police together had looted the property of the Munda, deprived them of Bhuinhari lands and captured many of them for forced labour. In some of these meetings Father Leivens and some representatives of the landlords were invited. Everybody agreed that in order to settle the disputes, it was necessary to get some inquiry done in one form or another. These meetings did not achieve anything beyond making the various aspects of the agrarian problem clear.

By this time the Sardars and the missionaries had drifted so far apart, that in October 1891 the Munda of ten Parganas submitted a petition to the government protesting against the oppressions of the German Mission. Many of the Munda had left the fold of the German Mission and joined the Baptist Mission. The German Mission was warned that it should not interfere with the religious, social and intellectual development of the Munda. Thus the Munda freed themselves from the influence of the German Mission.

The Sardars continued the agitation against the advice of their erstwhile supporters. They told their followers that they should stop payment of rent to their thikadars and should not present themselves to the local courts when summoned. The result was that the lands of many of the tenants were auctioned. The Sardars had spread a rumour according to which the Lt. Governor of Bengal would visit Ranchi and return their kingdom to the Munda. After that all officials, Rajas and landlords would leave Chotanagpur. Some Sardars openly began to talk of a revolutionary programme. At one time they even decided upon the date of the revolt in which landlords and German missionaries would be done away with. At this time the forest question also came up. The Sardars claimed that the Munda were the masters of the forests, but government officials did not allow them even to take firewood from them. The Sardars forcibly exacted contribution from people. In April 1894, a Sardar named Joshua was sentenced to two years' imprisonment for collecting contributions forcibly. Until that time the Sardars had believed that their kingdom would be returned to them. Since the missionaries opposed the agitation, all the Sardars turned into enemies of the Mission. Some Sardars began to cultivate lands belonging to the church by force. A large number of people gave up Christianity; some of them left one church to join another.

Some authorities have severely criticized the Sardars. They have been regarded as dishonest and fraudulent. The government officers were annoyed with them since they had to face the disturbances created by them. The missionaries were angry as many of the tribals had given up Christianity on account of the movement. The Sardar leaders had fallen into the clutches of Calcutta lawyers. Some Sardars were in fact dishonest and took advantage of the situation. They were not very careful about money matters. In the mammoth petitions a large number of forged signatures were made. They used to collect money by force and fraud. Various kinds of rumours were deliberately floated, but many of them sincerely believed in their programme and never had any doubt that they would not succeed.

The Sardari agitation helped the complete disintegration of the Khutkatti system. The view of the Sardars that the tenants should not pay rent to the landlord or the Raja proved fatal. In the Kulipiri Patti all the thirty villages were auctioned. A Hindu money-lender bought them. The result of stopping rent in Khunti and South Tamar, was also disastrous. Between 1888 and 1892 many Khutkatti villages were auctioned. Hoffman and Lister have produced many evidences of this.

The attitude of the Sardars had alienated the British officers. The leaders did not have confidence in each other or in the local government. Their folly had crossed all limits. Between 1890 and 1895 all the court verdicts were against the tribals. Some British government officials were convinced that obstinate Mundas were vexing the landlords without any reason. The Sardars thought that the local government was always on the side of the landlords. It may be said, however, that most of the Sardars were not dishonest. They did not understand the intricacies of the law. They had full hope that the government machinery would redress their grievances and relieve them from the tyranny of the landlords. In fact, most of them were loyal to the government. They had not taken the path of open revolt and wanted to achieve their objectives by constitutional means. They wanted that the system which was introduced in Kolhan should be adopted for them also. They wanted to be directly under British administration. They were themselves honest and loyal but the Bengali lawyers and court officials had made them stray from their path. They believed that if they could put forward their point of view before the Viceroy or Queen Victoria, they would surely succeed.

Two contradictory points of view have been advanced on the nature of Sardari agitation. The truth lies in between. The Sardari agitation was symptomatic of a special situation. It was the culmination of those trends which had disturbed Chotanagpur from 1830-31 to 1900-1901. It has been mentioned earlier that some of their leaders were the descendants of the Kol rebels who had left their hearth and home and settled in the central hilly region. Their claims were backed by tribal history. Their socialisation had engendered a deep consciousness of their past among them. For twenty years they had been looking for a way to ventilate their grievances. For this purpose they now adopted a perfectly legal path. Through petitions and memorials they wanted such lands restored as had been usurped by the landlords. They knocked at all doors for help. They went to the government, approached the Calcutta lawyers and sought guidance from the missionaries. But they were disappointed in all quarters. The Sardari agitation began in one form but gradually its character changed, and ultimately, its revolutionary dimension came to the fore. It became not only anti-government but also anti-missionary. The Sardars were convinced that they had been exploited and deceived by their patrons at Calcutta and that the British officials in Chotanagpur were so much in league with the Hindu landlords that their problems could not be solved by a legal agitation. Some Sardars began to believe that the root cause of their troubles was the British Government itself under whose patronage landlords and foreign missionaries flourished.

In 1892, they had made a plan to exterminate government officials and missionaries, but they did not have an all powerful leader. In 1895 most Sardars were waiting for the advent of such a leader. Thus the path was clear for the leadership of Birsa and his movement. The Sardar agitation had prepared the ground for the Birsa movement.

THE BIRSA MOVEMENT

The most important of the uprisings in Chotanagpur was

the Birsa movement of 1895—1900. It was, however, a complex of revivalism, political action and a search for utopia (Roy-Burman, B.K., 1974 : 47). Singh called it a resistance and religious movement at the same time (Singh, K.S., 1966). Its purpose was to satisfy the conditions of deliberately organised conscious efforts to construct a more satisfying culture. Of its two constituent elements, the movement was predominantly of the resistance type, organising violent attacks on the Mission, the *thana* etc. (Sinha, S.P., 1964 : 110).

The situational context of the Birsaite movement has been identified as follows : (a) encroachment on Munda Khutkatti lands of original village founders to an intolerable extent, (b) migration of thousands of labourers to the tea estates of Assam, being lured by Arkatas or recruiting agents, and (c) famine in Chotanagpur (Ekka, 1972 : 429).

Stephen Fuchs (1965 : 22) has termed the Birsa movement as a messianic movement. K.L. Sharma argued that the Birsa movement was basically transformative in terms of its ultimate goal. He adds that the basic instruments of the movement were no doubt messianic or revivalistic in nature, but the movement itself never aimed at a new religious order as such among the tribals (1976 : 38). This view is not true because the Birsa movement certainly had a religious element and a new religion, Birsa Dharam, came into existence with a new philosophy for the Munda.

Many factors were responsible for the emergence of the Birsa movement. The most important of these was the desire for economic liberation from the yoke of landlords and British rule. The movement had an organisational base with ethnicity and religiosity as the basis of mobilisation and involvement of the people in it. The Birsa movement may be regarded as a forerunner of the present Jharkhand movement.

Though the literature on Birsa and his movement has grown, the lines of approach to the subject have been shifting. K.S. Singh (1966) has reviewed the literature on the Birsa movement and published a detailed bibliography on the subject

The Birsa movement was basically agrarian and defensive. Driven by an irresistible self-defensive urge, the Munda had first sought shelter in Christianity, then broken away from the missions and turned to Calcutta lawyers, and finally clashed with the authorities. The controversy regarding the movement being political or agrarian emanated from a partial view of it. The movement was agrarian in its root, violent in its means and political in its end. Birsa in his speeches emphasised the agrarian factors and sought a political solution of the problem facing his people, i.e., the establishment of Birsa Raj under the "New King" (himself) (Ibid : 191).

Birsa Munda was born in or about 1874 in Gareria Ulihatu in the Tamar Police Station of Khunti sub-division. He was the fourth son of Sugna Munda, a peasant of very small means. His early childhood was spent in Khatanga where he first came in contact with Christian missionaries. It was in their association that he picked up reading and writing. He passed his primary and middle school examinations from Burju and Chaibasa mission schools. After some time Birsa joined Anand *panr* in Gaurbera as his domestic servant. The latter recited stories from the epics by which Birsa was greatly impressed. At this time he also visited the neighbouring village of Bamhani where a reputed Vaishnava saint gave discourses on Bhakti. He was so profoundly influenced by the doctrine of non-violence preached by the saint that he gave up hunting and non-vegetarian fooód. Birsa was deeply inspired by his Christian and Hindu teachers.

Birsa then went to live with his parents who had by then moved to Chalkad. He found the Munda steeped in ignorance and worshipping numerous gods and godlings. In the early monsoon of the year 1895, while Birsa was in a jungle with a friend, there was a thunderstorm, and lightning struck him and he was transfigured. Birsa said that at that moment he had received a divine revelation which related to the deliverance of his people. This news spread like wild fire. Soon after this he was attributed with having healing powers and crowds of suffering humanity began to seek his blessings. He began holding *Harikirtan* and giving religious discourses. He asked people to worship only one god i.e., Singbonga, abstain from violence and from eating animal flesh. All living beings, according to him, were children of Singbonga. He also forbade the drinking of wine and other intoxicants including rice-beer. He asked his followers to use the sacred thread and stressed purity of heart at the time of worship. This religion was known as the

Birsa *Dharam* (religion) and was a mixture of Hinduism and Christianity. He was called *Bhagwan* (God) as well as *Dharti Aba* or the Father of the World by his followers.

Old Munda of the village were perturbed by Birsa's activities and teachings, because if sacrifices were not offered to the village deities and harmful spirits were not propitiated, they believed that some calamity was bound to befall the village. Soon after, a small-pox epidemic broke out and people attributed it to the activities of Birsa. He was forced out of the village. Later on he returned and engaged himself in the selfless service of the sick. This earned him praise and respect from the entire neighbourhood as the pox victims were cured by his loving care. People came to believe that there was magic in his touch and the number of his followers began to swell. Vast numbers of people would congregate everyday to see him and hear his message.

Slowly the healer, the miracle worker and the preacher grew into a prophet. He preached that theft, deception, murder and drunkenness were sinful. He ordained that white pigs and fowl were unclean and thus should be destroyed. This order was promptly carried out by all Munda in the districts affected by the movement. Birsa prophesied that a deluge would flood the whole country leaving only one dry spot—Chalkad—where he stayed with his followers. Fire and brimstone would rain from the sky, those who stayed with him would be saved and the rest would perish. He forecast that this catastrophe would soon take place. It was a waste of labour, therefore, he suggested, to weed the crops and as the people would have no further use for ploughing, they should turn all their cattle loose. He further advised his followers to spend all their money in buying new clothes. People followed his instructions and a large number of them assembled on the appointed day at Chalkad and waited for hours for the events to occur. When nothing happened the crowds were disappointed. Birsa at last explained to them that the catastrophe had been postponed for some time.

In Birsa's time the Munda country was dominated by outsiders, zamindars, money-lenders and missionaries. Land was gradually passing out of their hands. The solidarity of the village was being broken up. Famine ravaged the area many times. Christian missionaries by their activities were creating dissensions in the villages. All these created a widespread feeling of discontent and unrest which also echoed in Birsa's heart. He raised his voice against the growing influence of the missionaries, the oppressions of the zamindars and the foreign rule which fostered these elements. He exhorted his followers to fight these forces of oppression. In order to restore the somewhat shaken confidence of his followers, Birsa's teachings gradually took a political turn. Thus out of the innocuous beginnings of the religious movement in 1895, an agrarian and political movement emerged, particularly when the Sardars inflated the ranks of his disciples. Though Birsa was influenced by the Sardars, it is difficult to say that he was their mouthpiece. The Sardars in the beginning professed loyalty to the British, even to the Raja of Chotanagpur and wanted only the elimination of intermediary interests. But Birsa's aim was that the Munda should rise against their oppressors, drive out or slay all aliens *(dikus)*—Hindus as well as Muslims and British —and establish a Munda raj, with him as leader and ruler and attain independence both religious and political. Birsa roused the apprehensions of the missionaries and they prevailed upon the government to take steps against him. A force was sent to Chalkad and there was a scuffle between it and Birsa's followers. Although a warrant for Birsa's arrest had been issued, it was not easy to do so. He was ultimately captured with the aid of Rev. Lusty in August 1895 and brought to Ranchi in chains. To strike terror in the hearts of the tribals it was decided to try him in the open. But the revolt was not crushed, through Birsa was sentenced to two and a half years imprisonment.He was released in November 1897 on the occasion of the Diamond Jubilee of the reign of Queen Victoria.

The four years following the first phase of the movement were marked by famines, the passage of ineffective agrarian legislation, the continuing Sardar agitation and the failure of the government to curb Birsa's activities after his release from jail. As a result, though the movement was driven underground, it gained in depth and emerged, at the end of the period, more powerful and potentially more dangerous than before.

On his release his influenee increased and he started the work of organising resistance in right earnest. Famine, scarcity and epidemic which hit the Munda country between 1897-99 provided him with an opportunity for social service. Birsa and his close followers came in contact with the suffering masses and gained their confidence. The landlords continued to oppress the people and Christian missionaries stepped up the work of conversion. Birsa went on a pilgrimage to Chutia, Jagannathpur and Naurantangarh between 1898-99. With these visits he established links with tradition and heritage. He brought holy water from one of the temples. This was known as *Birda* and was supposed to turn his followers into heroes. He exhorted people to fight injustice and to collect under his banner. Gradually, he started building up forces. Training in the use of bows, arrows and swords was given to the recruits. Birsa as a dynamic leader went from place to place looking after the training, organisation, and morale of his forces in Khunti, Ranchi, Chakardharpur, Bundu, Tamar, Karra, Torpa, Basia, Sisai etc. Meetings were held at various places and the grievances of the Munda were highlighted everywhere. The final meeting was held on the Dumbari Hill. Delegates from different parts of the Munda country came to receive directions and discussed the plan of operations with their leader. It was decided upon to start the movement on Christmas day in 1899 and to take revenge against Rajas, Hakims, Zamindars, Christians etc. Mission houses were attacked, police stations were stormed and pitched battles took place between armed Munda and the police.

When the news of the rising reached Ranchi, the authorities sent two forces towards Maranghada and Burju. The Deputy Commissioner wanted to make peace but the rebel forces rejected the offer. The rebels concentrated on the Dumbari Hill, and erected stockades at intervals to defend their position. They had with them their women and children and large stores of clothing, food and cooking untensils. Government forces surrounded the Dumbari Hill and opened fire on 9 January, 1900. The rebel forces retaliated with a shower of arrows, but they could not withstand the onslaught of the government forces for long. About 200 men, women and children were reported to have been killed. Ultimately, the rebels dispersed. People began to be arrested on suspicion for complicity in the rebellion. Missionaries became very active in rounding up suspects. Those who agreed to be converted were spared. In Maranghada, Saiko and Sarwada many Mundas were converted to Christianity in this way.

At the time of firing, neither Birsa nor his lieutenant Gaya Munda was on the Dumbari Hill. Birsa escaped to the jungles of Singhbhum and Gaya Munda was in hiding in village Etka and foiled arrest for two years in spite of the most vigilant search by the police. Later Gaya fell fighting while evading arrest in Etka. Birsa was finally arrested and sentenced to imprisonment in Ranchi jail along with eighty of his followers. Soon after, Birsa died of cholera in the jail pending his trial. His body was publicly cremated to convince his followers that he was no god but mere mortal. Yet to this day the Munda believe that Birsa would return some day to save his people. He lives in numerous Munda folksongs. When a Munda boy is to be named, Birsa is a favourite choice.

The perusal of Roy's account of Birsa and his movement creates the impression that he was a "cheat" and an "impostor" with the "pretensions" of a "prophet". It was alleged that he used to paint his body with turmeric to show that it changed into the colour of gold, a sign of divinity. His teachings were characterized as "mad" and his logic, "insane". His followers were said to behave like "infatuated fanatics". He was also said to have made false prophecies about the doomsday. The resistance movement led by Birsa was termed as 'folly' for which they had to pay a heavy penalty. At another place much later Roy (1931) offered a belated explanation that Birsa promised a kingdom of heaven in Chotanagpur by expelling the *dikus*, if not the *Sahebs* as well. Formerly, he had held that the movement was only against the alien landlords and not so much against European officials and missionaries.

Such an impression is not correct. The movement which Birsa led, or *ulgulan*, was the culmination of a long process of resistance to oppression both of landlords and of the administration. Since the missionaries took sides with the government the tribals were against them too. The movement must be viewed in the context of the conditions prevailing at that time and not with reference to concepts of nationalism or non-violence. The Munda had no comprehension of the nation as such, they were fighting for their own freedom from oppression and alien rule.

An immediate consequence of the Birsa movement was that the government became aware of the urgency of preparing a record of rights for the lands of discontented Munda. The survey and settlement operations were carried out during 1902-19. As a result of the settlement operations, the Chotanagpur Tenancy Act was passed in 1908 and it brought about a sense of security among the Munda. The Birsa movement also had implications with regard to administrative and other socio-religious movements in the Munda country.

Such movements and their consequences were supposed to help the tribals to assess the powers of Hindu society so that less violent means of contention were chosen for the continuation of the struggle, and make the Hindus realise that past oppressive practices would have to be avoided and thus leading to the emergence of a balance of power between the two groups, the social conflict essentially contributing to the process of social cohesion (Jay, E, 1958). This was, however, not true of the post-Birsa movement developments. The Mundas no doubt have not risen in arms since the Birsa movement but the ideal cohesive order has not yet emerged. The Birsa movement halted the rapid breakdown of the agrarian order. But the ameliorative measures, howsoever immediately effective, were merely palliative of the ills of the tribal society. Birsa's religious influence, in practice, remained confined to small groups of his followers. He was praised by an adoring posterity as the symbol of their awakening, but the onrush of alien influences and the rapid pace of urbanization and industrialization contributed to the process of detribalisation against which the Birsa movement like others had set its face. The politico-religious movement of Birsa summed up the Indian tribal people's reaction to their changing world in the nineteenth century (Singh, K.S. 1966 : 203).

11

MODERN POLITICAL CONSCIOUSNESS AND GROWTH OF THE JHARKHAND PARTY

THE MUNDA country in the present century has witnessed a distinct change in the pattern of the tribal movements and the rise of the separatist movement in terms of ethnicity and its transformation into a regional movement. As a result of the growth in education, land reforms and welfare programmes for the weaker sections of the population, the power structure in the tribal villages has undergone a change and a new elite has emerged among them. This elite is taking up leadership roles in shaping the destiny of the tribal masses. Since the beginning of the present century there has been a conscious effort on the part of the educated Munda elite to build up solidarity among the tribals of the Chotanagpur region.

Peasant revolts since the 1920s have been co-ordinated within the politics of regional parties. Political movements for independence or for national or regional autonomy have been occurring among the tribal people. The Jharkhand movement for the political autonomy of the Munda, Santal and Oraon is one such movement.

The rural bred charismatic and tradition-oriented Munda leadership, which worked for revitalising the tribals on the Hindu model was later disturbed owing to the devoted work of the missionaries, and their continuous effort to uplift the tribals brought about new standards for choosing leadership. During the last fifty years, it appears, the leadership has passed into the hands of the Western educated, urban bred Christian Mundas (Vidyarthi, L.P., 1967 : 130).

The Birsa movement and other rebellions not only highlighted the immediate problems and agrarian issues, but profoundly affected the people in terms of the tribal awakening and politicisation, antipathy to conversion among the Munda, the emergence of welfare institutions and associations, and finally the demand for the formation of the Jharkhand state in the Indian Union. However, it is emphasized that the Birsa movement was basically politically motivated and the demand for the formation of the Jharkhand state since 1938 and more specifically since 1950 testifies to the continuity of the same ideology. When the Jharkhand movement was at its peak in the early fifties, people thought that they were about to achieve their objective of a separate state under the command of the Munda leader Jaipal Singh, who had at that time a charismatic influence over the tribal people.

The institutionalised form of political consciousness among the Munda was first expressed in the Christian Students' Organisation set up in 1911-12, by J. Bartholmen, of the Anglican Mission, an orphan from Chaibasa and a student of St. Columba's College, Hazaribagh. He had attended the Students' Conference in Dacca. The Hazaribagh organization was a branch of the Dacca Students' Union and was specially formed to raise funds for the education of poor Christian students. The Chotanagpur Charitable Association was also organized to provide scholarships for both Christians and non-Christians. Voices, although feeble at that time, were raised for forging unity between the tribal and backward communities in Chotanagpur.

When constitutional reforms were in the offing, some Christian tribals took a lead in starting the Chotanagpur Improvement Society. The Society regretted that tribals were not secure and impressed on the government the need to preserve tribal identity in the changing political context. The aims and objectives of this cultural and social organisation were to improve the social, economic and political conditions of the Munda and other tribals in Chotanagpur. Its membership was restricted to tribals. For the first time, a formal organisation was established with the support of all the major tribal groups, especially the Munda and the Oraon. The earlier movements were, to a large extent, violent and nativistic, they were also the least organised and formalised, compared to the early twentieth century reformative movements which were well-organised and formally structured such as the Unnati Samaj. Some of the leading members of the Samaj were Theble Uraon, Bandi Oraon, Paul Dayal, Rev. Joel Lakra, Alfos Kujur, Elias Topno, Bir Singh Munda and Anand Masih. Though they had a strong devotion for their people, they lacked one who could lead them to their objective. The leaders organised meetings from time to time, and submitted reports of their grievances to the government. The objectives of the Samaj were propagated through a magazine called *Adivasi*, which was published in Mundari, Kurukh, Hindi and English. The Samaj contributed towards inter-tribal unity in the region, in the form of welfare organisations.

It sought to secure employment for educated tribals, reservation in the services and legislative bodies, and formation of a sub-state joined to Bengal or Orissa. Though it sought to spread its activities among the villagers, it remained essentially an urban movement. It is to this phase that we can trace the revival of *parhas* among the Munda. The Samaj was able to focus the attention of the authorities on the problems of the tribals (Singh, K. S., 1977 : 320).

The members of the Samaj asked for a separate state and submitted a memorandum to the Simon Commission demanding special privileges for the tribals. There was as yet no idea of a separate state for the tribals, but they were made to work and unite on the basis of ethnocentrism and the tribal brotherhood.

The members of the Samaj, however, differed among themselves on some issues and could not remain united for long. Ultimately, some of them left it and formed a parallel organisation called the Kisan Sabha to focus attention on the problems of the peasants. Its president was Theble Oraon and the secretary was Paul Dayal. These two organisations set up candidates for the general elections in 1937 without any success.

Until now the Catholics had kept aloof from these organisations. They had formed an organisation of their own known as Chotanagpur Catholic Sabha under the inspiration of the Archbishop of Chotanagpur. Thus for the first time, the Christian Church lent its active support to a purely political organisation. The Catholic Sabha set up candidates for the general election in 1937. Two of its candidates won the contest in which the candidates of the Unnati Samaj and of the Kisan Sabha were defeated. Its candidates swept the polls at the Ranchi municipal elections also.

Ignes Beck, their representative in Parliament, became distrustful of the Congress. The language policy of the Congress, to promote Hindi, was not to the liking of many of the then Chotanagpur tribal elite. Ignes Beck felt the urgent need of consolidating the solidarity of tribals transcending the denominational barriers. By stages, all the three organisations merged together to fight the *dikus* and improve the social, economic and political conditions of the tribals. Hence the Chotanagpur Adivasi Mahasabha came into existence and its first conference was held in Khunti in 1938. But as it was still riddled with leadership rivalry, it failed to impress upon the masses. But in early 1939, the second Mahasabha was convened under the presidentship of Jaipal Singh, an educated Munda leader and it was all success. From then onwards he became a regular member of the Sabha and later on was made its Chairman. Under his able leadership the gulf between the masses and the educated Christian Munda was bridged.

The immediate motivation for the formation of the Mahasabha was the experience of the first elections held in 1937 under the Government of India Act of 1935. The Congress had swept the polls. This persuaded Christian as also the non-Christian tribals to close their ranks, and form a joint body, the Adivasi Mahasabha. Two other sources of influence of the Mahasabha were the Bengali-Bihari controversy and the Muslim League politics. The Bengalis felt that their interests in Bihar were not safe and they could, therefore, combine with the tribals to form a separate state. The Muslim League in the mid 1940s played with the idea of forming a corridor, passing through the tribal areas, to link East and West-Pakistan. They sympathised with it and gave financial support to the Adivasi Mahasabha. The Mahasabha was led by professional political workers, some of them highly educated and articulate. It became a Chotanagpur movement extending over both urban and rural areas. It involved tribals other than the Munda and the Oraon. It demanded the formation not of a sub-state but its complete separation from Bihar. A series of violent incidents occurred during this period, which underlined the militant nature of the movement. But by 1947 the militancy subsided. The Sabha was routed by the Congress in the first elections held in 1946. The link with the Muslim League was broken, and the Bengali-Bihari controversy tapered off.

Jaipal Singh, who emerged as a prominent Munda leader of the Jharkhand movement in 1939, combined both local and cosmopolitan attributes in his personality. He was born in a Pahan family in Takra village near Ranchi. He had his education in Oxford University. He excelled in the field of sports. He obtained a Full Blue in Hockey at Oxford. He captained the Indian Hockey team which won the world championship at the 9th Olympiad at Amsterdam and received special congratulations from the Viceroy of India. He achieved distinctions in other fields as well. He was the first Indian to hold the post of a covenanted Mercantile Assistant in the Royal Dutch-Shell group, Calcutta. Later he became Revenue Commissioner and Acting Colonisation Minister in Bikaner State. To the educated tribals of Chotanagpur, therefore, he was the embodiment of their aspirations. Compared with his achievements, the local tribal leaders had very little to boast of. He was a welcome personality for another reason also. Prior to it, he was never involved in the local tribal politics in Chotanagpur. Hence he was expected to be impartial in his dealings. Before he became the President of the Second Mahasabha, the story of his remarkable career had spread all over Chotanagpur. Tribal masses who were leaderless for about four decades after the Birsa movement, accepted him as Marang Gomke, the Supreme leader. They looked upon him as the reincarnation of Birsa who was deified in his life time, as otherwise, it was argued he could not have achieved so many distinctions in foreign lands. These factors enabled him to consolidate the educated Munda under his able leadership. He made efforts to evoke the primordial sentiments of the tribals to unite them.

Very soon the Adivasi Mahasabha became a political organisation. It tried to have close relations with the Congress Party during the 1940s. The Mahasabha demanded representation in the Bihar Pradesh Congress Committee and its Working Committee. The Congress did not accede to this demand. As a result, a series of clashes took place between the Congress and the Adivasi Mahasabha workers, leading to some deaths, at Tapkara, Khunti and Ranchi during March 1946. Jaipal Singh contested a seat in the Provincial Council and lost. Many Mundas themselves had supported the Congress against the reactionary policies of the Adivasi Mahasabha. It was also reported in the newspapers that Jaipal Singh and his associates, the Christian missionaries and the Muslim League, openly fought the Congress with the connivance of some government officials.

After some time, some members realised the need for including the non-tribals of Chotanagpur in this organisation. They wanted to bring about a change in its constitution as well as its objectives. The non-tribals had already formed a separate organisation at Daltonganj to voice their demand for regional autonomy. Keeping these points in view, Justin Richard organised the United Jharkhand Block late in 1948. After resisting the idea for some time Jaipal Singh accepted it at last. In 1950, at Jamshedpur, the Jharkhand Party was formed as the political wing of theAd ivasi Mahasabha. Thus from a tribal organisation it became a regional political party.

There were certain factors underlying the creation of the Jharkhand Party. Apart from the failure of the militant movement in the early phase, there was also the experience of the framing of the Constitution of India. The tribals had been recognised as a minority and the fifth and sixth schedule had given them more than the anthropologists and the British administrators had prepared them for. The framers of the Constitution had given the country a secular system, which reassured the missionaries and the minorities. The Census of 1951, like the Census of 1931, showed that the tribals did not constitute a majority in the Chotanagpur region. Therefore, the Jharkhand movement was thrown open, at least in theory, to all residents of Chotanagpur. There was a transition from ethnicity to regionalism as the basis of the movement. This was, partly, a concession to the stand taken by the Congress Party that language and not ethnicity could determine the formation of a state. Many elements of the Socialist party and quite a few members of the money-lending community who could be identified as *dikus* joined the party.

The concept of Jharkhand was enlarged to include all the regions which once formed part of the Chotanagpur administrative division. Thus the tracts inhabited by the Chotanagpur tribals which formed part of Bengal, Orissa and Madhya Pradesh were included in the Jharkhand. The method adopted by the party was constitutional. Though Christians dominated the movement and provided the leadership, there was an unmistakable tribal core to it.

The Christian-oriented western educated model lost its exclusiveness and a new model of leadership emerged which symbolised the aspiration and needs of the local and regional people. It presented a somewhat secularised leadership before the masses of Chotanagpur, thus expressing its will for establishing regional identity in the wider frame of national integration.

K. Suresh Singh (1977 : 318) analyses a combination of factors to explain how Chotanagpur became the centre of the separatist movement. Firstly, Chotanagpur was the most advanced of the tribal regions in point of literacy, political consciousness and industrial progress. Secondly, the major tribal communities were concentrated in a geographically distinct region. Thirdly, Christianity made a great impact by converting major tribal populations like the Munda and giving them a sense of identity. It promoted education and also emphasized a sense of separateness from the rest. Next, the Chotanagpur tribes had a tradition of militant and organised struggles going back over a hundred years. Then, there was a rich corpus of anthropological literature to draw upon in order to create a new sense of history, which could legitimise the tribal's search for identity. Lastly, Chotanagpur was exposed to the operation of many interests. The Bengalis formed a sizable professional and landowning community and the Muslims were a significant trading and professional interest. The Bengali-Bihari controversy over employment in the late 1930s, and the Muslim League politics as mentioned earlier, also affected the development of the tribal separatist movement.

Jyoti Sen (1972 : 432) attributes the movement for the separate state of Jharkhand to : (a) the growing dicontent among the tribal people of Chotanagpur as a result of alienation of land; (b) exploitation by money-lenders etc.; (c) a strong antipathy towards *dikus* or non-tribals; and (d) political developments in the wider setting of the country. The emergence of the Jharkhand Party in 1950 lent the movement a strong political base to express its regional solidarity and emphasize the demand for a separate Jharkhand state.

With the formation of the Jharkhand Party and transition of the ethnic organisation to a regional one, the separatist movement was transformed into a party-based movement. The leaders of the party were mainly drawn from among the educated Mundas. The leaders of the party convinced the people of the need for a separate state, persuaded them to realise its importance and prepared them psychologically for it. The party won a spectacular success in the first general elections in 1952. The electorate went to the polls with religious zeal. The result was a resounding victory for the Jharkhand Party which secured over 70% of the Scheduled Tribe seats (24) in the election. The Congress was able to secure only 20% of the assembly seats reserved for the Scheduled Tribes in Bihar. The rest of the seats were divided between the Lok Sewak Sangh and the Janata Party. The Jharkhand Party emerged as the main opposition in the Bihar Legislative Assembly. Their members signed a memorandum which the party submitted to the States Reorganisation Commission (SRC) in January, 1955. The memorandum mentioned that besides 6 districts of Bihar, 9 districts of Bengal, Orissa and Madhya Pradesh would comprise the proposed state of Jharkhand. The SRC rejected the demand for a Jharkhand state. This slightly affected the election prospects in 1957 when the Jharkhand Party secured 21 (3 seats less than in 1952) out of 32 reserved seats. The Congress gained some more seats as compared to the previous elections. Some independent candidates also appeared on the scene.

From 1957 onwards the decline of the Party began which became evident in the 1962 elections. The Jharkhand Party suffered a further loss of seats. It secured only 19 seats out of 32. The Congress also suffered a heavy loss. It secured only 3 seats this time. The Swatantra Party made a good start. It won 6 seats. Of the rest, three seats went to the S.S.P. and one to the Communist Party.

There were a number of factors responsible for the declining influence of the Jharkhand Party after the 1957 elections. Firstly, there was the growing impact of development programmes on Chotanagpur and the increasing involvement of the tribals in the developmental process. Secondly, the split between the Christian and the non-Christian tribals began; the latter started looking to the Congress and the Jan Sangh for support. The All-India parties appeared on the scene. Next, the experience of Madhya Pradesh and Orissa which had given representation to tribal interests in the government and the Council of Ministers made it clear that all that was needed was a share in power to protect tribal interests, which could as well be secured by joining the Congress or by coming to some kind of understanding with it, as in Orissa. Lastly, the admission of the elements into the Jharkhand which could be identified as the *dikus*, the traditional enemies of Adivasis had never gone down well with the majority of the tribals (Singh, K.S., 1977 : 322).

The tribals have held the *diku* responsible for their misery and exploitation. They have struck with infallible precision at the money-lenders and land grabbers who continue to give offence. Of late, the extremist movement in tribal areas stretched the concept to cover all those who have deprived the tribals of the benefits of employment and of the fruits of the rich natural and mineral resources of their land. But the concept has been blurred in relation to those who have ceased to annoy. For instance, there is evidence that the initial bitterness against the peasantry which was so manifest in the first half of the nineteenth century has abated (Singh, K.S., 1972 : 377).

The concept does not extend to cover the category of exploitative elements in the tribal social structure or even among those groups which have been recognised as part of the larger social complex and the regional system such as Nagbansi chiefs. A distinction has also been always made by the tribes between the jagirdars and zamindars who have lived among them for centuries and those who came from outside in the first or second decade of the nineteenth century. The Hindu castes like Tanti or Swansi, Ghasi, Bhogta, Lohar etc. who had settled much before the coming of the alien landlords, and who respected the social and economic superiority of the Munda, were not looked upon as *dikus*, but as part of their communal life.

After the 1962 elections, Jharkhand leaders sensed the feeling of discontent among the people who had been promised a Jharkhand state if they voted for the party. As their desire remained unfulfilled, their faith in the leaders began to fade away gradually, and, it was clearly visible in the results of third general elections. Another reason for the people's discontent was that the "top brass" leaders were far away from them. They could not always place their grievances before them. The local leaders were not very helpful in this matter and a wide vacuum was created in the leadership.

Jharkhand leaders who were tired of sitting in the opposition believed that once in the ruling party they could actively pursue policies for the welfare of their people and could fight for a separate statehood. They also faced the difficulties in raising funds for their organisational work. They did not realise that their identity in the Congress would be lost and that the merger would aggravate the people's feelings of resentment. The merger of the Jharkhand Party with the Congress Party, effected in 1963, was thus a natural corollary of the operation of the forces mentioned above. Jaipal Singh, the Jharkhand leader, had not signed the memorandum for a separate state submitted to the SRC in 1955, a political decision hardly surprising, in view of the fact that the Jharkhand Party under his leadership merged with the Congress Party, and decided to withdraw the movement. They were welcomed in the Congress with open arms as the then Chief Minister of Bihar Binodanand Jha saw in it a convenient means of rehabilitating the sagging prestige of the Congress in Chotanagpur.

Factional politics in the Bihar Congress afflicted the merger from the beginning. With the resignation of Binodanand Jha under the Kamraj Plan, Jaipal Singh was dropped from the ministry and his lieutenant S.K. Bage was made minister by the new Chief Minister K.B. Sahay. The rank and file of the party was not happy with the merger and even Jaipal Singh occasionally held out threats of leaving the Congress. The merger was never officially ratified by the Party Conference.

In the fourth general elections in 1967, the erstwhile Jharkhand leaders suffered the blast of the anti-merger wind. S.K. Bage who was made a minister in place of Jaipal Singh by the Chief Minister K.B. Sahay, forfeited his security deposit and many tribal leaders lost their seats. Even Jaipal Singh narrowly escaped defeat in the elections. A number of leaders of the old Jharkhand who had not joined the Congress were more popular with the masses. Of the 29 reserved seats, 7 were won by them. The Congress held the largest share with 14, while the Jana Sangh had 5 seats. Socialist and Swatantra parties also won three seats.

After the fourth general elections, when the objective conditions of a movement were present and there were occasional spurts and, in some cases, even the sustained rhythm of a movement, there was no unified political expression of this. The structure of the Jharkhand Party had been fragmented i.e., the all-India body had broken up into smaller parties formed by tribal sub-ethnic groups. There was a movement, but no composite party. The Birsa Seva Dal, Vir Birsa Dal, Krantikari Morcha, the Chotanagpur Plateau Praja Parishad, the Adivasi Mahasabha, the Adivasi Chhatra Parishad and some splinter groups calling themselves as the Jharkhand Party appeared on the political scene.

In the late 1960's some national parties such as the Jana Sangh and the Communist Party extended their area of operation to Chotanagpur. As these parties were in the opposition to the ruling Congress Party, they were more popular with the masses. The Jana Sangh started its political activity only from the year 1966 through the Rastriya Swayamsevak Sangh which penetrated into the interior areas and got interested in the social and economic problems of the tribals. Within a short time it succeeded in attracting non-Christian educated tribals to its fold. During the 1966-67 famine, the local Jana Sangh workers distributed cooked food at a nominal price. In the 1967 elections the Jana Sangh emerged as a strong political party next only to the Congress in Chotanagpur. The ground for the penetration of the Jana Sangh was prepared by the communal riots of Jamshedpur in 1964, which spread into the interior of Singhbhum and Ranchi districts. It was followed by an intensive and extensive campaign by the Jana Sangh. The Jana Sangh was helped in this campaign by the Arya Samaj which launched the *Sudhikaran* (reconversion) movement. More than three thousand were reconverted by 1968 to Hinduism by them. While the Jana Sangh tried to expand its influence in all the tribal areas it concentrated mainly on non-Christian tribals. In the 1967 general elections it could secure five Assembly seats in Ranchi and Singhbhum. Communal riots in Ranchi in 1967 provided further ground for the Jana Sangh's expansion. But the Jana Sangh, despite its influence and organisation, could not give a lead to the tribals for the struggle for redressal of their main grievances, such as the restoration of land grabbed by Mahajans and others, exploitation by money-lenders and securing employment.

This phase also saw another trend, that of the emergence of the non-Christian tribal leadership. Prior to this, the Christian tribals, by virtue of their better education and organisational facilities afforded to them by the missionaries, came forward and fostered political consciousness in Chotanagpur, and therefore, dominated political leadership. It were the Christians who reaped most of the economic and educational advantages. Consequently, non-Chrristian tribals suffered neglect by the government in matters of economic and educational development. This roused a sense of resentment among them. In the Congress there were some non-Christian tribal leaders who advocated that in view of their progress in education and other fields, the Christian tribals should no more be allowed to enjoy safeguards and the privileges given by the Constitution. They demanded that the amount now spent on them should be diverted to the non-Christian tribals who were still very backward. During the visit of the Chanda Committee to Ranchi in November 1968, a big demonstration was held under the leadership of Kartik Oraon, sitting Congress M.P., to stress this point. In 1973 he also introduced a bill in Parliament with this object in view.

During the late 1960s there had been a distinct radicalisation of politics. This came about as a result of the articulation of the agrarian factor in the tribal situation. The Jharkhand in its constitutional role as a regional party, had played down the agrarian issue. During the intervening years the agrarian situation had become worse. The incidence of alienation of land belonging to tribals had shown an upward trend; more educated tribal youths were unemployed; the construction of industrial complexes had resulted in the displacement of tribals from their land and their absorption into industrial culture was slow. Though there was some progress in tribal regions, it was on a smaller scale than elsewhere, and it was also outstripped by rising aspirations among the new generation of the tribal community. The participation of a section of the tribal leadership in the government resulted in the distinct improvement in some matters, i.e., more tribals were employed in the government than before, the quotas reserved for tribals were, by and large, filled; more attention was paid to their region, and there was also a larger flow of funds. But, evidently this was not enough.

This radicalisation was also due to the influence of the Naxalite movement, and the entry of leftist parties in the region, in a big way. These parties had generally kept themselves out of tribal politics, and their interest had been limited to the sections of the workers engaged in mining and other industries. The leftist orientation to politics meant a greater stress on political education of workers and agrarian issues, a linking up of local and all-India politics, a measure of violence and militancy in means, and a better organisation. There was also commitment by all-India leftist parties to the concept of tribal autonomy as distinct from the formation of a tribal state.

The political character of the Jharkhand movement receded in the background and the agrarian aspects came into prominence. The formal political slogan of a separate state has not been given up, but there is greater stress on the nature and consequences of exploitation, isolation and neglect. As mentioned earlier, apart from the splinter groups of the Jharkhand Party, a number of small organisations have emerged in the changed situation competing for providing leadership to the tribal unrest. While each group has its own programme and has some vital differences with the other groups, all have been in agreement on one issue—the demand for a separate state of the tribals—the Jharkhand State. The Roman Catholic Church and the GEL Church also became very active in the agitation. Among these organisations, the Birsa Seva Dal, a youth wing of the movement, seemed to be more active and popular in Ranchi district. The Church commands a powerful influence on the Christian tribals. Taking advantage of the discontent among the tribals on their genuine grievances, the Church has been encouraging the demand for a separate state of the tribals. Apart from a demand for a separate Jharkhand state, the common demands of all tribal organisations were : (a) end of the exploitation of the tribals by Mahajans and traders, (b) restoration of lands grabbed by Mahajans and others, (c) employment of tribals in public and private sector industries, (d) end of official atrocities, (e) reservation of seats for tribal students in all colleges of Ranchi University, (f) appointment of tribals as Vice-Chancellor, Treasurer and Registrar of Ranchi University, and (g) declaration of Birsa Divas on June 3 as public holiday.

The Birsa Seva Dal was organised at the suggestion of Jaipal Singh in 1967. In the beginning this Seva Dal advocated the cause of tribal students and workers. They dealt with cases of delay in the payment of scholarships, difficulties in admission to the post-graduate classes and so on. Whenever they came to know about claims of employment or promotion of tribal candidates that had been overlooked, they brought it to the notice of the higher authorities and sought justice. When the communal riots broke out in Ranchi on 22 August, 1967, the Seva Dal organised a 'Peace Dal' which went round convincing the tribals that they should not be involved in this communal riot.

The Birsa Seva Dal, which was boosted by the missionaries in one area and the Communists in another, believed that Jharkhand could not be achieved by mere demands. Its leadership consisted of young educated tribals. Their slogans were *Jharkhand Hamara Hai* and '*Jharkhand Larke Lenge—* '*Teer Ke Bal Par*' or "Jharkhand will be won by a fight with the force of arrows". This exclusive tribal face of the Birsa Seva Dal was not relished by the old or new Jharkhand leaders as it takes the wind out of their call for a separate state consisting of both tribals and non-tribals. It was felt that the Seva Dal was gradually passing into the hands of the Communists who provided money and leadership. A few of the Muslim sufferers during the riots in 1967 had also sympathies with the Birsa Seva Dal and the separatist movement; they had supplied money to the Birsa Seva Dal and the Adivasi Mahasabha was recently organised by a section of the Jharkhandis. The student leaders in Ranchi felt disgusted with the self-interested power-seeking leaders who could be purchased by any party. They had faced police firing now and had shed their fear and were prepared to go to any extent for their own people. The veteran leaders of the Jharkhand Party claimed that it was far from dead. It was soon to be reorganised as 'Jharkhand Prant Dal' with its field of activity widened in the rural areas.

The rise of the Jharkhand and the Hul Jharkhand checked the influence of the Congress to a great extent. In the mid-term elections of 1969, the position of Congress came down to 10 seats. Jana Sangh appeared as a potential rival by winning six seats. Independent candidates secured 4 seats. The Jharkhand and Hul Jharkhand parties won 4 seats each. Socialist and Swatantra parties secured one seat each. Justin Richard the leader of the Hul Jharkhand Party, was an erstwhile colleague of Jaipal Singh. He took advantage of the anti-money-lender campaign of Sibu Soren, a leftist Santal worker, who had gone underground. He also organised forcible cutting of paddy from fields mortgaged by Santals to the money-lenders. He wielded great influence in Santal Parganas. The Jharkhand Party joined the coalition ministry in Bihar on the assurance that a statutory autonomous Board be formed for the development of Chotanagpur. The Hul Jharkhand Party sat on the fence.

After some time, the Jharkhand and Hul Jharkhand parties were in disaray. Progressive Hul Jharkhand, Prantiya Jharkhand and some other splinter groups appeared in this area. The tribals were thus left with no good party other than the Congress under whose banner they could organise themselves. The people also attributed India's victory in Bangla Desh to the leadership of the Congress Party. This led the Congress to win a spectacular success in the 1972 elections. 17 of the 29 reserved seats went to Congress. The number of successful independent candidates swelled to 7. The Jharkhand Party secured three seats and the Hul Jharkhand only one. The CPI also secured a seat. The Jana Sangh did not secure even a single seat.

From 1970 onwards efforts have been made towards inter-regional and inter-tribal solidarity and rejuvenation of the Jharkhand Party and the Jharkhand movement. Two memoranda were submitted to the Prime Minister of India during this period. Under the leadership of N.E. Horo, an ex-M.P. from Khunti and now MLA and the President of the Jharkhand Party (Horo Group), the movement has partially regained its lost prestige. The Bagun group of the Jharkhand Party under the leadership of Bagun Sumrai has regained influence in Singhbhum and has been opposed to the Horo group. The Birsa Seva Dal also renewed its demand for a Jharkhand State. An organisation called Jharkhand Mukti Morcha started *akli akharas* (places for intellectual discussion). The Morcha became quite active in restoring the lands from the money-lenders to the tribals. Another organization, called the Jharkhand Mukti Andolan, has come into existence recently and has also demanded a separate tribal state.

From the 1952 general elections onwards, Jaipal Singh was elected as M.P. from the Munda area in Ranchi district till his death in 1969. After his death, N.E. Horo, President Jharkhand Party (Horo group), won this seat in the 1970 bye-elections and in the 1971 general elections. As a result of an election petition by Jahan-Ara Jaipal Singh, Horo was unseated but he won the seat again in the 1974 bye-elections. In all these elections his nearest rival was the Jana Sangh candidate, Karia Munda.

During the movement led by Jayaprakash Narayan the Munda area responded with enthusiasm to the crusade against the evils of corruption, unemployment, rising prices etc. In Khunti, the movement was initiated and kept alive by the local Munda leaders. Chhatra and Jana Sangharsh Samitis were formed to carry out the programme of the movement. They took out processions and gheraoed the S.D.O. and B.D.O. They staged *dharnas* at several government offices such as the S.D.O's office, B.D.O's office, the Post Office etc. They also staged *dharnas* at the district government offices. It was during the movement period that N.E. Horo (then M.P.) and President of the Jharkhand Party took out a procession of 400 to 500 Chotanagpurias in New Delhi to press for his demand for a separate Jharkhand State.

With the proclamation of the internal emergency in June 1975, hectic police combing of the region started and about 40 prominent opposition leaders, local and national, were arrested. Some youths who had earlier participated in or had sympathy with the J.P. movement, formed a Youth Congress unit to evade arrest or police harassment and opened an office in Khunti town. As they failed to gain the support of the local

Congress workers, on the announcement of the March 1977 elections they closed down the office and some of them started working for the Janata Party candidate.

During the emergency, corruption and authoritarianism of the bureaucracy, the anti-encroachment drive and forced sterilization in the name of family planning, the imposition of a surcharge on land rent, encroachment on the powers of the judiciary etc. brought untold sufferings to the people. Under Twenty Point Programme some big landowners surrendered a few acres of their land above the ceiling. These lands were mostly infertile. However, the donors were keen to see that the lands were distributed among those who were and would remain loyal to them. Some government lands were also distributed, but these were also barren and no effort was made to make them cultivable. This was confirmed by important local Congress workers. However, there were some other measures under the Twenty Point Programme which proved fruitful. These included a number of agrarian measures which placed strong curbs on alienation of land and provided for debt redemptions and credit support, allotment of homestead land and restoration of land. After the announcement of the election on 18 January, 1977, and the formation of the Janata Party at the national level, the local unit of the Jana Sangh came to be known as the Janata Party.

In the Lok Sabha elections in March 1977 all the 5 Scheduled Tribe seats in Parliament went to the Janata Party. In the 1977 State Assembly elections, out of 29 Scheduled Tribe seats, the Janata bagged the major share with 18 seats, the Congress got only 4 seats, independents got 5 and the Jharkhand (Horo) and CPI won 1 seat each.

During the 1977 general elections the Congress, Janata and Jharkhand (Horo group) parties contested the Khunti parliamentary seat. T. Mochi Rai Munda, Karia Munda and N.E. Horo were the candidates from these three parties respectively. Earlier, an effort was made for an electoral adjustment between the Janata and Jharkhand Parties. But no such understanding could be reached between them. Karia Munda won the seat defeating N.E. Horo. His success showed that the non-Christian Munda leadership was more powerful than before. In the State Assembly elections out of 15 seats in Ranchi district, 8 went to the Janata, the Congress bagged 3, the Jharkhand (Horo) and the CPI(M) one each, and Independents two seats respectively. Out of 7 seats for Scheduled Tribes in Ranchi, the Janata got 5 and the Jharkhand and the Congress one seat each. Of the 6 Assembly seats in Khunti parliamentary constituency, 4 went to the Janata Party and one each to the Jharkhand (Horo) and Independent candidates.

In the post-election phase, the issue of a separate statehood for Chotanagpur and Santal Parganas, has surfaced again. Janata Party legislators of Chotanagpur and Santal Parganas had formed a nine-member Committee led by Lalit Oraon (Bihar's Forests Minister) for the creation of a separate state of Chotanagpur.

Meetings of different groups owing allegiance to different political parties have started taking place at Ranchi in a bid to gear up the demand for a separate Jharkhand State. A 42-member Sangharsha Samiti was constituted on 14 October, 1977 at a meeting of tribal leaders convened by Kartik Oraon, M.L.A.

These observations show that the issue of separate state for Chotanagpur and Santal Parganas has again come to the forefront. All the three parties, i.e., Janata, Congress and Jharkhand and their tribal and non-tribal leaders in the region have taken up this issue under three different groups, each led by Kartik Oraon, Jahanara Jaipal Singh and Lalit Oraon. Simultaneously, the C.P.M. and other extremist leftist workers have been supporting the cause for autonomy.

We have observed how tribal ethnicity, which provided the motivation of the Unnati Samaj and the Adibasi Mahasabha gradually developed into a regional movement. Tribal ethnicity in a multi-ethnic society characterised by economic interdependence and ritual ties among different communities had a different course of development in Chotanagpur as against the North-East ; separatism did not develop into secessionism. From 1947 onwards all movements have in their manifestoes spoken of regional and inter-ethnic programmes ; tribals have remained the dominant but not the exclusive element. This has been due to the realisation that the tribals do not form the majority in Chotanagpur as a whole, and that there are backward communities, in this backward region, who could also be brought together on a common political platform. However, the top leadership of the Jharkhand movement always remained with the educated Mundas from Jaipal Singh, the first President to N.E. Horo who leads the Horo group of the Jharkhand Party. The movement was most popular in the Munda area which had a safe ground for such a movement and had witnessed a number of revolts in the past. The Munda leadership and political consciousness were able to lead such a movement and sustain it through the changed political atmosphere in the nation, and transforming it from an ethnic movement to a regional movement thus expanding the horizon of its identity.

12

THE REALM OF BELIEF AND RITUAL

RELIGION is generally used to designate man's relation to supernatural powers and the various organised systems of belief and worship in which these relations have been expressed. There are no people, however primitive, who are without religion. Religion interacts significantly with other cultural institutions to such an extent that no social phenomenon presents a wider range of expression and implication.

The study of religion as manifested and expressed in its beliefs and rituals is more significant than as a body of doctrine on a mere mental force making for a highly organised attitude of mind. Beliefs and rituals are invariant factors in all religions. Every religion has some supernatural objects of belief, but religions differ in regard to their orientation. This is where particular beliefs and rituals of one society differ from those of another. As expressive actions of behaviour, rituals are symbolic and as such are not arbitrary but appropriate to a given culture.

MUNDA COSMOLOGY AND COSMOGONY

The problem of the origin of man and the world around him seems to have interested the human mind at all places and in all ages. All cosmogonic legends are the results of man's ambitious attempts at a solution of the eternal mystery of creation.

A well-known Mundari mythical legend starts with the creation of the earth. In the beginning of time, the face of the earth was covered with water. Singbonga, the Sungod (the supreme deity of the Munda) brooded over the waters and the first creatures that were born were a *kachua* (tortoise), a *karakom* (crab), and a *lendad* (leech). Singbonga ordered these creatures to bring him a lump of clay (*hasa*) from the depths of the ocean. The tortoise and the crab by turns tried their best, but all in vain. Then the leech succeeded in fishing out a bit of clay from underneath the ocean. And with this clay, Singbonga made the earth. At his bidding, the Earth brought forth trees and plants and herbs of different varieties. Singbonga then populated the earth with all types of birds and animals. The bird swan laid an egg. The first human-beings, a boy and a girl hatched out of this egg. These were the progenitors of the *horo honko* (human children) as the Mundas still consider themselves.

The first human pair were innocent of sex relations. So Singbonga pointed out to them certain vegetable roots and taught them to prepare *hanria* or rice-beer with it. They prepared it as directed and drank it. This inflamed their passions. In due course of time, the pair known as *Tota Haram* and *Tota Buria* (the naked male ancestor and the naked female ancestor) were blessed with offspring. Three sons were born to them, one after another. These were named Munda, Nanka and Rora respectively. According to another account, the three sons were named Munda, Nanka and Tenha. From the youngest Tenha, it is said, the *mati* or sooth-sayers of the Mundas are descended. All this happened at a place named Azamgarh. On their parents' death, the sons wandered about far and wide over the earth. Finally, they came to settle in Chotanagpur and established their villages by clearing forests.

A second version of this legend is given by some old Mundas of Sonepur Pargana. It runs as follows. The *horo honko* once cut off their association with the Singbonga. The Singbonga sent a warning to men on earth through his messenger bird Kaua Bhandari (crow, the steward) and Lipi Susari (*Lipi*, the cock). But men refused to obey him. Enraged at this act, Singbonga showered on the earth below a terrible rain of fire to destroy mankind. All the human-beings were destroyed except for a man and a woman, related as brother and sister to each other, whom the Singbonga Misi (the sister of Singbonga) saved by hiding them below a vast stretch of marsh. The Singbonga sent his servant birds to look out for any human-being that might have escaped the calamity. The birds at last found a leaf-cup, such as used by men, on the marsh and confirmed the existence of man. However, they could not see any human-being around. The birds then returned to the Singbonga with this information.

Thereupon Singbonga himself went down to the marsh and met Naga Era, the presiding spirit of the marsh from whom He wanted to know whether she had any human-beings in her custody. Naga Era handed over the surviving human pair to the Singbonga only after the Singbonga promised not to destroy mankind again. Singbonga placed them once more on the green earth. The man and woman were called Lutkum Haram and Lutkum Buria (the old man and the old woman ancestors) respectively. They lived as man and wife at Azamgarh. The world was peopled by their progeny. From Azamgarh their progeny went to various places and finally came to Chotanagpur.

It would not be out of place here to describe briefly the legend related with the origin of the element spirits or nature gods of Munda mythology. This is the Munda legend of Lutkum Haram and Lutkum Buria, otherwise known as the Asur legend.

Singbonga, the beneficent and Supreme Deity of the Munda, was once seated in heaven along with his consort. Soon they were disturbed by an intolerable heat which suddenly surcharged the heavenly atmosphere. The animals and birds on the earth also complained to Singbonga of the scorching heat coming out of the furnaces of the Asurs. Singbonga asked the Asurs through his servant birds like dhechua, karketa, lipi, kanu etc. to stop all work at their furnaces both in the day time and at night. The Asurs did not pay any heed to the advice, but insulted the messengers and continued iron-smelting in their furnaces day and night.

Finally, Singbonga himself set out in search of the Asurs. He changed himself into a boy affected with the itch or the Toro Kora. In Asur villages, He tried for the job of a domestic servant but the Asurs dreaded this contagious itch and did not give him a job. An aged Munda couple called Lutkum Haram and Lutkum Buria who lived in an Asur village took pity and kept him as a servant.

Once, during the Lutkumas' absence from home, the Toro Kora matched his 'egg-*gulis*' and his 'cake-*katis*' against the iron-*gulis* and iron-*katis* of the gods and the Asurs. The iron-*gulis* and iron-*katis* of the gods and the Asurs broke into pieces at a stroke of the egg-*gulis* and cake-*katis* of the Toro Kora. The defeated Asur boys complained to the Lutkums against Toro Kora saying that he did not heed his duties and the rice in the husking pit and in the basket was eaten away by the pigs and the fowl. To their surprise, the complaints were falsified by the discovery of plenty of rice in the husking-pit and in the basket and on the bamboo mats. The same experience was repeated once again and the itch covered boy came to be regarded as endowed with supernatural powers.

It was noticed that the output of the Asurs' furnaces declined. They were very distressed and they approached the Toro Kora for a remedy. As directed by him they sacrificed a white hen and the furnaces once again started functioning perfectly. But it was the beginning of their miseries; the old troubles with their furnaces recurred and were remedied by subsequent sacrifice of a white goat and a white sheep. At the time of another breakdown the Toro Kora asked for a human sacrifice for remedying the trouble. He offered himself for the sacrifice convincing them that He was fed up of his itching trouble and wanted to die for a noble cause.

As directed by Him, the Asurs put Him inside the furnace and worked the furnaces with newly made bellows. At the end of three days and nights, the fire was put out and the furnace opened up. The erstwhile Toro Kora came out with a shining figure decorated with gold and silver. The amazed Asurs were advised by Him to enter the furnace and bring out gold and silver for themselves. When all the men had got into the furnace, He ordered the Asur women to kindle the fire and work the bellows. While they worked the bellows, the screams of men came out of the furnace. The women were consoled by Singbonga saying that the men were quarrelling over the division of the spoils. When the blood started oozing out, He satisfied them by saying that it was the saliva spit out by the men after chewing betel leaves. Finally, when the furnace was opened up the women got horrified at the sight of the charred bones and ashes of their unfortunate husbands, sons and brothers. They wept and accused the Toro Kora of getting their men killed by their own hands.

At this, Singbonga told the women that this disaster was caused on account of disobedience of His orders. The women agreed to obey him henceforth, so He told them that the *pahan* would now onwards make offerings to them. When Singbonga was ready to depart the Asur women would not let him go. Thereupon Singbonga caught them by the hair and hurled them in different directions. Some were dropped on high mountains, some on rocks, some in deep waters, some on uplands, others again fell on wooded spots by the side of springs, and yet others were assigned pleasant meadows and groves for their future abode. Their disembodied spirits were to live for ever as presiding deities at these different places. Such is the origin of the nature-gods of the Munda pantheon. These include the Buru Bonga, the presiding spirit of the hills, the Ikir Bonga dwelling in the deep waters, the Nage Bonga who resides in the uplands and in the ravines, the Desauli Bonga who lives in woodlands and the Chandi Bonga whose abode is in shady groves, in the open fields or on hills.

THE MUNDA PANTHEON : THE HIERARCHY OF THE SUPERNATURAL

The Munda are aware that despite their existential knowledge and physical efforts, the course of nature is at times affected by agencies outside their sphere of control. To cope with this mysterious supernatural world, the Munda, like other tribes, have evolved a system of beliefs and practices. According to them, the supernatural world is peopled with a large number of supernatural spirits called *bongas* and a large number of impersonal powers. These are believed to shape the course of nature and of human events.

Munda beliefs in these supernatural spirits and the ways of entering into relations with them constitute their religion. It fits into Radcliffe-Brown's view that "religion is everywhere an expression, in one form or another, of a sense of dependence on a power outside ourselves" (1959: 157). It is precisely this urge to communicate with the higher supernatural world which has led the Munda to personify and, in certain cases, even individualise their spirits.

In Munda religion, the attitude towards these supernatural spirits is one of reverential fear, dependence, submission and propitiation. Communion with these spirits is concretely manifested mainly through supplications, rice-beer offerings and animal sacrifices made on behalf of a particular group, be it the whole village, lineage or household. To these must be added the ceremonial sharing of sacrificial food, besides certain special observances and taboos.

In his study on primitive religion in Chotanagpur, S.C. Roy remarks that though there is a general similarity in the religious systems of the tribes of Chotanagpur, what they really differ in is the relative weighing of the different classes of supernatural powers recognised in their respective pantheons. Thus, while the Oraon concentrate most of their religious thought and attention on their supreme god Dharmes and on the power of the evil eye, the Munda and other Mundari speaking tribes are particularly solicitous about their spirits or *bongas*.

It is from the authority of inherited traditions that present day Munda have derived their ideas and beliefs regarding these supernatural spirits and their modes of ceremonial approach and communion with them. The Munda are not mere worshippers of malevolent spirits as various scholars and missionaries have observed. To label Munda religion as a religion of uttermost fear is an over simplification and a misunderstanding. Many of the *bongas* of the Munda cannot be classified as evil spirits. On the contrary a good number of them are considered as *manita bongas* or beneficent deities. They are not only the protectors of the Munda but are also intimately involved in their welfare and moral behaviour.

A careful study of the Munda religious beliefs and ceremonies will show that the Munda believe in a Supreme Deity whom they call Singbonga, and whose blessings they invoke before every important religious ceremony. Besides Singbonga, the Munda pantheon includes a number of other deities and spirits. The Munda worship and propitiate these supernatural powers for bringing prosperity and averting misfortunes. They worship the spirits of their deceased ancestors (house gods) and the village gods. They also propitiate, as required, the *banita bongas* or malevolent spirits to avert their wrath. Nature gods like Buru Bonga, Ikir Bonga etc. do good and bad alike. They generally do good but when an individual Munda, or a family or a village offends them, they are annoyed and are to be propitiated by the *sokha* and sometimes by the village *pahan* to avert their ill effect.

Singbonga

Singbonga is the supreme deity of the Munda. He is worshipped before every religious function. He has no specific worship, but is reverentially remembered by the Munda when, before every meal, a Munda puts down on the ground a few grains of rice from his plate as an offering. In serious natural calamities, however, Singbonga is specially invoked and a white fowl is sacrificed to him. He is believed to accept white offerings. Therefore, He is offered white *gulainchi* flowers, white hen and white goat, white cloth, sugar, and milk etc.

Singbonga is considered to be the supreme creator. He has created the whole universe, the earth, the animals, the plants, rivers and seas. He created the human-beings to enjoy the fruits of His creation. He created the other *bongas* or deities and spirits and ruled over them. He is the ever beneficent god of gods, by whose authority the inferior deities hold their places and perform their functions. According to the good or bad life led by a man during his present life, he will be sent back to the world by Singbonga either as a man or as a beast, as a bird or as an insect. The most solemn oath of the Munda is *Sirmare Singbonga, ote re panch* (by Singbonga in heaven and the panch on the earth).

Village Gods (*hatu bongako*)

The village gods help the Munda in their agricultural operations and hunting excursions, and guide them in day-to-day life and order every human event. They are the *manita-bongas* or beneficent gods who bring prosperity to the village and ward off disease and other calamities. They are worshipped by the *pahan* or village priest, on behalf of the whole village, at specific times in the sacred groves or *sarna* of each village. They include the Dasauli-bonga, the Devibonga, and Jayar-bongako.

Dasauli Bonga: Dasauli bonga lives at a specific place in the fields. It is forbidden to fell the trees at the place she resides lest the *bonga* gets annoyed. In that situation she may cause death to women during pregnancy or confinement. The crops may also be lost due to the *bonga's* wrath. The village *Pahan* worships the Dasauli bonga at her abode with Arua rice. All the village households are supposed to be represented at the time of worship. Dasauli bonga is offered a black bullock for sacrifice but this practice has now disappeared.

Devi Bonga: The Munda have started worshipping some of the Hindu deities due to constant interaction with Hindus living among them. Once every year and at the time of epidemics, the Munda worship the Devi Mai (Devibonga) along with Buru-bonga and Ikirbonga. The three deities are worshipped together by the *pahan* at a specific place outside the eastern boundary of the village under a *golainchi* tree. A red he-goat for Buru-bonga, black he-sheep for Ikirbonga and two black pigeons and one black he-goat for Devibonga are sacrificed respectively for these three deities by the *pahan.*

A red and a white flag each are fixed at the place of worship for the Devi and Singbonga respectively. All the households are required to be represented at the worship. The sacrificial meat is cooked and enjoyed outside the village boundary near some spring or stream. The sacrificial meat is distributed equally among the participants.

Jayarbongako: Sarna or Jayar is a protected place in each Munda village. It is situated between thickly grown trees which are forbidden to be cut. Sarna represents the vestige of the original forest which was cleared by the original settlers of the village long back while establishing the village. The *pahan* worships the various deities of the Munda pantheon at the time of Sarhul in the Sarna for prosperity of the village.

Golainchi flowers are used for worshipping all deities other than Jayarbongako. However, at Sarhul *Sal*-flowers are used for worship. The *pahan* sacrifices a member of hens for different gods. He prays for good crops and for keeping the people and cattle-wealth of the village protected from diseases, epidemics and other misfortunes.

HOUSE GODS (ORABONGAKO)

The house gods are worshipped by the head of every Munda household in the *ading* of his house. When these deities are annoyed they cause trouble to the family members as well as to the cattle, it is believed.

These include ancestors or Haram Horoko of each family, and are worshipped once a year; and a light reddish (*sukra*) hen is sacrificed for them. These look after the welfare of the family.

(b) *Marangbonga* (*Mahadeo*) : Marangbonga of the Munda is synonymous with Lord Mahadeo of the Hindus. No hen, goat or sheep is sacrificed for Marangbonga, instead *urad* pulse and boiled rice are used as an offering. If fruit trees like *karanj*, mango and jack fruit do not bear fruit and the crops fail, the failure is attributed to Marangbonga's wrath.

On a particular day the *sal* twigs with leaves are fixed in front of the house. Two of these are taken inside the house and tied to two wooden structures of the house-roof. The worship is then performed at the place where the twigs are fixed in the ground. After worship, when all the members of that household sit for a meal they do not talk among themselves. Outsiders are not included in this feast.

Except Marangbonga, no other *bonga* is represented symbolically. In the *bari* (kitchen garden) attached to the house, a wooden stick about six feet long is fixed behind the wall of the house. An earthen pot smeared with rice flour paste is put upside down on the standing stick. This represents the Marangbonga. No one is supposed to touch it and children are kept away from it by covering it with thorny plants.

Gonra Bonga: This *bonga* looks after the welfare of the household cattle. A red hen is sacrificed in his name every year at a particular time. If he is not worshipped in a particular year, the cattle may be taken ill. On such occasions a red-goat is sacrificed. The sacrifice is made inside the cattle shed and the food is also prepared there itself on that very day. The meat of the sacrificed animal is not allowed to be taken by anyone other than a member of this household and the left over if any, is buried in the ground. Gonrabonga is known by four different names depending upon the method of worship. These are Gonra

Hankar, Hissi Hankar, Be-Hankar and Tundu Hankar.

BANITA BONGAKO

The view that the Munda are worshippers of malevolent spirits appears to have arisen from their offering worship to the *banitabongas*. But in addition to them, they also worship beneficent deities called *manitabongas*. The *banitabongas* are no gods at all, nor are they believed to be so by the Munda. These are the earth bound spirits of those persons who died an unnatural death. These malevolent spirits (*khachra bongako* or *pret*) include the *churinbongas* (spirits of women who died in pregnancy), *harsulivadbongas* (spirits of those who committed suicide), *muabongas* (those who were killed with a weapon), *nagdavabongas* (those who died as a result of snake bite), *kulachandi* (those killed by a tiger) and the *nasanbongas*. The propitiation of this class of spirits is the duty not of the Munda householder or of the village *pahan*, but of the ghost finders—the *mati*, *deonra* or *sokha*. Occasionally the earth bound spirits of some deceased member of a family haunt their old fields and may do some mischief; in such a case they have to be propitiated by sacrifices. But such a spirit does not form a part of the regular Munda pantheon.

Nature-gods

There is another class of supernatural powers known to the Munda. These are the elemental spirits or nature-gods. Such as the *Burubonga*, *Ikir bonga*, *Naga Era*, *Chandi bonga* and *Birbonga* etc. The origin of nature-gods has been described in the previous section. These stand between the beneficent deities and the malevolent spirits and they do good and bad alike. Their main function is to do good, but when an individual or a family or a village offends them, these spirits are annoyed and are to be propitiated by the *sokha* and sometimes by the village *pahan* to avert their anger.

Burubonga: Burubonga is supposed to reside on a hill. The rocks and the trees of that place cannot be destroyed. Burubonga helps the villagers in difficult situations. His help may be solicited by promising a sacrifice in his name and it is a must to give the due sacrifice immediately (at an already fixed date) after the trouble is over. Burubonga likes the sacrifice of a red hen and red goat. The Burubonga of wife's village helps the newly married couple more than that of his own village and thus the sacrifice of a red hen is offered by them after marriage. Once at Gitu Bera on the banks of the Koel river two brothers were engaged in fishing The elder brother caught a fish by his fish hook. When he took it out, the fish escaped. Both of them went searching for it and found it lying on the Hai-Buru near Bundu. They told the villagers that it was their fish. (A fish-like rock is still found on the Hai-Buru or fish hill). The villagers regarded them to be the men sent by God and requested them to settle there. They gave them land. These two brothers were known as Gutu Sahay and Bisu Sahay. They asked the villagers to do as they wished and the latter agreed. They were asked to worship Marang-buru and Hai-buru. All of them had a bath. These two brothers sprinkled mud on the body.

Marangburu was worshipped first followed by Hai-buru. After that Sukun Buru, Sandi Buru, Patra Buru are worshipped in Aghan and Hessa Buru in Posh. For their worship *kokro-cho* flower and rice-bread are used and men and women wear the flowers in their hair and over the ear. The *pahan* performs the worship. The Sukun Buru worship started when the Munda migrated to the Hasda area from Bundu area. Hessa Buru worship started when the Munda of Murhu once took away a Munda girl from Sukun Buru *jatra*. The next year they did not come to Sukun Buru *jatra* for fear of being taken to task and so they started the worship and *jatra* at Hessa Buru from that year.

The *pahan* while worshipping the Buru *jatra* chants *mantras* which mean 'Let the people fight each other and shed blood on the Buru. Let this blood be a token of sacrifice for the Burubonga and serve to expiate their sins, committed during the year.' Earlier the Munda used to take bamboo sticks with them to the *jatra* and picked up ritual fights leading to injuries. Burubonga is worshipped and called upon to help during fights.

Sukun Buru Jatra

This *jatra* or fair is celebrated to worship the Burubonga. Villagers from far and near flock to Sukun Buru. The seven *pahans* of seven villages around this hill viz., Dulmi, Sukandih,

Jonadih, Lotor, Buradih, Toladah etc. worship at the Sukun-buru in their respective boundaries on the hill in the morning of ninth day after the *purnima* (full moon) in the month of *Aghan* (December). In these villages there are separate *pahans* to perform the worship for the Buru-bonga at the village *sarna*.

On the eve of the *jatra* a camp-fire is arranged by the people of Dulmi, Sukardih etc., on the Sukunburu and the people in the distant villages come to know of it. The villagers start coming next morning in colourful clothes. Small shops appear on the hill. In the forenoon the *pahans* perform the worship, in the afternoon men and women dance and sing in the *akhra* at the top of the Sukunburu. The villagers approach the *jatra mela* with music played on instruments. At night the dance and song programmes are held in the *akhras* of the villages around the hill. This *jatra* lasts one day.

A similar *jatra* or fair is held on the Sandi Buru near Chondor where *Pahan* of Chondor performs worship. This *jatra* is smaller than that at Sukunburu and is held a day after the latter.

Ikir Bonga

Ikir (spring) *bonga* resides near some spring or field. The trees of that place are not destroyed and the field is left uncultivated. This *bonga* helps during troubles. Ikirbonga generally troubles married women and the Ikirbonga of the wife's village is more well-disposed towards the married man. A black sheep is sacrificed for the Ikirbonga. At Sarhul and Devi-bonga worship also, black hen and black sheep respectively are sacrificed for *Ikirbonga*.

Nage Bonga

Nagebonga resides around the fields or springs or rocks near the fields. The cultivated land where Nagebonga has its abode is harvested after sacrificing a black chicken in his name. Otherwise some person harvesting the crop may get a cut in the hand or develop stomach-ache while reaping the crop.

It is thought improper to visit the place of Nagebonga at mid-day as it may provoke his wrath. Sometimes his voice is heard like that of a crying baby. Itching is attributed to the anger of Nagebonga. The sufferer is advised to rub a copper coin on his body. At night, turmeric, rice dyed in turmeric and fire are placed on the path outside the village in the name of the angry *Nagebonga.* In case the deity is not pleased by this service a black chicken is sacrificed. In certain extreme cases the sacrifice of a pig becomes necessary to please the Nagebonga.

Chandi Bonga

Chandibonga resides generally near some trees or rocks. Children are not allowed to visit that place for the fear of being affected. Children under the spell of *Chandi* remain sick for most of the time. He may be seen in the form of a black dog, sheep, cat, human-being or tiger at night. He does not cause physical harm except by arousing fear in the mind of a person. Sometimes his presence may be felt when at night the sound of the footsteps of invisible animals is heard.

Chandibonga is offered sacrifice of ash coloured or white and black hen. The Mundas invoke Chandibonga's help in hunting expeditions by offering him sacrifices before setting out on the hunt. Chandibonga is also propitiated for acquiring desired success in a court case or against an enemy.

Sometimes Chandibonga is supposed to bring dust-storms and some persons may develop stomach ache subsequently. A black hen for Chandibonga and white hen for Singbonga are sacrificed to neutralise this effect.

Birbonga

Birbonga or Birsabonga is one and the same deity. The worship of Birbonga was initiated by the Munda to protect their fields from forest animals. Also Birbonga was invoked for help in hunting. These days the purpose of worship has changed. Those who desire wealth and good crops worship Birbonga. Not all households worship Birbonga. The worship is performed in front of the house or in the kitchen garden and not inside the house. Either a red hen or goat or both are offered as sacrifice every year. The neglect of Birbonga may cause failure of the crops or sickness in the family. In that case red goat is sacrificed to appease the annoyed Birbonga.

There is another class of beneficent Mundari deities. These

are the protective deities of particular families and groups. These are the Achraelbonga, Garasibonga etc. Achraelbonga presides over the interests of married women. If any such woman stealthily takes away any article from her parental house, the Achraelbonga would show its displeasure by bringing sickness to the house where the stolen goods are taken. Garasibonga looks after women during pregnancy and presides over child birth. To ensure the well-being of the expectant mother and the foetus, a red or grey hen is set apart by the head of the family, and a pitcher of rice-beer is prepared, in honour of Garasibonga, as soon as the first indications of pregnancy are observed. A date is fixed for the worship of the Garasibonga. On that date, the father, brother or uncle of the expectant woman comes to her house to perform the necessary worship. After offering prayers to the Garasibonga for the well-being of the expectant mother and of the child in the womb, he sacrifices the hen and makes offerings of its head, liver and tail, all boiled together, to the spirits of his deceased ancestors. This is followed by feasting and drinking.

RITUAL FUNCTIONARIES

Ritual activities are the best expressions of the religious life of human groups. As expressive aspects of behaviour, rituals are symbolic acts which are not arbitrary but appropriate to a given culture. These symbolic actions help men to enter into and reassert their social relationship with the supernatural world. The Munda believe that it is essential for every household, lineage, clan and village community to promote friendly relations with their supernatural powers. To do this, it is important to provide the *bongas* with offerings and sacrifices through which they enter into communion with their spirits. The contact between supernatural powers and the Munda is maintained by two kinds of functionaries known as the *pahan* and *mati, sokha* or *bhagat*. Besides these, the Munda have also felt the impact of Hinduism for several centuries. They have adopted a number of Hindu deities and rituals by imitating the lower caste Hindus living among them. In some areas, we find them employing Brahmins in their worship and rites de passage.

The *pahan* is the religious head of the village among the Munda. He is responsible for religious matters and enjoys great influence and prestige. He maintains amicable relations between the village and the village deities and other supernatural beings. The *pahan* is hereditary in Salehatu, Jojohatu and other villages in the Hasda area, while in Gutuhatu, Kalet and other villages in the Bhuinhari area, the *pahan* serves for a period of three years, and his selection is made by divination with the winnowing fan. Ordinarily he belongs to the *pahan* Khut, but failing a suitable candidate, he may be selected from the families descended from the original settlers of a different lineage. In various Oraon villages previously occupied by the Munda, a Munda is the hereditary *pahan*, because the Munda were the first settlers and the village deities must be propitiated by one familiar with the spirits of the locality.

The *pahan* holds *pahnai* service lands which may not be alienated. This land is rent-free and cannot be resumed by the government so long as any member of the village community is alive. The function of the *pahan* is to propitiate village deities, on behalf of the entire village and to ward off disease and misfortune. His assistant is known as the *pujar* or *pan-bhara*. The latter too is given the use of rent-free land which is known as the *pujarkhet*. He is elected every year from the *pujar* lineage or failing that from the ranks of the Bhuinhars.

The Munda like Santal, Ho and Oraon have a more elaborate system of village worship centred on the sacred grove or *sarna* where the village deities reside. The *sarna* consists of a cluster of *sal* trees which, it is taboo to cut down. The *pahan* worships these deities at *sarhul* with proper sacrifices. He fasts for a day prior to the *sarhul* and on the festival day worships all the g ods of the Munda pantheon in the *sarna* in the presence of the assembled Mundas and sacrifices a number of fowls. Food is cooked in new earthen pots at the *sarna*. The following morning, the *pahan*, with a number of *sal* flowers used at the worship on the previous day, visits each house in the village, inserts a bunch of *sal* blossoms in the door or roof of each house for which he receives a small fee. *Sal* samplings and flowers are hung at the door to ward off evils. In the afternoon a woman from each Munda household in the village goes to the *pahan's* house with a pot of water and a little oil. Each woman on her arrival washes *pahan's* feet, anoints him with oil, and washes his feet again. The *pahan* makes a present of two jars of rice-beer to the visitors. The *pahan* performs worship on the occasion of various other festivals. These include *phagu* festival, the *batauli, khalihan puja, Jom Nawa* and the *Ind parob*. In some villages in Hasda area there are different *pahans* to propitiate the village gods and the Burubonga respectively. At the Sukunburu, *pahans* of seven different villages perform worship in December. The ingredients of the worship performed by the *pahan* to establish communion with the *hatu bongako* and other deities of the Munda, include supplications, rice-beer offerings and animal sacrifices made on behalf of the village.

In Salehatu, Jojohatu, Gutuhatu and Kalet the institution of *pahan* is still viable and active. However, among the Hinduised Munda of Amlesa in Panch Parganas the village *pahan* does not worship the Hatubongako any more. The *pahan* of Jojohatu long back established relations with a Swanasi woman and he was socially boycotted by the villagers. As he did not agree to undergopurification ceremony he was not readmitted to the village community. The Munda of the village do not interdine with him even now, but he still worships the village gods at the *sarna* on Sarhul though the villagers do not participate in the worship. In Deori village in Tamar area the *pahan* performs routine worship at the Devi Temple and acts as the ritual sacrificer at the Dasehra festival.

In Birhu, the *pahan* had a Christian name even though he was a non-Christian. In the worship performed on the occasion of the Sarhul festival he stood on one leg. Since people were not taking as much interest in worship as before, life was becoming difficult for him. Formerly, at the time of worship the *sarna* used to be full of people. Not only the unconverted Munda but also the Christian Munda and even people of other castes and tribes used to come and attend it.

The *panbhara* assists the *pahan* during the worship at the village *sarna* especially at *sarhul* festival. He cleans the *sarna* and keeps two pitchers full of water there on the day prior to *sarhul* worship. During the worship he helps the *pahan*. It is the *panbhara* who officiates at the rain-making ceremony. All the villagers assemble at a nearby hill. There the *panbhara* worships the *burubonga* (rain god) with milk. Then he boils the milk in a new earthen pot hiding it from the assembled villagers on the hillside. If the milk soon boils up to brim it is considered a positive sign for bringing rain. Now the *panbhara* orders those assembled there to aim at the milk pot so as to break it into pieces and let the milk spill over. The moment the pot is broken the *panbhara* along with others return to the village. This ritual is believed to bring rain immediately. This is an example of homoeopathic magic.

As regards rain-making, there are also other rituals prevalent among the Munda. In some villages, the Munda go up a nearby hill and roll stones down the hill to produce a sound similar to the bursting of clouds to bring about rain. In Birhu the ceremony connected with rain-making is called the worship of Rajrogi Bonga. At Dudu Buru, one mile west of Birhu all men assemble for a dance. Before the dance begins a black goat or a fowl is sacrificed to Marang Buru. Rice-beer is served to all the boys and girls who then begin the dance. They dance for the whole day. By that time the clouds appear and when it is evening, it is believed it will rain so heavily that they will go back home completely wet.

MAGIC, WITCHCRAFT AND THE RITUAL FUNCTIONARIES

As observed earlier, the Munda believe in a class of mischivous impersonal spirits and evil powers which are not objects of worship, but which have to be scared away through exorcism or magic. Their attitude towards these spirits is mainly one of defiance, control and domination. Magic, unlike religion, is reserved only to the specialist. This distinction is also evident in the fact that among the Munda the ritual functionaries are different for religion and magic. This is similar to the case with other Chotanagpur tribes such as the Santal, the Ho and the Oraon. The Munda also distinguish between beneficent (white) and maleficent (black) magic.

Sokha

The minister of white magic is known as *sokha*, *mati*, *deonra*, *najo*, *vaidya* (medicine-man), *ojha*, or *bhagat* (diviner). The ministers of black magic are known as *dain* or witches and sorcerers. The *sokha* seeks to expose and counteract the anti-social activities of the sorcerer and witch and the evil influence of the impersonal forces. His magic is regarded as useful so long as he does not seek personal vengeance on his fellowmen through evil magic. A *sokha* is believed to possess special powers through which he is able to perform certain deeds that are outside the ken of the ordinary people. Among the Munda only men can become *sokha*. A woman who professes to having intimate relations with *bongas* is considered to be a witch and is persecuted. The services of the *sokha* are much sought af er at the time of disease or any other misfortune in the household. The *sokha* uses several methods of divination and exorcism to find out the cause of a sickness and to try and cure the patient, counteracting the mischief brought about by the evil spirits and powers.

Magic and religion are distinct in the sense that there are different functionaries such as *sokha* and *pahan* respectively. Not only are the objects of magic and religion different but the attitudes towards the *sokha* and *pahan* also differ. In spite of these differences, the Munda's attitudes towards religion and magic are not mutually exclusive. The *sokha's* mission is like that of the *pahan* in so far as both attempt at attaining certain results that accrue to the Munda. Magic and religion are often found together as parts of the same ritual and custom. In situations of emotional stress, both boost the people's morale by giving them hope and confidence.

As against the witch, the *sokha* is the only remedy. He is greatly respected in the villages around. The *sokha* possesses special powers by propitiating *Devi Mai* and *Mahadeva*. In a *sokha* or *bhagat's* house there is a sacred corner either inside the house as in Gutuhatu or in the courtyard as was observed in a non-Mundari *sokha's* house at Amlesa where the Lord Siva and Devi are established and worshipped regularly. A white flag or sometimes a red flag is fixed in the courtyard. The *sokha* of Gutuhatu worships these deities every Tuesday and Thursday with sweets (*sirni*), milk, water, *golainchi* flowers and incense. If possible, on *dasai* festival a white he-goat is sacrificed for *Mahadev* by the *sokha*.

The *sokha* among the Munda and Oraon propitiates Devi Mai, Mahadeva, Kali, Burubonga, Nagabonga, Jair Buru, Haram

Horo etc. Twice a week in the *ading* he worships deities with flowers, incense, *arua* rice and ghee etc. Sometimes, he sacrifices goats and fowl to these deities and if he fails to perform these weekly worships and the annual sacrifice, he thinks that he will lose his powers. He will not reveal his secret powers to anyone.

The *sokha's* power is said to be greater than that of the witch and so he can inflict injuries upon the witch. But if a witch possesses greater power than the *sokha*, then the latter has to suffer a lot. Therefore, a *sokha* has to be very accurate and careful in the practice of his art. Even the Christian tribals believe in witchcraft and employ the services of a Christian or non-Christian witch-finder to detect the causes of disease. The Christian *sokha* invokes divine help through divination, incantations, etc. The method of worship and the remedial measures clearly show the Christian influence.

The *sokhas* employ many occult methods to find out the spirit offended in any particular case. One of the methods described by S.C. Roy is that when a person believes that he is the victim of curse of some such angry spirit, he goes with some *arua* rice and a small quantity of oil to one of these *sokhas*. He lights a lamp with this oil and puts the rice in a winnowing fan. He now concentrates his gaze on the flame of the lamp. After few minutes he starts reciting *mantras* or incantations in which all the spirits are named and at each name some grains of rice from the winnowing fan are thrown into the flame. As soon as the flame flares up to more than its normal size at the repetition of the name of a spirit, that particular spirit is declared to have caused the affliction. Then the *sokha* suggests appropriate sacrifices for propitiating the offended spirit.

The other method of identifying the offended spirit is with *arua* rice and *sal* leaf. In another case the *sokha* lights a fire, and when the smoke rolls up and curls around him, he begins by slowly chanting *mantras* and quietly swaying his body, till at length he works himself up to a frenzy and announces that he has seen the witch who has incited a particular spirit to harm his client. The spirit, too, is named, as also the sacrifices required to appease him.

The *sokha* also plays an important part in performing the *soso tapa* (to ward off disease with *bhelva* twig) ceremony. When the crops of a Munda fail continuously over many years, *sokha* is consulted to find out the evil spirit or witch that is responsible for it. This ceremony is suggested by him to ward off the ill effects of the spirit, witch or the evil eye.

Soso tapa is performed at least a day or two before starting the paddy sowing. On that day the *sokha* draws a square on the ground in the courtyard of the Munda house. The drawing represents the earth and the sky. He, further, draws two circles each representing the sun and the moon. Some paddy is kept inside the square, a *bhelva* twig (*Semicarpus anacardium*) and an egg are placed on top of the paddy. The *sokha* along with other villagers sing Mundari songs in praise of Singbonga whole night. Early next morning before sunrise, he sacrifices an egg in the name of Singbonga and offers prayers standing with folded hands. He, then, touches the paddy three times with the *bhelva* twig. The paddy seed kept inside the house is similarly touched with the *bhelva* twig. Finally, he prays to the Singbonga to ward off the effect of evil eye from the crops. The paddy so purified is sown next day in the fields. In some cases the *sokha* performs *soso tapa* ceremony to protect the standing paddy crop from the evil eye. Then, the *bhelva* twig and the branch of the *keond* tree are planted by the head of the family, after the ceremony, in the middle of each of his paddy fields.

Witches and Sorcerers

Among the Munda, as among other tribes of Chotanagpur, there is a strong belief in the potent evil powers of a witch. In fact, most dreaded of magical effects are those resulting from witchcraft. Among Munda only women are believed to practice witchcraft and are known as 'Dain'. Besides, being expert in black magic, witches are believed to know sorcery, making use of material objects in influencing the evil spirits. This corresponds to Evans Pritchard's (1965) distinction based on his study among the Azande, between witchcraft as an influence and sorcery as a magic art using material objects.

There are many kinds of ailments caused by witches. No medicines, it is believed, can prove effective in diseases caused by spirits and witches. A *sokha* by his beneficent powers can discover the working of the witches and can name them. Witchcraft is not a quality inborn in a person, but it is acquired by deep meditation, labour, courage and propitiation of *bunita bongas*. A witch has to learn many rites. In early days, a woman discovered to be a witch was driven away from the village and her lands were confiscated by the village panchayat. As the witch cannot be banished from her village these days by law, she is only fined or severely beaten. Many cases have been known in which witches were poisoned to death. In Selda, a woman suspected of being a witch was secretly killed.

Unprovoked witchcraft directed against an individual or a family is usually considered a challenge to the whole society and the victim generally counts on his fellow clansmen and neighbours for assistance. Such witches as help the villagers against the mischief of other witches by counter spells and magic, are rewarded by gifts in kind after the harvest.

Though witchcraft is secretly practised in almost all the Munda villages, it is disapproved and decried publicly by others. Among the Christian Munda, the missionaries discourage the practice. In olden times, when a woman was accused of being a witch and ostracised by the village community, the Christian missionaries tried and succeeded in converting her and her family to Christianity and thus saved her from punishment. Cases related to witchcraft and *dain* are also instituted in the law courts in Khunti. Though the number of such accusations has gone down, the practice of witchcraft is still extant among the Munda.

The sorcerer uses a number of material objects to harm his victim. These are as follows : A person may be harmed through black magic by a twig tooth brush used by him. The dust from below the footstep, pared nails and hair are also used for this purpose. Rheumatism of the lower limbs may be caused by an enemy getting hold of a little dust of one's feet and uttering some magical formulae over it and sacrificing a fowl or making offerings of *arua* rice over the dust. Munda women, after combing, tie their waste hair and spit over it, before throwing, to make it ineffective for use in witchcraft. While a wall of a house is under construction, a witch may secretly take away some earth from the wall and tie it in a cloth, so that the wall may crack before completion. Another way of afflicting a person is to bury some medicinal herb or root using magic, on the path usually traversed by the victim. Some witches afflict their victims through incantations. Sometimes the chicken of the Munda may be stolen. The Munda keep a feather of each fowl. When a particular fowl is stolen, its feather is boiled with a belief that the thief would get stomach ache and thus will be identified.

The belief, that most of the diseases and misfortunes are due to maleficent *bongas*, impersonal powers, witches or sorcerers, does not dishearten the Munda. They have developed remedial measures to cope with such problems. Among the most potent remedies are white magic, omens and taboos.

The Munda believe in good and bad omens which are observed on all important occasions. The Munda while setting out to negotiate a marriage of their wards, observe omens. The effects of certain bad omens can be neutralised by offering the desired worship and sacrifices. Certain bad omens are liable to portend disaster and if such omens are encountered in the beginning, the negotiations are totally abandoned.

Some of the good omens are as follows : (1) a woman carrying paddy (a portent of wealth), (2) to see a woman carrying a pitcher full of water, (3) to hear the sound of the *panduk* (a bird), and (4) to see a *dhonr* snake, (5) a jackal crossing the path signifies that the potential couple would beget a large number of children, (6) seeing a funeral procession on the way to negotiate marriage, (7) a crow making a sound on the right side signifies happiness and crossing from right to left and cawing signifies dispute in the life of the potential couple.

The omens which are considered inauspicious are as follows : (1) to see a woman carrying an empty pitcher, (2) to hear the sound of a brass plate, (3) to see a man carrying a spade and other digging implements signifies impending death of one of the marriage partners, (4) to hear the sound of a barking dog and jackal, (5) coming across a *guturia* sparrow flying ahead on the way, (6) the sound of an owl, (7) sight of a person carrying a load of firewood, (8) the sound of the cutting of firewood, (9) a woman carrying ash-covered clothes for washing. It is not good to hear a cow mooing without an immediate response by the calf. Flames of fire, a woman with undressed hair, a new earthen pot lying on the way, and the falling off of a branch of a tree are considered bad omens. A woman throwing the ashes of her hearth and/or carrying a basket of boiled rice portend death. It is inauspicious if a cyclone rages or if a snake is seen entering its hole.

Other Ritual Functionaries

Tribal villages in the eastern part of Ranchi district have been under Hindu influences for a long time. One of the ritual functionaries is the Pattidar. The Pattidar is a person who visits the family whenever a death occurs. Seven or nine days after the event, the Pattidar visits the house with a notional drawing of the deceased and tells the family members that the latter had met him and had promised him a gift. The relatives of the dead person give him some rice, fuel and cash. It is believed that if the gift is withheld the departed soul remains with the Pattidar as a slave. The Pattidar in Serengdih comes from Herom, twenty miles east.

In Sirum it was found that the Brahmin is invited at the time of marriage and death. At death he officiates at the ceremony for offering *pind* to the dead. The Brahmin in this case comes from Beradih, a nearby village. He has a number of clients in the villages around. In Birhu, near Khunti, some Mundas used to invite the Brahmin to officiate at their marriage, but after some time the latter raised his fee. As a result, a barber from Khunti started performing rituals in place of the Brahmin.

Another ritual specialist is the *gosain.* In rank he is junior to the Brahmin and in those families which cannot afford to have the Brahmin, the former performs all the rites. The *gosain* is consulted before a marriage is settled. He performs worship to ward off evil spirits. Besides receiving his fee for particular services, he visits each of his clients at harvest time and claims a share.

The Brahmin and the *gosain* come for the purification ceremony on the seventh or ninth day after a death. The barber is called to shave the beard and head of all the male members of the family of the deceased. The Brahmin chants *mantras.* During the worship, copper coins and *tulsi* leaves are used. The Brahmin sprinkles water three times on the person who has offered *pind* to his ancestors and then it is sprinkled on all his relatives. On their way back from the river where they go for mortuary rituals, all persons chant *Haribol.* The *gosain* gets one-half and the barber one-fourth of what the Brahmin gets as his fee. These Hindu ritual functionaries have made the tribal villages part of a large and widespread ritual complex.

SEASONAL CYCLE OF RITUALS AND FESTIVALS

In the worship of the *bongas*, we can analytically distinguish two inter-related aspects, viz., the instrumental and the expressive. On the one hand, the performance of the religious rites expresses the recognition of the existence of the supernatural powers that can be exercised by the *bongas*. On the other hand, these powers are generally invoked to secure the goodwill of the benevolent *bongas* and to avert the displeasure of the malevolent ones. The expressive aspect is symbolised and manifested in a special manner in the various seasonal rites and festivals related with the annual agricultural cycle and the recurring rites of passage. Through these feasts, the Munda acknowledge in a most emphatic way, the spirits as their lords and protectors. These also give the Munda an occasion to thank their spirits and to rejoice with them.

The religious rites and festivals associated with the agricultural cycle are not only related to the immediate practical interests of life but also evoke emotion that goes beyond a mere response to practical needs. They bind the community together in their beliefs and give them a sense of the sacred. Collective ritual and rejoicing during these rites and festivals serve to intensify the emotional appeal of religion. In short, these are symbols of their beliefs in a communal setting.

The celebrations which accompany such collective rituals, in which people participate for the welfare of the entire group, are truly occasions for collective action. These act as channels through which cultural traditions are expressed and affirmed. It is on these occasions of collective seasonal rites, dances and festivals that a Munda experiences a deep religious feeling. His sense of security and also the feeling of belonging is intensified, thus strengthening the social solidarity in the community.

Munda seasonal rites and festivals have two aspects, i.e., religious and secular. The sacrificial offering is clearly at the centre of every Munda ritual and possesses both the communion and oblation elements which are ultimately inter-connected. The sacrificial communion symbolises a sense of presence and of fellowship with the spirits by sharing in the sacrificial food and drink. The oblation element symbolises the Munda's acknowledgement of their spirits as the real lords of their fields to whom tribute must be paid. It also manifests the Munda's dependence on these spirits who as in the case of the Trobriand Islanders must receive their share sacrificed from the general plenty.

As mentioned earlier, rituals are symbolic expressions of collective sentiments of a particular society. It is evident that there are certain common symbols repeated in various forms and under various circumstances in the different rites and festivals. A study of this symbolism provides us with an understanding of the meanings as prevalent in Munda society.

The first symbolic value is a sense of presence and of fellowship with the spirits. This is expressed in the libations and sacrificial offerings which are shared by the people and the spirits. The villagers get together for the worship of their village *bongas* and each household donates part of the sacrificial offerings. The sacred places associated with different *bongas* indicate a sense of special presence of the spirits and of their intervention.

These rituals also symbolise the Munda's dependence on their spirits. The oblation aspect of the sacrificial offerings, the dripping of the blood of the sacrificed animal on the whole village, symbolise the Munda's acknowledgement of their spirits as their lords and masters. The application of vermilion on the sacrificial animal symbolises that the animal is set apart for the spirits. The awe in which the spirits are held is perhaps most evident in the offerings of first fruits like the *sal*, and *mahua* blossoms and the winter paddy crop to the *bongas* during the *Sarhul* and other festivals. Similarly, if these *bongas* are defiled either through a birth or death in the village, no festivities can take place unless the spirits are first propitiated.

Another symbolic element that comes to the fore is a sense of new life and of harmony with nature, e.g., the *Sarhul* festival is a symbol of new life when nature is blossoming. The harmony with nature is manifested in the fact that most of the village feasts are connected with agricultural and seasonal cycles of nature. The table gives the periodicity, the corresponding agricultural operation and the kind of dance and music associated with it.

The main festivals among the Munda are *Mage*, *Phagu*, *Ba*, *Hon-ba Batauli*, *Karam*, *Dasai* and *Sohrai*. The main folk songs are *Jadur*, *Gena*, *Mage*, *Japi*, *Karam* and *Arandi* songs (marriage songs). These festivals and folk music are associated with specified periods of the year and are celebrated accordingly. The folk songs are accompanied by folk-dances associated and named after them.

Mage Parab is celebrated in the month of *Magh* with great pomp and show for the villagers do not have any work in the fields then and the houses are well stocked with paddy. The villagers in different villages celebrate the festival on different dates in this month according to their convenience.

Food and drink are offered to the ancestors. Rice flour *chapati* is made. Generally a he-goat is bought with the sum collected for the purpose and the meat is distributed keeping in view one's share in the contribution.

Mage Parab marks the end of the year and the beginning of the new year for the Munda. Domestic servants (*dhangar* and *dhangrin*) are kept on contract only up to *Mage Parab* and new contracts are made or renewed at this time.

In the afternoon of *Mage Parab* a game known as faudi or fudi is played by the adult males, with a stick and wooden ball, which is also known as *akash gend.* A match is played between two teams and the team which drives back the other from the middle point in either direction wins the game. In the evening the ball and the stick are kept in the *pahan's* house. He offers them rice-beer. Late in the evening the boys and the girls dance in the village *akhra.*

Phagu coincides with *Holi* festival of Hindus. It commences on *purnima* (full moon) in the month of Phalgun. A black hen is sacrificed by the *pahan* at the site of Chandibonga to help the Munda in hunting during the two days of the *phagu* festival. The *arind* and *semal* plants covered with straw and fixed on the way to the spring from the village *akhra* are set fire to and cut by the villagers on both the nights accompanied by drum beats and a *japi* folk song tune (*japi* is a hunting song). On the first night the *phagus* are cut starting from the *akhra* in the direction of spring while on the next night the process is reversed and the last *phagu* is cut near the village *akhra* and

Seasonal Cycle of Rituals and Festivals

Name of the Month		Name of Festival	Corresponding Agricultural operation	Corresponding Folk Dance and Music
English	*Mundari*			
Dec-Jan.	Mage	Mage		
Jan.-Feb.	Falgun	Phagu (Holi)-Purnima		Jadur
Feb.-Mar.	Chait	Sarhul (Ba)		
Mar.-Apl.	Baisakh	Hon-Ba	Manuring	Japi
Apl.-May.	Jeth	Jatra	Ploughing; Sowing of Summer Paddy	
May-June	Asarh	Batauli	Sowing the Kharif paddy and weeding the summer paddy	
June-July	Sawan		Transplantation of the Kharif paddy	
July-Aug.	Bhado	Karam (Bhado Ekadashi)		Karam
Aug.-Sept.	Aswin	Jom Nawa (Naya Khani) Inde (Bhado Purnima) Dasai (Hindu Dussehra)	Weeding the Kharif paddy, harvesting of Fora and Gondli	
Sept.-Oct.		Sohrai (Hindu Diwali)		
Oct.-Nov.	Aghan	Kolom Sing Bonga (Khalihan Puja)	Harvesting, Threshing	Japi
Nov.-Dec.	Poos	Sukun Buru Jatra (Hasda area) Hiburu or Poos mela (Panch Parganas)		

the boys and the girls then enter the *akhra* and dance throughout the night to the accompaniment of drums.

Bread made of rice flour is prepared in all the houses and the *Haram Horoko* are offered bread and rice-beer by the householder on this day.

Sarhul

Sarhul or *Ba* festival is celebrated in the month of *Chait* (at the end of March or in the beginning of April). The festival lasts from *panchami* to the day before *Purnima*. The date for *Sarhul* is fixed in different villages according to the convenience of the villagers.

Beginning of Sarhul: There are different versions regarding the beginning of *Ba Parab*. According to one version, the ancestors of the Munda once went to hunt in the jungle. Sudden rain forced them to take shelter under a *sal* tree. A tiger appeared and wanted to attack the Munda hiding under the tree. A cobra living in a hole on that *sal* tree came forward to rescue him from the tiger. The tiger was frightened and slunk away. The Munda believed that it was the *sal* tree which had saved him from the tiger and thus it became sacred for him. Since then *sal* flower is regarded as sacred. Its worship was begun and took the form of *Ba Parab*.

Worship in the ading: The association of this story of the origin of *Ba Parab* is related by people to the method of worship in this festival. The *sal* flower is worshipped. A special type of broom representing the tail of the tiger in that story is also kept at the place of worship. On the *Ba Parab* day if some member of the household were to enter the *ading*, in two or three days a *nag* snake is seen in the house which signifies that the ancestors are unhappy. On *Ba Parab* a light-red hen or *sukra sim* is sacrificed in every Munda household in the name of the ancestors.

The festival is celebrated for three consecutive days. On the first day, fish is cooked and offered to the Orabonga in the *ading*. On the next day *urd dal* is cooked without frying and *sal* branches with new leaves are brought from the jungle. *Urd dal*, cooked rice and leafy branches of *sal* are offered to the ancestors. They are supposed to take their meals sitting on the *sal* branches that day. *Sal* and *gurul* flowers (*gudul*) and leafy branches of *keond* and *char*, are brought home from the forest. All these flowers and leafy branches are kept at the place of worship. A pink-coloured hen is offered as sacrifice to the ancestors. The head of the household performs the worship and sacrifice in the *ading*. After worship all the family members are offered *sal* and *gurul* flowers to be put on the ears and hair. Visitors are also offered the *sal* flowers.

Worship in the sarna by the village Pahan : On the third day the *pahan* performs the *Ba-puja* in the village *sarna*, as a representative of the village community for the common benefit of the villagers and cattle and good harvest. His assistant, the *panbhara,* keeps two new pitchers of water full to the brim in the *sarna* on the previous night. Two *sal* branches are kept in each pitcher to measure, if the water level has changed the next morning. If the water level is found lower than the previous night, less rains are expected during the next monsoon, if the level remains the same the rains are predicted.

The *pahan* sacrifices 12 hens in the *sarna* on that day in the name of many gods. He sacrifices a white hen for Singbonga, red for Burubonga, pink for Orabongako, ash coloured for Ikirbonga, white black mixed *(hende purta)* for Chandibonga and *ara purta*, i.e., red and white mixed for Nagebonga. The other six hens may be of any colour. One member from each village household is supposed to be present on the occasion.

The sacrificed hens are cooked in the *sarna* and *pahan's* family eats the food there itself. The cooked meat is not given to any one other than those belonging to the *pahan's* family. In the evening after worship the villagers bring the *pahan* to his home with due respect. The village women wash his feet. The *pahan* offers the *sal* and *gurul* flowers to the visitors. He offers the rice-beer and also food. On the fourth day *Giri-ba* is celebrated and the flowers are thrown at the place known as *Giri-ba*. The *pahan* offers the *sal* and *gurul* flowers to all the villagers that day.

Boys and girls sing and dance in the village *akhra* on four consecutive nights and during the day. Munda youth go from village to village for dancing. *Jadur* folk-songs and dances are performed during *Sarhul.* Rice-beer is taken by every one as it gives them stamina for dancing the *jadur* which is strenuous. The villagers put on new clothes according to their means.

Hon-ba is *Sarhul* on a smaller scale. On the first day, fish is offered in worship. The next day boiled rice, and *urd dal* is offered and a pink hen is sacrificed by each Munda householder. Villagers bathe after anointing themselves with turmeric and mustard oil. They are purified before entering the house with four different things : (a) first rice-beer is sprinkled with *bel* leaves; (b) then the leg of the hen is sprinkled with water by *bel* leaves; (c) water with fish is sprinkled with *bel* leaves; and finally, (d) pure water is sprinkled with grass from the fourth *sal*-leaf cup. *Hon-ba* is celebrated in every household. In the evening *jadur* dance and song are performed by young men and young girls in the village *akhra*.

Batauli is celebrated in *Asarh* when the crops germinate. A pink hen is sacrificed to the ancestors to get better crops. The *pahan* prays to the Singbonga and other *bongas* on behalf of the whole village for a good harvest. He also sacrifices a pink hen for his ancestors. Women observe fast on the first half of the day before *Batauli*. Young men and women dance in the village *akhra* at night.

The *Karam* festival is one of the most important festivals among all the tribes of Chotanagpur. This festival has been adopted from the Hindu castes. It is celebrated on the eleventh day of *Bhado* (August-September). It is believed that one can achieve wealth, prosperity and joy in life by celebrating this festival. It is celebrated at the village level and all the villagers co-operate in it. The preparations start days before the festival. All unmarried girls bring sand from the field in the early morning in baskets. They put some paddy, *urd*, maize, *gangai* seeds in the baskets. From that day they water it every morning with *haldi* water. After a bath on the *Karam* day, a man goes to the forest with some unmarried girls to cut a *Karam* branch. All of them fast and sing *Karam* songs to the accompaniment of musical instruments while going to the forest. They bring the *Karam* branch and plant it in the courtyard of the house in the evening. The *pahan* of the village performs worship with the virgins. The girls bring the sprouted seeds in the basket with earthen lamps and offer them to the *Karam*. After the worship the *pahan* recites the *Karam* story. Then they take their meal and the virgins take out the *Karam* branch and consign it in the stream with singing and dancing. On that day all the villagers go door to door and are received with rice-beer.

An interesting legend is connected with the origin of the *Karam* festival. In the early days, this world was known as Manchpur. Dancing was not known then. It was limited only to Indrapur, the palace of king Indra. There, fairies danced day and night during the *Karam* festival.

Two brothers, Anayashri and Dhanyashri ruled in the kingdom of Manchpur. They were fathers of Karma and Dharma respectively. They had a beautiful flower garden near the palace. A gardener was appointed to look after the garden. One day Anyashri and Dhanyashri saw that some flowers had been plucked and destroyed by someone. On enquiry the gardener told them that the fairies of Indrapur used to pluck these flowers every night. They came every night in a chariot. The King asked the gardener to spray a special kind of magical ash on the flowers so that the fairies would not return to Indrapur. The gardener did so. The thieves were thus caught. King Indra himself came to the garden and disclosed his identity and said that the flowers were used as ornaments by the fairies when they performed the *Karam* dance, which was supposed to be the source of all their wealth and prosperity. He, therefore, asked them to perform the *Karam* dance. From that day *Karam* began to be observed in this world.

King Indra then requested them to free his chariot. Anayashri and Dhanyashri told him that the chariot could move only if it was touched by a virgin who had been on fast that day. Luckily they found such a girl in the same village. King Indra requested her to touch his chariot. The girl came and touched the chariot and it began to move. Thus King Indra returned with the fairies to his palace. Since then Anyashri and Dhanyashri began to perform the *Karam* festival and became very rich. Unfortunately, salt was scarce in their kingdom. People were in great need of salt. Anyashri sent Karma to fetch salt. Karma proceeded in search of salt with 700 servants. He met many merchants but all of them refused to sell salt to him. At last he reached Cuttack in Orissa and bought salt from a big merchant. Karma returned happily with all the salt laden on bullocks and servants. As he approached his village, he sent a messenger to inform his brother, Dharma. Dharma was then engaged in the worship of the *Karam* god. He, therefore, requested the messenger to ask his brother to wait for some time. But as it was getting late Karma sent a messenger again but the messenger returned with the same reply. Karma became angry and went himself to Dharma leaving the bullocks and servants behind and cut down all the branches of the *Karam* tree and threw them away. Because of Karma's such rude behaviour, Dharma split from him the same night. Karma went back to bring his salt but was surprised to find everything gone. When he returned home, he found that his building was in ruins and his wife and children were crying of hunger. Karma went to his brother Dharma who was then serving food to guests as is usual after the performance of the Karma festival. Dharma, therefore, asked Karma to wait as the guests were to be given precedence over the family members. After some time, he went again but got the same reply. He became disappointed. The next morning he went with his wife and children to work in his brother's fields. After work, he went to Dharma for his wages. This time Dharma was distributing wages to his labourers. He, therefore, asked Karma to wait. This enraged Karma again and he went back to the fields and began uprooting all the plants he had transplanted for his brother. But he was surprised to see the plants being planted again by some unseen hand. At that time he heard a divine voice saying that he should worship Karam Raja, to get rid of all his troubles. Karam Raja lived in 'Hiri-hiri Sagar'.

On hearing this voice, Karma went out in search of Karam Raja. On the way, he met a tortoise hanging from the branch of a tree. The tortoise requested Karma to pray before Karam Raja for its salvation. There Karma saw a spring and wanted to drink water. But when he took some water, it became red like blood and full of insects. So he could not drink it. Going further, he met a woman carrying fire on her head. She was in great trouble and requested him to ask Karam Raja for her salvation. Karma was very hungry and wanted something to eat. He was very happy to see a *dumar* tree laden with fruits. But he was disappointed as these were full of vermin. Proceeding further, he met a milkman milking his cow. Karma asked him for milk but the bucket was tucked in between the milkman's thighs. He beat Karma with a stick. So Karma went away. Thereafter Karma met a man with a bush on his shoulder. The man requested him to pray before Karam Raja for his salvation. Thereafter, Karma reached a tank and saw a crocodile with a big palm tree growing from its body. This crocodile also requested him to pray for him to Karam Raja.

At last, Karma reached Hiri-hiri Sagar. He saw Karam

Raja floating in the sea. He jumped into the water to touch his feet, but could not do so because of his sins. He became very tired and was on the point of drowning. Afterwards Karam Raja took pity on him and saved him. Karma then prayed to Karam Raja and all his troubles were over. He also prayed to Karam Raja for the tortoise, the woman, the man, the milkman and the crocodile whom he had met on the way and they too got rid of their troubles.

Karma returned home happily with Karam Raja. On approaching his village he saw his brother Dharma who welcomed him graciously. Karma found his palace again in good condition and his wife and children were very happy. They were wealthy and prosperous. Thus the people began to worship Karam Raja and observed the *Karam* festival every year on the eleventh day of *Bhado*. This is an adaptation of a Hindu festival and is common in many parts of Bihar. The story of the two brothers Karma and Dharma clearly indicates this.

Dasai (Dasehra)

This festival is borrowed from the Hindus again. The Hinduised Munda celebrate *Durga Puja* like their Hindu neighbours, especially in the *Panchparganas.* For other Mundas it is a festival in which new clothes are worn. *Dasai Karam* is fixed in the village *akhra* where the young men and women dance. Unlike *Karma* of *Bhado* (where the deity is worshipped by the head of each household) the *pahan* performs worship in the name of Singbonga and other deities. The dance goes on for the whole night around the *karam* plant in the *akhra*. The *karam* is immersed in the river or pond the next evening before sunset.

In the Tamar area, the Hinduised Munda perform *Durga Puja* or *Dasai* and goats are sacrificed at the Durga Temple at Diuri and other places The *pahan* acts as the ritual sacrificer.

Sohrai : The Munda like the Hindus celebrate *Sohrai* for the protection of cattle from diseases. It is celebrated on the *Kartik Amawasya*. Ploughing is stopped about a fortnight before the *Sohrai* festival to give rest to the cattle.

On the first day *Sarguja* oil is anointed on the horns of the cattle in the evening. On the next evening the cattle are anointed with *sarguja* oil and *sindur* to the accompaniment of musical instruments. People sing and request the cattle to forgive them for any trouble they might have given them during the year and also to accept their offerings.

On *Sohrai* morning all cattle are taken for grazing. In the evening they return singing and the cattle are washed in the village pond. They wait outside the house. From the courtyard to the cattleshed, foot prints of cattle are made with rice flour paste. Near the door of cattleshed, a peg about six inches long is fixed where deities such as Jhetha Mara and Von Kuari (the goddess of the jungle) are worshipped. A black hen is sacrificed for these *bongako.* A red hen may be sacrificed by a family having buffaloes. The hen is beaten to death by striking it with a cattle horn. On other occasions the hen is killed by cutting its throat.

All the villagers make circular imprints of rice flour paste with a vermilion spot in the centre on the body of all the cattle before sunset. The horns are decorated with bands of *sarguja* and green paddy plants and marigold-flower garlands are put round their necks. The decorated cattle are brought to the centre of the village before sunset. At this time songs are sung with the beat of drums and the cattle are put on show. Women sprinkle rice in the pond or the river where the cattle are taken for drinking water. They are brought home and given grass to eat. Again in the evening *sarguja* oil and vermilion are applied on the horns. At night young men and women dance in the *akhra.*

This festival is mainly celebrated for the worship of cattle. The story behind this festival is narrated below. Once there lived an old Munda couple. At that time there was no agriculture and people were foodgatherers. One day the old man went to a river bank and found some calves playing in the dirt. They looked ugly. He washed them and they came out beautiful and clean. They told him to go away lest their parents kill him. But he said that he wanted to see their parents, and he climbed a tree. In the evening when the cows and bulls returned they found the calves very clean. They asked the calves as to who had washed them. They told them after being promised that the man who washed them would not be punished. The man came down and the cattle thanked him. They were so impressed that they went with him to his house and lived there.

The bulls and cows told the Munda to build a plough and till the field with their help and sow paddy. At the year-end there was a bumper crop. The old couple cooked rice and pulses and had their meal. They did not give anything to the cattle. At this the cattle got angry and left the house in distress.

On the way God appeared and persuaded them to return home and admitted that it was his mistake as he had not taught man to care for his benefactors. God appeared before the Munda couple and told them that they should take care of the bullocks and cows as they were useful. He asked the couple to cook rice and *urd* on full moon day in *Ashwin* and feed it to his bullocks and cows. He asked them to be kind to the cattle and worship them every year. *Sohrai* has been celebrated from then onwards. The Hindus worship other deities and the Supreme God as well on the *Sohrai* day. Munda also light a lamp in the cattle shed to show God that they care for their cattle.

Another story about the origin of *Sohrai* is about a king who was very poor. He had seven sons. When the king died, the sons could not decide on the succession. One by one all the brothers became kings but they remained poor. Then the youngest son became the king. He wanted his orders to be followed. The six elder brothers agreed to obey him. He (Lita) ordered them to go out and bring any dying, dead or living animal. Once they brought a dead non-poisonous snake. They kept all these on the roof.

One day a young girl was washing clothes in the river. A king who passed that way also took his bath there. But he left his diamonds there unknowingly. When he remembered, he returned and enquired from the girl about his diamonds. She said that a bird had taken them away. The bird went to the poor king Lita's house and told the Raja this story. But Lita said that if the other King would not celebrate *Sohrai* that year he would return the diamonds.

That year this King did not celebrate *Sohrai.* All the cattle then came out of the sheds and collected under the *mahua* tree and decided to go to that country where *Sohrai* was celebrated that year. The *mahua* tree also decided to accompany them. All of them went to King Lita's city and were greeted as *Sohrai* was being celebrated there. With them came the agriculture diety, Lakshmi. King Lita became rich by celebrating *Sohrai* and the other King became poor by not doing so. There were no rains and no crops in his kingdom. This shows the importance of *Sohrai* and this story can be heard in Mundari folk songs even today.

JATRA

Jatra dances are full of hopping and jumping sequences and are in tune with the nature of the song. The dance appears as though they are challenging the enemy for war. Munda young men and women after the day's long work go to perform *jatra* dances at night, sometimes as far as 7 to 8 miles. This dance is held everyday, though not at the same place. It is performed in different villages on each consecutive night.

The *jatra* dance has four forms and each is performed at different periods of the year : *Jathura Jatra*—from the second fortnight of *Baisakh* up to the onset of the rainy season. Then the *Asarhi* or *Bharno Jatra* dances are performed in *Asarh* (June-July) and at the time of the *Ind*-festival around *Dasehra* the *Ind Jatra* or *Dasai Jatra* is celebrated. The fourth one is *Sohrai Jatra* which starts after the *Sohrai* festival (*Kartik-Amawasya*). The songs of these four forms are set to different tunes. Young men come out in an unusual costume with facial make-up, feathers or flowers in their turban, wearing flowers as ear-rings, holding tinkling bells and other sound-making instruments and fixing mirrors to the waist. These gaily dressed young men dance with great enthusiasm. Girls also adorn themselves with the same zeal as boys. They wear flowers in their hair, a thick sari with a red border and put on *jhutia* (toe rings), many bangles on the forearms and armlets on the upper arms, *hansuli* round their necks and *tarki* in the ears (ear-rings made from rolled red colour palm leaves fitted with small mirrors on both sides) and a red coloured blouse.

ESCHATOLOGY : LIFE AFTER DEATH

As stated earlier, the Munda believe in a host of deities

and spirits. According to the good or bad life led by a man during his present life, it is believed he will be sent back to the world by Singbonga either as a man or as a beast, as a bird or as an insect. On death the *roa* or soul is carried away by the Jom Raja (the god of death) to his abode in the south. Such is the Munda's idea of rebirth which is less elaborate than that of his Hindu neighbours. The Munda believe that when a man's time is over he must die. After death, heart and mind leave the body and mingle with air.

The Munda strongly believe in the soul as distinct from the body and as surviving the latter. They have various names to denote soul, e.g., *ji, mon, roa* and *umbul.* The first three are loan-words. *Umbul* is a Mundari word which denotes primarily any shade or shadow. This is probably the term by which the Munda originally denoted the soul as distinct from the body. The *ji* is the principle of life found not only in men, but also in plants and animals. When a plant or animal dies its *ji* mixes with air. The *ji* of man is immortal and when he dies, it goes to the *bitarpur*, there to receive from Singbonga its reward or punishment. The *ji* being the principle of life, cannot leave the body without causing death, except for a very short time during a collapse; if it comes back at once, life will not be lost and the man will revive.

A distinction is made between the *ji* and *roa* by the Munda. Unlike the *ji,* the *roa* is not bound to remain continually in the body during life. In fact, nearly every night when the body lies down to sleep and the *ji* has to remain there, the *roa* is off on an outing. A dream is just what the *roa* sees and hears when it wanders about. The *roa,* like the *ji,* is immortal, but after death it does not go with the *ji* to *bitarpur*, it remains on earth and becomes a *bonga.* It is the disembodied *roa* which is called *umbul,* or shade by the Mundas. Excepting Singbonga, who is truly the only God, all the *bongas,* (not those borrowed from Hinduism) are nothing more than disembodied *roas* or shades of men or women, they are not devils at all, nor even minor gods. The tutelary spirits are the shades of the wives of the Asurs, and the *ora bongako* are the shades of the ancestors.

The *bonga* or disembodied *roa* is not as immaterial as the *ji,* since it is supposed to be still in need of food and drink. That is why when the Munda bury their dead, some rice and coins are kept with the corpse to enable the *roa*, still present, to pull on until it is introduced into the inner room *(ading)* of the house and worshipped as *orabonga* and offered sacrifices. In case the *roa* is not brought home, it may live on tree tops and rocks. It gets its food, as it harms people and forces them to offer sacrifices to it. As the *roa* does not have a body any-more to keep up, it needs very little.

Every human *roa* is endowed by Singbonga with a single *gun* or a quality. The *gun* causes the *roa*, when seen by another *roa* (in a dream) to take the shape of an animal. It influences man's temperament and fate, and causes in his life affinity with the special habits, appetite or efficiency which characterises the animal, the shape of which the *roa* has taken. It is impossible to find out what kind of *gun* a man has. However, for some, at least, this question is solved to the satisfaction of the Munda's mind when, the *roa* is introduced into the house by the *umbul ader* ceremony. On this occasion, the floor is strewn with ashes and when the ceremony is over, they are scanned eagerly for any traces which will show that the shade has entered the house and taken its abode therein. Now, it happens that the traces they find, or thing they find, are or resemble, those of a cat or dog or some other animal. This is at once considered a proof that the *roa* of the deceased was and is cat-like or dog-like etc.

SOCIAL FUNCTIONS OF RELIGION

No religion can be fully understood in isolation, apart from the society in which it is found. Any study of religion must begin by observing and describing belief systems and behaviour patterns, but these data will become significant only when they are related to their social meanings and functions.

The study of functions in the social sciences is the study of the social consequences of an institution. The function of religion, i.e., in this sense, means the relationship it bears to family patterns, political and economic organisations, social values and the social structure as a whole. Social conditions affect the forms and values of religions, and these, in turn, influence social organisation and social institutions. The strength of these inter-relationships is not always equal. Religion is much more pervasive in some cultures than in others, and within a given cultural system, religion may have greater bearing on some institutions than on others.

Although religion always relates to other social institutions and values, in no society is the totality of social life manifestly governed by religion. Several nineteenth century scholars imagined that this was the case in early or non-literate societies; that the mentality of primitive man was such that they gave to all activities, experiences and observations, a supernatural interpretation. Modern anthropologists have found, however, that all societies have secular areas that are not considered to be under supernatural jurisdiction.

Among the Munda there exists a strong interrelationship between family organisation and religious structure. The Munda worship the spirits of their deceased ancestors (house gods). These are called Orabongako. The social functions of ritual sacrifices offered to the ancestor spirits is that their solemnity and collective expression help to reaffirm and strengthen the family solidarity. As Radcliffe-Brown (1959 : 164) puts it, they give stability to the social structure by giving solidarity and continuity to the lineage, past, present and future. The Munda is made to feel a certain dependence on his ancestors, who, in turn, watch over him with loving care as they are remembered and venerated. Otherwise, they will not only stop showering their blessings but will visit him with illness or other misfortune. The motives involved in ancestor worship, though not always the same, are mainly : (a) a desire to show reverence to the dead ; (b) a longing for their blessings and protection; (c) a fear of their revenge. In short, the feelings of the living towards their dead relatives are ambivalent; compounded of affection and fear.

Munda religion provides an example of how religion may function to uphold the norms of a society, thus contributing to the maintenance of the social order. This function of religion is a universal one, but the specific procedures by which it is accomplished differs from culture to culture. Every society approves of certain types of behaviour and disapproves of others, even though a rigid distinction between right and wrong may not be conceptualised. Though the moral codes of different societies may be highly divergent and even contradictory, there is still the universal sentiment, that it is appreciable to conform to the code of one's own society and unworthy to disregard its prescriptions. The reactions of different societies to offenders against established custom may range from mild disapproval, perhaps only verbally expressed, to drastic punishments and even excommunication. But religion remains the focus for the phenomenon of the emotional involvement of a group, however small, in the actions of its members.

In any society, certain activities seem to be considered as morally neutral while others are subject to moral assessments, even though these may only take the form of malicious gossip or silent admiration. The type of conduct which gains a man social merit varies from society to society, but the principle of public recognition of a socially desirable conduct is extremely widespread. Rewards no less than punishment represent a society's reaction to the conduct of individuals.

The Munda distinguish between right and wrong action, conduct or behaviour. While public approval rewards a right conduct there are a number of negative sanctions that follow on misconduct or bad behaviour. These may be the internal sanctions, the sanctions of the society and lastly the supernatural or automatic sanctions. The last set of sanctions are involved by way of breaking a taboo and may affect the offender, his family, clan or village.

A Munda youth, from his early days, acquaints himself with the social values and ethics that govern the Munda way of life and he knows in general terms the conduct that is expected of him. This he learns through myths and lore and informal education, through the family and the larger circle of the village and the tribe. If he does not conform to his social environment and breaks the tribal laws or offends against custom and tradition, he knows that his behaviour will invoke sanctions which, when set in action, will work to his disadvantage.

As noted above there are certain offences against the existing moral order which expose not only the culprits, but also their entire community to supernatural or automatic sanctions. Such offences are believed to bring evil in their train as well as natural calamity and are penalised with severe punishment by the village panchayat or *parha* panchayat. Drought, epidemics or other disasters may be caused by an undetected case of incest or the desecration of the sanctuary of a god. The punishment can be averted if the offender propitiates the enraged deities with sacrifices, but to do so he must discover the cause of misfortune and the identity of the offended god. The contact between supernatural powers and the human-beings is maintained by the *pahan* and *sokha* who worship and propitiate these supernatural powers for bringing prosperity and averting misfortunes.

The common viewpoint of anthropologists is that religion and economy are, indeed, everywhere functionally inter-related but that the magnitude of these relationships varies. Economic and religious changes arise from a multitude of factors and functions and are mutually reinforcing, so that economic ideas influence and adjust themselves to religious concepts and *vice versa*.

The Munda perform various rites and ceremonies by which they seek to ensure safety and prosperity to the village community as a whole at each new stage in the annual cycle of its economic pursuits, and the feasting and rejoicing and social rituals that mark their successful termination. These pursuits are mainly agriculture and cattle-tending. Fishing and hunting are not the regular pursuits of the tribe but are occasionally practised by the Munda. The only occasions on which fishing and hunting are regarded as something of a sacred ceremony are in connection with the Sarhul and Phagu festivals respectively. The agricultural cycle serves not only the immediate material interests of life but also arouses emotion that goes beyond mere response to practical needs. It binds the community together in their beliefs and gives them a sense of the sacred. Collective ritual and rejoicing during these occasions help to intensify the emotional appeal of religion.

The Munda perform the rain making ceremony by worshipping Buru Bonga to ensure or to increase the yield of crops. The various rituals associated with agriculture mark the agricultural stages of sowing, germination, harvesting and threshing. They also worship the Devi Bonga once a year to ward off diseases and bring them prosperity through good crops of paddy, mango, mahua, jack fruit etc.

Economic distribution deals with the ways in which goods

once produced are exchanged or allocated. Society could not function if individuals produced goods exclusively for their own use. Though the family is a small economic unit, the exchange patterns are universally extended well beyond family bonds. In all human groups there are specialists of some kind, men or women who have skills which others do not have and who are regularly called upon to render services. Among the Munda there are the *pahan*, *panbhara* and *sokha* who are religious and ritual specialists whose special ability is in their effective communication with supernatural powers. The *pahan* and the *panbhara* are given rent free *pahanai* and *panbhara* lands for their maintenance for their services, i.e., worshipping the village deities on behalf of the village community. Other ritual functionaries such as the Brahman, the barber, the *gosain* etc. are also employed by the Munda on various occasions such as birth, marriage and death in a family. They are paid for their services on these occasions along with the customary share of paddy after harvesting.

Similarly, the distribution and exchange of economic goods takes place at different ceremonies and festivals. Gifts are given on different occasions. Whenever a child is born in a family all the invitees to the *chhati* ceremony generally bring some gifts for the child. Marriage is also an occasion for the exchange of gifts not only between the offines, but also between the family in which the marriage is taking place and the kin group of which it is a part. Presents are also made at the time of a funeral. After harvesting the Munda go on good will visits to their relatives and also receive them. This is a time of plenty and a time for returning obligations. The *Jatras*, ceremonial dances and other religious occasions provide an opportunity to entertain guests and relatives and strengthen the inter relationships.

[illegible]umption refers not merely to the ways in which goods [illegible] up, but also the role, property and wealth play in the [illegible] their consumers. Property may consist of previleged knowledge or rights, including methods of dealing with the supernatural. Everywhere, the use of property takes on meanings beyond the satisfaction of primary biological needs. Comfort, security, prestige, status, power, pride and pleasure are but some of the intangible benefits of ownership and consumption. In a Munda family, women are not allowed to worship the family deities (Ora bongako) and the ownership of landed property does not include them. The male head of the household offers worship to the family gods on different occasions associated with the individual life cycle and festivals. Similarly the *pahan* is a ritual specialist and only he can establish relationship with the supernatural powers.

The Singbonga, the Ora bongako, the village gods and other categories of supernatural powers in the Munda pantheon are believed to guard them against misfortune and bring prosperity to them. They are worshipped to secure their blessings. Communion with these spirits is manifested mainly through supplications, rice-beer offerings and animal sacrifices made on behalf of a family, clan or a village. At the *Jom Nawa* festival certain ceremonies are performed in September or so, at the time of eating of the new harvested rice crop. *Chura* made of new rice is eaten with milk or curds and molasses. Rice-beer and hens are offered to the ancestors and the sacrificial food is shared ceremonially. It is forbidden to eat new pulses like *kurthi* before *Sukan Buru* festival in December, otherwise the offender may be killed by a tiger.

The Munda attribute diseases or misfortunes to the supernatural, human and physical actions, such as those of *bongas*, witches and sorcerers and nature. They have developed remedial measures to combat such problems. The social function of religion with regard to diseases and other calamities is to avert these events through magic, omens and taboos. When an epidemic or disease visits a Munda village, all the village women collect the old cooking pots, old worn out winnowing fans and brooms from their respective houses and go collectively to the village boundary and throw these things there in the belief that all the spirits which caused the diseas[illegible] been driven out of the village boundary.

The symbolic value of rituals is a sense of pres[illegible] fellowship with the spirits. This is expressed in the li[illegible] and sacrificial offerings shared by the people and the spirits. The rituals also symbolise the Munda's dependence on their spirits. The praise of these deities in the *mantras* shows their supremacy. It is manifest in the offerings of first fruits like the *sal*, *mahua* and crops to the *bongas* at the *Sarhul* and other festivals. Rituals and festivals symbolise a sense of new life and harmony with nature. This is manifest in the fact that most of the village feasts are connected with agricultural and seasonal cycles.

The idea of community solidarity is expressed in collective feasting, drinking, singing, dancing, mutual visits and exchange of gifts. The mutual stimulation of collective public worship gives meaning and enhances value to the Munda way of life. They become conscious of their unity and are at the same time dependent on their spirits. These expressions of religion are techniques for entering into, continuing and reasserting social relationship with the invisible world. The collective celebrations are an affirmation of all the values that the community holds dear. They are the creative self-expression of the community's life and identity.

13

HINDUISM AND CHRISTIANITY IN THE LIFE OF THE MUNDA

IMPACT OF HINDUISM

THE EVIDENCE of the prevalence of Hinduism and its cults of the Sungod and Mother goddess in Tamar dates back to the early medieval age. Culturally, the plains of Panch Parganas were the gateway of Vaishnava influence to the Munda country. Hindu Vaishnavism left a permanent impression on the Mundas of this area. Towards the close of the medieval period, like tribals elsewhere they were influenced by Hindu religious movements. Mahaprabhu Chaitanya on his way from Nilachal to Mathura passed through Jharkhand and made converts among the tribals. Benand Das composed and recited Mundari songs based on Vaishnava themes. A number of poets composed their works in Sadani and Panchpargania. The best known of them was Budu Babu of Babai Kundi in Tamar. His songs are very popular in Panch Parganas. The waves of new religious and social forces completely submerged the Munda way of life in Panch Parganas. The communities of Gosain, Manjhi, Tanti, Swansi and Adhikari played an important role in spreading Vaishnavism throughout the Munda country and they still are its distant outposts among the Mundas.

The religious interaction of the Hindu and Munda systems led to Siva being accepted as Mahadev Bonga and Parvati as Chandi Bonga. To the Munda festivals, the Hindu influence added *Dasai*, *Karam*, *Phagu*, *Jitia* and *Mahadev Manda mela*. The lyrical *Karma* songs were accepted by the Munda due to their wide appeal and popularity. To the Munda dances of *Jadur*, *Mage*, *Japi* and *Racha* the new influence contributed *Lahsua*, *Domkach* and *Paika*. The wide gamut of *mantras* or incantations recited by the *sokha* which are mostly in the Sadan language are further indications of the partnership of the Munda and non-Munda in the sphere of magic. Some of the marriage ceremonies of the Mundas have Hindi names and are of Hindu origin. Like their Hindu neighbours, the Munda on the east of Ranchi-Chaibasa Road do not take beef. For a long time the tribal and non-tribal living in the Munda country had been brought into a socially and economically integrated pattern. The latter respected the social and economic superiority of the Munda, and through their supplementary economic roles, gave a fullness and an economic self-sufficiency to the tribal village. These Sadans were the Swansis, the Ghasis, Bhagtas and Lohars etc.

The Munda, in turn, did not consider them as aliens (*dikus*) but accepted them as an essential part of their communal life. The extent of this integration at the lower level is apparent from the similar pattern of life led by the tribals and the non-tribals. The social occasions such as the name-giving ceremony, marriage, names of days and months, household utensils, tools and weapons, dress, houses and even language are almost, common to both. The *pahan* presides over the communal life of the village.

Sirum was under the strong influence of Hinduism which came from the east, i.e., Bundu and Tamar, which have been important centres of Vaishnavism for a long time. The impact is observable in the beliefs and practices of the Munda. Some Hindu practices have been adopted without understanding their real significance and beliefs connected with these practices also undergo a change by the time they reach the tribals.

In the Maranghada and Sirum area a majority of the Munda wear the sacred thread. Though wearing of the sacred thread has been imitated from the Brahmins, the imitation is not complete. There is no sacred thread ceremony. Many Vaishnava mendicants visit this area frequently. This explains the influence of the Bhakti cult. They have been for a long time the channel of communication between devotional Hinduism and the Munda. There is a marked departure from traditional beliefs in tribal deities or *bongas*. It is believed that the *bongas* have lost most of their powers. They believe that an illness or other misfortune caused by the wrath of evil spirits can be averted not only by the sacrifice of goats or hens or by propitiation but can also be neutralized by the purification of the body.

The Munda in the Panch Parganas area have been Hinduised for a long time. They speak Panchpargania, Hindi and Bengali and the use of Mundari is least among them. Mahadev temples, Devi Mandaps and temples of Radha Rani are found in almost all the villages. They keep the *tulsi* plant in their courtyards and worship it. The *pahan* of village Diuri officiates as a priest at the Devi Mai temple of that village. At the *Dasehra* festival the *pahan* performs the function of the ritual sacrificer at the Diuri temple. Pattidar, Brahmins, Gosains and barbers are employed by Mundas in some areas during life crisis occasions.

In Selda some of the Munda have declared themselves to be the adherents of Sheoli Dharam. The number of such people, however, does not exceed half a dozen. Those who professed this creed did not seem to have any clear idea of its content. On enquiry it was revealed that it drew its inspiration from Buddhism. This religion has been named after the village Sheoli which is situated near Gaya. In fact, one of these persons visited Sheoli. The place has a Hindu monastery where the present exponent of that sect lives. In spite of their having adopted the new faith, they continued to worship the old deities. The only change that has occurred is that they do not sacrifice chicken, goats or offer rice-beer to the deities. The sect was said to have spread from Singbhum where some people of Selda had affinal relatives. These people do not plough their fields on Thursday and burn incense on that day. Those who can afford, offer milk and sweets to the deities.

In some areas, the Munda belong to Birsa Dharam, Tana Bhagats and Muni Samaj, a reformist sect of Hinduism. In the three study areas Birsaites were found in Jaipur in Torpa Block and Sirum Serengdih in Khunti Block. In Kalet there were two Munda households belonging to Tana Bhagats. Tana Bhagats are mostly found among the Oraons. In Salehatu two households belonged to Muni Samaj—a reformist Hindu sect which has its head office at Gorakhpur in U.P. This religion is popular among the Swansis of Maranghada area and they are agents for its spread among the Mundas. Chota Rai of Salehatu, who belongs to Muni Samaj does not worship the Munda deities, or offer sacrifice or take meat and rice-beer. He has a framed photograph of the Muni Samaj Guru displayed in his house and offers incense and prayers to him every morning and evening. Members of this sect in this area hold occasional congregations at a place and sing in praise of their *Guru.*

BIRSA DHARAM

Birsa Dharam was propagated for the first time among the Mundas of Chotanagpur by Birsa Bhagwan during the closing years of nineteenth century. In formulating the tenets of his faith, he was influenced by Hinduism and Christianity; however, the soul of his religion remained completely Munda. The new religion preached that God was one and He was Singbonga. He called for a belief in one God in place of numerous deities. The followers were to abstain from the worship of innumerable spirits. They were not to sacrifice fowl or flesh for the deities, but were to pray to Singbonga who was Almighty and the Creator of all. Arua rice, a few coins etc. could be used for the purpose of worship. They should love all creatures and venerate the cow. They should eat neither flesh nor fish nor fowl and should give up taking rice-beer. They should lead simple lives and should not tell lies or steal. Birsaites were asked to be united. They were directed to take weekly rest from work such as ploughing etc. and devote the day in worship and meditation. Birsa asked his followers, male or female, to wear the sacred thread of the Hindus and take their meals after purifying themselves by taking a bath. They were also directed not to interdine with non-Birsaites and not to take impure food. They were further asked not to inter-marry with non-Birsaite Mundas. Birsa also wrote a book of prayers for the use of his disciples. He came to be known as *Bhagwan* or *Dharti Aba* by his followers.

The Birsaites are spread over more than one hundred villages of Porahat (Singbhum), Karra, Torpa, Khunti, Murhu and Tamar police stations of the Khunti sub-division, Kolebira and Bano of Simdega sub-division, Bero and Lapung of Sadar sub-division of Ranchi district. The Birsaites are everywhere a compact and closely-knit community, living in small groups in hamlets.

The original faith exists in three sub-sects today, their followers taking their respective day off. The members of the two schools, Thursday and Sunday would gather and offer prayer in the house of a *Guru* or *Pracharak*. Thursday, being the birthday of Birsa, became more popular among his disciples and was substituted for the Christian Sunday on a wide scale. However, due to the vulnerability of their Thursday congregations to detection by the authorities, Sundays and Wednesdays were preferred as days of rest and prayer. There is also another line of distinction between those who pitch flags and those who worship the *tulsi* plants in the courtyard of their houses. The former group corresponds to the Thursday school and the latter to the Sunday school respectively. At present, there are preachers in Bortodih, Serengdih, Poseya, Jaipur, Jalmai, Khandajui and Rogoto etc. Their activities are limited to the propagation of Birsa's religion and conversion to his faith which are not very large in number. On the face of it, the nature of the Birsa religion ranges from the puritan Thursday to the somewhat liberal Sunday school. However, the differences are small and the outlines of Birsa Dharam are clear and its ingredients common to all sub-sects.

Faith in Birsa as the messenger of God or prophet and his prayers replace propitiation of spirits as the road to happiness. The prayers of the Birsaites subsequently apotheosized him into God himself. In the early days of the prophethood of Chalkad, he was *Dharti Aba* and later *Bhagwan* or God incarnate.

The exclusion of the *pahan*, purification ceremonies, prayers and puritanism pervade the Birsaite's approach to social occasions. The *pahan* is replaced by the *panch*, who presides over the functions in the individual and social life. The traditional concept of ceremonial purity was emphasised by Birsa and given a new significance. The Birsaites do not spit in fire, water and river nor do they abuse the air, water and fire as other Mundas do. The purification ceremony is performed with water in a clean pot. It is sprinkled on a person or all over the house with a mango stalk or some grass. Before that the water is purified with the touch of the grass and a piece of copper put into it. A Birsaite, when he returns home, is received by his wife, who sprinkles the purified water on his person. Saturday is a day of preparation for Sunday when the Birsaites of the Sunday school wash their clothes and clean their homes. The place where they take their food is cleansed with cowdung before and after taking the food. Food is normally taken only after a bath. Purification and prayers are essential parts of all rituals in the social and personal life of the Birsaites. The barber and the washerman play an important role at ceremonies like death rites, births and marriages, especially among followers of the Sunday school.

The three vital events i.e., birth, marriage and death in the life cycle of a Birsaite are marked by the same features as the role of new functionaries, *panches* or preachers, purification ceremonies, prayers, abstention from sacrifice, drinking and spirit worship, wearing of a new sacred thread and sandal paste. Apart from these, there is a marked difference in the rituals by a Birsaite and a Sansar Munda or a follower of the traditional Munda religion.

Conversions to Birsa's faith are not a common occurrence. The ceremonies on such occasions take place as follows : The preacher is given a new *dhoti* to wear for the occasion; he brings a brass pot full of water and sprinkles it all over the house. Old utensils are removed and replaced. The intiate is given the sacred thread after a ritual bath. The ceremonies end in prayers and a common feast to celebrate the occasion. The preacher is paid a fee in which the *Guru* has a share.

The traditional Munda festivals, for Birsaites, are occasions for prayer and purification ceremonies. They celebrate *Phagu*, *Dasai* and *Sohrai*. The festival of *Jomnawa* fits in with the Birsaite concept of purification, the occasion symbolises the new crop. The house is cleaned. New clothes and sacred threads are worn, the old utensils and hearths are replaced. Only a few Birsaites celebrate the *Ind* festival. They fast for the day and pray. The *Mage Parab*, the *Sarhul*, the *Honba* and the *Batauli* festivals are not celebrated by Birsaites.

Presently, however, the Birsaites themselves are losing faith in their religion. By departing from the traditional religion they can neither have relations with the non-Birsaites nor can they claim to stand at par with the Brahmins. The non-Birsaites do not give any consideration to the religious convictions of the Birsaites. It is difficult for them to believe that there is only one God and that the *bongas* of the *sarna* should not be worshipped. In illness and other misfortunes they continue to take the help of the *sokha* who necessarily must be from the non-Birsaites. On receiving the advice of the *sokha* they have to propitiate the offended spirit by sacrificing a goat or a hen. While they abstain from animal food, they cannot abstain from animal sacrifices. Unmarried boys and girls, even in a Birsaite family, take sacrificial meat. Even the drinking of rice-beer is not forbidden. It was observed that the Birsaites in Serengdih village had lost their land and, therefore, were dependent on the people of the Pahan Khut for borrowing money and other things. In the panchayat also the Pahan Khut played a leading role. The Birsaite felt so isolated that seven families from their village have now ceased to be Birsaites. The Birsa religion, which once gave new philosophy and hope to the Munda during a crisis, does not seem to have much prospects for transforming the Munda society in the face of the new forces of urbanization and industrialization

IMPACT OF CHRISTIANITY

The Advent of Christian Missionaries

Christian missionaries first arrived in Chotanagpur in 1845. They belonged to the Gossner Mission and came from Germany. The four pioneer missionaries, Pastors E. Schatz, F. Bastch, A. Brandt and H. Janke, who arrived at Ranchi in November 1845, preached among the Munda and the Oraon for about 5 years before they succeeded in converting any one to Christianity. Four Oraon families received baptism on 9 June, 1850. On 26 October, 1851, Sadho Munda, bhuinhar of village Bandhea, and Mangta Munda of village Balalong were baptised by the Rev. Schatz. They were the first Munda converts to Christianity. On 18 November, 1851, the foundation stone of the Gothic building popularly known as the German Church, on the Ranchi-Chaibasa Road, was laid. This Church, was consecrated on Christmas 1855, and called Christ Church. It is the first Christian church built in Chotanagpur.

With the spread of Christianity, the Munda and Oraon

became more aware of their rights to the land and of the persistent suppression and victimization at the hands of lease-holders and landlords. It caused displeasure to the alien landlords who used every possible means of persecution against these converts with no other effect than the spread of Christianity.

When, therefore, the Sepoy Mutiny broke out in 1857, the Christians had to face the worst. Out of fear, the German missionaries left Ranchi and stayed in Calcutta. They returned to Ranchi only by the close of that year. During the Mutiny, the native Christian community was broken up, but their dispersion over the district seems to have given a considerable impetus to Christianity as the number of converts largely increased after the restoration of order. The German Mission Report claimed at the end of 1860 about 1700 baptized converts, to whom were added in the coming seven years on an average, 1225 every year. It was also held that most of the new inquirers looked to the secular benefit the Christians enjoyed rather than to the spiritual side of the new religion. With the increase in the number of converts among the tribals, the Hindu landlords became more hostile in their attitude lest the former began disobeying them. So they began to oppress and torture the Christians in various ways. Contemporary official reports stated that for these conflicts both the Christians and the landlords were to be blamed equally. Towards the end of 1855, the conflict became serious and a detachment of native infantry had to be sent from Ranchi to Govindpur for the preservation of order in Pargana Basia and Sonepur, both largely inhabited by Mundas.

The missionaries took steps to educate the tribals of Chotanagpur. In the year 1868, the German Mission split up due to a disagreement between the senior German missionaries at Ranchi and the Home committee at Berlin, regarding the constitution and organisation of the mission. The Home committee sent out a band of younger missionaries from Germany; and the then senior missionaries with a larger number of Christian converts requested Bishop Milman of Calcutta to receive them into the Church of England and were duly entered. The new missionaries were known as the Baptist or the Anglican Mission. In 1890, Chotanagpur was formed into a separate Diocese under the Right Rev. J.C. Whitley as its first Bishop.

He learnt the Mundari language, wrote the first Mundari Grammar in English and translated portions of the New Testament and the Prayer Book into Mundari. Rev. A. Nottrott wrote the first primer and a Mundari Hymn book printed at Banaras in 1871. In 1871, the Rev. A. Nottrott published the first Mundari Grammar in the German language to assist young German missionaries coming to Ranchi and it was translated into English by the Rev. P. Wagner. From the very beginning of their existence in Chotanagpur the various missions established schools to educate Indian boys and girls. The German Mission Primary School at Ranchi was raised to the Matriculation standard in January, 1896. This school and the German Mission Girls' School have been entirely boarding schools. Boarding schools were opened at Lohardaga, Govindpur, Koronjo and Takarma etc. Teachers' training schools and a theological seminary were opened at Ranchi. Numerous religious and educational books in Mundari, Oraon and Hindi have been published by the German Mission since its establishment. Under the auspices of the Calcutta Bible and Tract Society, Dr. Nottrott brought out a translation of the New Testament and of the Old Testament.

The German Mission Hospital and Dispensary were opened at Ranchi (1890) and Lohardaga. Asylums for lepers were started at Lohardaga (1882) and Purulia (1887). In September 1907, the Rev. E. Muller started co-operative credit banks in the Ranchi district at every mission station in the division to improve the living conditions of the Christian converts of the Mission.

Besides the three old mission stations at Ranchi, Lohardaga and Govindpur, new mission stations were started at various other places, viz., at Burju (1869), Takarma (1873), Chainpur (1892), Khuntitoli (1895), Gumla (1895), Kinkel (1899), Tamar (1901), Koronjo (1903), all within Ranchi district. Other places are Hazaribagh (1853), Purulia (1863), Chaibasa (1865), Porahat (1867) and Chakradharpur (1893).

The total number of baptised converts of the GEL Mission was 74,626 at the end of 1909. Of this number, as many as 55,650 belonged to the Ranchi district, besides a large number of Munda and Oraon Christians working in the Duars and in Assam as coolies.

Similarly, the Baptist or the S.P.G. Mission opened schools, hospitals and co-operative banks among the Mundas and Oraons of Chotanagpur and started mission stations at Ranchi, Maranghada, Murhu, Dorma, Soparom, Purulia, Hazaribagh, Chaibasa etc. In about 40 years, from 1870—1909, the number of baptised converts rose more than three times and reached 18,117 and that of communicants multiplied more than four times to 8349 by 1909.

In the year 1869, the Rev. Father A. Stockman, S.J., opened the first Catholic Mission station at Chaibasa in Chotanagpur division but organised work among the tribals began some fifteen years later. In 1883 the Central Mission Station was established at Doranda and then removed to Ranchi by 1888. By the year 1885, the number of baptised Mundas of the Chotanagpur Catholic Mission rose to 2,092. With their conversion to Christianity, the Mundas and Oraons came to appreciate in a better way their rights as men and as tenants and believed that they would certainly rebut the oppression of the landlords by adopting the new religion. The number of Christian converts to the Catholic Mission swelled to about one lakh and half by 1909. The number of Catholic converts of the Munda tribe alone exceeded 30,000 in 1909, as against 2092 in the year 1885. The important Catholic Mission centres in Ranchi district were located at Ranchi (1887), Sarwada (1882), Torpa (1885), Mandar (1893), Noatoli (1890), Khunti (1891), Rengari (1901) etc. The Chotanagpur Roman Catholic R.C. Mission organised various educational and industrial training institutions for the tribals at various places in and around Ranchi. Female education was also stressed greatly. Dispensaries were attached to each mission station for the health and medical care of the tribals of the adjoining areas. The Chotanagpur Catholic Co-operative Credit Society (CCS) (started by the Rev. Father J. Hoffmann) was one of the most significant institutions of the R.C. Mission set up for improving the economic conditions of the tribals and releasing them from the clutches of money-lenders. Thus R.C. Mission with its beneficent educational and various other institutions and elaborately organised mission work among the tribals of Chotanagpur became most popular among them as compared to the G.E.L. and S.P.G. Missions and even attracted Christians of other denominations.

The work of the Roman Catholic Mission in giving help and strengthening the economic base of the Munda is described below :

Chotanagapur Catholic Mission Co-operative Credit Society

The Chotanagpur Catholic Co-operative Credit Society (CCS) was started by the Rev. Father J. Hoffmann in the first decade of this century. The society was registered under Act X of 1904, on 2 December 1909. The society was started to improve the material condition of the Catholic Munda. It is a large centralized society embracing the whole Roman Catholic population of Ranchi and formed with the object of enabling the members of the mission to constitute themselves into a system of federated and autonomous societies within the central institution. The society is managed by a central committee of management with headquarters at Ranchi. The area of operation is divided into circles corresponding to missionary circles, each in charge of a missionary. The circles are again divided into villages or groups of villages, each of which forms a rural unit. The unit has its own panchayat and supervisors, and keeps its own accounts and administers its own loans.

Initially, the society had 16 circles and within 6 months the number of rural units reached 229 and the society had realised a 'capital of Rs. 22,845 which grew in proportion with time. Father Hoffmann travelled throughout Chotanagpur explaining to the Christians the advantage of Cooperative Banks. The initial capital of the society came from the deposits of those Munda who were working in the Assam tea gardens and in the Andaman Islands. The society became inactive during the 1940's and was activized around 1950. The non-Christian tribals are also members of the society, specially, in Jitutoli circle. Earlier the non-Christian tribals were also given loans but it was difficult to realise these from them for they were not under the social or religious pressure of the mission to repay the loans.

According to the Director's report of 6 March 1975, the society experienced a considerable rise in the number of its circles, units and members during 1965-75. In 1965 there were 42 circles, 855 units and 29425 members. The corresponding figures in 1975 increased to 55 circles (+31% increase), 1144 units (+34%) and 48,724 members (+65%). There was a 61% increase in the deposits of the members reaching Rs. 81,50,000 in 1975 and the deposits of non-members increased by39% to Rs. 52,77,386 in 1975. The society contributed Rs. 10,001 to the National Defence Fund in 1972. In the Munda areaalone there are at present about 10 circles and 228 rural units. These are at Khunti, Karra, Torpa, Sarwada, Mahugaon, Bandgaon, Lachragarh, Kutungia, Jitutoli and Anandpur.

One of the main problems of the society has been that the loans advanced to the members could not be fully realised in any of the years. During the 47 years between 1915-1957 the loans fluctuated around Rs. 1,00,000. It was due to persistent non-payment of loans which was always 30 to 50% and never less than 25%. During the 15 years from 1957 to 1972 the situation regarding the realisation of loans improved somewhat. This progress was due to stern discipline in forwarding the loans. However, 1969 onwards the situation again deteriorated and outstanding loans amounted to 18% of the total in all the years. till 1974. The CCS had given more than 1,00,000 loans till 1973 at the rate of 6%.

It has consistently advocated the practice of taking loans only for productive purposes. Apart from the urban maintenance loans, with which wage earners buy cheap rice, very small amounts of loans had been advanced towards meeting the expenditure on marriage feasts, and maintenance etc. It is clear from the percentage of outstanding loans in different years given above, that the CCS failed to bring about a change in the attitudes of its members.

Some of the shortcomings in the functioning of the Co-operative Society are noted below :

1. The members do not state the real purpose of the loan they apply for. They apply for the purchase of a bullock, but buy rice and eat away the loan.

2. Many people, when asking for a loan for a justified purpose, apply for a larger sum than required, just to have some spare cash to spend.

3. Many people take loans from traditional sources like the grain *gola*, etc. and keep the CCS in reserve to cover other emergencies.

4. A loan is not sufficiently understood as a burden to be cast off as quickly as possible, some members delay the refund, and frequently a new emergency overtakes them.

Along with these persisting old attitudes of the members, the inability of the CCS in realising the loans is responsible for the high and constant percentage of defaulters over the years.

5. The CCS does not take prompt action against small accounts of unpaid loans.

6. It sometimes sanctions loans for purposes other than those emphasised by the CCS.

7. Grants of loans are characterized by favouritism, lack of leadership and making the panchayat a scapegoat for personal incapabilities in checking corrupt practices.

The nature of CCS loans clearly shows that the society, as a matter of policy, advances loans mainly for productive purposes. That the total number of loans given by the CCS were more than 10,000 during 1970-71, but the number decreased to less than 10,000 in 1973-74. The total amount as well as the average size of loans were higher in 1973-74 than in 1970-71. The average size of loan was Rs. 232 in 1973-74 and Rs. 182 in 1970-71. As regards the specific purpose of loan, about 50% were given for cultivation expenses in 1970-71 and 53% in 1973-74. The next item was the purchase of cattle and accounted for one-fifth of the total loans for this purpose in 1970-71. The percentage declined in 1973-74. There were no loans on marriage expenses in 1970-71 while 8 such loans (3.2%) were given in 1973-74.

It was mentioned by the Director of the CCS that the society should act like a school, teaching better socio-economic attitudes to all, and leadership to many. The central leadership should, whenever possible, refrain from imposing hard and fast rulings, but after giving strong advice to the circle managing committees, rely on them for action. The managing committees should influence the unit *panchs* and in the same way, the *panchs* should influence the individual members.

The CCS will achieve its final objectives of improving the socio-economic status of the tribals only by changing their socio-economic attitudes, by implementing its well planned economic policy, and by educating the tribals to check their improvidence and propensity for consumption and to encourage them augment their savings.

Catholic Employment Agency

Catholic missionaries also opened a Labour Bureau at Ranchi to organize the tribals, and put them in touch with the employers at distant places as well as to arrange all the facilities for them. The Bureau also collected half the money earned by the labourers and sent it to their families or remitted it to them on their return. However, the Bureau was closed down after 1947 and its functions ceased except for the collection of savings of the labourers still living in far off places. Collection is done through the missionaries stationed there, now on behalf of the Catholic Co-operative Society, and such collections are annually deposited in the bank of the Society or remitted to their relatives through parish priests. Lakhs of rupees are thus deposited in the Bank of the Society every year. In 1958 the Labour Bureau was renamed under the name of "Catholic Employment Agency". The missionary in charge of it collects relevant information regarding employment, training and apprenticeship from different newspapers, local, civil and military employment exchanges, railway offices, educational institutions, private industries and factories, private contractors, labour employers and such other sources which, along with relevant instructions, are sent to different parish Fathers who read it in the gathering of village Catechists and teachers in the parish church once a month. The villagers then get this news through their catechists or teachers and contact the parish Father if interested or, in many cases, directly go to Ranchi for necessary guidance from the Father-in-charge.

Since the year 1967, the Christians of Ranchi have been running a Council known as the Council for Christian Vocational Guidance and Employment, Ranchi. It is a joint venture of the Catholics, Lutherans. Anglicans and the Syrians. The Council meets once a month to discuss the various vocational problems of the students and to devise ways and means to solve them in the light of the prevailing position of the employment market. Presently, a few informative and instructive printed hand bills have been distributed by the Council among the students and sent to various Christian schools in interior villages for information. In due course, the Council aims to provide its services to the converts of the entire Chotanagpur district in a more planned and systematic manner.

Missionaries also concentrate on the improvement of the agricultural system of the converts which is the main source of their livelihood. With this end in view in the beginning, agriculture lectures were arranged among the Catholics with the co-operation of the Agriculture Department of the Government and people were asked to use improved variety of seeds and chemical manure in their fields and to adopt the Japanese method of cultivation. Some educated and enlightened converts, since then, can be found in some villages using such manure in their fields or practising the Japanese method of cultivation.

The missions have also done excellent relief work during the drought and famine in 1967. The Central Development and Relief Committee of the G.E.L. Mission, Ranchi did a commendable job for the development of tribal converts. The developmental activities included the repairing of village roads, sinking irrigation and drinking water wells etc. under the food for work scheme. In late 1975, the committee selected village Marcha near Torpa and started a nutrition project for expectant and nursing mothers and children below seven years of age. The project was financed by the Lutheran World Service, Geneva.

Political Consciousness

It is certain that the Christian missionaries have brought among the Christians a consciousness of their past exploitation, their rights and privileges and thus injected in them a feeling of self-confidence. Since the beginning of this century, the tribal leadership has been in the hands of the western-educated Christian tribals who are essentially rational in interpreting and tackling the political situation. The growth of Christian tribal leadership has been discussed in detail earlier. The other aspect of the impact of missionary activity has been the impetus given to political organisations. There are some pockets of missionary influence where the traditional political institutions of the tribals are being revived and put on a sound footing. In Koenara, Birhu, Khatanga, Kotbo etc. the *parha* organisation is still quite influential. The functioning of the *parha* has been put on sound lines and all the Munda, both unconverted and converted take pride in solving their own problems through the *parha* rather than taking their cases to the *gram* panchayat. In 1953 some of the tribal leaders had organised a *parha* training camp at Tangarbansali near Ranchi to train workers for reorganising the *parha* in the Munda and Oraon areas. Recently educated Christian tribals have attempted to modernise the village panchayat (*Hatu sabha*) and Parha Sabha in line with the socio-economic and political changes taking place in the tribal area and the country. Efforts are being made to incorporate modern democratic value and strengthen the existing traditional values with a view to promote the welfare of the tribals. *Masclant Topno* a Christian Munda school teacher is the moving force in framing a new constitution for the Bais Parha consolidating different *parhas* under a *Parha Hadri* and getting it registered as a registered society.

Conversion to Christianity has introduced new ideas, new values and several new practices among the Munda and have reoriented their personal and social lives. A Christian starts his day with prayers when he dedicates all his work, joys and sorrows to Jesus. He expresses his gratitude to God for protecting his life at night, thus enabling him to see the new day and further invokes His aid so that he may not commit any sin and may do everything according to His sacred desire.

A Christian offers prayer before and after doing his work, before and after taking his meal. Among the Catholics some godfearing people make the sign of cross over the body even before drinking water and rice-beer. Prayers are offered by the Catholics also at night when they finish their dinner and go to bed. The members of the family collect in a room and offer prayers before the picture or image of Jesus Christ, St. Joseph or other saints. In their prayers, they introspect whether they committed any sin on that day, express regret for whatever sin was committed and pray to God that it should be expiated. The soul is then 'handed over' to the Lord, and prayers are offered to the Patron Saint to guard the soul at night. After offering the evening prayers they go to sleep.

The Lutherans also offer evening prayers and entrust their

soul to God for the night, but instead of doing it in their respective families, they assemble at the village church before having their evening meals. The prayers are usually led by the village *panch*. In Amlesa Mission toli, the evening prayer is held in turn at the house of each Lutheran. If there is an ailing person in the hamlet, the evening prayer may repeatedly be held at his place for several days, so as to secure the special blessings of God on that family. Prayer is a part of Sunday service at the church and it is offered on all the socio-religious occasions such as festivals, birth, baptism, sacrament, marriage and death.

Whenever one goes to attend a Church service, a person must change his dress and put on clean clothes. The usual dress of the Christian is a *dhoti* and shirt. Shorts and trousers are also used by young people; mostly by those who have been to school and college. Urban bred educated tribals, both converts and non-converts, prefer cotton and terrycot trousers and shirts. Educational and economic status also affects attitudes towards dress. Millimade saris, blouses, brassieres and petticoats constitute the dress of young Christian girls, while children below two years of age are invariably dressed either in frocks or shirts and shorts. Christian Munda women do not cover their heads.

The most remarkable change which can be found among Christian girls is their hairdo which makes a contrast with that of the unconverted ones. Christian girls freely use moden things like ribbons and *choti* and hair is arranged either in two long plaits or just braided in a chignon at the back of the head.

Another great change in the hair style of the males which took place after conversion to Christianity was the cutting of the top knot of the hair on the head and the tuft of hair hanging down to neck.

Christian women are more particular about their dress than about their ornaments. Education has made them look upon heavy ornaments as a waste. Modern trinkets like ear-rings, nose-studs, chains, necklaces, etc. are being widely used. Tattooing was common among women on the face and on other parts of the body. With conversion this custom is dying out. Educated Christian tribals do not like their daughters and sisters to be tattooed. They hold that besides being painful it disfigures the body.

Christianity has introduced a new way of greeting among the Christian Munda. Among the non-converts when two persons meet, the younger bows to the elder, bringing his right hand up to his forehead or folding his hands and saying *johar*. The older Munda responds by repeating the greeting in a similar manner. When a non-convert woman greets a man she will kneel down with both her hands on the head and whisper the word *johar*. Men only fold their hands slightly and bend in response to this greeting. The Christian Munda, irrespective of age and sex, shake hands and remember Lord Jesus when they meet another Christian or an outsider. The Catholics say *Jai Yisu* (Hail Jesus or Glory Jesus) and the Lutherans say *Yisu Sahai* (May Jesus help you) while shaking hands. Among the Lutherans, after the Church service is over, the priest shakes hand with the congregation one by one and the latter shake hands with each other with the words *Yisu Sahai*.

Christians refrain from doing manual work on Sunday. They attend the Church for Sunday service. The type of manual work, forbidden on Sundays, may include any professional or agricultural activity such as ploughing, husking, threshing harvesting, sowing or carrying manure to the field, digging of wells, thatching of roofs etc. However, odd and light jobs like repairing one's fishing net, minor carpentry work, making of *mora* (paddy receptacle), or watching over the fields etc. are not objected to.

The most important activity of the Christians on Sunday is their Church service. The Church service at the GEL Parish, Tapkara is held at noon so as to enable the Christians from distant villages to reach the Church easily. In Gutuhatu R.C. Mission the service is held at 7 A.M. The proceedings of the service may last from one hour to two hours. In GEL Parish, Tapkara a Sunday school is held in the Church hall for boys and girls. The Sunday service serves many purposes, since Sunday is an off day, the people are free from their usual agricultural work and the Church service provides a good opportunity for the villagers to get together. In the Church they listen to the religious discourse. They bring with them some contributions in the form of paddy, rice, vegetables, fruit or cash for the Church fund or *siryni*. A record is maintained of the weekly contributions. News about marriages, baptism, sacrament or the announcement of important festivals and other important information is given during the Church service. The monthly meeting of the Parish is held after the Church service in the first week of the month. This sitting is held to discuss the social, economic, religious and other problems of the Parish villages.

Hockey and football are favourite pastimes for the Christian boys and hockey for the Christian girls, and Sunday provides a good occasion for it. At Tapkara, every Sunday, there used to be a hockey match either for boys or for girls. The winners were given a fowl as a prize, while the losers were given half the price of the fowl. After the match, the winner boys and girls danced, and sang to the beat of the *Mandar*. Once when the boys' hockey team of Bhandar Toli won the match, the village girls brought water, sprinkled it with mango leaves on the winners, washed and anointed their feet with oil and garlanded them. They danced together till dusk.

Christianity does not prohibit the use of liquor or rice-beer but restricts its use to moderate quantity. It is thought that if taken in excess, drink must lead to many social vices such as quarrels, illicit sexual relations, economic hardship, theft and such other things. It is also feared that such persons would fail in their duty and not live up to the ideals of Christianity.

Drinking is completely prohibited among the Lutherans by the Church Council. However, many Lutheran Munda were found taking *mahua* liquor and rice-beer on different occasions. The Lutherans, however, have found a substitute for liquor and rice-beer in tea which is taken at festivals, marriage and other occasions. At the *lotapani* ceremony of a young Lutheran Munda it was observed that a big pot of tea and not rice-beer was exchanged and the tea was then served to the gathering by the couple. However, many among the visitors had taken rice-beer or *mahua* drink on their way to the bride's house. Tea has gained popularity as a cheap beverage not only among the Christian tribals, but also among those not converted but somewhat urbanised. Many tribals have opened tea stalls at roadside bus stops and market places.

Christianity and education have worked against the popularity of dancing. These factors have induced a change of values among the tribals. It was envisaged that free mixing of the Christian boys and girls at night during the *akhra* dance encouraged moral degradation leading to illicit sexual relations. Hence it was opposed by Christian missionaries. Converts were also prohibited from joining non-Christians in the dances at the village *akhra*. However, in spite of this, the Christians dance very often in an open space in the village or in the courtyard of a villager. It was observed that the young Christian boys and girls used to dance every night in the courtyard of a villager during the months of August, September and October. They also dance and sing at other Christian festivals such as Christmas. Dancing and singing are also common at the time of *lotapani* and marriage festivities. At Christmas, it was observed at the GEL Church Amlesa, that girls and young women sat in rows on the ground with legs stretched in front singing and swaying their bodies to the rhythm of the drum beat. At the *lotapani* ceremony of a Lutheran Munda the boys' party and the girls' party arranged a competition in singing Geet Gobind accompanied with drums and hand clapping throughout the night. Geet-Gobind are songs in Mundari and Sadani on themes from the Bible. Similarly, on other occasions the songs or prayers are sung in praise of Jesus Christ and on related themes.

Conversion to Christianity has made the tribal give up his old beliefs and practices. His faith in the power of his own traditional gods and spirits to save him and his family from troubles was already shaken and the adoption of a new theology and beliefs and practices gave him the necessary strength. The Christian rituals to be followed varied with the dictates of the particular denomination to which the convert belonged. There is nothing new about the religious practices followed by the converted tribals. They observe the different Christian festivals, such as Christmas, Easter, All Saints' Day, Israel Jatra etc. Resistance is perhaps the strongest in the realm of ideas.

One of the biggest achievements of the Christian missions has been in the field of education. It is a fact that a large number of tribals would have remained illiterate in the absence of the missionary's work in this field. The schools wherever, they are, admit the Christians and non-Christians alike; though the converted tribals may. be given some advantage over the other. So while education has changed the life of the converts, it has also brought awakening to the non-converts. The education which Birsa received at the G.E.L. School at Chaibasa deeply influenced his ideas and contributed to the making of his faith. Most of the tribal leaders of today have been educated in Mission schools. Education has, therefore, given them something more than knowledge. It has opened up a vast horizon for getting employment in Government and elsewhere. Those who took advantage of these facilities have been able to enhance their social status in the eyes of not only their fellow-tribals but also in those of the non-tribals.

Among the converts also, the belief in witchcraft is still present. In case of a disease or misfortune in the family, a Christian *bhagat* or *sokha* is called to detect and cure the disease. A Christian woman school teacher at Tapkara was suffering from a feminine disease *chhutka*. After trying the allopathic medicine for months without any relief, finally a Christian *bhagat* was called who through divination attributed the cause of disease to a witch. He suggested massage of oil prepared by him by mixing some indigenous herbal roots and advised her to perform some magical rites to ward off the evil effect of the witch. Some relief was observed in the ailing woman.

Besides administering medicines, prayer is also offered to God for the recovery of the ailing person. It was seen in some cases that a picture of Christ or Mary or a Cross or a Rosary was placed near the bed of the patient. When a man falls seriously ill, a parish Father or any other missionary who is available is called for the Last Sacrament or *Prabhu-Bhoj*. This is the last sacrament a man gets. Sometimes a patient recovers after the administration of the Last Sacrament.

The impact of Christianity on the life cycle of an individual has been dealt with earlier. Among the Lutherans of Koenara, if a person is deemed to be on his death bed and recovery seems impossible, prayers are offered which are believed to help in his recovery. There are people who still believe that spirits cause death and that if they are propitiated by prayers, the ailing man would survive. The Christians bury their dead in the village graveyard which is meant for Christian Mundas. They raise an earthen or concrete grave over the dead. A child who dies unbaptised and a Christian who has been expelled from the Church are buried outside the Christian burial ground.

Christianity has helped in widening the horizon of the consciousness of Munda and a new link has been forged between the tribal villages and Christendom. A number of Churches in the Munda area are engaged in the work of evangelization and they have their own organizations in the interior. These organizations are affiliated to the larger territorial units of the Churches. In this way regular contact is maintained between the converted Munda and the Indian and European agencies of the different missions through their missionaries, literature, teachers etc. Sometimes brilliant Christian Munda and other tribals are sent abroad to be trained as missionaries and when they come back they bring with them new ideas which they are eager to apply to the conditions obtaining in India. Wherever there are Churches, a number of villages are included in a parish. On Sundays all the priests of the parish are invited to attend all important festivals and functions. The influence of the missionary is not only limited to matters of religion but extends over secular affairs as well. Thus through the Church, the Christian tribals come to form a part of the world Christian ritual complex. They draw inspiration from Christian beliefs and get infused with western philosophy and scholarship.

Although the missionaries had much to give in exchange for conversion, which has not been without its material and economic value to the tribes, they have contributed to the destruction of the social unity and commual life of the village. Catholic missionaries in Chotanagpur preach loyalty to the Church as being more important than loyalty to the tribe. A breakdown in the communal life of the tribe or the village has reduced its effectiveness in its struggle against disruptive influences. Tribal dances in the *akhra* have been abolished by the Lutheran and Anglican Churches and the Catholic Mission allows them only under severe restrictions. The *akhra* as a social institution has disappeared in purely Catholic villages and in the dances at night only girls of the same village are permitted to dance together and one of the village *panchas* has to be present to give the signal for the termination of the dance in the evening. Non-Christian religious dances like *Karma* or *Sarhul* have been forbidden.

In villages where the Christians are in a majority the entire village organization has come under their control. The traditional village officers like the *Munda* and the *pahan* have become insignificant and have been replaced by church *mandlis* and panchayats. These *mandlis* work under the direction of the local pastor. In those villages where there are a large number of non-Christians in addition to converts, the Christians have their own *mandlis* and they do not take part in the affairs of the village panchayat.

In social relations, there is an estrangement between Christians and non-Christians. Their dress, standard of living, method of greeting and other behaviour-patterns are different. A non-Christian cannot accept food at the hands of a convert. Thus a village having both non-Christians and converts is divided into two factions. When the village is faced with any problem or presented with a programme for development, there are always two divergent points of view. In a village consisting of both these groups no decision can be taken or social action to follow them up taken at the village level. The converts regard themselves as being outside the pale of the village headman's authority and consider the missionary as their sole guide.

The condition of a village where more than one mission has converts, is even worse. In Birhu and Gutuhatu villages all the three missions, e.g. G.E.L., R.C. and S.P.G. are functioning at the same time. In Birhu there are three primary schools run by the three missions and the rivalry between them is quite sharp. This has resulted in the formation of three factions among the Christians. Even in a village like Koenara where all the Christian Munda were Lutherans, a split occurred in 1938 and they established two village Churches. In 1958, reconcilation was reached between the two factions and the Sunday services started being held in a single Church. However, the two factions hardly agree on issues of common concern.

14

THE MUNDA TO-DAY : AN OVERVIEW

SARAT CHANDRA ROY passed away in 1942, thirty years after the publication of his book on the 'Munda'. In his lifetime he witnessed many changes in Munda life and thought, some of which he recorded in long papers, either on the Munda or on allied tribal problems in Chotanagpur. He had also expressed a desire to revise his book on the Munda but on account of continued ill-health and pre-occupations, both academic and non-academic, he could never fulfil his cherished wish.

Roy loved the Munda with the core of his heart. He was always full of sympathy for their cause and devoted all his efforts towards their welfare. If he were to return to the land and the people he loved for a short visit in the late seventies, he would witness many changes among the Munda, some of which may be the fruition of trends that began in his days while yet others may be entirely new.

He would first of all have noticed some changes in their material culture. These would include the popularity of tea as a cheap beverage not only among the Christian tribals but also among those who have developed urban contacts. He would also have been surprised at tribals flocking to tea stalls at roadside bus stops. Instead of thick handwoven clothes he would have found men and women wearing mill-made *dhoties* and saris. Young men not only in the urban centres but also those with a smattering of education in villages are found donning bushshirts and trousers. Little girls would be dressed in frocks. Instead of using flowers in their hair and rolled palm leaves in their ear lobes, girls would be using bead-necklaces and cheap trinkets. In the villages, instead of using the *gungu* as a cover for rain, cloth umbrellas would be found in large numbers. In almost all villages there would be a few transistor-radios tuned to music in Hindi. Some villages would also be electrified and now most villages would have primary schools.

In villages affected by urban contact, young men use many fancy goods such as fountain pens, torches, sun glasses, cameras etc. Among women, glass bangles are now more popular than the traditional lac bangles or heavy brass ornaments. Those who can afford to, use soap, plastic combs, shoes etc, Tattooing is now less popular. Married women, both Christian and non-Christian, have begun using vermilion in the parting of the hair like Hindu women.

The popularity of dancing among the Munda has been adversely affected by education and Christianity. School-going children consider dancing an old-fashion. Sometimes parental injunction discourages song and dance in children, as it is believed, these interfere with their studies. Dancing is decried by school teachers who are generally outsiders. They hold it responsible for promoting sexual immorality. At many places Munda children have forgotten the art. Even when they know it, they are too shy to dance as it carries the stigma of tribalism. The Munda proverb *Sen ge susun, kaji ge durang* (to walk is to dance, to speak is to sing) seems to have lost its meaning.

The opening of roads connecting villages to highways and of the railway line from Ranchi to Bondamunda passing through the heart of the Munda country, have revolutionized spatial mobility. Fast buses run on these roads and distances, which formerly had to be covered on foot and took hours and days are now covered easily by public transport. In almost all villages there are a number of bicycles which extend people's horizon without additional expenditure and brings them into contact with the Community Development Block headquarters or the nearest town.

The growth of education has been phenomenal. The number of matriculates in Sarat Chandra Roy's time could be counted on the fingers of one hand; but now the number of graduates runs into thousands. The number of schools has multiplied. The government, the missionaries and the social welfare agencies have joined in this effort. Among the Christian Munda literacy is almost cent per cent and among the non-

Christians the number is rising at a fast rate. Munda women have also taken to education and although the numbers are still small the rate of increase is very well comparable to that in non-tribal area.

Education has given them not only literacy but enlightenment in all aspects of life. It has paved the way to individual social mobility. It has opened up a vast horizon for getting employment and for the diversification of occupation. Those who have received education rise in the esteem of their fellow men and acquire a social status. However it has a debit side too. It is drawn from a different social system and inculcates in the child, a language, a mode of thought, a scale of values and a behavioural pattern that are different from his own. Children who stay in schools for a number of years become misfits in their homes and look to the town for some employment. The alien school teacher who oftener than not, has no understanding or sympathy, derides the tribal way of life which creates in the students an inferiority complex. He is the model to be emulated in thought, behaviour and action. Education makes a difference in the tribal way of life and level of aspirations.

The growth of education has led to a psychological phase in which the tribal rediscovers his culture or sets in motion the process of contra-acculturation. His first reaction has been to bring his religious beliefs into line with those of the lower Hindu castes and this he did by shedding those practices which he thought were incongruent to those of his neighbours. On a mass scale this led to religious movements such as those initiated by Birsa. But this phase was followed by a marked reawakening of pride in certiain aspects of Munda culture. Some of the Munda dances and institutions have received a new appraisal. Troupes of dancers from different areas take part in the divisional, State and National festivals and have, on many occasions, secured prizes for the State of Bihar. Tribal songs and folklore have received an impetus through the opening of the Ranchi Station of the All India Radio. All these instances are sporadic attempts of a newly enlightened people to reawaken a sense of pride in the traditional Munda culture.

Education also led to the emergence of a middle class among the Munda. Its ranks are swelled by educated Mundas who are in government service or in profession like teaching, medicine and law. Brought up in liberal and democratic traditions and conscious of their rights as citizens in a free India, this middle class is desirous of participating in the processes of government. It is keen that its voice receives the attention it deserves. It serves as the mouthpiece for the aspirations of the Munda. It is also from this elite that the demand for a separate state of Jharkhand emerges.

SOCIAL STRUCTURE

Sarat Chandra Roy mentioned the process of clan segmentation. This process has gone on, with the result that now the Munda have more than one hundred and fifty clans. The reasons for segmentation are the same as in Roy's days. The close identification between the clan and clan territory is no longer there. Nor do the Munda care to take the bones of the dead to the original habitat of the clan. The *sasandiri* no longer serves as title deeds of the Munda.

Although Roy casually referred to the greater extent of acculturation and Hindu impact in the Panch Parganas, he did not mention the social stratification in those parts. At least in Tamar, Munda society has ceased to be homogeneous. We can easily discover the existence of five or six classes which differ not only in wealth but also in status. We also find the exploitation of one class by another with the result that people conceive of indigenous exploiters. In other areas, individual families have become rich but the process of class formation is not evident.

The basic pattern of the domestic group is the nuclear family with one or two dependents. There are a large number of patrilineal extended families also. Joint families are very few. By and large, in the Naguri area and in Tamar, Hindu kinship terminology as it obtains in non-tribal Bihar has made serious inroads in the Mundari vocabulary. There are now a larger number of cases of sexual relations inside the clan. The sentiment for village exogamy has considerably weakened. The village and the *parha* Panchayats are satisfied with fines to make up for social wrongs. In some cases such liaisons do not tend to be permanent, the elders even wink at it. There are now a larger number of arranged marriages, in the initiation of which the marriage partners do not have a role. Most of the pre-marital friendships do not result in marriage. The arranged marriage with payment of bride-price enjoys the highest social approval. Some love marriages, mostly of the runaway type do take place, but they are soon formalised. All marriages, however, are adult marriages.

The traditional bride-price consisting of two heads of cattle, Rs. 12 and a few clothes has now been converted into cash in the Naguri area. In Tamar, however, in the case of educated bridegrooms, not only is the bride-price skipped but a small dowry is also expected and given. This is obviously the result of the long standing Hindu impact in that area.

NEW ECONOMIC HORIZONS

The process of the breakdown of the Khutkatti, or the communal land system of the Munda had been noticed and lamented by Sarat Chandra Roy. This process has continued. Now there are just over a hundred communal villages in Munda areas which survive as islands. The bulk of the tribals are now proliferating as small farmers and landed labourers. With each division of the holding on account of the pressure of population, the proletarianization of the tribal peasant is increasing. Land alienation is a phenomenon that has plagued the tribal scene for a long time. There have been transfers of land from tribals to non-tribals and from tribals to tribals. In spite of the Chotanagpur Tenancy Act, which was passed in 1908, the process continued. This has been possible on account of the several loopholes in the legislation, advantage of which was taken both by tribals and non-tribals. The growing improvidence of the Munda leading to indebtedness lies at the root of land alienation. This process was stepped up after independence with large scale settlements of lands, which were once in the possession of tribal communities, by the ex-landlords with either migrant or non-migrant groups of people in the forties and later. The growth of urbanization and the necessities of industrial complexes accentuated the problem. The Dhebar Commission in 1960 noted the acuteness of this problem and in 1969 an ordinance was made to plug the loopholes in the Chotanagpur Tenancy Act and to provide certain safeguards to the tribal people against alienation of land. There is no doubt that the process has been slowed down to a great extent with the passing of this ordinance.

An interesting result of the restriction on land transfers from tribals to non-tribals was the rise of a small class of tribal money-lenders. Thus, certain families became rich and some differentiation became evident in Munda society.

The dependence on the forests has been reduced to some extent on account of the fact that there has been a great deal of destruction of forests. It has been calculated that Chotanagpur has lost 18% of its forests in recent years. But wherever there are forests they provide part of the sustenance for the Munda. Forests are the source of food, such as edible roots, fruits and flowers. They are also the biggest employer. The rights of the village in the neighbouring forests has been recognized. However, the tribals are no longer the masters of the forests and their rights have been restricted to a large extent. Steps have been taken to improve agriculture in the Munda areas. In those parts where the tribal population was two-thirds of the total population, tribal development blocks were created. Large funds were made available under the Community Development Programme. There were impressive achievements in communication, extension of education and medical facilities, but the development in agriculture was not remarkable. Some Munda began to use improved seeds, chemical fertilizers and also better techniques of agriculture. Since most of the Munda areas are one-crop areas, the process of self-generating and self-sustaining growth could not be set in motion. On account of poor resources most tribal families could not be involved in agricultural development. There is, however, no doubt that there was some improvement in the situation which is evident from the fact that there has been some decline in the extent of indebtedness. Local surveys indicated that 73% of the tribal households were indebted. In three villages studied by us the percentage of indebted families is only 52. The improvement in situation may be due to the fact that with the growth of education people are moving out of the village to seek urban employment. Part of the income derived from this may have been transferred to the rural areas for wiping out debts.

The migration to North Bengal and Assam tea gardens has now been reduced to a trickle. The people who go during the slack agricultural season to Calcutta or to other areas return when it is time for ploughing the land for the Kharif crop. Hundreds of labourers have now started going to Punjab where, besides food and clothes, they are assured of a monthly salary of Rs. 60. Each labourer, therefore, is able to save Rs. 300 in the five months that he remains outside his home. Besides giving him the cash income, the seasonal migration to Punjab makes him familiar with improved agricultural practices which in itself is a great gain, provided credit facilities are available. Monetization of the economy is proceeding fast and now for most of the services performed, payment is made in cash. The practice of money barter is restricted only to certain goods. Monetization has also affected inter-group relationships in Munda villages which were analogous to the *jajmani* system.

Industrialization, which is one of the prime movers of change, came to the Munda area in the early sixties. The first effect of industrialization was not happy at all, since it resulted in the displacement of the Munda from his hearth and home. On a rough estimate, about 5,000 acres of land were acquired and nearly 5,000 families were displaced. It is true that the displaced families got compensation but they did not know how to use it, nor was any provision made for them to be absorbed into the industrial complex. The spread of industries and the emergence of markets hastened the decline of village industries and traditional crafts with which many primitive artisans were associated. This is reflected in the fall in the percentage of workers engaged in household industries from 4% to 2.9%. Thus, a large number of displaced tribals and impoverished artisans were reduced to a status of paupers. Industrialization also opened the flood-gates of immigration. This led to conflict between the local tribal people and the outsiders. In view of their poor technical abilities the employment of tribals in higher posts in the industrial complex continues to be inadequate.

The Munda who have been in the vortex of industrialization have been greatly transformed. The industrial ethic changed the traditional communal goals of extended kinship groups to those of personal achievement and individual careers. The newly achieved status in industry affected the form and nature of village leadership. Vertical mobility, which was unknown in the traditional Munda society, came to be seen as an established norm. Industrialization also led to the growth of consciousness of one's rights and privileges. The industrialized Munda have more opportunities of voicing their grievances and demanding a right to mould their own destiny. Another important change is the loss of homogeneity, which is a tribal attribute. Munda labourers constantly interacting with non-tribal labourers have lost some of their distinctively tribal characteristics. Crime is on the increase in such areas and the village leaders are powerless to deal with the situation. To escape punishment one has only to join a labour camp. The enormity of the crime is lost in the atmosphere of anonymity in the town.

In the industrial area there is a tendency for the expansion of group identity beyond tribe. Inter-tribal marriages, association in political organizations and trade unions cut across tribal lines. The radio, movies and newspapers bring news and views of the world which were beyond the comprehension of the Munda before industrialization. His universe has expanded and so have his world-view and levels of aspiration. Changes have been observed in the food habits, dress and personal decoration of the Munda on account of the impact of industrialization and urbanization. There is free mixing between the tribals and the non-tribals. A number of marriages have been reported between tribal girls and non-tribal men. Besides this, there have been a large number of illegal unions which has led to the birth of illegitimate children. When the non-tribal father leaves, the mother and children are left destitute. The mother most often falls from virtue and the children become delinquents. Industrialization has also promoted linguistic acculturation. Workers who have remained for quite some time in the industrial settlement are able to speak Hindi and do not take an interest in their native tongue.

The impact of industrialization is, however, confined to the areas which are closer to industrial complexes. Researches have shown that industrial complexes remain like islands making little difference to the rhythm of life beyond the core in the vast countryside. In the interior areas life continues to be much as before.

Another feature which deserves notice is the growth of entrepreneurship among the Munda. In a recent study, conducted largely in the Munda area, it was found that hundreds of entrepreneurs were engaged in different sectors of activity. At least 40% of them have continued in the business year after year. The enterprises they have engaged in are the running of flour mills, photography, grocery shops, tailoring, homoeopathy, radio and cycle repair, cloth shops, watch-repair, sale of ready-made garments, fertilizers and seeds as well as pump repairs. With some training and promotional effort, many more tribals can be brought into this field. This will reduce the dependence on agriculture and also the pressure on land. The informal urban sector has a great capacity for absorbing a larger number of entrepreneurs than the large industries.

EMERGENT POLITICAL CULTURE

In recent years there has been a tremendous rise in the political consciousness of the Munda. A number of general elections have been held. On such occasions, workers from different political parties approach the people for votes. Formerly the Munda were acquainted only with the Congress and the Jharkhand parties but now the Janata Party has also made serious incursions in the tribal village. The Jharkhand Party has been plagued by fragmentation and factionalism. Since the merger of the Jharkhand Party and the Congress, a number of splinter groups appeared, each claiming to be the Jharkhand Party. The party was rent by cleavages based on communal and denominational factors The noticeable development was the rise of urban pressure groups led by educated tribals mostly Christian Munda from the industrial complex. These pressure groups highlighted the problems of unemployment and demanded jobs for the tribal youth in the administration and in industrial undertakings. The most potent of these groups was the Birsa Seva Dal. The Seva Dal sometimes used violent methods. Its meetings and processions consisted of youth armed with bows and arrows. But after some time the Seva Dal pledged itself to a constitutional role. A number of other organizations grew up. These were characterized by political extremism, agrarian radicalism and cultural revivalism. They wanted the expulsion of the non-tribals from Chotanagpur, the ending of the exploitation of tribals by non-tribals and the securing of preferential treatment for the sons of the soil in employment.

There has been an erosion in the influence of Christian tribal leaders. With the spread of education among the non-Christian tribals, the leadership among them has also emerged. This leadership challenged the old Jharkhand Christian leadership. The entire Munda country has been exposed to the operation of Pan-Indian forces including the macro-political systems. Some of the non-Christian tribal leaders are coming up with an appeal to the traditional institutions of the Munda such as the *sarna*, the *akhra* and the *parha*. They have begun advocating the view that only the non-Christian tribals should be given the status of a Scheduled Tribe. Thus, Christianity has come as a wedge in tribal solidarity.

An articulate and effective political elite has emerged in the Munda areas. It has not only acquired a taste for politics, but is also vigorously contributing to the emergence of a new political idiom. It is not constrained by the conventional rules of the game. It is conscious of tribal rights and is capable of making shrewd and calculated moves to gain their acceptance. Tribal problems are being politicised. Politics has emerged as the principal avenue through which the tribal leaders look forward to finding solutions to their many problems. Some of these problems have recently acquired a sharp edge. With the rise in aspirations, the inventory of tribal needs has become longer. Their leaders are aware that in politics competitive pressures determine one's place and share in the decision-making processes. By being a part of this process, they can ensure not only the preservation of their self-respect but also gain a larger share of resources for economic development. There has been a noticeable shift in their political attitudes and strategies. From the politics of compliance and affirmation they have moved over to a politics of pressure and protest. The leaders are now adopting a radical posture and fomenting militant agitation. The politicization of the tribal scene is a natural and logical culmination of the democratic process. Tribal leadership is in a state of transition. They are emerging from a subject of parochial political culture and becoming a part of participant political culture.

An important development has been the assertion of ethnicity in industrial urban centres. This is one way of staking and maintaining economic claims. Thus, while the clothes he wears, the food he eats and the way in which he lives may conform to an urban pattern, this does not signify that the tribal has renounced his traditional identity in his social and political commitments. This explains the great exuberance with which tribal festivals are celebrated in towns.

RELIGION IN FERMENT

In recent years there has been a newly awakened interest in religious festivals and in identifying with the *sarna* religion. Many educated Munda claim sarnaism as their religion. In urban centres too the tribal festivals of *Sarhul* and *Karam* are celebrated with great enthusiasm. This may be due to the resurgence of ethnicity. In most areas, however, the pantheon of the Munda has been enlarged by the inclusion of popular Hindu deities like Ram, Krishna, Hanuman, Mahadeva, etc. The life-cycle rituals like *chhati*, marriage and death rituals follow broadly the caste Hindu pattern. In the families of middle class Munda the Brahmin priests perform all the rituals. Hindu festivals like *Holi, Ramnaumi, Dusehra* and *Diwali* are celebrated with great enthusiasm in many areas.

The missionaries played an important role in bringing about social change among the Munda. Christianity gave them an ideology and a myth and a sense of history. It had also sharpened the feeling of separateness and emphasized the distinctive identity of the convert tribals. In this process the tribal community was split up and its solidarity was affected. The gulf between the Christian and non-Christian groups widened. During British rule the missionaries had helped the tribals to regain their self-respect and dignity. They were regarded as the guardians of the tribals. They took a number of measures for the welfare of the tribal people in the field of education and health, but they were all the time regarded as allies of the British rulers and they saw to it that the bulk of the tribals did not join the freedom movement. In the early years of independence the missionaries were largely anti-Congress. With the passage of time the conflict between the Christians and the non-Christians developed. Its main cause was the realization that the Christians being more advanced had cornered the bulk of the benefits of development as well as of employment offered by the government or other agencies.

WHITHER MUNDA ?

Any significant change in culture necessarily involves changes in social integration in the social structure. Social change consists essentially in processes of integration and disintegration. Disequilibrium and maladjustment are the result of uneven change, a failure to fit traditions to novelty or an alteration of one aspect of culture without alteration in other aspects. It involves pressure to change, and so long as it continues, there must be change. As a force of change, disequilibrium must always press towards its own resolution, towards equilibrium. Social structures of tribal societies present a similar picture of breaking down and building up.

Anthropologists have hitherto devoted most of their attention to the disintegration of tribal social structures. They are sometimes more eager to preserve the traditional structures than the members of the particular societies themselves. They look wistfully to the past and lament the passing of the traditional society. The fact that integration is also taking place, though in terms of another type of structure, has often been overlooked. The anthropologist is obliged to probe deeper to discover it. Despite the obscurities, the analysis of re-integration is just as essential for the understanding of social change as the investigation of disintegration. We need both if we are to know how one type of social structure develops out of another.

The Munda are undergoing the process of integration in terms of another type of social structure. With the growth of education, the tribals are being drawn into the services and professions in larger numbers. In literacy the figures show a definite upward leap. Development effort in the Munda area as well as the statutory privileges given to tribals has helped in the emergence of a tribal middle class. Such a middle class family living at Ranchi or Khunti for a generation or two is indistinguishable from others of the same class. Their standard of living compares favourably with others of their income level. Most of the tribals are bilingual and there is no difficulty of communication between the tribals and non-tribals except in the deep interior. In social mixing also there is no difference and tribals and non-tribals meet on equal terms.

Modernization may have challenged the traditional ties of tribes or kinship but it seldom succeeds in overthrowing them completely. These primordial forces show a resilience in the adaptation to new conditions. With increased economic and political competition there is more to gain than lose. This encourages people to fall back upon and, where necessary, modify familiar and trusted principles of association. In the urban centres, people of different backgrounds are thrown together. There is a constant threat to security in an alien environment. In such a situation the urban tribesman is encouraged to seek the support and security found in tribal ties. Voluntary tribal associations come up. These are not only mutual aid societies but also provide a platform for cultural meets as well as a forum to articulate their grievances. However, the situation is not very simple, since in towns new class identifications cut across traditional barriers of tribe and community. Successful political manipulators ingeniously exploit the new and old types of relations to suit their interests in different contexts. In some cases the worst pedlars of tribalism are usually the most articulate educated elite.

In India the situation is somewhat more confusing. The government seeks to encourage inter-caste unions by offering cash inducements to those who contract marriages with members of the Scheduled Castes and Scheduled Tribes. The Scheduled Tribes themselves are entitled to special statutory benefits designed to afford them some compensation to set off their handicaps. This places tribesmen in a quandary. They want to escape from the stigma of tribal status, but by doing so they risk losing those special benefits to which their birth specifically entitles them. The Munda are in such a quandary.

There is no doubt, however, that the Munda are proceeding towards the mainstream but this by no means requires them to shed such items of their culture which they consider important and valuable in terms of their identity. In India there are numerous castes and communities which are a part of the mainstream but which still retain some of their traditional ways and institutions.

The direction of change is unmistakable. The Munda, like

other small communities living in a multi-ethnic society, are approximating the styles of living prevalent in the dominant community. Their ways of thought, their world view and level of aspirations are also changing more or less in the same direction. The Munda have a number of problems but so have the others. All of them are part of a backward economy whose rate of growth is extremely slow. The solutions the Munda may seek to their problems would also be of the same nature as that of other disadvantaged people of the region. This is evident in the way the class consciousness has been sharpened and politics has been radicalised in tribal areas. Modern forces are so strong that they have involved Munda society in a way that its problems can only be viewed in a pan-Indian frame. Even the demand for a separate state of Jharkhand is being justified by the argument in favour of small states for speedy development.

Through all these years, marked by peace and amity and punctuated with conflict and confrontation, the Munda have exhibited a tenacity in some aspects of culture and resilience in others. Their genius for adjustment is superb. They have been wafted by winds of change from all sides but they have not been swept off their feet. With patience and understanding they are moving towards a destiny which gives them a place of honour in Indian polity.

APPENDICES

APPENDIX I

List of Munda Clans

Sl. No.	Name of Clan	Sl. No.	Name of Clan
1.	Barjo	26.	Huni Purti
2.	Jhora-Barjo	27.	Kali Purti
3.	Bodra	28.	Lupu Purti
4.	Lang-Bodra	29.	Sandi Purti
5.	Ramra-Bodra	30.	Sarukad Purti
6.	Sakiri-Bodra	31.	Soso Purti
7.	Tebo-Bodra	32.	Toroe Purti
8.	Campia	33.	Sanga
9.	Digi Campia	34.	Edel Sanga
10.	Guria	35.	Dere Sanga
	(a) Aratone	36.	Tiru Sanga
	(b) Salkar	37.	Soe
11.	Sandi-Guria		Tuing Soe
12.	Mundu		Ged ,,
13.	Pande-Mundu		Sama or
14.	Murum		Jang ,,
15.	Sandi-Murum		Patrapete ,,
16.	Soe-Murum		Ated ,,
17.	Orea		Til ,,
18.	Cauli Kutung Orea		Or ,,
19.	Sukuri Putur Orea	38.	Sole Soe
20.	Purti		Ged ,,
21.	Chutu Purti		Sama ,,
22.	Chupud Purti		Patrapete ,,
23.	Enga Purti		Ated ,,
24.	Hasa Purti		Til ,,
25.	Holong Purti		Or ,,

Sl. No.	Name of Clan	Sl. No.	Name of Clan
39.	Tuti/Bajra/Bajrai	75.	Salu meena
40.	Jom-Tuti/Bhojroj	76.	Singha
41.	Baba/Dhan	77.	Sirka
42.	Bale	78.	Tani/Barwa
43.	Bale-Mucu	79.	Taraeba
44.	Baru	80.	Tilming
45.	Bhus	81.	Tao
46.	Bulung	82.	Terom
47.	Cauria	83.	Tero/Lakra
48.	Dang/Dhang/Dahang/ Dahanga	84.	Tandaya
		85.	Tirung
49.	Dungdung/Aind	86.	Thuria
50.	Gari	87.	Tiru
51.	Hapadgara	88.	Barla
52.	Hasa/Hassara	89.	Bengra/Bhengra/ Bhengraj
53.	Hau/Topno/Demta		
54.	Hans	90.	Dodrae/Dodorae
55.	Hansda	91.	Kandir
56.	Hemrom	92.	Seta Kandir
57.	Here	93.	Kandulana
58.	Horo/Kachhap/Singh/ Shital	94.	Kongadi
		95.	Kamal (Hinduised)
59.	Jojo	96.	Sal (Hinduised)
60.	Jojohar	97.	Sandil (Hinduised)
61.	Kaua	98.	Surin
62.	Kerketa	99.	Bading
63.	Kuda	100.	Bage/Baghe/Baghi
64.	Kujuri/Kujur	101.	Bagear/Baguar/Bagraila
65.	Kula/Bagh	102.	Bhut/Kuar
66.	Kungkal	103.	Bur
67.	Lang	104.	Duduria
68.	Barlanga	105.	Danguar
69.	Maukal	106.	Dunduar
70.	Nisha	107.	Ergat
71.	Pandu Bing	108.	Ham Soy
72.	Putam	109.	Holo
73.	Ramra/Rambra	110.	Kauriar
74.	Runda/Bando	111.	Lugun

Sl. No.	Name of Clan	Sl. No.	Name of Clan
112.	Mundri	133.	Gograi
113.	Nagruar	134.	Gomi Buru
114.	Samad	135.	Hembo
115.	Sandigarai	136.	Herenj
116.	Sanguar	137.	Hobo
117.	Sankura	138.	Hurum Suku
118.	Tirki	139.	Jate
119.	Tiro	140.	Jatrom
120.	Jhoreya	141.	Jaria
121.	Bando	142.	Kadiyar (Hinduised)
122.	Bagsuria	143.	Lada
123.	Binda	144.	Langchere
124.	Bhalu	145.	Linda
125.	Baray-ood	146.	Lipi
126.	Bodoso	147.	Manaki
127.	Budu	148.	Saragat
128.	Bhuinya	149.	Sisigi
129.	Captain	150.	Tuyu
130.	Chekha	151.	Nag
131.	Choreya	152.	Patra-Kukuri
132.	Dhechua		

APPENDIX II

Munda Kinship Terminology

English term	Kinship terms			English Term	Reciprocal Kinship terms		
	Mundari Term				Mundari Term		
	Salehatu	Gutuhatu	Amlesa		Salehatu	Gutuhati	Amlesa
1	2	3	4	5	6	7	8
Father	Aba, Apu	Aba, Apu	Ba, Bap (Hindi)	Son Daughter	Beta (H) Beti (H)	Kura Hon, Kuri Hon, Mai	Beta(H) Beti(H)
Mother	Eang	Eanga, Uma, Ma	Ma (H)	Son Daughter	Beta (H) Beti (H)	Kura Hon, Babu Kuri Hon,	Beta (H) Beti (H)
Brother (m.s.)	Haga	Haga	Bhai	Brother (m.s.)	Haga	Haga	Bhai
Brother (w.s.)	Haga	Haga	Bhai	Sister (m.s.)	Misi	Misi	Bahi
Brother-child of own father and another mother	Haga	Bhai	Sautania Bhai	—			
Brother-child of own mother and another father	Haga	Bhai	Sautania Bhai	—			
Sister (w.s.)		Nanaing, Anjhing	Bahin (Bohin)	Sister (w.s.)		Nanaing Anjhing	Bohin (Bahin)

Contd.)

1	2	3	4	5	6	7	8
Sister-child of own father and another mother		Nanaing Anjhaing	Sautania Bohin	—			
Sister-child of own mother and another father		Nanaing Anjhaing	Sautania Bohin	—			
Elder-Brother (m.s.)	Daaa	Marang Haga, Dada	Dada	Younger Brother (m.s.)	Bhai (H) Huding Haga	Unding,	Bhai (Chhota)
Elder Brother (w.s.)	Dada	Marang Haga	Dada	Younger Sister (m.s.)	Bahin (H), Misi	Unding	Bohin
Elder Sister (m.s.)	Didi, Dai	Nanaing, Didi	Didi	Younger Brother (w.s.)	Bhai (H), Haga	Unding	(Chota) Bhai
Elder Sister (w.s.)	Didi, Dai	Nanaing, Aji	Didi	Younger Sister (w.s.)	Bahin, Misi	Unding	(Choti) Bohin
Father's Brother	Bada, Bodo, Huding Aba, Kaka	Kaka, Marang/ Huding Apu	Chhota Ba, Bara Ba	Brother's Child (m.s.)	Bada (Male), Badi (Female), Bodo, Beta, Beti	Babu, Mai, Bhatija, Bhatiji (Hindi)	Bhatija, Bhatiji
Father's Brother's Wife	Badi, Huding Eang, Kaki	Kaki, Badi	Chhoti Ma Bari Ma	Husband's Brother's Child	Bada, Badi, Bodo, Beta,	Babu, Mai, Bhatija, Bhatiji (H)	Bhesur Beta, Beti Devar

					Beti,	Bada, Badi	Beta, Beti
Father's Brother's Child	Dada, Haga, Misi	Dai Dada, Nana, Unding	Bhai, Bahin	—			
Father's Sister	Hatum (Elder and Younger)	Fufu, Gungu	Fufu	Brother's Child(w.s.)	Bhagina (Male), Bhagini (Female)	Bhagina, Bhagini, Gere	Beta, Beti
Father's Sister's Husband	Mamu	Fufa, Kuma	Fufu	Wife's Brother's Child	Bhagina, Bhagini (Hindi)	Bhagina, Bhagini, Gere	Fufu —
Father's Sister's Child	Dada, Didi, Dai Haga, Bhai Bahin, Misi	Dada, Nana, Unding		Mother's Brother's Child	Dada, Didi, Dai Haga Bhai, Bahin, Misi	Dada, Nana, Unding	
Mother's Brother	Mamu	Mamu, Kuma	Mama	Sister's Child (m.s.)	Bhagina, Bhagini	Bhagina, Bhagini, Gere	Bhagina, Bhagini
Mother's Brother's Wife	Hatum	Mani, Kumaing Mami		Husband's Sister's Child	Bhagina, Bhagini	Bhagina, Gere	Bhagina, Bhagini

(Contd.)

1	2	3	4	5	6	7	8
Mother's Brother's Child	Dada	Dada, Bhai, Haga, Unding	Bhai, Bahin	Father's Sister's Child	Dada	Dada, Bhai, Haga, Unding	Bhai, Bahin
Mother's Sister	Marang, Huding Eang	Badi, Kaki, Bari Ma, Mausi	Bari Ma, Mausi	Sister Child (w.s.)	Bada, Badi, Beta, Beti	Babu, Mai, Bada, Beta, Beti	Beta, Beti,
Mother's Sister's Husband	Bada, Kaka	Bada, Kaka	Bara Ba, Mausa	Wife's Sister's Child	Bada. Badi, Beta, Beti	Babu, Mai, Bada, Badi, Beta, Beti	Mausa, Mausi
Mother's Sister's Child	Dada, Didi Bhai, Bahin	Bhai, Haga, Unding Nana, Behin Unding	Bhai, Bahin	—	—	—	—
Father's Father	Nana, Boora, (Saking)	Aja	Mita, Aja	Son's Son (m.s.)	Boora, Nana	*Jaing Kura. Kuri*	Nati,
				Sons' Daughter (m.s.)	Boori, Nani	Jaing Hon tani	Natin
Father's mother	Nani, Boori	Aji	Mitin, Aji	Son's Son (w.s.)	Boora, Nana	Jaing Kura	Nati

				Son's Daughter (w.s)	Boori, Nani,	Jaing Kuri	Natin
Mother's father	Nana, Boora	Nana	Nana	Daughter's Son (m.s.)	Nana, Boora,	Jaing Kura,	Natin
				Daughter's daughter (m.s.)	Boori Nani	Kuri Jaing	Natin
Mother's mother	Boori, Nani, Saking	Nani	Nani	Daughter's Son (w.s.)	Nana,	Jaing Kura	Natin
				Daughter's Daughter(w.s.)	Boori,	Jaing Kuri	Natin
Husband	Anjh-Kura, Kisan	Anjh Kura, Anjh	Pati (H)	Wife	Anjh-Kuri,	Anjh Kuri,	Patni, Mor
					Ora-Hope	Gharni	Ghareya
Wife's father	Aba, Hunjar Aba, Hunjar Apu, Sasur (H)	Hunjar, Bada, Hunjar	Sasur	Daughter's husband (m.s.)	Hon Aratani	Artani, Damad	Beti Damad
Wife's mother	Hanar Eang, Hanar Boori, Hunjar Boori	Hanar, Badi Hanaring	Sas	Daughter's husband (w.s.)	Hon Aratani	Aratani, Damad	Beti Damad
Husband's Father	Hunjar Aba	Hunjar	Sasur	Son's wife (m.s.)	Hon	Kimin	Beta
				Sas, San's wife (w.s.)	Kimin		Putohu

1	2	3	4	5	6	7	8
Husband's mother	Hanar Eang,	Hanar,					
Wife's Brother	Tenjang kura, Bau Hunjar	Tanjaing Kura	Sara Jethsara	Sister's husband (m.s.)	Bonai (younger) Aratani (Elder)	Bhatu, Tenjaing	Bohnoi, Bohin Damad
Wife's Sister	Tenjang Kuri, Aji Hanar	Aji Hanar, Tenjaing Kuri	Jethsari, sari	Sister's husband (w.s.)	Bonai (Younger) Aratani (Elder)	Bhatu, Tenjang	Bohnoi, Bonin Damad
Wife's Brother's Wife	Dai, Boko, Boe	Aji, Nana, Unding	Didi, Bohin	Husband's Sister's husband	Aratani, Huding, Haga,	Dada, Aja, Erilkura	Dada, Bhai
Husband's Brother	Bau Hunjar, Eril Kura	Bau Hunjar, Eril Kura	Bhesur, Devar	Brother's wife (m.s.)	Hiling Bu, Hili Haga Kimin	Hiling, Nanaing, Kimin Unding,	Bahu, Bhaiputohu
Husband's Sister	Aji Hanar, Eril Kuri	Aji, Eril Kuri	Nanad	Brother's wife (m.s.)	Hiling Bu, Hili, Haga Kimin	Hili, Nana, Kimin Unding	Bahu, Bhai Putohu
Wife's Sister's Husband	Saragin, Sarhu	Saragin, Sarhu	Sarhu				
Husband's Brother's Wife	Dai, Bokokuri. Naning	Nana, Hiling, Erilkuri, Unding	Jethani, Devrani				

Brother's Wife's parent's other Children		Yar (among Boys) Gayee Ram (among Boys and Girls) Gayee (among girls)	Sangat Sangat-Sangatin Sangatin	Sister's husband's parent's other Children.		Year (among boys) Gayee Ram (among boys and girls) Gayee (among girls)	Sangat Sangat, Sangatin Sangatin
Bride	—	Kanya (H)		Bride groom		Dulha (H)	Var (H)

BIBLIOGRAPHY

Basu, N.K., "Munda festivals of Chotanagpur", *Journal of the Asiatic Society of Bengal*, Vol. 30, 1934.

Beteille Andre & T.N. Madan, (ed.), *Encounter and Experience-Personal accounts of Fieldwork*. Delhi : Vikas Publishing House Pvt. Ltd., 1975.

Bhaduri, M.B., "Astronomy of the Munda and Their Star Myths", *Man in India*, Vol. II, No. 1., 1922.

Bogaert, M. Vanden, "Entrepreneurial Patterns in the Urban Informal Sector: The case study of Tribal Entrepreneurs", *Social Action*, Volume 27, No. 3., 1977.

Bowles, G.T., "Linguistic and Ritual Aspects of the Munda Problem" in *Studies in the Anthropology of Oceania and Asia* presented in the memory of Dixon. Cambridge, 1943.

Burman, B.K. Roy, "Ethnicity in Chotanagpur with Particular Reference to the Tribal Communities" : A Source paper prepared for a UNESCO Expert Committee meeting on Race Relations in Asia and Oceania, 1974.

Census of India, Series-I, Paper I of 1975, Scheduled Castes & Scheduled Tribes, 1971.

Census of India, Bihar. Unpublished Census Tables on Scheduled Tribes, Tables STI—STV, 1971.

Chotanagpur Catholic Mission Co-operative Credit Society, Ranchi. Director's Reports for the years 1972, 1973 and 1975; Balance sheet for the year 1975.

Choudhury, N.C., *Munda Social Structure*. Calcutta : Firma KLM Private Limited, 1977.

Dalton, E.T., *Descriptive Ethnology of Bengal*. Calcutta: Office of the Superintendent of Government Printing, 1872.

Dhan, R.O., "Problem of Land Alienation in the District of

Ranchi", Bihar Tribal Research Institute (Mimeographed), 1966

Dass, B.L., Census of India, 1971, Series-4, Bihar, Paper I of 1971 : Provisional Population Totals. Delhi : Manager of Publications, 1971.

Ekka Phillip, *Revivalist Movements Among the Tribals of Chotanagpur* in Singh, K.S. (ed.), : Tribal Situation in India. Simla, Indian Institute of Advance Study, 1972.

Firth, Raymond, *Elements of Social Organisation.* London : Vatts & Co., 1956.

Forde, C. Daryll, *Habitat Economy and Socity.* London : University Paperbacks, Methuen. (first published in 1934), 1963.

Fuchs, Stephen, *Rebellious Prophets : A study of Messianic Movements in Indian Religion.* Bombay: Asia Publishing House, 1965.

Goode, William J., *Religion Among the Primitives.* London : Collier—Macmillan, 1964.

Gough, Kathlean, "Indian Peasant Uprisings", *E.P.W.*, Vol. IX, Special number, 1974.

Herskovits, M.J., *Man and His Works.* New York: Alfred, A. Knopf, 1956

Hoffmann, John and A.V. Emelen, *Encyclopaedia Mundarica.* Patna : Superintendent, Government Printing, Bihar, 13 Vols., 1950.

Hoffmann, John, "Principles of Succession and Inheritance among the Munda", *Man in India*, Vol. XXXXI. (Reprinted from the Journal of the Bihar and Orissa Research Society, Sept., 1915), 1961.

Kala Rani, Munda Women, Unpublished M.A. dissertation Bihar University, Ranchi, 1955.

——, "Coming of Age Among Munda Girls", *Bulletin of Anthropology*, Bihar University, Ranchi, 1957.

Koichi, Sugiyama, *A Study of Munda Village Life in India.* Tokyo: Tokai University Press, 1969.

Kumar, N., Bihar District Gazetteers, Ranchi. Patna: Government of Bihar, Gazetteers Branch, Revenue Department, 1970.

Lewis, Oscar, *Village Life in Northern India : Studies in a Delhi Village.* New York : Vintage Books—A Division of

Random House, 1958.

Mandal, B.B., The Parliamentary Election, 1977 : A Case Study of Khunti (ST) Constituency in Ranchi District (Bihar)-a Report prepared as a part of ICSSR Project on General Election Study, 1977. (Typed).

Munda, Ram Dayal and Norman Zide, "Revolutionary Birsa and Mundari Folk Songs", *The Journal of Social Research*' Vol. XII, No. 2, 1969.

Mundari, Lal Singh, "A Munda Birth", *Man in India*, Vol. 36, No. 1, 1956.

Murdock, G.P., *Social Structure*. New York : Macmillan, 1949,

National Institute of Community Development, Perspectives of Tribal Development and Administration—Proceedings of the Workshop held at the NICD, Hyderabad, 18-20, April, 1974.

——, "New Stirrings in Adivasi Politics", *Main-stream*, Vol. VI, No. 47, 1968.

Prasad, Ranchor, *Selected Plan Statistics—Bihar*. Patna : Government of Bihar, 1976.

Prasad, S.D., "Jojohatu, a Munda Village", *Bihar Village Survey Monograph* No. 1 : Manager of Publications, Delhi 1963.

——, Census of India, 1961, Vol. IV, Bihar, Part V-A, Special Tables for Scheduled Castes and Scheduled Tribes. Delhi : Manager, Publications, 1965.

——, Census of India, 1961, Bihar, District Census Handbook, 15, Ranchi. Patna : Government of Bihar, 1968.

Radcliffe-Brown, A.R., *Structure and Function in Primitive Society*, London : Cohn and West Ltd., 1959.

Radcliffe-Brown, A.R. and Forde Daryll (ed.), *African Systems of Kinship and Marriage*. London : Oxford University Press, 1964.

Roy, M., "A Parha at Work", *Bulletin of Deptt. of Anthropology*, Bihar University, Vol. 1, No. 1, 1957.

Roy, S.C., "The Divine Myths of Mundas," *Journal of Bihar and Orissa Research Society*, Vol. II, 1916.

——, "The Theory of Rent Among the Mundas of Chotanagpur," *Man in India*, Vol. XXVI, Nos. 3 & 4, 1946.

——,"The Administrative History and Land Tenures of the Ranchi District under British Rule," *Man in India*, Vol. XXXXI, No. 4, Oct-Dec., 1961 (Reprinted from The

Calcutta Review, 1911)

——, *The Munda and their Country*. Bombay : Asia Publishing House. (First Published in 1912), 1970.

Sachchidananda, *Culture Change in Tribal Bihar—Munda and Oraon*. Calcutta : Bookland, 1964.

——, *Profiles of Tribal Culture in Bihar*. Calcutta : Firma K. L. Mukhopadhayay, 1965a.

——, *Survey of Tribal Development Blocks, KARRA* (Ranchi). Ranchi : Bihar Tribal Research Institute (Mimeographed), 1965b.

——, *Tribal village in Bihar : A study in Unity and Extension*. New Delhi : Munshi Ram Manohar Lal, 1968. "Tribal Situation in Bihar" in Singh K. S. (ed), 1972 :

——, *Tribal Situation in India*. Simla : Institute of Advanced Study, 1972.

——, *Tribal Voter in Bihar*. New Delhi : National Publishing House, 1976.

——, Studies in Economic Anthropology in India : Search for New Perspectives—A research paper presented at a Seminar at the Anthropological Survey of India, Calcutta, 1977.

Sahay, K. N., *Under the Shadow of the Cros*. Calcutta : Institute of Social Research and Applied Anthropology, 1976.

Saran, A.B., "Murder Among the Munda: A few Case Studies", *Bulletin of the Bihar Tribal Research Institute*, Ranchi, 1960.

——, "Munda and Oraon Murderers in Jail", *Bulletin of the Bihar Tribal Research Institute Ranchi*, No. 3, 1963.

——, *Murder and Suicide Among the Munda and the Oraon*. Delhi : National Publishing House, 1973.

Sen, Jyoti, "The Jharkhand Movement" in Singh, K. S (ed.), *Tribal Situation in India*. Simla : Indian Institute of Advanced Study, 1972.

Sharma, K. L., "Jharkhand Movement in Bihar", *Economic and Political Weekly*, Vol. XI, Nos. 1 & 2, 1976.

Singh, K. S., *The Dust Storm and the Hanging Mist—A Study of Birsa Munda and his Movement in Chotanagpur* (1874-1901). Calcutta : Firma K. L. Mukhopadhyay, 1966.

Singh, K. S. (ed.), "Agrarian Issues in Chotanagpur" in Singh, K. S. (ed.), *Tribal Situation in India*. Simla : Institute of Advanced Study, 1972.

Singh, K. S. (ed.), *Tribal Situation in India*. Simla : Indian Institute of Advanced Study, 1972.

——, Tribal Ethnicity in a Multi-ethnic Society : A Study in the Processes of Conflict and Integration in Colonial and Post Colonial Chotanagpur. Unpublished Draft submitted to UNESCO.

Singh, K. S., "From Ethnicity to Regionalism : A study in Tribal Politics and Movements in Chotanagpur from 1900 to 1975" in *Malik*, S.C. (ed).

——, *Dissent, Protest and Reform in Indian Civilization* Simla : Indian Institute of Advanced Study, 1977.

Sinha, D.P., *Culture Change in an Inter-tribal Market*. Bombay: Asia Publishing House, 1968.

Sinha, S.P., *Life and Time of Birsa Bhagwan*. Ranchi : Bihar Tribal Research Institute, 1964.

——, Report on Mundari Khutkatti System in Chatonagpur. Ranchi, Bihar Tribal Welfare Research Institute, 1965 : (typed).

——, Portrait of a Munda Leader : Birsa Bhagwan (1895-1900) in Vidyarthi, L.P.(ed.), *Leadership in India*, Bombay; Asia Publishing House, 1967.

Spencer, D. M., "The Munda Theory of Legal Punishment," *Bulletin of Bihar Tribal Research Institute*, 1959.

Topno, Sem, "The Changing Pattern of Munda Personal Names", *The Eastern Anthropologist*, Vol. XXIII, No. 2, 1970.

Trigunayat, Jagdish, *Bansuri Baj Rahi*. Patna : Bihar Rashtrabhasha Parishad, 1957.

Verma, K.K., *Culture, Ecology and Population*. New Delhi : National Publishing House, 1977.

Vidyarthi, L.P., *Cultural Contours of Tribal Bihar*. Calcutta : Punthi Pustak, 1964.

——, Aspects of Tribal Leadership in Chotanagpur in Vidyarthi, L.P. (ed.), *Leadership in India* Bombay : Asia Publishing House, 1967.

Vidyarthi, L.P. (ed.), *Leadership in India*. Bombay : Asia Publishing House, 1967.

——, Socio-cultural Implications of Industrialisation in India —A case study of Tribal Bihar. New Delhi : Research

Programmes Committee, Planning Commission, 1970.

Vidyarthi, L.P., "An Appraisal of the Leadership Pattern Among the Tribes of Bihar" in Singh, K S. (ed.), *Tribal Situation in India*, Simla : Institute of Advanced Study, 1972.

Vidyarthi, L.P. & Rai, B.K., *The Tribal Culture of India*. Delhi: Concept Publishing Company, 1977.

INDEX